HANDLING COMPLEXITY IN LEARNING ENVIRONMENTS: THEORY AND RESEARCH

ADVANCES IN LEARNING AND INSTRUCTION SERIES

Series Editors: **K. Littleton, C.P. Constantinou, L. Mason, W.-M. Roth and R. Wegerif**

Further details: www.elseviersocialsciences.com

Published

HAKKARAINEN, PALONEN, PAAVOLA AND LEHTINEN
Communities of Networked Expertise: Professional and Educational Perspectives

TERTTU TUOMI-GRÖHN AND YRJÖ ENGESTRÖM
Between School and Work — New Perspectives on Transfer and Boundary-crossing

DE CORTE, VERSHAFFEL, ENTWISTLE AND MERRIËNBOER
Powerful Learning Environments: Unravelling Basic Components and Dimensions

VAN SOMEREN, REIMANN, BOSHUIZEN AND DE JONG
Learning with Multiple Representations

DILLENBOURG
Collaborative Learning: Cognitive and Computational Approaches

BLISS, SÄLJÖ AND LIGHT
Learning Sites: Social and Technological Resources for Learning

KAYSER AND VOSNIADOU
Modelling Changes in Understanding

SCHNOTZ, VOSNIADOU AND CARRETERO
New Perspectives on Conceptual Change

SMITH
Reasoning by Mathematical Induction in Children's Arithmetic

KOZULIN AND RAND
Experience of Mediated Learning

ROUET, LEVONEN AND BIARDEAU
Multimedia Learning: Cognitive and Instructional Issues

GARRISON AND ARCHER
A Transactional Perspective on Teaching and Learning

COWIE AND AALSVOORT
Social Interaction in Learning and Instruction

VOLET AND JÄRVELÄ
Motivation in Learning Contexts

Related journals — sample copies available online from:
http://www.elsevier.com

Learning and Instruction
International Journal of Educational Research
Computers and Education
The Internet and Higher Education
Early Childhood Research Quarterly
Journal of Early Childhood Teacher Education
Learning and Individual Differences
Educational Research Review

HANDLING COMPLEXITY IN LEARNING ENVIRONMENTS: THEORY AND RESEARCH

EDITED BY

JAN ELEN

Katholieke Universiteit Leuven, Belgium

RICHARD E. CLARK

University of Southern California, USA

Published in Association with the European Association for Learning and Instruction

Amsterdam • Boston • Heidelberg • London • New York • Oxford
Paris • San Diego • San Francisco • Singapore • Sydney • Tokyo

ELSEVIER

Elsevier
The Boulevard, Langford Lane, Kidlington, Oxford OX5 1GB, UK
Radarweg 29, PO Box 211, 1000 AE Amsterdam, The Netherlands

First edition 2006

British Library Cataloguing in Publication Data
A catalogue record is available from the British Library.

Library of Congress Cataloging in Publication Data
A catalog record is available from the Library of Congress.

ISBN-13: 978-0-08-044986-9
ISBN-10: 0-08-044986-7

For information on all book publications
visit our website at books.elsevier.com

Printed and bound in The Netherlands

06 07 08 09 10 10 9 8 7 6 5 4 3 2 1

Working together to grow
libraries in developing countries
www.elsevier.com | www.bookaid.org | www.sabre.org
ELSEVIER   BOOK AID International   Sabre Foundation

Contents

List of Figures

List of Tables

Contributors

Mireille Bétrancourt
TECFA, Department of Psychology and Education, University of Geneva, Geneva, Switzerland

Geraldine Clarebout
Centrum voor Instructiepsychologie en -technologie, K.U. Leuven, Leuven, Belgium

Richard E. Clark
Center for Cognitive Technology, Rossier School of Education, University of Southern California, Los Angeles, CA, USA

Gemma Corbalan
Educational Technology Expertise Center, Open University of the Netherlands, Heerlen, The Netherlands

Ulrike Cress
University of Tuebingen, Applied Cognitive Psychology and Media Psychology, Tübingen, Germany

Erik De Corte
Centrum voor Instructiepsychologie en -technologie, K.U. Leuven, Belgium

Ton de Jong
Faculty of Behavioral Sciences, University of Twente, Enschede, The Netherlands

Fien Depaepe
Centrum voor Instructiepsychologie en -technologie, K.U. Leuven, Belgium

Pierre Dillenbourg
Swiss Federal Institute of Technology, École Polytechnique Fédérale de Lausanne (EPFL), EPFL — CRAFT, Lausanne, Switzerland

Sean Early
Center for Cognitive Technology, Rossier School of Education, University of Southern California, Los Angeles, CA, USA

Jan Elen
Centrum voor Instructiepsychologie en -technologie, K.U. Leuven, Leuven, Belgium

Friedrich W. Hesse
Knowledge Media Research Center, Tübingen, Germany

Keith Howard
Center for Cognitive Technology, Rossier School of Education, University of Southern California, Los Angeles, CA, USA

Slava Kalyuga
Educational Assessment Australia, University of New South Wales, Rosebery, Australia

Richard E. Mayer
Department of Psychology, University of California, Santa Barbara, CA, USA

M. David Merrill
Center for Instructional Technology and Outreach, Brigham Young University Hawaii, Laie, HI, USA

Fred Paas
Educational Technology Expertise Center, Open University of the Netherlands, Heerlen, The Netherlands

Gavriel Salomon
Faculty of Education, Haifa University, Haifa, Israel

Norbert M. Seel
Faculty of Economics and Behaviour Sciences, Department of Education, Research on Learning and Instructional Design, University of Freiburg, Freiburg, Germany

Educational Psychology and Learning Systems, Florida State University, Tallahassee, FL, USA

Dominique Sluijsmans
Educational Technology Expertise Center, Open University of the Netherlands, Heerlen, The Netherlands

John Sweller
School of Education, University of New South Wales, Sydney, Australia

Colin Tattersall
Educational Technology Expertise Center, Open University of the Netherlands, Heerlen, The Netherlands

Jeroen J. G. van Merriënboer
Educational Technology Expertise Center, Open University of the Netherlands, Heerlen, The Netherlands

Jan D. Vermunt
IVLOS Institute of Education, Utrecht University, Utrecht, The Netherlands

Lieven Verschaffel
Centrum voor Instructiepsychologie en -technologie, K.U. Leuven, Belgium

William Winn
University of Washington, Seattle, WA, USA

Philip H. Winne
Faculty of Education, Simon Fraser University, Burnaby, British Columbia, Canada

Preface

Working on this book was a challenging and rewarding experience that generated a lot of respect and gratitude on our part. We are much obliged. First of all, we are grateful that we could work with a group of top researchers each of whom not only immediately accepted our invitation, but also submitted their chapters often long before the deadlines and proactively co-operated during the consecutive stages of the editing work. Thanks to these authors, the book now presents a rich variety of research and theory with respect to complexity in learning environments. Second, the editing process could not have been accomplished without the valuable support of two marvellous persons. Sean Early from the University of Southern California has taken care of most if not all of the language editing. All authors have graciously used his advice, impressed by the relevance and linguistic proficiency of his suggestions. Betty Vanden Bavière from the K.U. Leuven has taken care of the layout with a lot of good humour and patience, and backed up by years of experience. She took all the necessary initiatives to deliver a professional manuscript to the publisher. We also would like to thank Karen Littleton and the other members of the editorial board of the *Advances in Learning and Instruction Series*. They created an opportunity for us to compose and edit this book. Finally, we are also indebted to the Fund for Scientific Research, Flanders, which provided substantial financial support to organize workshops that have brought about ideas expressed in this book.

Lastly, we would like to thank the eminent scholar and researcher who on retiring created, maybe not the reason, but in any case, the occasion for preparing this book. Inspired by his person and his work; his sensitivity for interrelationships, methodological vantage points, and theoretical gateways; encouraged by his open mind, and supported by his great sense of humour, we started to work on 'his' book. We now dedicate this book to him as a token of our recognition and gratitude:
Joost Lowyck, we thank you.

Jan Elen and Richard E. Clark
Leuven — Los Angeles
October 2005

Introduction

Setting the Scene: Complexity and Learning Environments

Jan Elen and Richard E. Clark

As the mind learns to understand more complicated combinations of ideas, simpler formulae soon reduce their complexity; so truths that were discovered only by great effort, that could at first only be understood by men capable of profound thought, are soon developed and proved by methods that are not beyond the reach of common intelligence.

Marquis de Condorcet (1743–1794)

This edited book is a tribute to Joost Lowyck on the occasion of his retirement as professor of Educational Technology at the Katholieke Universiteit Leuven, Belgium. By focusing on complexity and revealing its diversity from different perspectives, the chapter authors recognize and try to extend Professor Lowyck's work, in which complexity is a prominent and recurrent theme (e.g., Lowyck, 1998, 2002a,b,c; Lowyck & Elen, 2004).

In this introduction, we first analyze the notion of 'complexity'. Next, we wonder whether learning and instruction have indeed become more complex and if so in what sense. Finally, the structure of the book is highlighted by briefly previewing the different chapters.

Complexity

Complexity itself is far from an evident notion. In this book, complexity of learning, learning tasks, and learning environments are discussed. With respect to learning and learning tasks, two related but different approaches to the definition of complexity can be taken. A first approach defines complexity in reference to the features of a learning task (Dörner, 1996; Spector, 2000). It is argued that a task becomes more complex when it has (1) an increasing number of elements; and/or (2) more relationships between elements; and/or (3) more diverse relationships between elements; and/or (4) more changes over time in elements,

Handling Complexity in Learning Environments: Theory and Research
Crown Copyright © 2006 Published by Elsevier Ltd.
All rights of reproduction in any form reserved.
ISBN: 0-08-044986-7

relationships and interrelationships between elements. While agreeing that all four elements are critical to operationalizing complexity, the different contributions in this book tend to locate complexity not in the environment — not in external tasks but instead in the interaction between the characteristics of tasks and the characteristics of individual learners. It is claimed that complexity of learning tasks results from the requirement that learners consciously and deliberately process elements, relationships, diversity or changes in order to handle tasks.

Implied in this second definition is the position that the amount of complexity in any task changes depending on the prior task-relevant knowledge or experience and aptitudes of individual learners. What is highly complex to one person may be much less complex for another one. The suggestion here is that rather than being mainly a feature of the environment; complexity primarily seems to be in the eye and the mind of the beholder.

In research on learning and instructional complexity, the environmental complexity definition suggests detailed analyses of tasks, phenomena and situations. Examples are the analytic detail one finds in studies of programmed instruction (e.g., Lane, 1965), question asking behavior of teachers (e.g., Lowyck, 1974, 1976), or the use of video as a research instrument (e.g., Lowyck, 1971, 1980, 1986). The second approach builds on these analyses and stresses that the analysis itself is determined to a great extent by the theoretical perspective adopted such as studies of the different levels of cognitive load experienced by novices when compared with the load of more experienced people (van Merriënboer, 1997) or the extent to which discovery or unguided constructivist learning strategies are helpful for learners whose prior task-relevant experience leads them to experience excessive complexity (Mayer, 2004). The theoretical perspective one selects determines what tasks, phenomena and situations are relevant and what level of detail is required in the analysis.

Complexity and Learning Environments

All contributions in this book can be said to adopt a cognitive perspective toward learning and instruction. Consequently, the importance of considering the cognitive architecture (e.g., Sweller, this volume, Chapter 1; van Merriënboer et al., this volume, Chapter 11) as well as the cognitive and motivational processes involved in learning (e.g., Clark, Howard, & Early, this volume, Chapter 2; Cress & Hesse, this volume, Chapter 4; de Jong, this volume, Chapter 6) is stressed. Winne (this volume, Chapter 12) clearly specifies that adopting a cognitive perspective reveals the developing nature of multiple models currently used. Current models may be both too specific and not sufficiently granular. Critical components of instruction and learning are missing and for each component multiple layers of specificity need to be more carefully considered.

Modeling Learning Environments

In line with specifications in the literature on learning and instruction, the different contributions in this book point to at least two aspects that should be considered more deeply in order to 'model' learning environments for people concerned with interests in school-based instruction.

First, various contributions show that learning tasks are the most central active ingredients of instruction. Learning tasks constitute the common ground for instruction and learning. Various authors stress the importance of carefully selecting and sequencing learning tasks as inadequate decisions in this respect may actually hamper learning (see Clark, Howard, & Early, this volume, Chapter 2; van Merriënboer et al., this volume, Chapter 11; Merrill, this volume, Chapter 15). The nature of learning tasks and how they are interpreted by learners determine to a large extent whether instruction will be successful (see Luyten, Lowyck, & Tuerlinckx, 2001; Vermunt, this volume, Chapter 9).

Second, the contributions suggest that for learners learning tasks not only consist of formal, often *domain-specific, problem statements.* Evidently, support provided in the instructional setting is part of the learning task (Elen & Clarebout, this volume, Chapter 10). The *medium for delivering instruction* may also be considered to be part of the learning task. In contrast to what the classical literature on learning and instruction suggests, the classroom with a teacher as the main instructional agent is no longer the evident medium for instruction. Information and communication technology (ICT) has become an integral part of learning and instructional processes (De Corte, Verschaffel, & Lowyck, 1994, 1996; Dillemans et al., 1998; Lowyck, 1993, 2000a,b,c; Lowyck, de Gelder, & Vanmaele, 1987; Lowyck & Elen, 1999; Lowyck, Pöysä, & van Merriënboer, 2003; Lowyck & Vanmaele, 1992; Lowyck & Utsi, 2004). The specific role of ICT and more specifically their impact on the effectiveness or efficiency of learning and instruction has been heavily debated (see the media-debate: Clark, 2001). The availability of powerful technological tools calls for new approaches to scaffolding learners (de Jong, this volume, Chapter 6; Winn, this volume, Chapter 13) and provides new opportunities for studying learning processes (Winne, this volume, Chapter 12). The classroom context is also argued to be part of the learning task. By favoring some and discouraging other actions, the classroom context (see Depaepe, De Corte, & Verschaffel, this volume, Chapter 10) and the peers (Dillenbourg & Bétrancourt, this volume, Chapter 8; Cress & Hesse, this volume, Chapter 4), in that context affect the interactions of the learner with the task. Although far from evident, interactions with peers may create opportunities for making prior knowledge explicit, discuss viewpoints and, hence, for conceptual change. Finally, the classroom itself is no longer the unique anchor point for learning tasks. Research in recent years has illustrated the potential impact of the broader context by studying learning and instruction in a more diversified set of contexts, for instance corporate education (Lowyck, 1994; Lowyck & Clark, 1996a,b).

Need for Fine-Grained Analyses

In addition to identifying a more extended and more diverse set of elements learning tasks consist of, the cognitive perspective has also highlighted the need for more fine-grained analyses of the various elements and interactions between the elements that influence learning from instruction.

The learner   A multitude of variables affect the activities of learners in instructional settings as illustrated by research on the architecture of the mind (e.g., Sweller, this volume, Chapter 1), prior knowledge (e.g., Driscoll, 2005; Seel, this volume, Chapter 3), motivation (e.g., Clark, Howard, & Early this volume, Chapter 2), and metacognition (e.g., Winne, this volume, Chapter 12; Elen, Lowyck, & Proost, 1996). This research on factors that affect learners' activities in instructional settings reveals the multi-dimensional and multi-layered nature of human functioning as a consequence of multiple and diverse interrelationships. One critical but more or less ignored factor is growing evidence about the automated and unconscious quality of many cognitive, self-regulatory processes and the prior knowledge that supports new learning (e.g., Sweller, this volume, Chapter 1; Clark, Howard, & Early, this volume, Chapter 2). More emphasis in the future on these automated strategies and knowledge types — and increased effort to study how they are developed and applied during learning- may enlarge the impact of instructional research.

The teacher   A second element, which importance is generally recognized — the teacher — has become more diversified in at least two ways. First, research on teacher thinking has revealed the complex decision-making processes teachers engage in while teaching (Lowyck, 2003a,b). Second, the notion of 'teacher' has been replaced by a more abstract and multi-dimensional notion of 'support' (e.g., Elen, 1995). Support does not refer to any specific element of the learning environment but to a function that has to be accomplished by a teacher and any other instructional agent in the learning environment. The teacher is no longer the unique instructional agent, but has become one of many possible support delivery systems. As already indicated, the importance of computers in general and multimedia in particular (Mayer, this volume, Chapter 7), as delivery systems for support has increased. Replacing the notion of 'teacher' by the notion of 'support' has made educational researchers aware of the multitude of learning environments' features that can be deliberately designed to support learning (Elen & Clarebout, this volume, Chapter 10; Lowyck & Elen, 1990, 1991, 1993a,b, 1994a,b; Elen et al., 1996; Lowyck, 2002b).

Interrelationships   Cognitive research on learning and instruction has also revealed the large number and the diversified nature of the relationships between different relevant variables. Learning and instructional variables are interrelated in numerous and diverse ways. For instance, it has been shown that in contrast to intuitive reasoning schemes that favor linear relationships, a number of relationships between task features and motivational variables as well as learning results are curvilinear. While the Yerkes–Dodson law expressed this already a long time ago, researchers still seem to be surprised to find out that support that is functional for novice learners, may actually become detrimental to expert learners (see Dillenbourg & Bétrancourt, this volume, Chapter 7). The dynamic and reciprocal nature of the interrelationships also adds to complexity. Changes in one variable may affect changes in other variables, which in turn affect the original variable. Learning tasks that are highly complex to novice learners become gradually less complex as learning develops over time. The changing and evolving nature of learning and the complex interactions of variables that influence the process over time pose extraordinary challenges for the design of research and practice. Clear research questions (Merrill, this volume, Chapter 15), a layered research design (Salomon, this volume, Chapter 14), and considering a multitude of data (Winne, this volume, Chapter 12) from multiple sources and perspectives (Winn, this volume, Chapter 12) are a few of the strategies that are suggested in this volume to meet this challenge.

Structure of the Book

This book consists of three parts. A first part addresses complex learning primarily from the perspective of learning and the learner. The second part tackles complexity in learning and learning environments. The third part deals with handling complexity in empirical research.

Complexity: Learning and the Learner

Cognitive architecture   The first part starts with a fresh discussion of cognitive archi-tecture and its implications. In his chapter, Sweller discusses how the cognitive system handles complexity. Cognitive load theory is suggested as an explanatory system that helps integrate knowledge of the evolutionary origins of human cognitive architecture with the instructional consequences that flow from that architecture. Cognitive load theory nor-mally identifies three sources of cognitive load: Extraneous, germane and intrinsic. Sweller's chapter is concerned primarily with intrinsic cognitive load, which is argued to be determined by the complexity of the information to be learned or in other words by the extent that elements of information that must be learned interact. If element interactivity is high, then interacting elements must be processed simultaneously in working memory imposing a high intrinsic cognitive load. Under these circumstances, instructional designs and their associated extraneous cognitive load become critical.

Motivation   While Sweller focuses on the cognitive architecture of mind, the interrela-tionships between complex tasks and motivation are elaborated by Clark, Howard and Early. Clark et al. first define complexity from a cognitive perspective and distinguish between learning and motivation problems associated with complex educational environ-ments. The chapter then describes examples of research on five motivational problems that students appear to experience when working on complex tasks. It is specified that when per-ceived complexity increases: (1) excessive working memory load may cause motivational 'defaults' that are automated, largely unnoticed and destructive to learning; (2) students with inappropriately high or low task self-efficacy tend not to persist and invest very low mental effort to learn; (3) more learners experience negative emotional reactions and those who lack emotional self-regulatory skill tend to become distracted from learning goals; (4) stu-dents who have learned to attribute mistakes and other learning difficulties to fixed and uncontrollable causes such as inadequate intelligence reduce their effort; and (5) students who value learning but are victims of prejudice in culturally diverse educational settings, are more susceptible to learning and testing deficits due to 'stereotype threat'.

Prior knowledge   Seel addresses the role of prior knowledge by discussing the role and functioning of mental models in complex problem solving in the field of dynamic systems. Mental models are defined as an idealized reduction of the relevant attributes of phenom-ena to be explained or learned. Mental models enable one to express complex and abstract phenomena in concrete terms. According to Seel, the construct of mental models as well as their external representations helps us understand the learning-dependent transitions between different states of knowledge as learners interact with the environment. Seel describes different kinds of model-oriented instructional methods that interact with the autonomy and adaptability of learners. Chapters in the second part of the book describe research on learning environments.

Complexity: Learning Environments

Simulations and multimedia   de Jong opens the discussion in his chapter by presenting a framework for instructional scaffolds. de Jong argues that inquiry or scientific discovery learning with computer simulations is a difficult, but promising learning approach. It is promising since it may lead to more deeply rooted and intuitive knowledge. It is difficult because the processes that constitute scientific discovery learning are not very familiar to students with the result that students make characteristic mistakes. The ineffectiveness of unsupported or unguided discovery learning is in this respect a well-established fact. With this in mind, de Jong describes several key scientific discovery learning processes such as orientation, hypothesis generation, experimentation and evaluation. For all of the processes mentioned, software scaffolds have been developed that are meant to turn ineffective unsupported discovery into effective guided discovery. de Jong presents a clear overview of scaffolds for scientific discovery learning with computer simulations and summarizes the results of empirical evaluations.

Mayer discusses another kind of context — the new electronic multimedia used for instruction and describes a set of clear, research-based design guidelines. Mayer starts from a number of very practical questions: How can we help people understand cause-and-effect explanations of how complex systems work, such as how the human respiratory system works, how lightning storms develop or how an electric motor works? Mayer suggests ways to translate research on learning from instruction so that we can succeed in multimedia environments. He argues that a major challenge for instructional designers is to provide explanations of complex systems that capture the system's complexity without overwhelming the learner.

Instructional methods   Dillenbourg and Bétrancourt highlight the importance of, and the complexity related to collaboration between learners in classrooms and informal learning environments. They ask whether collaboration increases or decreases the complexity of a learning environment and its associated cognitive load. On one hand, collaboration might enable some degree of division of labor that may reduce cognitive load. On the other hand since collaboration-related activities such as interacting, expressing thoughts or monitoring another person's understanding are processes that induce some extraneous cognitive load, these activities may create cognitive overload and impede learning mechanisms. Dillenbourg and Bétrancourt contend that the trade-off between productive or intrinsic versus counter-productive or extraneous load of collaboration is not specific to collaborative learning.

Cress and Hesse further explore the problems that may be related to collaboration by investigating the factors that affect learner's inclination to contribute to an information pool when learners work collaboratively or when they make use of varied information resources. In these situations, the exchange of information between students becomes relevant. One way to enable knowledge exchange in classes or larger groups, they suggest, is to establish a common information pool. Cress and Hesse consider that such an information pool can be established as a by-product of another activity (like in a newsgroup), or it can be an explicit goal as in organizational knowledge management projects creating an organizational memory by using databases. This chapter focuses on people's motivation for participating in this kind of knowledge exchange.

Considering learners   Vermunt addresses the question how to provide support in order to help students cope with task complexity. First, a theoretical model on balancing support for various forms of student learning is presented. The model is based on an analysis of congruence and friction between students' self-regulated learning and the external regulation of learning exerted by teachers and teaching methods. Empirical research pertaining to the model is discussed. The case of secondary school reforms in the Netherlands, new learning, is then discussed from the perspective of the model. Finally, implications for theory, practice and further research are inferred.

The issue of adaptation to learners by selecting learning tasks in learning environments is addressed by van Merriënboer, Sluijsmans, Corbalan, Kalyuga, Paas, and Tattersall. These authors start from the observation that contemporary educational programs aim at increased flexibility by dynamically adapting the succession of authentic learning tasks to individual student needs. This chapter discusses how such adaptation can best be achieved, i.e. how the most optimal learning task can be selected. They propose that well-designed assessments should not only take overall performance into account, but also the costs (time, effort) needed to reach this performance, and the many qualitatively different aspects that can be distinguished in complex behavior. They suggest three different systems to implement adaptive learning tasks. In system-controlled models, an educational agent (teacher, eLearning application) selects the optimal learning task; in shared-responsibility models, an educational agent selects a subset from all available tasks after which the student makes a final selection, and in advisory models, the student is given helpful advice on task selection.

Classroom context   Depaepe, De Corte, and Verschaffel open their discussion by pointing at the complexity of the context in which learning occurs. They highlight the importance of considering not only deliberate but also implicit and unintentional instructional interventions. Their chapter outlines the impact of the culture of the mathematics classroom on students' development of mathematics-related beliefs and on their performances on mathematical tasks. The interpretative framework of Cobb and his colleagues is exemplary proposed as an appropriate lens through which one can look at mathematical classroom processes. Their concepts of 'norms' and 'beliefs' reflect respectively the social and individual level of the mathematics classroom. They argue that the classroom mathematics culture, as a determinant of students' mathematical learning and performance, emerges during successive interactions between the teacher and the students.

Instructional interventions   Elen and Clarebout also ask to broaden the focus of instructional research by more directly considering the actual rather than the planned use of instructional interventions. These authors acknowledge that instruction assumes that learning can be enhanced by well-targeted support. At the same time, they stress that research on learner control and tool use reveals that support is often either inadequately used by learners or not used at all. The lack of (adequate) use of instructional interventions reduces the effectiveness of the learning environment. Elen and Clarebout argue in favor of more studies that actually reveal the functionality of instructional interventions and of designing lean learning environments in order to avoid additional load for the learners.

Complexity: Research Issues

The third part of this edited book raises the question of 'complex' research. The different chapters address methodological issues, research design questions and make concrete proposals.

Model-building   Winne highlights new research strategies and points to problems related to misspecification of models. He actually deals with modeling complexity and argues in favor of more data and more ecological data. Winne starts from a brief review of three broad models of learning from instruction — teacher effects, cognitive and self-regulated learning — as representative of the field. The three-part model provides a backdrop for his proposition that the field is not as advanced as it might be expected to be. Winne proposes three reasons for the lack of progress. First, models of learning from instruction are misspecified; that is, relevant variables are excluded from a model, irrelevant variables are included, and measures of how much one variable affects another are inaccurate. Second is the problem of focus. This problem arises because, when variables co-vary with one another over time, focusing on (designating) one variable as cause and the other as effect is arbitrary. The third problem is granularity, that is, the level of detail at which a researcher should gather data that contributes to validly testing models about events that comprise learning. Winne proposes a remedy that builds on the notion of a conventional time-series experiment. Specifically, he recommends recording and analyzing an individual learner's data about temporally unfolding events that reflect or *trace* theoretically critical forms of cognition that comprise learning. A method for analyzing trace data is illustrated.

Research design and research methods   Winn extends in his chapter the argument that simplifying the observations may not help to understand the complex processes involved in learning and instruction. He illustrates that data from different sources may help us to understand the variables involved and the processes that play a role. Learning, Winn argues, is very complex, and students are coupled to learning environments in complex ways. To understand and study this complexity, ideas from system theory to learning can be profitably applied.

In his chapter, Salomon argues that learning environments are complex systems. Learning environments are *composites*, not just lists or clusters of variables, which entail *relations* among the variables. A satisfactory description of a learning environment, in his view, must include these relationships without which its structure cannot be understood. This chapter proposes that studying variables one by one and comparing in that way among different learning environments leads to the identification of *patterns of differences* that can inform us of the net contribution of the presence or absence of, say, test anxiety, to achievement. On the other hand, when whole configurations are compared, including the relations among the variables or components, *differences of patterns* emerge showing how the configurations of the learning environments differ from each other. In this case, however, Salomon points out that the net contribution of an isolated variable cannot be determined. He clearly claims that research of learning environments needs both approaches to complement each other such that both causal relations and configurational structures of learning environments can be fully understood.

Research questions Research that actually deals with complexity in learning environments needs both a well-thought of methodology and a series of pertinent and relevant questions. Merrill completes the research section by arguing in favor of a research agenda that would focus on validating a set of so-called first principles. The author identifies a set of instructional strategy principles that have been prescribed by a number of different instructional theories and recommended practices. He then proposes a set of hypotheses for the interrelationships among these principles. While many of these instructional design principles have been supported by individual experimental studies, the author was unable to find an integrated body of research that has studied the interrelationships among these instructional principles. Merrill proposes a scaled series of theory-based hypotheses that may provide a framework for integrated research on learning and instruction.

A synthesis of major findings and critical research questions, and an attempt to identify guidelines concludes this edited book on 'Handling complexity in learning environments: theory and research'.

References

Clark, R. E. (Ed.) (2001). *Learning from media. Arguments, analysis, and evidence.* Greenwich, CT: Information Age Publishing.

De Corte, E., Verschaffel, L., & Lowyck, J. (1994). Computers and learning. In: T. Husèn, & T. N. Postlethwaite (Eds), *International encyclopedia of education* (pp. 1002–1007). Oxford: Pergamon Press.

De Corte, E., Verschaffel, L., & Lowyck, J. (1996). Computers, media and learning. In: E. De Corte, & F. Weinert (Eds), *International encyclopedia of developmental and instructional psychology* (pp. 695–700). Oxford, UK: Pergamon Press.

Dillemans, R., Lowyck, J., Van der Perre, G., Claeys, C., & Elen, J. (1998). *New technologies for learning: Contribution of ICT to innovation in education.* Leuven: Leuven University Press.

Dörner, D. (1996). *The logic of failure: Why things go wrong and what we can do to make them right.* New York: Holt.

Driscoll, M. P. (2005). *Psychology of learning for instruction* (3rd ed.). New York: Pearson Education.

Elen, J. (1995). *Blocks on the road to instructional design prescriptions: A methodology for I.D.-research exemplified.* Leuven: Leuven University Press.

Elen, J., Lowyck, J., & Proost, K. (1996). Design of telematic learning environments: A cognitive mediational view. *Educational Research and Evaluation: An International Journal on Theory and Practice, 2,* 213–230.

Lane, H. (1965). Programmed learning of a second language. In: R. Glaser (Ed.), *Teaching machines and programmed learning. Data and directions* (pp. 584–643). Washington, DC: Department of Audiovisual Instruction, National Education Association of the United States.

Lowyck, J. (1971). Les moyens audio-visuels et la pédagogie de groupe. *Eurodidac, 2,* 26–32.

Lowyck, J. (1974). De vraagstelling als een mogelijke strategie voor het helpen bereiken van cognitieve en affectieve doelstellingen. *Tijdschrift voor Catechese, 4,* 223–240.

Lowyck, J. (1976). Die Analyse des Fragenstellens als Instrument für ein abgestuftes Fertigkeitentraining. *Unterrichtswissenschaft, 1,* 53–73.

Lowyck, J. (1980). *A process analysis of teaching* (Report n°21). Leuven, K.U. Leuven, Departement Pedagogische Wetenschappen, Afdeling Didactiek en Psychopedagogiek, (EDRS-ED 190513).

Lowyck, J. (1986). Post-interactive reflections of teachers: A critical appraisal. In: M. Ben-Peretz, R. Bromme, & R. Halkes (Eds), *Advances of research on teacher thinking* (pp. 172–185). Lisse: Swets & Zeitlinger.

Lowyck, J. (1993). Increasing access and participation: The use of new educational methods, media and technology for course presentation and for student support. In: C. de Vocht, & P. Hendrickx (Eds), *Conference proceedings European conference "Flexible responses in higher education"* (pp. 111–115). Brussel: Studiecentrum Open Hoger Onderwijs.

Lowyck, J. (1994). Learning in industrial settings. In: T. Husèn, & T. N. Postlethwaite (Eds), *International encyclopedia of education* (pp. 3302–3306). Oxford, UK: Pergamon Press.

Lowyck, J. (1998). *Van instructie-omgevingen naar leer-omgevingen: de slogan voorbij? Leerstoel Ererector L. Verhaegen.* Diepenbeek: Universiteitsfonds Limburg.

Lowyck, J. (2000a). Van personal computer naar e-leerplatform: Implicaties voor een ontwerpkunde. In: R. Koper, J. Lowyck, & W. Jochems (Eds), *Van verandering naar vernieuwing: Onderwijstechnologische grondslagen van elektronische leeromgevingen* (pp. 51–69). Heerlen: Open Universiteit Nederland.

Lowyck, J. (2000b). The challenge of ICT for the innovation of university education: A case-study. In: EADTU (Ed.), *Proceedings of the EADTU millennium conference: Wiring the ivory tower. Linking universities across Europe, Paris, France, 28–30 September 2000* (pp. 438–444). Heerlen: EADTU Secretariat.

Lowyck, J. (2002a). Ontwerpen van complexe leeromgevingen. In: J. Binon, P. Desmet, J. Elen, P. Mertens, & L. Sercu (Eds), *Tableaux vivants. Opstellen over taal-en-onderwijs* (pp. 533–550). Leuven: Universitaire Pers Leuven.

Lowyck, J. (2002b). Pedagogical design. In: H. H. Adelsberger, B. Collis, & J. M. Pawlowski (Eds), *Handbook on information technologies for education and training* (pp. 199–217). Berlin: Springer.

Lowyck, J. (2002c). Teaching methods, knowledge, technology and assessment: An interlinked field? *Universities Coimbra Group Newsletter, 19,* 11.

Lowyck, J. (2003a). Teacher thinking and teacher routines: A bifurcation? In: M. Kompf, & P. M. Denicolo (Eds), *Teacher thinking twenty years on: Revisiting persisting problems and advances in education* (pp. 101–110). Lisse: Swets & Zeitlinger.

Lowyck, J. (2003b). Post-interactive reflections of teachers: A critical appraisal. In: M. Kompf, & P. M. Denicolo (Eds), *Teacher thinking twenty years on revisiting persisting problems and advances in education* (pp. 295–306). Lisse: Swets & Zeitlinger.

Lowyck, J., & Clark, R. E. (Eds). (1996a). New research directions for training in organizations. *International Journal of Educational Research, 25*(Special issue), 383–471.

Lowyck, J., & Clark, R. E. (1996b). Corporate training design: Past, present, and future. *International Journal of Educational Research, 25,* 465–471.

Lowyck, J., de Gelder, E., & Vanmaele, L. (1987). Schrijven met een computer in het Beroepssecundair Onderwijs: Een pedagogisch-didactische benadering. *VVM-Berichten, 3,* 8–31.

Lowyck, J., & Elen, J. (1990). Self-study packages, vantage points for a new instructional design. *International Journal of Educational Research, 6,* 565–579.

Lowyck, J., & Elen, J. (1991). Wandel in der theoretischen Fundierung des Instruktiondesigns. *Unterrichtswissenschaft, 19,* 218–325.

Lowyck, J., & Elen, J. (1993a). Hypermedia for learning cognitive instructional design. In: A. Oliveira, & D. Jonassen (Eds), *Structures of communication and intelligent help for hypermedia courseware* (pp. 131–144). Berlin: Springer.

Lowyck, J., & Elen, J. (1993b). Transitions in the theoretical foundation of instructional design. In: T. Duffy, J. Lowyck, & D. H. Jonassen (Eds), *Designing environments for constructive learning* (pp. 213–229). Berlin: Springer.

Lowyck, J., & Elen, J. (1994a). Instructional psychology (as a contributing field to instructional design). In: T. Husèn, & T. N. Postlethwaite (Eds), *International encyclopedia of education* (pp. 2870–2874). Oxford, UK: Pergamon Press.

Lowyck, J., & Elen, J. (1994b). Modelling ID-research. *Proceedings of the first Workshop of the Special Interest Group on Instructional Design*, EARLI, Leuven: K.U. Leuven.

Lowyck, J., & Elen, J. (1999). Learners and learning in information and communication technologies (ICT) environments. In: C. M. Feyten, & J. W. Nutta (Eds), *Virtual instruction. Issues and insights from an international perspective* (pp. 65–105). Englewood, CO: Libraries Unlimited, Inc.

Lowyck, J., & Elen, J. (2004). Linking ICT, knowledge domains, and learning support for the design of learning environments. In: N. M. Seel, & S. Dijkstra (Eds), *Curriculum, plans and processes in instructional design. International perspectives* (pp. 239–256). Mahwah, NJ: Erlbaum.

Lowyck, J., Pöysä, J., & van Merriënboer, J. (2003). Conditions of ICT-based design for learning communities. *Technology, Instruction, Cognition and Learning (TICL), 1*, 153–182.

Lowyck, J., & Utsi, S. (2004). Exploring the features of multimedia learning. In: H. Niegemann, D. Leutner, & R. Brünken (Eds), *Instructional design for multimedia learning. Proceedings of the 5th International Workshop of SIG 6 Instructional Design of the European Association for Research on Learning and Instruction (EARLI) 2002* (pp. 211–221). Münster: Waxmann Verlag.

Lowyck, J., & Vanmaele, L. (1992). How to put language in a child's mind. The development of 'Scriptor' as a computer tool for writing. In: P. A. M. Kommers, D. H. Jonassen, & J. T. Mayer (Eds), *Cognitive tools for learning* (pp. 215–226). Berlin: Springer.

Luyten, L., Lowyck, J., & Tuerlinckx, F. (2001) Task perception as a mediating variable: A contribution to the validation of instructional knowledge. *British Journal of Educational Psychology, 71*, 203–223.

Mayer, R. E. (2004). Should there be a three-strikes rule against pure discovery learning? *American Psychologist, 59*, 14–19.

Spector, J. M. (2000). Introduction. In: J. M. Spector, & T. M. Anderson (Eds). *Integrated and holistic perspectives on learning, instruction, and technology. Understanding complexity* (pp. xi–xxii). London: Kluwer Academic Publishers.

van Merriënboer, J. J. G. (1997). *Training complex cognitive skills: A four-component instructional design model for technical training.* Englewood Cliffs, NJ: Educational Technology Publications.

Chapter 1

How the Human Cognitive System Deals with Complexity

John Sweller

Introduction

This chapter considers complexity from a cognitive load theory perspective. It is divided into three sections. The first section discusses how complexity is defined, measured and handled by cognitive load theory. The concepts of intrinsic cognitive load and element interactivity are examined. The second section considers how complexity is dealt with by natural information processing systems in general and human cognitive architecture in particular. This section places an emphasis on the evolutionary reasons why our cognitive system deals with complexity in its seemingly counter-intuitive way. The third section considers the instructional implications that flow from the interaction between complex information and the human cognitive system. In the language of cognitive load theory, this section is concerned with extraneous cognitive load and techniques to reduce it in order to allow the imposition of germane cognitive load.

Defining and Measuring Complexity within a Cognitive Load Theory Framework

Cognitive load theory deals with complexity using a single construct: element interactivity (Sweller, 1994). An element is anything that needs to be understood and learned. If elements interact, they cannot be understood in isolation whereas non-interacting elements can be understood and learned independently of each other. If many elements interact, element interactivity is high; if few interact, element interactivity is low. Levels of intrinsic cognitive load depend entirely on levels of element interactivity. In other words, the intrinsic complexity of information that a learner is attempting to assimilate is determined by the levels of element interactivity.

Handling Complexity in Learning Environments: Theory and Research

All rights of reproduction in any form reserved.
ISBN: 0-08-044986-7

An example of a task that is low in element interactivity is learning the symbols of chemical elements. One can learn that the chemical symbol for copper is Cu without learning the symbol for any other chemical element. In contrast, one cannot learn to balance a chemical equation without simultaneously taking into account all of the symbols of that equation. In this case, element interactivity is high.

Element interactivity can be estimated for all tasks faced by learners by counting the number of interacting elements (e.g., Sweller & Chandler, 1994; Tindall-Ford, Chandler, & Sweller, 1997). Learning the symbol for copper consists of three elements (copper = Cu). Learning how to multiply out a denominator in order to make the numerator the subject of an equation includes 17 interacting elements, as the following example demonstrates.

$a/b = c$ [5 symbols = 5 *interacting elements*]

$(a/b)b = cb$ [*b* in the original expression is a denominator (= *1 element*); a denominator can be removed from an expression in an equation (= *1 element*); by multiplying by the denominator (= *1 element*); any transformation on one side of an equation (= *1 element*); must be matched by the equivalent transformation on the other side (= *1 element*); in order to retain the equality (= *1 element*); accordingly, the right side of the equation (= *1 element*); must be multiplied by the denominator on the left (= *1 element*)]

$a = cb$ [*b* in the numerator (= 1 element); can cancel (= 1 element); *b* in the denominator leaving the numerator (= 1 element); as the subject of the equation (= 1 element)]

Note that these 17 elements are an estimate based on the assumption that the learner is a novice just beginning to learn algebra. For expert algebra problem solvers and indeed, most readers of this chapter, the entire procedure is likely to be encompassed within a single element. The procedure by which expertise alters the number of elements and the consequences of that procedure are critical to cognitive load theory and indeed, to human cognition. The consequences of expertise will be discussed in detail in the next section. For the moment, the salient point is that element interactivity can vary considerably and that element interactivity can be defined as complexity. Complex material includes a large number of interacting elements that must be considered simultaneously in order to be understood.

It should be emphasised that element interactivity, while it affects task difficulty is not synonymous with difficulty. Learning a large number of chemical element symbols is a difficult task. The task is difficult because many elements must be learned. On the current definition, it is not a complex task because the elements do not have to be considered simultaneously. Learning how to multiply a denominator is also a difficult task but for a different reason. The task is difficult because it is complex and that means there are many interacting elements that need to be simultaneously considered. It is a much more complex task than learning the symbols of chemical elements, not because many elements are involved — there are far fewer elements than learning chemical symbols — but because the relatively few elements interact and must be considered simultaneously.

How Human Cognitive Architecture Evolved to Handle Complexity

The manner in which the human cognitive system evolved to deal with complexity is, at first sight, surprising. We might expect that the obvious structure to deal with complex information is a large structure capable of handling many interacting elements. In fact, when dealing with novel, as opposed to well-learned information, we do not have a structure capable of handling many interacting elements and indeed, as is argued below, it may have been impossible for such a structure to evolve. In this section, some critical characteristics of human cognition when dealing with complex, high element interactivity material will be discussed.

Human cognition can be characterised as a natural information processing system. Any information processing system that can be found in nature is a natural information processing system. Evolution by natural selection is one such system as is the cognitive system of any animal, including human cognition (Sweller, 2003). While such systems differ from each other depending on the context in which they must function, they also share several common characteristics. Those characteristics can be described in the form of basic principles that constitute the underlying logic of natural information processing systems. The principles are:

- *The information store principle*. Natural information systems include information stores that determine all activity with the exception of random activity.
- *The randomness as genesis principle*. Information in a store can be altered by randomly proposing an alteration and testing it for effectiveness with effective alterations retained and ineffective alterations jettisoned. This principle is the initial source of all information in the store of a natural information processing system.
- *The narrow limits of change principle*. All alterations to a store by random alterations must be small relative to the size of the store in order to ensure that functionality of the store is retained.
- *The borrowing principle*. Much larger alterations to a store can occur by adding information from another store that has already been tested for effectiveness.

In this section, the evidence and arguments supporting these principles will be provided.

The Information Store Principle

Natural information stores deal with complexity by storing huge amounts of information. In the case of biological systems, a genome, as is well known, provides that store of information. The massive amount of information stored in an individual's DNA determines biological activity. Genomic complexity is required to handle biologically complex activities.

Long-term memory provides a similar function in human cognition. It has taken our field a very long time to realise the central importance of long-term memory in human cognition. Because at any given time we are unaware of most of the contents of long-term memory, many people intuitively feel that the sole function of long-term memory is simply to store more or less random, unconnected memories. The reconceptualisation of the role of long-term memory can probably be traced to the work on chess by De Groot (1965) and Chase and Simon (1973). They established that the only discernible difference between chess grand masters and weekend players was in memory of chess board configurations taken from real games. That difference disappeared when dealing with random board configurations.

Chess grand masters have stored tens of thousands of board configurations in long-term memory (Simon & Gilmartin, 1973). That store of information in long-term memory permits chess experts to recognise most of the configurations they encounter and tells them which move is the best for that configuration. This finding has been replicated on several occasions in a variety of different, educationally relevant domains (e.g., Egan & Schwartz, 1979; Jeffries, Turner, Polson, & Atwood, 1981; Sweller & Cooper, 1985). It suggests that information held in long-term memory is not simply unstructured snippets of information but rather consists of massive amounts of integrated information that is central to thinking and problem solving. The purpose of long-term memory is to allow us to deal with very complex, very high element interactivity material in the same manner, as the purpose of immensely complex genomes is to permit organisms to function in a very complex environment. Natural information processing systems functioning in complex environments require similarly complex stores of information.

The manner in which information is structured in long-term memory is a matter of ongoing-research concern. For present purposes, schema theory will be used as a guide. A schema integrates multiple elements of information into a single element that informs us what actions we should take under given conditions. Chess experts can recognise board configurations and the best moves associated with each configuration because they have schemas for board configurations. Those schemas integrate the many elements that go to make up a board configuration into a single, schematic element. The importance of schemas for problem solving skill was recognised in the early 1980s (Chi, Glaser, & Rees, 1982; Larkin, McDermott, Simon, & Simon, 1980). A person has problem-solving skill in a given domain because they have accumulated many schemas in that domain. On this view, most of our intellectual behaviour is schema based. We have perceptual schemas that permit us to recognise the infinite variety of shapes that constitute handwritten versions of the letters of the alphabet and higher-order schemas that allow us to recognise combinations of letters that go to make up words or combinations of words that go to make up phrases or even sentences and combinations of sentences. Other schemas allow us to derive meaning from these shapes that almost certainly exceed chessboard configurations in their complexity. We have large numbers of schemas that permit us to recognise and solve algebra problems like the one discussed above. Together, schemas such as these are central to our cognitive lives and in that sense, schemas held in long-term memory are central to human cognition.

The Randomness as Genesis Principle

While schemas can be transmitted from one individual to another via education (as discussed below), how are they initially constructed? Before being transmitted to other people, where does the first schema come from? If one treats the human cognitive system as a natural information processing system, the answer to these questions is quite different to those normally provided in psychology and education. It is an answer that is both logically unavoidable but likely to be seen by many as confrontational.

In natural information processing systems, random generation followed by effectiveness testing is the only conceivable process by which the large store of information discussed in the previous section can be initially built. While likely to be controversial in psychology and education, this principle is now universally adhered to by evolutionary biologists. All genetic differences both between and within species were initiated by a process of random mutation. A random mutation that increases the fitness of an individual to survive in its environment is likely to be passed on to future generations and so retained as part of the genome. A mutation that decreases the fitness of an individual to survive in its environment is likely to be lost.

This generate-and-test procedure is quite unavoidable. Natural information processing systems do not have and cannot have an executive-type structure that determines what alterations to the store of information are or are not to be considered (Sweller, 2003). The test part of generate-and-test can determine what will be retained but there is no conceivable process that can determine what will be generated other than random generation. Random mutation has been accepted by biologists because there is no alternative mechanism that can be used to determine which mutations are likely to be beneficial before the mutation has occurred. That "decision" only can be made after a mutation has occurred with no executive process available to determine what future alterations to the store of information might be beneficial. In other words, all the immense complexity to be found in the biological world was built by a simple, random generation and test procedure.

If human cognition is another example of a natural information processing system, the same logical imperatives that lead to the random generation and test procedure in evolution by natural selection must also lead to random generation and test in human cognition. And indeed, a simple analysis suggests that this procedure is just as unavoidable in human cognition as in biological evolution.

Consider a person faced with a novel situation in which the person is unsure what action to take. In other words, the person is faced with the complexities inherent in a problem-solving context. How does the person determine what problem-solving moves are required to solve the problem? Failing someone showing the person which moves to make (a situation discussed below), there are only two move generating sources. Either the person uses previously acquired schemas held in long-term memory or failing those schemas being available, moves must be generated randomly and tested for effectiveness. In some combination or other, there are no other possibilities available. The level of complexity of the problem faced does not alter this choice. To the extent that knowledge held in long-term memory is not available to assist in generating moves, they must be generated randomly. Once generated, they can be tested for effectiveness using a process such as means-ends analysis (Newell & Simon, 1972) but their potential effectiveness cannot be determined prior to their being generated. As is the case for biological evolution, there is no conceivable executive system that could make such determination (Sweller, 2003). Random generation followed by effectiveness testing is the genesis of all information held by natural information processing systems.

The Narrow Limits of Change Principle

There are structural consequences that flow from the random elements associated with altering the information store of natural information processing systems. Specifically, it is essential that any alterations to the store are small. A large change is likely to destroy the functionality of the store. The larger the change, the less likely it is to be effective. A complex organ such as the eye can evolve by random alterations over a long period because each incremental change can be tested for effectiveness with only effective alterations retained. The probability that such complex structures and functions could evolve randomly in a simultaneous fashion is effectively zero.

Human cognition has a specific structure, working memory, to ensure that alterations to the contents of long-term memory at any given time are small. When dealing with novel information that could potentially alter the contents of long-term memory, both the capacity (Cowan, 2001; Miller, 1956) and the duration (Peterson & Peterson, 1959) of working memory are very limited. As indicated above, it may seem peculiar that the structure that is central to dealing with complex information should have evolved with such severe limits. The need to ensure that the integrity of long-term memory is preserved dictates working memory limits. Given these limits, how does working memory deal with complexity? It is critical to note the nature of those limits.

The basic cognitive architecture central to most models is the one first outlined by Atkinson and Shiffrin (1968). In that architecture, working memory can receive information either from sensory memory or from long-term memory. The limitations discussed above only apply to novel information coming via sensory memory. The well-known characteristics of working memory apply only to such information. Working memory limitations disappear when dealing with previously organised information coming from long-term memory. The quite different characteristics of working memory when dealing with information fed from sensory as opposed to long-term memory provide the key to how human cognitive architecture deals with complexity.

While working memory can only deal with a limited number of elements, what constitutes an element varies depending on what has been learned. Schemas are elements. As was found with chess grand masters, if someone has stored in long-term memory a complex schema consisting of many interacting lower order schemas or elements, that schema can be brought into working memory and treated as a single element. Working memory capacity is not strained because under these conditions, working memory is dealing with only one element rather than the multiplicity of interacting elements that make up the schema. Complex schemas may necessarily take a long time to develop but once they have been developed, their effects on working memory can be quite startling. Indeed, the effect is so large that it induced Ericsson and Kintsch (1995) to postulate a separate structure, long-term working memory. As indicated above, the current treatment, rather than assuming a separate structure, postulates a single working memory structure that is able to deal with information with different characteristics depending on whether it is sourced from sensory or long-term memory.

The interaction between working and long-term memory provides the core explanation of how the human cognitive system deals with complexity. It does not deal with complexity by a structure that can take large numbers of random elements and impose order on them. It deals with complexity by incrementally building up complex schemas in long-term memory. The elements that go to make up these schemas must first be processed in working memory but working memory is structured to only process a very small number of those elements at a time. It can only process a large number of elements once they have been incrementally structured and then stored in long-term memory. There are no known limits to the size of a schema that has been stored in long-term memory and can be brought into working memory. That knowledge in long-term memory is central to human intellectual skill. We are skilful despite our inability to deal with more than a few elements of novel information at any given time.

The Borrowing Principle

In natural information processing systems, the initial construction of bodies of information by random generation followed by tests of effectiveness is necessarily a very slow and lengthy process. In evolutionary biology, while random mutation is the ultimate source of all genetic material, it is possible for genetic material to be borrowed by one species from another species and so short-circuit the slow, generate-and-test procedure. Furthermore, any genome borrows almost its entire structure from its immediate ancestors with random mutation playing a quite insignificant role.

In human cognition, the borrowing principle constitutes a major procedure in that it is the most common form of learning. While random generation followed by tests of effectiveness provide the ultimate source of all human knowledge, for any individual, learning by means other than generate-and-test is necessarily the norm. An individual cannot use random generate-and-test to provide the huge knowledge base held in human long-term memory. While, as is the case for any natural information processing system, the information that constitutes that knowledge base was initially generated by the random generate-and-test mechanism, that knowledge can be transmitted to others indefinitely and it is that transmission that inevitably constitutes the bulk of knowledge acquisition. Any individual's knowledge base depends almost entirely on information transmitted from others either directly or by print, rather than on random generate-and-test. The borrowing principle requires us to learn almost everything from others rather than to discover for ourselves. Expecting individuals to discover complex, high element interactivity information by a random generate-and-test procedure rather than have it transmitted is futile.

How does the borrowing principle apply to human learning? Whenever an individual provides guidance to another individual, the intention is the transfer of information or knowledge held in long-term memory. Before the advent of writing, the spoken word was the primary means of transfer. Since the advent of writing, the written word along with pictures and diagrams are more common. In either case, a large amount of information held in any individual's long-term memory is likely to have been transferred from the long-term memories of other individuals by communication in either spoken or written form. In other words, instruction, broadly defined is the most important source of any human's knowledge even though that knowledge had to be initially generated by a random generation and test procedure, frequently over many generations. Finding ways of organising that instruction to take into account, human cognitive architecture has been the goal of cognitive load theory and is discussed next.

Instructional Implications

The previous two sections on defining and measuring complexity and on the evolution of human cognitive architecture provide the cognitive base that underlies cognitive load theory. The theory uses our knowledge of information structures and cognitive structures to generate instructional principles. It assumes that the major purpose of instruction is to effect alterations in long-term memory by the acquisition of large numbers of domain-specific schemas. It assumes further that the instruction must be structured to reduce any extraneous load on working memory where an extraneous load is defined as one that does not contribute to schema acquisition. By reducing extraneous cognitive load, capacity is freed for germane cognitive load, which is cognitive load that is necessary for schema acquisition. These two sources of cognitive load are additive, along with intrinsic cognitive load caused by element interactivity and discussed above. Together, all three sources of cognitive load cannot exceed total working memory capacity.

Cognitive load theory has generated a large number of specific instructional design principles. Because there are several recent summaries of those principles (e.g., Sweller, 2003, 2004), they will not be repeated here. Rather, the general consequences of cognitive load theory for the design of instruction dealing with complex, high element interactivity material will be discussed. Mayer (this volume, Chapter 7) has used his theory of multimedia learning, which has close ties to cognitive load theory (Mayer, 2005; Sweller, 2005a), to provide complementary instructional design principles.

Human cognition deals with complex material by slowly building schemas in long-term memory that can then be processed as a single element in working memory. Until those schemas have been constructed, it is quite impossible for working memory to deal with complex, very high element interactivity material. The randomness as genesis principle ensured that working memory had to evolve with severe limits on its ability to simultaneously process many elements. Those limits, in turn, are an example of the narrow limits of change principle. Accordingly, instructional material must be structured to reduce working memory load when dealing with complex, high element interactivity material presented to novices. Most instruction is directed to novices because novices are in most need of instruction. But novices, by definition, do not have the extensive schemas in long-term memory that can be used to reduce working memory load. They are being presented with instructional material in order to acquire those schemas. If that instructional material ignores the working memory limitations of novices, it will be deficient. Once some degree of expertise has been attained in a particular domain, the characteristics of working memory alter in that working memory limits expand or even disappear entirely. At that point, instructional procedures that may be necessary for novices are no longer essential and may even have negative consequences (Clark, 1989; Kalyuga, Ayres, Chandler, & Sweller, 2003). Furthermore, instructional procedures based on the need to reduce working memory load are only likely to be necessary for complex, high element interactivity material that imposes a heavy intrinsic cognitive load in the first place (Sweller, 1994). If intrinsic cognitive load is low, designing instruction to reduce extraneous working memory load is likely to be irrelevant because working memory will be able to handle such instruction even when it imposes high levels of extraneous cognitive load.

What classes of activities are likely to reduce extraneous cognitive load? One of the earliest recommendations of cognitive load theory was the suggestion that most standard problem-solving activities imposed a very heavy working memory load (Sweller, 1988). In order to solve a problem by means-ends analysis (Newell & Simon, 1972), a problem solver must simultaneously consider the current problem state, the goal state, extract differences between them and find problem-solving operators that will reduce those differences, as well as maintaining a stack of subgoals. All of these activities must occur in working memory and this act of searching for a problem-solving move that will bring the problem solver closer to a goal state bears little relation to schema acquisition. While problem-solving schemas indicate how a problem should be solved, searching for problem solving moves is a different cognitive activity to learning which moves will best lead to a problem solution and as a consequence, problem solving through means-ends analysis is a technique that interferes with learning (Sweller, 1988). Schema acquisition is vastly enhanced by having learners study worked examples rather than solve problems (e.g., Sweller & Cooper, 1985; Cooper & Sweller, 1987). This finding is known as the worked examples effect. Experimentally, it occurs when a group of learners given worked examples to study perform better on subsequent tests of problem solving than learners given the same problems to solve. The current educational fad of recommending problem solving during discovery or constructivist-based learning makes no sense given our knowledge of human cognitive architecture and has no empirical support from controlled experiments (Kirschner, Sweller, & Clark, in press; Mayer, 2004).

Another general recommendation of cognitive load theory is to reduce unnecessary search for referents in instructional material. If X refers to Y, firstly, does it need to refer to Y and secondly, if it does need to refer to Y, can we reduce the need for learners to search for the nature of the relation between X and Y? For instance, assume a geometry diagram and its set of explanatory statements. Normally, neither the diagram nor the statements can be understood in isolation. They must be mentally integrated before they can be understood. The act of mental integration requires working memory resources that consequently become unavailable for schema acquisition. In contrast, if the explanatory statements are integrated within the diagram so that learners do not have to search for referents, extraneous cognitive load is reduced and learning enhanced, providing an example of the split-attention effect (Ayres & Sweller, 2005). The effect is demonstrated experimentally when a group of learners provided with information in a split-attention format perform better on a subsequent test than another group with identical information in an integrated format. It is an effect that is only obtainable with complex, high element interactivity material that imposes a heavy intrinsic cognitive load (Sweller & Chandler, 1994). Using simpler, low element interactivity material, Sweller and Chandler (1994) found no differences between conditions. The extraneous cognitive load imposed by split-attention is irrelevant when intrinsic cognitive load imposed by element interactivity is low because total cognitive load does not exceed working memory resources.

Not all diagrams and their associated statements are unintelligible in isolation. Sometimes, a set of statements merely redescribes the diagram. The statements may be redundant and unnecessary. Requirement of learners to process and integrate such statements with the diagram requires working memory resources that could better be deployed in schema acquisition. Eliminating the redundant statements improves learning providing an example of the redundancy effect (Sweller, 2005b). Experimentally, the effect is demonstrated when learners presented material without redundant information perform better on a subsequent test than learners presented the same material with additional, redundant or irrelevant information. Again, the redundancy effect is only obtainable using high element interactivity material (Sweller & Chandler, 1994) with no differences between conditions using simple, low element interactivity material. When dealing with low element interactivity material cognitive load may not exceed working memory resources even when redundant material is included. The redundancy effect is not only obtainable using diagrams and redundant text but can be obtained using any redundant, unnecessary material such as redundant information that appears on both a screen and in a manual, or identical text that is presented in both written and spoken form.

Cognitive load theory has also been used to recommend that when two sources of related information are unintelligible in isolation, rather than integrating them to reduce split-attention, a verbal source should be presented in spoken rather than written form. A diagram and written text can be presented as a diagram and spoken text, for example. Controlled experiments have demonstrated the superiority of dual modality presentation over single modality presentation (Low & Sweller, 2005). The effect occurs when a group of learners presented, for example, a diagram and essential text in spoken form, obtain higher test scores than a group of learners presented the same diagram along with written rather than spoken text with the diagrams and written text presented in split-attention format. This effect is caused by the expansion of working memory available under dual, auditory and visual modality presentation over a uni-modal presentation such as a diagram and written text. The modality effect, too, is only obtainable when dealing with complex, high element interactivity material (Tindall-Ford et al., 1997). Simple, low element interactivity material results in no differences between conditions demonstrating again that the important consideration is working memory load (Tindall-Ford et al., 1997).

The previous effects all demonstrated that extraneous cognitive load is only important when dealing with complex, high element interactivity material that imposes a high intrinsic cognitive load. Together, they provide examples of the element interactivity effect, which occurs when extraneous cognitive load becomes irrelevant due to a low intrinsic cognitive load. Intrinsic cognitive load has also been studied independently of extraneous cognitive load. Pollock, Chandler, and Sweller (2002) studied the learning of very high element interactivity material. (See van Merriënboer & Sweller, 2005, for a review of cognitive load theory and very complex information.)

Cognitive load theory assumes that very high element interactivity material can be easily handled by experts in a domain because the interacting elements are all subsumed within a schema which can be treated as a single element in working memory resulting in a minimal cognitive load. The question immediately arises, how are such complex materials handled initially, before schemas have been acquired? The interacting elements cannot be manipulated in working memory because of the limitations of working memory when dealing with novel material. Schemas that incorporate those elements have not as yet been formed. Pollock et al. (2002) suggested that the material must initially be learned as isolated elements, ignoring the interactions between them. By ignoring interactions between elements, understanding of the material is compromised but working memory can handle the isolated elements. Once they have been learned, interactions between elements can be further learned resulting in full understanding. In other words, it was hypothesised that understanding would be facilitated by first learning the elements in isolation followed by the interactions between them rather than attempting to learn the elements along with their interactions from the beginning of instruction.

Pollock et al. (2002) tested this hypothesis by having one group of learners who presented the learning elements in isolation followed by the same group of elements with the interactions between them emphasised. Another group was presented the interacting elements immediately. This group was presented the interacting elements twice in succession to ensure equality of learning time. The results on subsequent tests indicated superior learning by the isolated/interacting elements group compared to the interacting elements group alone. When dealing with highly complex material, it is better to present it in isolated elements form even though understanding is initially compromised. By subsequently presenting the material with full emphasis on understanding the interacting elements, learning and understanding are facilitated compared to presenting the material with all interactions emphasised. For novices, the working memory load of interacting elements will prevent understanding. This result provides an example of the isolated/interacting elements effect.

There are many other effects generated by cognitive load theory that have not been discussed in this chapter (see Sweller, 2003, 2004). Most, though not all, are compounds or interactions of the above effects. It should be noted that most of these effects are only obtainable with novices. As expertise increases, the effects first begin to narrow and disappear and then may reverse, giving another effect, the expertise reversal effect (Kalyuga et al., 2003; see also Clark, 1989). As an example, one of the consequences of the expertise reversal effect is that while novices require many worked examples, those worked examples should be faded with increasing expertise (e.g., Renkl & Atkinson, 2003) by first using completion problems in which learners must complete the solution to a partially solved problem (e.g., Paas & Van Merriënboer, 1994) and then presenting full problems. This procedure fits in precisely with our knowledge of how human cognition deals with complexity. Initially, a learner without relevant schemas held in long-term memory, must solve a complex problem using inefficient random generate-and-test procedures. Guidance from worked examples deals with complexity and obviates the need for generate-and-test. As schemas build up in long-term memory, they can deal with complexity instead. Guidance can be provided by those schemas rather than by instruction. At that point, the learner is ready to solve problems without external guidance because the element interactivity that leads to complexity is embedded within schemas that can indicate relevant actions without exceeding working memory capacity.

Conclusions

At their base, all cognitive-load theory derived effects depend on the interactions between the information structures and cognitive structures discussed above. Information is complex when learners are required to process many interacting elements simultaneously. Our cognitive architecture evolved to handle complex information, not by the seemingly obvious route of a large working memory but rather, by incrementing knowledge in long-term memory that could then be brought into working memory as a single element consisting of an unlimited number of organised sub-elements. In this way, providing it has already been organised in long-term memory, massively complex information can be dealt with by just a few elements in working memory.

Organised information held in a very large, permanent store appears to be a central characteristic of natural information processing systems. These systems share an underlying logic in the sense that the function of the store and the manner in which it must be built and altered are common.

Some unavoidable characteristics of natural information processing systems have instructional implications. When dealing with novel information for which previous knowledge is unavailable, it is impossible to determine the consequences of an action until after it has been chosen. Accordingly, actions must be chosen randomly and tested for effectiveness. Unguided teaching techniques, currently popular in some quarters, appear to unwittingly encourage learners to engage in such random search. The obvious alternative is to provide guidance and so eliminate random search.

Random search requires working memory to have a limited capacity when dealing with novel information. Those capacity limitations disappear when dealing with previously organised information from long-term memory. Cognitive load theory uses the relations between working and long-term memory to devise instructional techniques intended to facilitate the acquisition of knowledge in long-term memory. In turn, the success of the theory in generating instructional techniques suggests that the informational and cognitive structures assumed by the theory realistically reflect reality.

References

Atkinson, R., & Shiffrin, R. (1968). Human memory: A proposed system and its control processes. In: K. Spence, & J. Spence (Eds), *The psychology of learning and motivation* (Vol. 2, pp. 89–195). New York: Academic Press.

Ayres, P., & Sweller, J. (2005). The split-attention principle in multimedia learning. In: R. E. Mayer (Ed.), *The Cambridge handbook of multimedia learning* (pp. 135–146). New York: Cambridge University Press.

Chase, W. G., & Simon, H. A. (1973). Perception in chess. *Cognitive Psychology, 4,* 55–81.

Chi, M., Glaser, R., & Rees, E. (1982). Expertise in problem solving. In: R. Sternberg (Ed.), *Advances in the psychology of human intelligence* (pp. 7–75). Hillsdale, NJ: Erlbaum.

Clark, R. E. (1989). When teaching kills learning: Research on mathematics. In: H. N. Mandl, N. Bennett, E. De Corte, & H. F. Friedrich (Eds), *Learning and instruction. European research in an international context* (Vol. 2). London: Pergamon Press.

Cooper, G., & Sweller, J. (1987). The effects of schema acquisition and rule automation on mathematical problem-solving transfer. *Journal of Educational Psychology, 79,* 347–362.

Cowan, N. (2001). The magical number 4 in short-term memory: A reconsideration of mental storage capacity. *Behavioral and Brain Sciences, 24,* 87–114.

De Groot, A. (1965). *Thought and choice in chess.* The Hague, Netherlands: Mouton (Original work published in 1946).

Egan, D. E., & Schwartz B. J. (1979). Chunking in recall of symbolic drawings. *Memory and Cognition, 7,* 149–158.

Ericsson, K. A., & Kintsch, W. (1995). Long-term working memory. *Psychological Review, 102,* 211–245.

Jeffries, R., Turner, A., Polson, P., & Atwood, M. (1981). Processes involved in designing software. In: J. R. Anderson (Ed.), *Cognitive skills and their acquisition* (pp. 255–283). Hillsdale, NJ: Erlbaum.

Kalyuga, S., Ayres, P., Chandler, P., & Sweller, J. (2003). Expertise reversal effect. *Educational Psychologist, 38,* 23–31.

Kirschner, P., Sweller, J., & Clark, R. (in press). Why minimally guided learning does not work: An analysis of the failure of constructivist, discovery, problem-based, experiential and inquiry-based learning. *Educational Psychologist.*

Larkin, J., McDermott, J., Simon, D., & Simon, H. (1980). Models of competence in solving physics problems. *Cognitive Science, 4,* 317–348.

Low, R., & Sweller, J. (2005). The modality principle in multimedia learning. In: R. E. Mayer (Ed.), *The Cambridge handbook of multimedia learning* (pp. 147–158). New York: Cambridge University Press.

Mayer, R. (2004). Should there be a three-strikes rule against pure discovery learning? The case for guided methods of instruction. *American Psychologist, 59*(1), 14–19.

Mayer, R. (Ed.), (2005). *The Cambridge handbook of multimedia learning.* New York: Cambridge University Press.

Miller, G. A. (1956). The magical number seven, plus or minus two: Some limits on our capacity for processing information. *Psychological Review, 63,* 81–97.

Newell, A., & Simon, H. (1972). *Human problem solving.* Englewood Cliffs, NJ: Prentice-Hall.

Paas, F., & Van Merriënboer, J. (1994). Variability of worked examples and transfer of geometrical problem solving skills: A cognitive-load approach. *Journal of Educational Psychology, 86,* 122–133.

Peterson, L., & Peterson, M. (1959). Short-term retention of individual verbal items. *Journal of Experimental Psychology, 58,* 193–198.

Pollock, E., Chandler, P., & Sweller, J. (2002). Assimilating complex information. *Learning and Instruction, 12,* 61–86.

Renkl, A., & Atkinson, R. (2003). Structuring the transition from example study to problem solving in cognitive skill acquisition: A cognitive load perspective. *Educational Psychologist, 38,* 15–22.

Simon, H., & Gilmartin, K. (1973). A simulation of memory for chess positions. *Cognitive Psychology, 5,* 29–46.

Sweller, J. (1988). Cognitive load during problem solving: Effects on learning. *Cognitive Science, 12,* 257–285.

Sweller, J. (1994). Cognitive load theory, learning difficulty and instructional design. *Learning and Instruction, 4,* 295–312.

Sweller, J. (2003). Evolution of human cognitive architecture. In: B. Ross (Ed.), *The psychology of learning and motivation* (Vol. 43, pp. 215–266). San Diego: Academic Press.

Sweller, J. (2004). Instructional design consequences of an analogy between evolution by natural selection and human cognitive architecture. *Instructional Science, 32,* 9–31.

Sweller, J. (2005a). Implications of cognitive load theory for multimedia learning. In: R. E. Mayer (Ed.), *The Cambridge handbook of multimedia learning* (pp. 19–30). New York: Cambridge University Press.

Sweller, J. (2005b). The redundancy principle in multimedia learning. In: R. E. Mayer (Ed.), *The Cambridge handbook of multimedia learning* (pp. 159–168). New York: Cambridge University Press.

Sweller, J., & Chandler, P. (1994). Why some material is difficult to learn. *Cognition & Instruction, 12,* 185–233.

Sweller, J., & Cooper, G. A. (1985). The use of worked examples as a substitute for problem solving in learning algebra. *Cognition and Instruction, 2,* 59–89.

Tindall-Ford, S., Chandler, P., & Sweller, J. (1997). When two sensory modes are better than one. *Journal of Experimental Psychology: Applied, 3,* 257–287.

Van Merriënboer, J., & Sweller, J. (2005). Cognitive load theory and complex learning: Recent developments and future directions. *Educational Psychology Review, 17* (2), 147–177.

Chapter 2

Motivational Challenges Experienced in Highly Complex Learning Environments

Richard E. Clark, Keith Howard and Sean Early

Introduction

One of the greatest challenges facing education today is to find more effective and efficient ways to support the learning of highly complex knowledge. As Richard Snow described the issue: "... learning to learn, learning to reason, learning to find and solve problems, learning to be interested and industrious, to persevere, to achieve in the face of novelty, complexity, adversity, and change ... increasingly becomes the principal goal of education" (Snow, 1996, p. 536). Snow goes on to define general ability as the capacity to deal effectively with novelty and complexity. "Intelligence is ... an organization of aptitudes for learning and problem solving, particularly in situations involving novel or complex meaningful information and incomplete instruction about it" (p. 537). To advance the goal of understanding how to support the learning of complex knowledge, most discussions emphasize the use of structured teaching strategies or the design, development and delivery of strongly guided instruction and other educational services (for example, Kirschner, Sweller, & Clark, 2006; Mayer, 2004). This chapter will describe the various ways that motivation to learn is influenced by complexity and a few of the special motivational challenges students experience as they attempt to learn complex knowledge in challenging environments. Motivation has been found to make a highly significant contribution to learning from instruction, accounting for approximately 20 percent of the variance in achievement and about 29 percent of the variance in transfer of knowledge (Colquitt, LePine, & Noe, 2000). Considering that instructional strategies account for about the same proportion of learning variance (Snow, 1996), motivational processes may deserve more attention from researchers concerned with complex learning. Our discussion begins with a definition of complexity and a description of current motivation theory. We then go on to describe five different research areas where task complexity may interfere with the motivational processes that support learning. Where possible, we will also describe the evidence for ways to overcome motivational problems.

Handling Complexity in Learning Environments: Theory and Research
Copyright © 2006 by Elsevier Ltd.
All rights of reproduction in any form reserved.
ISBN: 0-08-044986-7

Defining and Measuring Complexity and Novelty

Current attempts to provide a cognitive definition of learning complexity (Salomon, 1983, 1984; Lohman, 1989; Snow, 1996) have focused on the number of non-automated cognitive operations or strategies that students must implement to achieve a specific learning goal. Thus as learning tasks require more non-automated operations, cognitive complexity increases. Sweller (this volume, Chapter 1) refers to this process as element "interactivity" and provides examples from mathematics tasks where more complex learning requires the mastery of many related steps in an operation.

While it is possible to measure the explicit cognitive steps or strategies required to achieve well-defined tasks such as a mathematics problem, it has been a challenge to measure the extent to which student prior experience has led to automated cognitive strategies that can be applied without placing a load on working memory (Anderson, 1983, 1990). Students with more prior knowledge learn more quickly in part because they do not experience as much complexity as students with less prior knowledge. When poorly defined tasks or problems are tackled, cognitive load is a significant factor for most students (Singley & Anderson, 1989). Lohman (1989) described the problem of estimating the amount of complexity that confronts any learner in any task situation very well when he cautioned that: "What is novel for one person may not be novel for another person or even for the same person at a different time … [thus] … inferences about how subjects solve items that require higher level processing must be probabilistic, since the novelty of each [item] varies for each person" (p. 348).

In addition to the number of non-automated operations, individual assessments of complexity must also consider the amount of processing space available in working memory for each learner. While the availability of working memory space appears to be very limited (Cowan, 2001), the actual space available to any learner varies considerably due to both motivational and learning processes (Bandura, 1997).

Recognizing that complexity must be defined by reference both to the prior knowledge and to the motivational processes a learner brings to bear on a task, is a necessary step in understanding how to support learning. Lohman (1989) made a compelling, research-based argument that for learners with diverse cultural backgrounds and different levels of prior knowledge, any given learning goal could be excessively complex for some but routine for others. Historically, reviews of research on motivational processes that support (or fail to support) learning suggest that as complexity increases, a learner's motivation becomes a much more significant predictor of learning (Pintrich & Schunk, 2002). It seems important, therefore, to examine some of the most important motivational challenges posed by complexity. After defining motivation and its role in learning, the chapter will describe five motivational challenges students face when pursuing complex learning goals.

Defining and Measuring Motivation

Motivation is most often defined as "… the process whereby goal-directed activity is instigated and sustained" (Pintrich & Schunk, 2002, p. 4), and, in addition, as the amount and quality of the "mental effort" people invest in achieving learning and performance goals (Salomon, 1984). Mental effort is defined as "the number of non-automatic elaborations necessary to learn or solve a problem" (Salomon, 1984, p. 785) or "interactivity" (Sweller, this volume, Chapter 1). Thus, motivational research and theory tends to focus on three primary dependent variables or "indexes": (1) starting (instigating) new behaviors; (2) persisting (sustaining) in the face of distractions once started on a goal and; (3) investing mental effort in order to accomplish goals that are novel and complex (Pintrich & Schunk, 2002) since routine goals can be achieved with a minimum of mental effort. It is useful to view motivation research and theory as an attempt to understand the precursors of one or more of these three "index" variables or their contribution to learning and problem solving. There are variables that influence starting, persisting or investing mental effort (Clark, 1999a) during learning. Presumably, learners with high ability will not learn unless they start, persist and invest adequate mental effort during learning. All other motivational variables are presumed to influence one or more of these three indexes.

Current motivational theories and models The theoretical models in current educational use derive, in part, from an early analysis of motivation research by Salomon (1983, 1984), more recent reviews by Pintrich and Schunk (2002); and the model building effort of Martin Ford's (1992) Motivational Systems Theory (MST) as well as the more familiar Social Cognitive Theory proposed by Bandura (1997). Some of these efforts have been summarized by Clark (1999a, 2003, 2004, 2005, in press; Clark & Estes, 2002), who has described a theory called CaNE (Commitment and Necessary Effort) where commitment is a joint function of starting and persisting at a task, and effort reflects the number of novel cognitive operations needed to achieve a goal. Evidence for the theory comes from various sources including meta-analytic reviews of motivation studies (e.g., Colquitt et al., 2000) and direct tests (e.g., Condly, 1999; Gimino, 2000; Flad, 2002; Yildir, 2004).

Until recently, motivation research has tended to be fragmented and motivation theories seem often to overlap and researchers seem to examine similar constructs with different names and different constructs with similar names. Ford's (1992) review of motivation research and theory identified over 30 different theories of motivation. Pintrich and Schunk (2002) describe six different motivation research groups who were investigating very similar goal-orientation variables but using different construct names. Efforts by theory builders such as Ford (1992), Pintrich and Schunk (2002) and Bandura (1997) to integrate diverse yet overlapping theories has recently made it possible to better understand the motivational processes that occur during learning and problem solving. One model that attempts to integrate many of the variables in a number of current theories is presented in Figure 2.1.

The motivational challenge of complexity Routine, well-learned tasks when practiced in a familiar environment, apparently do not place heavy demands on motivation (Bandura, 1997). What is clear from studies that support many motivation theories is that when we learn successfully, motivation has provided the initiation and energy that led us to start pursuing a goal, persist in the face of distractions and competing goals and invest adequate mental effort to master the range of complex cognitive operations needed to achieve the goal. Thus, hypothesizing a motivational origin of failure to learn seems reasonable when otherwise able students fail to achieve learning goals. What aspects of motivational processes are challenged when learning tasks grow increasingly complex? Are some learners more vulnerable to motivationally based learning problems? The

Figure 2.1: Integrated model of motivation variables.

discussion turns next to five areas where motivation seems to account for a great deal of learning variance.

Task Complexity and Motivation

The first issue to be discussed draws on the cognitive load theory of Sweller and colleagues (Sweller, this volume, Chapter 1), and on theory generated and research conducted in psychotherapy settings on automated "ironic" processes in cognition (e.g., Clark, 1999b; Wegner, 1997) to highlight research on automated and unconscious cognitive processes that may inhibit motivation and learning when working memory is overloaded by the learning environment.

> As task complexity increases, excessive working memory load may cause cognitive "defaults" that are automated, largely unnoticed and destructive to learning

Wegner (1997) has provided evidence for a process he calls "Ironic" mechanisms in mental control. He presents evidence that when working memory is overloaded by complex tasks, anxiety about performance and/or a number of conflicting goals, the result is that a hypothesized "ironic monitoring system" causes an automated cognitive default in working memory. These defaults are often experienced as gaps in attention, "day dreaming" or inappropriate "off task" behaviors. Examples of default behaviors are sitting with a book one intends to study and turning pages but recognizing at some point that the content of pages cannot be recalled because our mind has "wandered" to thinking about problems or other distractions. Wegner (1997) presents evidence that overload defaults are due to an unconscious, uninterruptible, cognitive process that "... searches for mental content signaling a failure to create the intended state of mind" and introduces "... different, unwelcome and unintended behavior" (p. 148). Shoham and Rohrbaugh (1997) draw on cognitive expectancy-control motivation theory and attribute the ironic process to a perceived loss of control. They describe the downward spiral of control loss that afflicts many people who seek psychological help because they cannot learn to control intrusive thoughts, fears, or test anxiety. They note that expressing these fears often leads helpful friends to urge the person to "stop thinking about it". Yet the more a person tries not to think or worry about something negative, the more that cognitive overload occurs and unwelcome, intrusive thoughts occur in working memory. The more that these thoughts are experienced, the greater the perceived loss of control which lowers our self-efficacy for control of our own thinking. The result is that intrusive thoughts actually increase.

The ironic monitoring system is contrasted with an opposing, "intentional monitoring system", that is "... conscious, effortful and interruptible ... [and] searches for mental content consistent with the intended state of mind" (Wegner, 1997, p. 148). This system is the one that we hope is operating when learning is taking place. It focuses attention on assigned learning goals and activities and encourages the retrieval and reorganization of appropriate prior knowledge schemas. In order to maintain the intentional system, students must believe that they are experiencing a personally manageable level of complexity in instructional displays (Clark, 1999b).

Another motivational area where belief plays an important role in the amount and type of motivation available to support complex learning is described in social cognitive theories concerning the influence of self-efficacy on persistence and mental effort during learning.

> As task complexity increases, students with inappropriately high or low
> task self-efficacy tend not to persist and reduce their mental effort

As task complexity increases during learning, persistence and mental effort also increase (Pintrich & Schunk, 2002). Yet Bandura (1997) and Salomon (1984) provide evidence that when tasks are highly complex and yet perceived as familiar, mental effort decreases. This implies that the relationship between perceived self-efficacy and mental effort is negative when highly complex tasks are perceived as familiar and easy. At inappropriately high self-efficacy levels, overconfident learners apparently stop investing effort because they perceive tasks as familiar and so use inappropriate previously acquired learning strategies. Weiner's (1985, 1986) attribution theory provides evidence that unexpected and negative events provoke attempts to explain why failure occurred. His theory could be interpreted to suggest that people who make overconfident mistakes may be difficult to help since they generally can be expected to avoid taking responsibility for their use of inappropriate knowledge. They may project the blame for their mistakes to teachers, instructional materials, tests or other aspects of the learning environment. Heckhausen and Schultz's (1995) developmental theory of motivation points to reliable age differences in the way students can be expected to react to learning problems caused by overconfidence. They offer evidence that younger learners tend to choose "primary" or external projection strategies when faced with negative feedback about their performance under conditions of excessive challenge or conflict, whereas adults tend to select more "secondary" and internal projection strategies in the same context. Their theory predicts an interaction between age and the locus of causal attributions after overconfident failures.

Sarbin (1997) describes research on five types of strategic action that are deployed by most people to handle threats to efficacy: (1) Instrumental acts that seek to change the external environment such as appeals to others for help. (2) Tranquilizing and releasing acts that attempt to change internal states through acts such as the use of tranquilizing drugs, physical exercise and meditation. (3) Attention redirection that focuses attention on consistent input (to balance the conflict) through neurotic behaviors such as conversion reactions, imaginary worlds, hypochondriasis, or external projection of blame. (4) Changing beliefs and values that attempt to modify perceptions of the event so that the new perception disconfirms the threat or conflict such as "reframing" or "reinterpreting" the event. (5) Finally, escape behaviors such as depression, helplessness and quitting or dropping out. Each of these reaction strategies provide alternatives that are helpful (reframing the event) and those that are potentially harmful and destructive (addiction to tranquilizing drugs). Additional research on the use of reframing information during feedback about errors may be beneficial.

In addition to self-efficacy, the current emotional state of an individual or group is also hypothesized to influence task persistence and mental effort when task complexity increases (Bower, 1995; Ford, 1992; Helmke, 1987; Weiner, 1985).

> As task complexity increases, more learners experience negative emotional reactions and those who lack emotional self-regulatory skill tend to become angry or depressed and distracted from learning goals

The general hypothesis resulting from research on emotion suggests that as mood becomes more positive, both starting and persisting become more likely, frequent and stronger in the face of increasing complexity (Boekaerts, 1993; Bower, 1995; Ford, 1992). Negative moods are characterized as sadness, fear, depression and anger (Ford, 1992). These negative mood states inhibit persistence and mental effort (Bower, 1995). Positive moods are characterized by happiness, joy, contentment and optimism. Positive emotions have been found to foster persistence and mental effort (Bower, 1995; Ford, 1992). In research, mood states are indicated by people's memory for information congruent with their self-reported mood state; ratings of the enjoyableness of mood-congruent information or commitments; affiliation preferences for associating with people who are also experiencing positive mood states; and social comparisons with mood-congruent people in social and educational contexts (Bower, 1995). Expectancy-control theories (Eccles & Wigfield, 1995, 2002) suggest that negative mood states reduce value for learning goals; lead to lowered expectations that success or control will be achieved in complex environments, and negative moods focus people on past errors and failures

(Boekaerts, 1993; Bower, 1995). In fact, there are suggestions (e.g., Shapiro, Schwartz, & Austin, 1996; Weiner, 1986) that one of the origins of negative emotions is the perception that we are denied adequate control in specific situations. For example, Weiner (1986) suggests that depression sometimes results from the self-perception that we are lacking in, critical skills or ability to achieve a necessary goal, and that anger is the emotional product of the cognitive belief that some external agent has threatened our self-control.

Izard (1993) has presented evidence of four separate mechanisms that generate the same emotion in any individual. Only one of those systems is cognitive and under the control of the individual. Other, non-cognitive emotion activation systems include habitual or automated emotional reactions to events (Anderson, 1990, 1983) plus neural, biochemical and hormonal processes (Izard, 1993). Izard's research suggests that the origins of emotions are not always under our direct control. Yet, Bower (1995) makes the point that emotions can be influenced by environmental and cognitive events even when their origins are biological or neurological. This claim seems to be supported by recent evidence concerning the extent of the placebo effect in mood disorders such as depression. For example, Enserink (1999) reviews the meta-analyses of antidepressant drug trials and concludes that as much as 75 percent of the effects of new drugs such as Prozac are due to expectancy beliefs and not due to biological factors.

Interventions that have been found to change negative mood states have included listening to music that is perceived to be positive; writing or telling about a positive mood-related experience; watching a movie or listening to stories that emphasize positive mood states (Bower, 1995); and emotion control training through "environmental control strategies" including the choice of learning context and "positive self talk" (Corno & Kanfer, 1993). There are also indications that trusted enthusiastic, positive, energetic teachers and learner "models" encourage positive emotions in others and support learning goal persistence (Bandura, 1997).

In addition to beliefs about our capabilities and positive emotions, beliefs about the causes of our errors and failures also have been found to have a major impact on learning in complex environments.

> As task complexity increases, those who have learned to attribute mistakes and other learning difficulties to fixed and uncontrollable causes (e.g., inadequate intelligence) reduce their effort

Weiner (1985, 1986) described a system for understanding the ways in which learners responded to successes and failures in complex learning environments "… in the hope of modifying instructional practice to improve achievement" (1985, p. 567). Weiner's (1985) attribution theory responded to prior motivational theories, expectancy-value theory in particular, by locating the attribution within the individual, in a temporal context, and under the control of affective responses to success or failure. According to attribution theory, each attempt at task completion occurs within an individualized context of expectations (for success or failure) and values (importance of irrelevance). These expectancy values are confirmed or disaffirmed by perceived task outcomes which in turn trigger affective responses such as joy, exuberance or contentment for successes, or guilt, shame, frustration or anger for failures. The affective response in turn leads to a search for causality by the individual. Weiner theorizes that three conditions are most likely to lead to a sponta-neous effort to find a cause or reason (attribution) for events that are classified as when events are unexpected, negative and/or novels. Events that are classified as unexpected, negative and/or novel are very common in highly complex learning environments. In the tradition of social psychology, attribution searches for causes of events are conscious, and rational attempts to explain perceptions that are located simultaneously in three attribution dimensions: locus (internal/external — "Was the cause internal or 'in me' or external and 'in my environment'?"), stability (stable/unstable — "Was the cause stable or reliable or was it unstable and unreliable?"), and controllability (controllable/uncontrollable — "Was the cause under my control, or not?").

Attribution Bias in Complex Settings

Weiner (1985) provided evidence that during socialization most people learn causal beliefs or attribution biases about common experiences to protect their self-image. Multiple forms of attribution bias are hypothesized including: fundamental error bias and self-serving or positivity bias. Attributions that contain fundamental errors are those that incorrectly ascribe positive events to the self, while discounting other possible causes that might have contributed. Self-serving bias forgives our own errors as situational and tem-porary while attributing other people's errors to durable, reliable and negative traits. Recent meta-analyses of the effect size of self-serving bias (also referred to in the litera-ture as the hedonistic bias), by Mezulis, Abramson, Hyde, and Hankin (2004) found that its mean weighted effect is 0.96 SD across large and diverse samples. It is reasonable to hypothesize that an effect so large may indicate that this bias may be highly automated in human cognitive processing architecture. This meta-analysis is one part of an increas-ingly large body of research summaries that documents the connections between particu-lar types of attributions and subsequent performance on learning tasks. These reviews also contain strong indications that the more complex the learning task and environment, the more likely that inaccurate and damaging attribution biases will be used to explain mistakes and failures.

Mezulis' summary of so many studies provides considerable evidence to support the hypothesis that students who make external, stable, uncontrollable attributions for failures (for example, "This teacher always gives impossible mathematics tests") are significantly less likely to start or persist at subsequent tasks in that context or invest mental effort in a way that leads to success. Alternatively, students who make internal, unstable, and con-trollable attributions for their failures (for example, "I did not invest enough time and effort studying for the test") are more likely to increase their effort for similar, subsequent tasks; a strategy that often leads to increased success. This is not to say that all internal, unsta-ble, controllable attributions lead to success. Linnenbrink and Pintrich (2002) describe evidence of situations where unstable, internal attributions that discount other significant causes of failure (for example poor instruction, distracting or disruptive task contexts, hunger or illness) can lead to future learning problems. Linnenbrink and Pintrich suggest that attributions related to effortful strategy use are particularly effective in increasing motivation and task engagement because they "help dispel the inappropriate belief that effort always leads to success, but still helps to convey the ideas that success is possible"

(2002, p. 317). Wilson and Linville (1985) demonstrated that giving college students information about the instability of the sources of poor performance created both short- and long-term improvements in achievement outcomes including grade point average and reduced dropout rates. In addition to supporting adaptive attributions through structured discussions with students, Cleary and Zimmerman (2004) and Hall, Hladkyj, Perry, and Ruthig (2004) document the important role that more structured attribution retraining programs can have in increasing student success.

Attribution Retraining

In attribution retraining programs, student are generally given specific information about attribution processes, shown videotaped simulations of attributions using actors, and subsequently engaged in discussion about the ways in which they might make attributions in a variety of situations (Hall et al., 2004). The content provided by videotaped simulation could be delivered by live actors, or trained volunteers with the same results (Clark, 2001). In other programs, causal attributions are one phase within a larger cycle of self-aware analysis of learning strategies and outcomes (Cleary & Zimmerman, 2004). In all cases, however, attribution retraining has been shown to have significant positive effect sizes across multiple aspects of performance and achievement. Although not examined in the current body of research on attribution, we hypothesize that as the conscious cognitive processes related to making adaptive attributions become automated, their effects would stabilize in a positive direction across multiple performance domains. However, there are complex task domains where the suggestion of negative attributions can cause performance difficulties for the most capable learners. This appears to be the case when negative stereotypes about test taking are communicated to learners who have been the target of prejudice in educational settings.

> As task complexity and saliency increases students who are victims of prejudice in diverse educational settings are more susceptible to "stereotype threat" in complex learning environments

It appears that negative cultural, national and racial stereotypes, when they are made salient in testing situations, can harm the test motivation and performance of socially stigmatized groups (Steele & Aronson, 1995). The so-called "stereotype threat" is activated when an individual runs the risk of confirming an unflattering or negative stereotype generally held about the social group to which he or she belongs (Steele, 1997).

Experimental manipulations of stereotypes in experiments reported by a number of researchers (e.g., Spencer, Steele, & Quinn, 1999; Steele, 1997; Steele & Aronson, 1995) have consistently documented decreases in academic test performance that result when individuals are faced with potentially confirming negative stereotypes that might apply to themselves. In the typical experiment, very capable students who are members of a race, gender or national culture that has been stereotyped as weak performers in the area being tested are taking a "high stakes" test in a setting where a majority of students are members of a race, gender or culture commonly perceived as more capable. When an authority in the test environment points out the negative stereotype, measured test performance by minority students is often significantly reduced. The finding seems to occur even when an attempt is made to argue against the negative stereotype. Most troubling about these studies is the fact that stereotype threat seems to have a greater impact on the most motivated and capable students (Steele, 1997).

Although this area of research started with the examination of the test performance of African-Americans in North America, subsequent research has documented the stereotype threat effect with students of both African and Latin origins in academic performance (Aronson, 2002; Steele, 2003), females in mathematics (Brown & Josephs, 1999; Spencer et al., 1999), low socioeconomic groups in academic tasks (Croizet & Claire, 1998), and white males in math performance when compared with Asian students (Aronson et al., 1999). Simply having test-takers identify their race on a pretest questionnaire has been found to result in lower test performance when race membership is associated with lower test performance (Steele & Aronson, 1995).

How is Stereotype Threat Related to the Testing Environment?

At first glance, these results may suggest that by not making race, nationality or gender salient in a testing environment, the problem would be solved. However, the impaired performances do not appear to be the result of only mentioning stereotypes. Similar results are observed when researchers manipulate the manner in which an assessment is presented to test-takers. Informing African-American subjects that a test is a measure of intelligence results in adverse effects on performance, whereas presenting the same test as an information-gathering instrument does not (Steele & Aronson, 1995). It may very well be that a stereotype of African-American intellectual inferiority creates a threat for a test-taker that he or she might confirm the stereotype. Similar results have been obtained by informing female test-takers that a math test has historically resulted in lower performances by females (as compared to men) which results in females performing significantly worse than equally qualified men (Spencer et al., 1999). But when told that the same test has not resulted in gender-related differences, females perform equal to their male colleagues. This suggests that by presenting a test in a different manner, the threat of confirming a negative stereotype can be removed and performance apparently does not suffer.

The fact that this phenomenon has been observed in populations for which there are fairly well-known negative stereotypes raises the question as to the specific motivational process is at work. Is the effect due to situational anxiety and/or symptomatic of some internal feelings of inferiority or low self-esteem on the part of the test-takers? It is interesting to note that the same type of performance impairments are observed with highly math identified, Caucasian male test-takers when given pre-test information that white males historically perform worse in math than Asian students (Aronson et al., 1999). This suggests that situational pressures alone can create the effect, since this population (White males) is not presumed to have general low self-esteem or feelings of intellectual inferiority.

Research on stereotype consciousness in middle childhood (McKown & Weinstein, 2003) suggests that in North America, African-Americans and Latinos (traditionally academically stigmatized groups) are aware of these stereotypes even as early as ages 6−10. Stereotype threat effects have been observed in girls aged 11−14 in math performance (Ambady, Shih, Kim, & Pittinsky, 2001). The fact that stereotypes may be so well known at such an early age suggests that the stereotype threat phenomenon might be an important but hidden process that operates when complex knowledge is tested at all levels of education.

Hypotheses About the Causes of Stereotype Threat in Complex Testing Situations

Different theories as to the underlying processes or mechanisms that lead to stereotype threat have emerged. The role of anxiety has been examined (Osborne, 2001; Spencer et al., 1999; Steele & Aronson, 1995), as well as the possible combined roles of anxiety and diminished working memory (Schmader & Johns, 2003), but exactly how the two interact to affect performance has yet to be fully explicated. Anxiety as a trigger seems to have the most significant support for being at least a contributor to the observed effects, though its exact role in the process continues to be investigated.

Expectancy has been suggested as perhaps playing a role in these threat situations (Stangor, Carr, & Kiang, 1998). It is plausible that when a test-taker is given a seemingly credible reason why they might not perform well, their self-efficacy may decrease along with their expectancy for success. This reduced expectancy may result in lower performance. However, further research on examining the role of expectancy in stereotype threat has been met with mixed results (Cadino, Maass, Frigerio, Impagliazzo, & Latinotti, 2003).

Although some critics have challenged some of the underpinnings of stereotype threat theory, the effect has been demonstrated in robust fashion in several studies for almost a decade. Yet some of the issues mentioned by critics warrant further investigation. Just how large a part stereotype threat plays in the overall performance of poor and minority students has yet to be clarified. Whether it operates alone, or in concert with the myriad of other factors that contribute to the underperformance of this segment of the student population is still an open question. For example, it is reasonable to hypothesize that student's who have minimal motivation to succeed on high-stakes tests as a result of early academic failures would presumably not be affected, since they no longer identify with the academic domain.

The most important potential outcome of stereotype threat research would undoubtedly be to find ways to prevent stereotype threat from affecting test performance. In order to do so, it will be necessary to clarify the mechanism or mechanisms responsible for the reduction in performance of affected individuals. Research into anxiety is appealing and somewhat promising, given the established research that links anxiety to hampered academic performance. Insofar as anxiety is generated by uneasiness about some future outcome, research into how expectancies might play a role in the process would also be in order.

How can Tests be Structured to Counter the Effects of Stereotype Threat?

The apparent situational nature of the effect suggests that by altering the manner in which assessments are presented, test facilitators might better enable students to perform up to their capabilities. Stereotype threat research on athletic tasks suggests one way that outcomes might be improved by way of test presentation. Black and White elite athletes showed opposite patterns of performance on a laboratory miniature golf course, depending on which of the two groups was put under stereotype threat (Stone, Lynch, Sjomeling, & Darley, 1999). When the task (ten holes of golf) was presented as a measure of "natural athletic ability", Blacks outperformed Whites. When the same task was presented as a measure of "strategic sport intelligence", Whites outperformed Blacks. In addition to demonstrating that this phenomenon may apply in settings other than academic performance, this research suggests that presenting material in a way that emphasizes a group's perceived strengths can improve that group's performance.

As the stakes continue to be raised for testing results, and the emphasis on testing outcomes continues to increase, researchers interested in complex learning environments must examine contributing factors to the underperformance for different subgroups of students. Stereotype threat appears to be one of those potential factors, and solving its mystery might contribute to reducing error in high-stakes tests.

Conclusion

Complex learning tasks and environments present a significant challenge to both cognitive learning ability and learner motivation to persist at the task and invest adequate mental effort to learn. While considerably less developed than cognitive learning research, the testing of motivation theories and the design of systematic research on motivational variables have increased dramatically in the past two decades. As a result of these studies, it appears that in most learning environments, motivation accounts for almost as much learning variance as cognitive aptitude, and thus requires more consideration in both educational research and practice.

Studies of the cognitive processes that underlie learning have provided strong evidence that learners risk cognitive overload and failure in their attempts to assemble novel strategies to support their own learning. Yet it appears that the problem is confounded by motivation issues that accompany cognitive challenges. For example, there is compelling evidence that for some students, cognitive overload causes unconscious, automated motivational "defaults" that reduce their persistence at a learning task and reduce their mental effort by switching their attention to less demanding and irrelevant stimuli. These defaults appear to happen without conscious awareness and may have a negative impact on learning. Evidence also suggests that complexity may lead students with inappropriately high or low self-efficacy to reduce their mental effort and either attempt to find an "excuse" to withdraw from learning and/or refuse to accept responsibility for mistakes.

Other areas of motivation research suggest that some learners experience strong negative emotions during cognitive overload, and when their emotional self-regulatory skill is low, negative emotions reduce task persistence and mental effort. Negative emotions are more likely for students who have learned to attribute mistakes and failures to stable and uncontrollable causes (such as a lack of intelligence). These students interpret learning difficulties as evidence that they cannot succeed and reduce their persistence and effort. A very damaging variety of this belief is explored by researchers concerned with "stereotype threat", In this research, the most capable and motivated students appear to experience anxiety, and increase their level of concern in high-stakes testing situations when they are reminded that their race, gender, or culture is expected to perform poorly on the test they are taking. This increased and perhaps distracting concern leads to significantly reduced performance.

Many motivational studies have explored treatments that help to overcome motivational deficits on complex tasks when complexity cannot be reduced to a more manageable level. Many of these interventions focus on self-regulatory skills such as the reattribution of beliefs about failure to more controllable causes or the management of strong negative emotions and/or adjustments in inappropriately high or low self-efficacy. Future research in this area would benefit from attempts at building and validating more comprehensive theories of motivation to learn with particular reference to the learning of complex tasks.

References

Ambady, N., Shih, M., Kim, A., & Pittinsky, T. L. (2001). Stereotype susceptibility in children: Effects of identity activation on quantitative performance. *Psychological Science, 12,* 385–390.

Anderson, J. R. (1983). *Rules of the mind.* Hillsdale, NJ: Erlbaum.

Anderson, J. R. (1990). *The adaptive character of thought.* Hillsdale, NJ: Erlbaum.

Aronson, J. (2002). Stereotype threat: Contending and coping with unnerving expectations. In: J. Aronson (Ed.), *Improving academic achievement* (pp. 279–301). San Diego: Academic Press.

Aronson, J., Lustina, M. J., Good, C., Keough, K., Steele, C. M., & Brown, J. (1999). When white men can't do math: Necessary and sufficient factors in stereotype threat. *Journal of Experimental Social Psychology, 35,* 29–46.

Bandura, A. (1997). *Self efficacy: The exercise of control.* New York: W. H. Freeman.

Boekaerts, M. (1993). Being concerned with well-being and with learning. *Educational Psychologist, 28,* 149–167.

Bower, G. H. (1995). *Emotion and social judgments* (Monograph). Washington, DC: The Federation of Behavioral, Psychological and Cognitive Sciences (Science and Public Policy Seminars).

Brown, R. P., & Josephs, R. A. (1999). A burden of proof: Stereotype relevance and gender differences in math performance. *Journal of Personality and Social Psychology, 76,* 246–257.

Cadino, M., Maass, A., Frigerio, S., Impagliazzo, L., & Latinotti, S. (2003). Stereotype threat: The effect of expectancy on performance. *European Journal of Social Psychology, 33,* 267–285.

Clark, R. E. (1999a). *The CANE model of motivation to learn and to work: A two-stage process of goal commitment and effort.* Invited paper presented at a conference on training in work settings at the University of Leuven, Belgium.

Clark, R. E. (1999b). Yin and Yang cognitive motivational processes operating in multimedia learning environments. In: J. van Merriënboer (Ed.), *Cognition and multimedia design* (pp. 73–107). Heerlen, Netherlands: Open University Press.

Clark, R. E. (2001). *Learning from media: Arguments, analysis and evidence.* Greenwich, CT: Information Age Publishers.

Clark, R. E., & Estes, F. (2002). *Turning research into results: A guide to selecting the right performance solutions.* Atlanta: CEP Press.

Clark, R. E. (2003). Fostering the work motivation of individuals and teams. *Performance Improvement, 42*(3), 21–29.

Clark, R. E. (2004). What works in distance learning: Motivation strategies. In: H. O'Neil (Ed.), *What works in distance learning: Guidelines* (pp. 89–110). Greenwich, CT: Information Age Publishers.

Clark, R. E. (2005). Five research-tested group motivation strategies. *Performance Improvement Journal, 5*(1), 13–17.

Clark, R. E. (2006). Motivating individuals, teams and organizations. In: J. Pershing (Ed.), *Handbook of human performance improvement* (3rd ed.). San Francisco: Jossey-Bass Pfeiffer.

Cleary, T. J., & Zimmerman, B. J. (2004). Self-regulation empowerment program: A school-based program to enhance self-regulation and self-motivated cycles of student learning. *Psychology in the Schools, 41*, 537−550.

Colquitt, J. A., LePine, J., & Noe, R. A. (2000). Toward an integrative theory of training motivation: A meta-analytic path analysis of 20 years of research. *Journal of Applied Psychology, 85*, 678–707.

Condly, S. J. (1999). *Motivation to learn and to succeed: A path analysis of the CaNE model of cognitive motivation.* Unpublished Ph.D. dissertation, Faculty of the Rossier School of Education, University of Southern California, Los Angeles.

Corno, L., & Kanfer, R. (1993). The role of volition in learning and performance. In: L. Darling-Hammond (Ed.), *Review of research in education* (Vol. 19, pp. 81−107). Washington, DC: American Educational Research Association.

Cowan, N. (2001). The magical number 4 in short-term memory: A reconsideration of mental storage capacity. *Behavioral and Brain Sciences, 24*, 87–114.

Croizet, J.-C., & Claire, T. (1998). Extending the concept of stereotype threat to social class: The intellectual underperformance of students from low socioeconomic backgrounds. *Personality and Social Psychology Bulletin, 24*, 588–594.

Eccles, J., & Wigfield, A. (1995). In the mind of the actor: The structure of adolescents' achievement task values and expectancy-related beliefs. *Personality and Social Psychology Bulletin, 21*, 215–225.

Eccles, J., & Wigfield, A. (2002). Motivational beliefs, values and goals. *Annual Review of Psychology, 53*, 109–132.

Enserink, M. (1999). Can the placebo be the cure? *Science, 284*, 238–240.

Flad, J. (2002). *The effects of increasing cognitive load on self-report and dual task measures of mental effort on problem solving.* Unpublished Ph.D. dissertation, Faculty of the Rossier School of Education, University of Southern California, Los Angeles.

Ford, M. E. (1992). *Motivating humans: Goals, emotions and personal agency beliefs.* Newbury Park, CA: Sage.

Gimino, A. E. (2000). *Factors that influence students' investment of mental effort in academic tasks: A validation and exploratory study.* Unpublished Ph.D. dissertation, Faculty of the Rossier School of Education, University of Southern California, Los Angeles.

Hall, N. C., Hladkyj, S., Perry, R. P., & Ruthig, J. C. (2004). The role of attributional retraining and elaborative learning in college students' academic development. *Journal of Social Psychology, 144*, 591–612.

Heckhausen, J., & Schulz, R. (1995). A life-span theory of control. *Psychological Review, 102*, 284–304.

Helmke, A. (1987). Affective student characteristics and cognitive development: Problems, pitfalls, perspectives. *International Journal of Educational Research, 13*, 915–932.

Izard, C. E. (1993). Four systems for emotion activation: Cognitive and non-cognitive processes. *Psychological Review, 100*, 68–90.

Kirschner, P., Sweller, J., & Clark, R. E. (2006). Why minimally guided learning does not work: An analysis of the failure of discovery learning, problem-based learning, experiential learning and inquiry-based learning. *Educational Psychologist, 41*(2).

Linnenbrink, E. A., & Pintrich, P. R. (2002). Motivation as an enabler for academic success. *School Psychology Review, 31*, 313–327.

Lohman, D. F. (1989). Human intelligence: An introduction to advances in theory and research. *Review of Educational Research, 59*, 333–373.

Mayer, R. E. (2004). Should there be a three-strikes rule against pure discovery learning? *American Psychologist, 59*(1), 14–19.

McKown, C., & Weinstein, R. S. (2003). The development and consequences of stereotype consciousness in middle childhood. *Child Development, 74,* 498–515.

Mezulis, A. H., Abramson, L. Y., Hyde, J. S., & Hankin, B. L. (2004). Is there a universal positivity bias in attributions? A meta-analytic review of individual, developmental, and cultural differences in the self-serving attributional bias. *Psychological Bulletin, 130,* 711–747.

Osborne, J. W. (2001). Testing stereotype threat: Does anxiety explain race and sex differences in achievement? *Contemporary Educational Psychology, 26,* 291–310.

Pintrich, P. R., & Schunk, D. H. (2002). *Motivation in education: Theory, research and applications* (2nd ed.). Englewood Cliffs, NJ: Prentice-Hall.

Salomon, G. (1983). The differential investment of effort in learning from different sources. *Educational Psychologist, 18*(1), 42–50.

Salomon, G. (1984). Television is "easy" and print is "tough": The differential investment of mental effort in learning as a function of perceptions and attributions. *Journal of Educational Psychology, 76,* 774–786.

Sarbin, T. R. (1997). On the futility of psychiatric diagnostic manuals (DSM's) and the return of personal agency. *Applied and Preventive Psychology, 6,* 233–243.

Schmader, T., & Johns, M. (2003). Converging evidence that stereotype threat reduces working memory capacity. *Journal of Personality and Social Psychology, 85,* 440–452.

Shapiro, D. H., Jr., Schwartz, C. E., & Austin, J. A. (1996). Controlling ourselves, controlling our world: Psychologies role in understanding positive and negative consequences of seeking and gaining control. *American Psychologist, 51,* 1213–1230.

Shoham, V., & Rohrbaugh, M. (1997). Interrupting ironic processes. *Psychological Science, 8*(3), 151–153.

Singley, M. K., & Anderson, J. R. (1989). *The transfer of cognitive skill.* Cambridge, MA: Harvard University Press.

Snow, R. E. (1996). Aptitude development and education. *Psychology Public Policy and Law, 2,* 536–560.

Spencer, S. J., Steele, C. M., & Quinn, D. M. (1999). Stereotype threat and women's math performance. *Journal of Experimental Social Psychology, 35,* 4–28.

Stangor, C., Carr, C., & Kiang, L. (1998). Activating stereotypes undermines task performance expectations. *Journal of Personality and Social Psychology, 75,* 1191–1197.

Steele, C. M., & Aronson, J. (1995). Stereotype threat and the intellectual test performance of African Americans. *Journal of Personality and Social Psychology, 69,* 797–811.

Steele, C. M. (1997). A threat in the air. *American Psychologist, 52,* 613–629.

Steele, C. M. (2003). Stereotype threat and African-American student achievement. In: A. G. Hilliard, T. Perry & C. M. Steele (Eds), *Young, gifted, and black : Promoting high achievement among African-American students* (pp. 109–130). Boston: Beacon Press.

Stone, J., Lynch, C. I., Sjomeling, M., & Darley, J. M. (1999). Stereotype threat effects on Black and White athletic performance. *Journal of Personality and Social Psychology, 77,* 1213–1227.

Wegner, D. M. (1997). When the antidote is the poison: Ironic mental control processes. *Psychological Science, 8*(3), 148–150.

Weiner, B. (1985). An attributional theory of achievement motivation and emotion. *Psychology Review, 92,* 548–573.

Weiner, B. (1986). *An attributional theory of motivation and emotion.* New York: Springer.

Wilson, T. D., & Linville, P. W. (1985). Improving performance of college freshmen with attributional techniques. *Journal of Personality and Social Psychology, 19,* 287–293.

Yildir, I. (2004). *Group motivation and performance indicators in an online, team role-playing game.* Unpublished Ph.D. dissertation, Faculty of the Rossier School of Education, University of Southern California, Los Angeles.

Chapter 3

Mental Models and Complex Problem Solving: Instructional Effects

Norbert M. Seel

Introduction

How does the immune system respond to constantly changing bacterial and viral invaders? How do birds achieve their flocking formations? Can a butterfly influence the weather? Why do traffic jams form and how can traffic flow be improved? How do galaxies form? These questions asked by Jacobson (2000) focus on phenomena that may be regarded as complex systems. They present unique challenges for people because the more complex a system is the more difficult it is to understand it and operate effectively with it. Therefore, the process of coping with complex systems, such as power plants or industrial systems, is closely related with problem-solving. However, problems vary not only in their complexity but also in their structuredness. Depending on the transparency of criteria and the degree of familiarity of means to solve problems, they can also be ill-structured or well-structured (Dörner, 1976). In a narrow sense, the complexity of a problem depends on the number of variables it involves, the degree of connectivity among these variables, the type of functional relationships among them, and the stability of the problem over time (cf. Funke, 1991). Simple problems such as most textbook problems are composed of few variables, while complex problems such as international political problems, may include many factors that interact in unpredictable ways.

Most people can cope effectively with a complex system by constructing and main-taining a *mental model* that provides them with enough understanding of the system to control it. In this sense, the notion of mental models is interrelated with the investigation of problem-solving in complex systems, which provides a unique challenge for research in the field of learning and instruction (cf. Jacobson, 2000). This can be illustrated by the dis-cussion on higher-order instructional objectives concerning problem-solving and discov-ery learning in schools. Several scholars, such as Lesh and Doerr (2003) and Schauble (1996), encourage the pursuit of higher-order objectives and argue that helping students to develop their own "explanatory models" should be among the most important goals of

Handling Complexity in Learning Environments: Theory and Research
Copyright © 2006 by Elsevier Ltd.
All rights of reproduction in any form reserved.
ISBN: 0-08-044986-7

math and science education. A recommendation often made in recent learning theory and research is to involve students, either individually or in groups, in actively working on challenging problems. If it is true that knowledge about complex systems poses a special learning challenge for students, it seems likely that students should experience difficulties when given problem-solving tasks involving phenomena in complex systems. However, to date there have been only few reports on students solving problems dealing with complex systems (e.g., Resnick & Wilensky, 1998).

   This chapter will include a description of the approach of *model-oriented learning and instruction*. This approach is based on theories of *mental models* and focuses on *complex problem solving*. The central idea is that complex problem solving is guided by explanatory mental models designed with a specific end in mind. Students explore these models by developing hypotheses and then varying input parameters to investigate how well their conjectures align with the models. More generally, model-oriented learning is considered an important kind of information processing that occurs when people actively construct meaningful representations, such as coherent *mental models*, that represent and communicate subjective experiences, ideas, thoughts, and feelings. By means of such representations an individual is also able to simulate real actions in imagination (in the sense of thought experiments). Therefore, mental models can be considered an effective means of problem-solving in complex systems. However, to date only few studies have examined the learning-dependent progression of mental models in the course of complex problem-solving (cf. Mayer, Mathias, & Wetzell, 2002; Penner, 2001; Seel, Al-Diban, & Blumschein, 2000).

   This paper will begin with a general discussion of mental models and their functions for complex problem-solving. The discussion will describe why complex problem-solving presupposes mental models. Following this, we will provide an overview of the approach of model-oriented learning and instruction. Third, we will describe several quasi-experimental studies in that novices were asked to solve a set of problems dealing with complex and dynamic systems. The paper will conclude with a consideration of the findings of these studies in relation to recent instructional psychology and a discussion of the implications of this research for instructional design.

Information Processing and Mental Models

Cognitive psychologists agree that people have abilities that are essential for processing information and acting successfully in different environments. According to Rumelhart, Smolensky, McClelland, and Hinton (1986), one of these abilities is that humans are very good at pattern matching. They are evidently able to quickly "settle" on an interpretation of an input pattern. This ability is central for perceiving, remembering, and comprehending. It is probably *the* essential component for most cognitive behavior and is based on schemata. However, humans are also very good at modeling their worlds. That is to say they can anticipate the new state of affairs resulting from actions or from an event they observe. This ability is based on building up expectations by "internalizing" experiences and is crucial for inferential learning. Thirdly, humans are good at manipulating their environments. This can be considered as a version of man-the-tool-user and is perhaps the crucial skill in forming a culture. Especially important here is the ability to manipulate the environment so that it comes to represent something. Rumelhart et al. argue that these abilities are grounded on the interplay between *schemata* and *mental models*, which fulfill — as described in Piaget's epistemology — the basic cognitive functions of assimilation and accommodation (cf. Seel, 1991).

Schemata assimilate new information into cognitive structures and constitute the fundamental basis for constructing models of the world that aid in the process of accommodation (Seel, 1991). In keeping with this idea, Rumelhart et al. (1986) divide the cognitive system into two modules or sets of units. One module — called an *"interpretation network"* — is concerned with the activation of schemata, and the other one is concerned with constructing a "model of the world". It takes as input some specifications of the actions we intend to carry out and produces an interpretation of "what would happen if we did that". Part of this specification might be a specification of what the new stimulus conditions would be like. Thus, the interpretation network (i.e., an activated schema) takes input from the world (to be explained) and produces relevant reactions, whereas the second module, i.e., the "model of the world", predicts how the input would change in response to these reactions. In cognitive psychology it is common to speak of a *mental model* that would be expected to be operating in any case, insofar as it is generating expectations about the state of the world and thus "predicting" the outcomes of possible actions. However, it is not necessary for world events to have really happened. In the case that they have not, the cognitive system replaces the stimulus inputs from the world with inputs from the mental model of the world. This means that a "mental simulation runs" to imagine the events that would take place in the world if a particular action were to be performed. Thus, mental models allow one to perform entire actions internally and to judge the consequences of actions, interpret them, and draw appropriate conclusions.

Mental models represent the structure of the world because they are generated to structure it and not to reproduce or copy a given external structure. In other words, mental models *represent* the subject's knowledge in such a way that even complex phenomena become plausible. From an epistemological point of view, the theory of mental models is based on the assumption that an individual who intends to give a rational explanation for something must develop practicable methods to generate appropriate explanations on the basis of both principally restricted domain-specific knowledge and a limited capacity for information processing. The individual constructs a model that both integrates the relevant bits of domain-specific knowledge step-by-step and meets the requirements of the phenomenon to be explained; the model then "works" and can explain a specific phenomenon. Basically, comprehension and reasoning in specific situations necessarily involve using mental models of different qualities to understand the world (Greeno, 1989; Seel, 1991). Accordingly, the learner makes a mental effort to understand complex systems and in doing so constructs appropriate mental representations to model and comprehend these systems. Certainly, this kind of learning may also involve the accumulation of domain-specific knowledge, but its main purpose consists in the construction of causal explanations with the help of appropriate mental models. Stated in the terminology of Piaget's epistemology, it is a mode of accommodation rather than of assimilation. Consequently, the construction of a mental model in the course of learning often necessitates both a restructuring of the underlying representations and a reconceptualization of the related concepts. Of course, there is no need for a mental model as long as the learner can assimilate the learning material into the structures of his or her prior knowledge. Therefore, a substantial *resistance to assimilation* is a prerequisite for constructing a mental model, and the degree of this resistance depends greatly on the complexity of the topics to be learned.

Problem-Solving in Complex Systems

Since its beginning, research on problem-solving has demonstrated that processes of problem-solving evidently are not always identical because different individuals usually reach distinctly different solutions (cf. Krems, 1995). This variability is also characteristic of a particular person (cf. Nair & Ramnarayan, 2000). However, individual differences in problem-solving also depend on the characteristics of the problem, i.e., its scope, structuredness, and complexity, which correlates with the cognitive operations necessary for solving a problem. Problems can be differentiated in accordance with the specific type of barrier one has to pass to reach a solution. A helpful classification of problems and the barriers involved in them has been provided by Dörner (1976), who argues that the type of a problem depends on the transparency of the goal criteria and how familiar the means of solving it are (see Figure 3.1).

Several scholars, such as Raudenbush, Rowan, and Cheong (1993), have pointed out that the most common problems that students solve at schools, universities, and training institutions are well-structured problems that require the application of a limited and known number of concepts, rules, and principles being studied within a restricted subject-matter domain.

According to Rumelhart et al. (1986), well-structured problems, such as Duncker's X-ray task and the Tower of Hanoi task, can be solved by means of activating or modifying an available schema (see, for example, Sweller, 1988), whereas ill-structured problems often possess aspects that are unknown. Additionally, such problems might have multiple solutions, varied solution methods, or even no solutions at all. Ill-structured problems often require learners to make judgments and express personal opinions or beliefs about the problem and presuppose the construction of mental models. In contrast to well-defined problems, the initial state, the desired end state, and the barriers are all complex and change dynamically during the process of problem-solving. For instance, policy making is just such a dynamic, complex problem; that is to say that the task environment and its factors change over time and don't "wait" for a solution as they do, for instance, in the case of a chess problem. When the conditions of a problem change, the solver must continuously adapt the understanding of the problem while searching for new solutions because the old solutions may no longer be viable. For example, investing in the stock market is often difficult

		Clarity of objectives	
		High	*Low*
Certainty of resources	*High*	Interpolation barrier	Dialectic barrier
	Low	Synthetic barrier	Dialectic & synthetic barrier

Figure 3.1: Classification of problems in accordance with both the clarity of objectives and certainty of resources (Dörner, 1976).

because market conditions, such as demand, interest rates, or confidence, tend to change, often dramatically, over short periods of time. All this cannot be done by means of schemata that can be activated from long-term memory but rather demands the ad hoc construction of a mental model in the sense described above.

According to Funke and Frensch (1995), complex problem solving (CPS) implies effective interaction between the problem solver and the situational requirements of the task. Accordingly, CPS depends on both internal subject factors and external factors. CPS appears to vary with the amount of experience the individual has with similar problems that can be recalled from memory (e.g., Krems, 1995). Additionally, CPS is affected by cognitive variables such as the available domain-specific knowledge, metacognitive strategies, and cognitive styles as well as non-cognitive variables, such as self-confidence, perseverance, motivation, and enjoyment (Dörner & Wearing, 1995). In general, complex problems require more cognitive operations than do simpler ones. The necessity of balancing multiple variables during problem structuring and solution generation constitutes a heavy cognitive burden for problem solvers. Therefore, the question comes up as to whether cognitive load theory could be applied to comprehend CPS. From my point of view, the answer is a clear *NO* because cognitive load theory is applicable to conventional problems but not to complex problems, for which the implications of cognitive load theory might be different. At the moment, cognitive load theory recommends the use of means-end analysis and worked examples, which are presented to students to show them directly, step by step, the procedures required to solve different problem types (Sweller, 1988). Studying worked examples may impose a low level of cognitive load because attention needs only be given to two problem states at a time and the transformation that links them. In contrast, the definition of CPS includes a focus on the distance or "gap" between the task and the problem solver rather than a focus on the nature of the task itself (Funke & Frensch, 1995). According to this "gap" definition, a complex problem is not defined by the task features, but rather by the interaction between task characteristics and individual characteristics. In general, gap definitions imply that the same task may constitute a problem for one person but not for another, whereas "task" oriented definitions (as involved in cognitive load theory) assume that a task either constitutes, or does not constitute, a problem for all solvers.

The methods we teach to students for solving conventional problems cannot be used effectively to teach people to solve ill-structured problems. Some very ill-structured problems probably cannot be taught at all. They must be experienced and dealt with using general intelligence and world knowledge. Mental models fulfill several functions in this context: (1) They guide the comprehension of the system as well as the concrete operations with it; (2) they allow the system's states to be explained; and (3) they allow predictions about the system's behavior and the effects of intervention in the system to be derived (cf. Greeno, 1989; Young, 1983). Therefore, model-oriented learning can be considered an important "tool" for learning and complex problem solving.

Model-Oriented Learning and Instruction

Models are representations of something: They represent natural or artificial objects, so-called originals, which can in turn be models of something. A person constructs models in accordance with specific intentions in order to "map" the environment in many respects. To illustrate this one can refer to globes, which are models of the earth. Naturally, a particular globe is not a little earth. Rather, it is constructed and designed to give answers to questions concerning the locations of different places or distances between places. With regard to the chemical composition of the earth, a globe is not relevant. Other examples of modeling can be taken from the field of physics, such as Rutherford's atomic model or Newton's models of gravitation.

From the formal point of view of semantics, modeling can be defined as a *homomorphism* between two relational systems. A *relational system* $\mathcal{A} = [A, R_1^A, \quad, R_n^A]$, i.e., the base domain or original, may be mapped onto another relational system $\mathcal{B} = [B, S_1^B, \ldots, S_n^B]$, i.e., the target domain, with the aim of explaining the target domain with the help of the base domain. In epistemology and cognitive psychology, this mapping is grounded on *analogical reasoning* and presupposes the construction of two internal models of the base and target domain. This can be illustrated by an example provided by Holyoak and Thagard (1995, p. 33): "… Our knowledge of water provides us with a kind of internal model of how it moves. Similarly, our knowledge of sound provides us with a kind of model of how sound is transmitted through the air. Each of these mental models links an internal representation to external reality. But when we consider the analogy between water waves and sound propagation, we are trying to build an isomorphism between two internal models. Implicitly, we are acting as if our model of water waves can be used to modify and improve our model of sound." The structural features of model building and the inherent analogical reasoning have been described in more detail by Seel (1991) in terms of structural mapping. On this basis, four general functions of model building can be distinguished: (1) Models aid in the *simplification* of an investigation to particular and relevant phenomena in a closed domain. (2) Models aid in the *envisioning* (or visualization) of complex structures or systems. (3) Models aid in the *construction of analogies*, which help to identify the structure of an unknown domain with the help of the structure of a known domain. In this way, a well-known explanation (e.g., Rutherford's atomic model) can be mapped onto a phenomenon to be explained (e.g., quantum mechanics). Such models are called *analogy models*. (4) Finally, models may aid in the *simulation* of the processes of a system. This occurs when an individual interacts with the objects involved in a situation in order to manipulate them mentally in such a way that the cognitive operations simulate specific transformations of these objects that may occur in real-life situations. These *simulation models* operate as thought experiments that produce qualitative inferences with respect to the situation to be mastered.

According to these functions we can distinguish between two main classes of mental models: *perceptual models* and *thought models* (cf. Stachowiak, 1973). Glaser, Lesgold, and Lajoie (1987) as well as Johnson-Laird (1983) refer to perceptual models as *appearance* or *structural models* that represent the external world and mediate between images and propositional representations, whereas *thought models* also include qualitative process models and inductions aiming at the construction of artifacts that may represent complex systems and their causal relationships in a dynamic manner. Perceptual models do exhibit characteristics similar to picture-like representations, but they go beyond mental images. This can be illustrated by the following example (from Markman, 1998, p. 248): "Imagine a situation in which a boy stands at the top of a hill, makes a snowball, and rolls it down the snow-covered side of the hill. A person may never have witnessed an event like this, but one can construct the event and talk about it. One can imagine that the snowball rolls down the hill and gets larger and larger as it rolls, because snow sticks to it. A mental image of this event occurring might be formed. … But this situation goes beyond a mere mental image; it requires reasoning about the physics of the situation to determine how the image changes over time." Thought models go beyond such perceptual models insofar as they presuppose processes of inductive reasoning to approximate a solution of a problem. A central part of the construction of thought models, defined here as qualitative process models, is a continuous process of model formation, its use and reinforcement, and revision or rejection (cf. Buckley & Boulter, 1999): The problem solver forms an initial model of the problem's content, either intentionally to meet some learning goal or spontaneously in response to some task. When the model is used successfully, it is reinforced and may eventually become a precompiled, stable model. If the model is not satisfactory in use, it may be revised or rejected.

Norman (1983) has pointed out that we must also distinguish between our conceptualization of a mental model and the mental model we think a person might have. To capture this idea, he separates the concept of "conceptual models" from that of "mental models". Accordingly, Kluwe and Haider (1990) distinguish between different kinds of models: (1) For a (complex) system S of the world there is a subjective internal or *mental model* of S, $MM(S)$, which represents the knowledge a person has or can reconstruct with regard to S. (2) There are also "objective" models, $OM(S)$ — developed by scientists on the basis of their subjective mental models. We consider them to be *conceptual models*, $CM(S)$, which represent the shared knowledge of a discipline. They result from the mental models of scientists. (3) Cognitive psychologists develop *psychological models* of the mental models of a system: $PM[MM(S)]$. Interestingly from an instructional point of view, Kluwe and Haider (1990) introduce a fourth kind of model: (4) *Designed instructional models, DIM[CM(S)]*. These models can be understood as instructionally designed conceptual models of a system S that are used for the construction of interfaces (learning tasks, manuals, and training) in order to guide the learners' construction of mental models. These "designed instructional models" of conceptual models are constructed by instructors with the aim of teaching the shared knowledge of a discipline (cf. Seel, 2003). However, they do not correspond one-to-one with the conceptual models of a discipline but rather are simplified versions of conceptual models that guide the learners' comprehension of the learning material and evoke intended conceptual changes in the learning-dependent progression of mental models from preconceptions to causal explanations. Thus, "designed instructional models" mediate between the learners' mental models and the conceptual models of a subject matter.

Can We Influence Model-Oriented Learning through Instruction?

The question of whether and how we can influence model-building activities through instruction has long been at the core of various educational approaches (see, for example, Karplus, 1969), and in the field of research on mental models we can also find a strong pedagogical impetus from the very beginning. According to Johnson-Laird (1989) and other authors we can distinguish between several sources for the construction of mental models: (1) the learner's ability to construct models in an inductive manner, either from a set of basic components of world knowledge or from analogous models that the learner already possesses; (2) everyday observations of the outside world combined with the adaptation of cultural models; and (3) other people's explanations and their adaptation. Among these sources, the third one seems to be especially relevant for instruction.

According to Carlson (1991), it is possible in principle to design instruction to involve the learner in a process of inquiry in which facts are gathered from data sources, similarities and differences among facts noted, and concepts developed. In this process, the instructional program serves as a facilitator of learning for students who are working to develop their own answers to questions. On the other hand, instructional programs can present clearly defined concepts followed by clear examples. A designed conceptual model may be presented ahead of the learning tasks in order to direct the learner's comprehension of the learning material. More generally, we can distinguish between different paradigms of model-oriented instruction depending on whether they aim at (a) *self-organized discovery and exploratory learning*, (b) *guided discovery learning*, or (c) *learning oriented toward the imitation of an expert's behavior* or the adaptation of teachers' explanations.

Clearly, there might be environments that can initiate a form of learning based on free exploration by invention, but in instructional contexts we regularly operate with well-prepared and designed learning environments that constrain the student's learning processes to various extents. Accordingly, at the beginning research on model-centered instruction focused on the pedagogical idea as expressed by Mayer (1989, p. 47), which suggests that "students given model-instruction may be more likely to build mental models of the systems they are studying and to use these models to generate creative solutions to transfer problems". As a consequence, many studies on the learning-dependent progression of mental models have focused on the internalization of conceptual models provided to students in the course of instruction (Mayer, 1989; Seel et al., 2000). In this research the emphasis is on learning oriented toward the imitation of an expert's behavior or the adaptation of teachers' explanations.

An alternative approach emphasizes the role of guided *discovery learning* for the construction of mental models (cf. Penner, 2001). According to this approach, the learner has to search continuously for information in a given learning environment in order to complete or stabilize an initial mental model that corresponds to an "a priori understanding" of the material to be learned. The goal of instruction is to create micro-worlds in which objects follow specific sets of rules. One example is a micro-world in which balls fall in accordance with Newton's laws of motion (White, 1993). Students explore this model by developing hypotheses and then varying input parameters to investigate how well their conjectures align with the model. In mathematics education the defining characteristic of this kind of discovery learning is that students explore conventional mathematical symbolizations in experientially real settings. More generally, Doerr (1996) states with regard to the various settings of discovery learning that students have to develop *expressive models* to explain phenomena using a variety of tools. According to Doerr, this model building begins with the students' informal understanding and progressively builds on it. In other words, discovery learning occurs as a multi-step process of model building and revision (Penner, 2001). This is closely related to the reinforcement and consolidation of a model based on a continuous examination of whether a model can be replaced with an alternative model or not. Seel (1991) describes this process as a test of reduction to absurdity and refers to the metaphor of a gold digger who is washing away the sand to find the gold nugget. As long as there is no better model, the model builder operates with the model at hand. This process corresponds, to a large extent, with discovery learning as described in the literature (Hammer, 1997).

However, discovery learning is very ambitious as the learners must have previously achieved sufficient problem-solving and metacognitive skills to guide their learning process. Therefore, for beginning students it can be argued that self-organized discovery learning is closely associated with learning by trial-and-error but not with deep understanding. In addition, Briggs (1990) demonstrated in a case study that an instructional strategy directed at discovery learning may dramatically increase the probability of stabilizing initial faulty mental models. Consequently, a substantial conceptual change does not take place, and relatively stable intermediate states of causal understanding often precede the conceptual mastery intended by instruction. In sum, self-organized learning aimed at the creation of mental models can indeed be rather pretentious — see, for example, the studies of Kafai and Ching (2004) and Kolodner et al. (2004), in which the learners were provided with minimal guidance in the process of model building. However, pure discovery learning is a process that even an expert might sweat over sometimes. Therefore, in order to be effective, learning environments aiming at model-building activities must be designed carefully (cf. Seel, 2005). This precept corresponds with the current discussion on fallacies of pure discovery learning as described by Mayer (2004) and Kirschner, Sweller, and Clark (in press). Indeed, these authors make it evident why minimal guidance during instruction does not work.

Designing Effective Environments for Model-Oriented Learning

Decades ago, Wertheimer (1959) pled for learning environments designed to help learners solve new problems effectively. In the 1960s and 1970s, several educational psychologists argued in a similar vein in accordance with Piaget's epistemology. For example, Bruner (1966) introduced the idea of guided discovery learning into the educational discussion, whereas Farnham-Diggory (1972) favored "free learning environments" and Stolurow (1973) developed his conception of *transactional instruction*, according to which learning environments should provide opportunities for reflective thinking. These different conceptions agree on the point that learning can be supported externally but not forced. In contrast to the current discussion about discovery learning (Kirschner et al., in press; Mayer, 2004), Stolurow argued that if we want to improve exploratory learning and problem-solving we need well-designed environments that provide the learners with optimal conditions for the development of initiatives and reduce external guidance to a minimum.

These different lines of argumentation can be summarized by stating that successful model-oriented instruction presupposes effective learning environments, which may be designed in accordance with two different conceptions: First, there is a goal-oriented design of learning environments, which aims at the internalization of "designed instructional models" provided to the students. Second, there are instructional approaches that emphasize the self-organized construction and revision of models by students in the course of guided discovery learning. Gibbons (2001, 2003) integrates both lines of argumentation: "The events of instruction, which are the structures we design, serve human learning processes under the ultimate control of the individual. Instruction, therefore, does not *cause* learning but *supports* learning intentions the learner commits. ... Some of these processes (such as the initial processing of visual or auditory information) are involuntary, but many of them (focusing attention, finding and selecting associations, etc.) are completely voluntary" (p. 3). In accordance with this precept, Gibbons formulates seven principles of model-centered instruction, which correspond with several other approaches of model-oriented teaching, such as the cognitive apprenticeship approach or Gravemeijer's approach for math education (Gravemeijer, Cobb, Bowers, & Whitenack, 2000). Moreover, Gravemeijer et al. argue that *emergent models* play a central role in individual students' learning and in the collective mathematical development of the classroom community. The notion of emergent models encompasses some aspects of the exploratory approach insofar as students are encouraged to develop their own models but do so in situations that are chosen by the teacher to support the realization of a proposed learning trajectory. Thus, it is possible for the designer to propose a developmental route for the classroom community in which students first model situations in an informal way (this is called a *model of* the situation) and then formulate their informal modeling activity mathematically (this produces a *model for* reasoning). Whereas Gravemeijer's approach can be situated between externally guided learning and discovery learning, another current movement in instructional research is closely related to the idea of pure *model-based discovery learning* (cf. Bhatta & Goel, 1997) that is currently under controversial discussion in the literature (cf. Kirschner et al., in press; Mayer, 2004). In contrast to the idea of pure discovery learning, our instructional research on the learning-dependent progression of mental models follows Bruner's precept of guided discovery learning as well as the cognitive apprenticeship approach and aims at the reflective adaptation of an expert's conceptual model.

Lessons Learned from Research

The following paragraphs describe several projects focused on model-oriented learning in various instructional settings. The projects investigated three main topics (cf. Al-Diban & Seel, 1999; Seel & Schenk, 2003): (1) The learning-dependent progression of mental models in the course of instruction; (2) how this progression can be guided by way of particular instructional interventions, such as the cognitive apprenticeship approach, and (3) how to assess mental models and their learning-dependent progression as influenced by instruction.

The first project was realized between 1994 and 2001[1] and was concerned with the *adaptation of "designed instructional models"* provided to students in the course of multimedia learning. The focus of the second project[2] was on the *use of mental models as devices for complex problem solving and discovery learning.*

[1] I gratefully acknowledge financial support for this research from a generous grant by the Deutsche Forschungsgemeinschaft (i.e., the German Research Association) with Grant-No Se399/4. The research group consisted of Dr. Sabine Al-Diban, Susanne Held, Claudia Hess, Dr. Wolfram Lutterer, Christoph Nennstiel, Katharina Schenk, Ralph Siegel, and Susan Wilcek.

[2] Again I gratefully acknowledge financial support for this research from a generous grant by the Deutsche Forschungsgemeinschaft (i.e., the German Research Association) with Grant-No Se399/8. The research group consists of Bettina Couné, Ulrike Hanke, Dirk Ifenthaler, Dr. Katharina Schenk, and Susanne Steiner.

Research on the Adaptation of Conceptual Models

This research consisted of a series of replication studies that were conducted to investigate externally guided model-oriented learning in a comprehensive multimedia learning environment designed in accordance with the principles of the cognitive apprenticeship approach (Collins, Brown, & Newman, 1989). The subject matter domain was situated in macroeconomics and dynamic economic systems. More specifically, the focus of the multimedia program was on the financial politics of the European Central Bank, including (1) the financial system of nations, and (2) the approaching European monetary union because the introduction of the *Euro* (money) provides the wider context for European financial politics. Both topics are concerned with highly complex systems. After a series of evaluation studies (cf. Al-Diban & Seel, 1999), we know that this multimedia program fulfills the criteria of modeling in complex systems. We considered the cognitive apprenticeship approach to be a promising instructional strategy. This instructional approach provides students with instructionally designed conceptual models to encourage them to imitate an expert's explanatory model. Moreover, it prescribes in detail what the learner has to do in each sequence of learning in order to achieve particular objectives.

According to the cognitive apprenticeship approach, effective learning environments can be characterized by 18 features in four broad dimensions: *Content, methods, sequencing*, and the *sociology of teaching*. We placed special emphasis on the "methods" dimension. However, we also isolated a fifth dimension of cognitive apprenticeship by emphasizing the important aspects of motivation and the need for a motivational design of learning environments (cf. Seel & Schenk, 2003). As the cognitive apprenticeship is mainly concerned with macro-aspects of planning, we combined it in a further step with Jenkins' (1979) tetrahedral model, which we consider relevant for the micro-level of the design of learning tasks. The result of the combination of both approaches can be described as in Table 3.1.

The emphasis of this research was on the methods of the cognitive apprenticeship approach: In *modeling*, the learners were provided with an expert's solution to a complex problem with the intent of encouraging them to adapt the conceptual model of the expert. In *coaching*, students are supervised and given guidance as they try to find solutions to a given task in an adaptive manner. In *scaffolding*, the students are offered process-oriented assistance to improve their cognitive skills for problem-solving. The heuristics taught in this phase of instruction consisted of the decomposition of a complex problem into sub-problems and the construction of analogies between the sub-problems. Following these steps, *articulation* aims at "thinking aloud" while working on a task, whereas the next step, *reflection*, aims at the comparison of the problem-solving procedures applied by the learner and the expert. Collins and colleagues (1989) maintain that these methods contribute greatly to the development of reflective thinking and metacognitive control of learning. For our purposes, articulation and reflection were integrated into a "teach-back" procedure (Sasse, 1991) in a social learning situation. Finally, in *exploration* the students had to apply the problem-solving procedures they had learned to new, but similar, tasks. The intention of this was to improve the students' cognitive problem-solving skills.

On the whole, the results of five different evaluation studies with more than 400 subjects (secondary school students with an average age of 17) allow the conclusion that the cognitive apprenticeship approach can be considered a sound framework for the instructional

Table 3.1: Intersection between the cognitive apprenticeship approach and the Jenkins' tetrahedral model.

Cognitive Apprenticeship	Jenkins			
	Personal variables	**Learning tasks materials**	**Activities of learning**	**Results of learning, criteria**
Contents	Declarative knowledge Heuristic knowledge	Curriculum of a subject matter topic	Acquisition of declarative and procedural knowledge	Schemata Mental models
Methods	Control strategies Learning styles	Modeling Coaching Scaffolding Articulation Reflection Exploration	Generative, procedural learning Metacognition	Rules Principles Proceduralization
Sequencing	Knowledge organization	Sequencing of learning steps	Increasing complexity and variety	Learning hierarchies
Motivation	Intrinsic motivation	Difficulty of tasks	Need for achievement	Interests Attitudes
Sociology	Cooperation Competition	Authenticity Contextuality	Culture of expert practice Team spirit	Social behaviors and skills Attitudes

design of model-based learning environments. The recommended sequence of the methods, "modeling — coaching — scaffolding — exploration", significantly improved the learning outcomes and achieved significant results in accomplishing the learning tasks and the complex transfer tasks in exploration. These results correspond with observations and results of other studies, such as of Casey (1996) and Chee (1995) — but with the reservations that it proved to be difficult to realize the methods of articulation and reflection in a multimedia environment as well as to optimize the methods of scaffolding and exploration in order to improve self-regulated learning (for more details, see Seel & Schenk, 2003).

Beyond the evaluation of the cognitive apprenticeship approach as a suitable framework for the design of model-oriented learning environments, we especially investigated the stability and change of the mental models the learners constructed in the course of learning.

In accordance with the situated cognition approach, it is assumed that a learner constructs a mental model in order to simulate relevant properties of the situation to be cognitively mastered. An assumption of the situated cognition approach with far-reaching implications for instruction is that a mental model is not a fixed structure in the mind, but rather is constructed when needed — for example, to master the specific demands of a new learning situation. In accordance with this, numerous studies in the research field of conceptual change (cf. Dole & Sinatra, 1998) indicate that students dynamically modify and restructure their conceptual structures when they evaluate externally provided information as being more plausible and convincing than their prior knowledge. Clearly, this depends to a large extent on the externally provided information, e.g., in the form of a conceptual model for constructing an appropriate mental model to master a new situation and its cognitive demands. In accordance with this idea, we investigated how permanent and stable the mental models generated after a learner's early exposure to an appropriate conceptual model are. We assessed the learners' mental models at four different points of time: (1) Pre-test prior to the experimental treatment; (2) intermediate-test after the phases of *articulation* and *reflection*; (3) post-test after the experimental treatment; and (4) a stability test after a period of four months. As a major assessment method we applied the technique of "causal diagrams", i.e., a special kind of structure-spreading technique that requires the learners to draw the causal relationships between the main sectors of the dynamic system to be taught, either on a flip-chart wall or a sheet of paper (cf. Seel, 1999). This procedure proved to be a reliable and valid instrument for measuring the students' causal explanations of a dynamic system.

It has been argued that it is often easier for a learner to assimilate an explanation (provided by a conceptual model) than to induce one independently (Mayer, 1989). In this case, the conceptual model provided was integrated into the thinking process functionally, and related information could be integrated progressively in a more or less consistent manner to achieve substantial conceptual changes. Actually, several studies have demonstrated that the presentation of a conceptual model really does affects the construction of a task-related mental model, depending on the stage in the learning process at which a conceptual model is presented (Mayer, 1989; Seel & Dinter, 1995). In contrast with these findings, the results of our more recent investigations, reported on here, indicated that the learners exhibited only a minor tendency to adopt the conceptual models they were provided within the instructional program, preferring instead to extract information from the learning environment in order to construct their own explanatory models. Evidently, these models displayed only minor similarities with the provided conceptual models. Beyond this, a comparison of the models constructed by the learners at the different points of measurement shows only minor correspondences between the different models the learners constructed in the course of the instructional program. This stable result from five replication studies justifies the conclusion that mental models measured by means of causal diagrams are situation-dependent constructions. Although they were not constructed fully independently at the various points of measurement, their structures were obviously highly different. Maybe it was cognitively less demanding to construct a new model than to remember a previously constructed model. This result contradicts, to some extent, Anderson's (1983) ACT theory, according to which the contextualized nature of model-based learning indicates the immediate availability of routines for retrieving content from declarative and procedural memory. Rather, the results of our experiments indicate that the time needed for successful model-based learning was not sufficient with regard to the emergence of a schema, defined here as an automated routine that does not require mental effort to access and apply stored knowledge structures. We are currently investigating this aspect of model-based learning in a quasi-experimental study (Darabi, Nelson, & Seel, in press).

On the whole, these results are consistent with the theory of mental models, which does not suppose a factual persistence of a stagnant mental model over time, but rather a situation-dependent construction of ever new idiosyncratic models. Nevertheless, it is plausible to assume that a repetition of similar situations will evoke similar mental models that become stable cognitive structures or schemata at a certain point in time. However, until today this has not been investigated in the field of mental model research.

Model-Based Problem-Solving and Discovery Learning

Parallel to the instructional research inspired by the pedagogical precept to provide students with model-relevant information (Mayer, 1989), an alternative approach has emerged in recent years that emphasizes the *construction of explanatory models* and gives primacy to students' inquiry processes of analysis, experimentation, and simulation — especially in math and science education (cf. Lesh & Doerr, 2003). At first glance, this approach seems to correspond with the "learning by design" approach, which also focuses on students' construction of models by discovery processes (cf. Kafai & Ching, 2004; Kolodner et al., 2004), but the explanatory model approach does not pay any attention to what it is that is being discovered. Therefore, Schauble (1996) argued that if instruction and learning are to focus on models and modeling, then it is absolutely critical to focus on models that correspond to the "big ideas" or main constructs and conceptual systems that underlie the curriculum in mathematics and science. Otherwise students invent models of their own that are often incomplete and incorrect (cf. Brown & Clement, 1989). However, this research camp does not refer to *mental models* as means of private representations, but to forms of representations and inscriptions that are constructed or adopted as conventions within a community to support disciplinary practices. In Norman's (1983) vocabulary, this approach refers to "conceptual models". From our point of view, this approach corresponds to a large extent with the mental model research as a significant challenge for the understanding of how to nurture, accommodate, and respond to the partial and incomplete models that students are likely to build in designed learning environments.

Accordingly, the focus of the second comprehensive research project to be reported on in this chapter was on *mental models as devices for problem-solving and discovery learning*. Again the major focus of this research was on the assessment of the learning-dependent progression of mental models within a learning environment for complex problem solving. The learning environment we used in this research was designed in accordance with the principles of model-oriented learning and instruction (Seel, 2003). The learning environment is modular in structure and can be divided into declarative and heuristic modules.

The declarative modules contain all information needed to solve the problems. The heuristic modules primarily support the model-building process and analogical reasoning. The essential heuristic module is a *Model-Building-Kit* (*MoBuKi*), which provides students with information about models, model building, and analogical reasoning as well as with examples of analogies applied successfully on a meta-level. In this respect, the

MoBuKi offers a heuristics for model-based problem-solving which can be transferred to various content. Four supplementary modules complete the learning environment. A curriculum module contains scientific information on the prevailing content. Here the learners can navigate through different topics. However, there are no models available within this module, and thus learners have to construct their own models using the information provided. The module *"wissen.de"* includes various text documents, audio recordings, and pictures to complement the information in the curriculum module. Another module is the presentation of the problem and learning task, where the learners are requested to solve a complex problem. The task the students are provided with is to construct two models — one model that explains the problem (*explanation model*) and a second model with relations and functions similar to the *explanation model*, which we call an *analogy model*. The toolbox *"MS PowerPoint"* is the module in the multimedia learning environment that allows students to externalize their mental models for the problem they are trying to solve.

To collect data concerning the learning-dependent progression of mental models we measured the students' models at pre-defined stages of their learning process. To date, we have conducted two comparable studies with different disciplines (ecology and geophysics). In both studies we experimentally varied two factors of model-based discovery learning: (1) individual vs. collaborative learning and (2) self-guided vs. scaffolding-based learning (cf. Ifenthaler & Seel, 2005). The instructional intervention during the experiment was realized as follows: The scaffolding-based group received specified learning aids from (a) the multimedia learning environment and (b) from an expert. The learning aids from the multimedia learning environment were realized as automated information inputs on significant points within the learning environment. The learning aids from the expert were provided individually in written form. These written expert notes consisted of an elaborated explanation of the model built at an earlier measuring point and further information about the problem. In study one, the written expert note was given before measuring point 72, in study 2, the expert note was given before measuring point 41. The self-guided group received no learning aids from the multimedia learning environment and a very simple individually written expert note at the same measurement points as the scaffolding-based group.

In the first study, 52 secondary school students (9th grade) took part in a quasi-experiment. The subject matter domain of this study was ecology, and focused on the "forest as a complex system". The main task of the students was to construct explanatory as well as analogy models in order to solve complex problems they were provided with in the learning environment. Owing to the aforementioned experimental variation, 26 students took part as individual learners, whereas the other students worked as collaborative learners. We selected the stored student models of the individual learners in order to measure their learning-dependent progression. To indicate significant changes in the learners' models, we asked experts to determine the degree of similarities or differences in the structures of the models produced by the learners. The learners' task was to construct two models: (1) An *explanatory model* to explain the phenomenon in question; and (2) an *analogy model* to detect similarities between the structures of different domains. A total of 50 experts evaluated 416 explanatory and analogy models constructed by the students. In order to control the reliability of the ratings, the raters had to evaluate the same set of models on two separate days (with a delay of four days). On the whole, the learners had to construct or revise models at eight different points of measurement in the course of the instructional program: The first measurement involved the learners' *preconceptions* (i.e., the "a priori" model; constructed before they worked with the learning environment); then they had to construct and revise six models; finally, they had to construct the so-called *take-home model* without using the learning environment or the preceding models.

For the evaluation (on the explanatory models), MR_{eml}, the coefficient of internal consistency calculated using Cronbach's coefficient alpha was 0.84 ($n = 5642$). For the second evaluation (for the analogy models), MR_{aml}, the coefficient of internal consistency calculated using Cronbach's coefficient alpha was 0.86 ($n = 3822$). These findings demonstrate that the method instrument we applied can measure similarities or differences between models reliably.

Table 3.2 provides an overview of the probabilities of change. As expected, the probability of change decreased continuously as long as the students were concerned with elaborating the models they had constructed. In other words, the models became increasingly stable. However, when the students could not refer to the preceding models (i.e., the take-home model), the probability of change increased significantly.

Beyond this, we also found a significant effect due to the experimental variation (scaffolding-based vs. self-guided learning). A one-way ANOVA revealed a significant effect for the comparison of the models between measuring point 6_2 and 7_2, $F = 11.45$, $p < 0.05$ with an effect size of $Eta^2 = 0.323$ (see Figure 3.2). Evidently, this result can be explained by the specific instructional intervention given in the scaffolding-based learning group immediately before measurement 6_2.

The results for the *analogy models* revealed a slightly different picture (see Figure 3.3). Unlike the results for the explanatory models, the measurements did not show a continuous decrease for the analogy models. However, the probability of change from *model* (8_1) to the *take-home model* (8th) increased significantly with $p8_1\_8th = 0.86$, which is consistent with the results described above.

We were able to replicate these results in a second study attended by 79 secondary school students. As in the first study, the students had to construct explanatory models as well as analogy models for complex problems within the subject matter domain of plate tectonics. The overall task consisted in constructing several scenarios of tectonic effects on the Black Forest. This task proved to be a cognitively demanding and complex problem.

Table 3.2: Average probability of change in explanatory models *(n = 26 students)*.

Measuring point (mp)	Ø Probability of change
$2pc$-3_2	0.99547511
3_2-4_2	0.77375566
4_2-5_2	0.57013575
5_2-6_2	0.30542986
6_2-7_2	0.27149321
7_2-8_1	0.15158371
8_1 - 8th	0.80090498

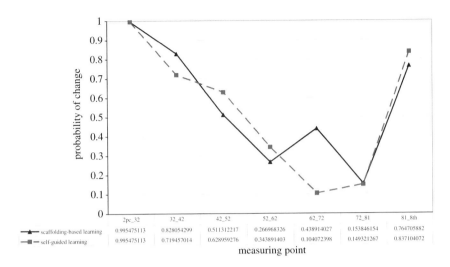

Figure 3.2: Measurement of change for the explanation models of study 1.

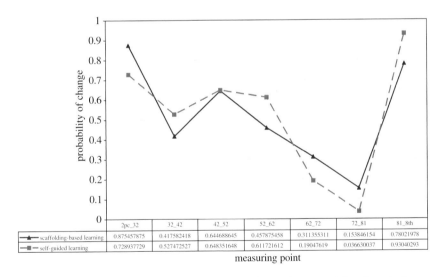

Figure 3.3: Measurement of change for the analogy models of study 1.

As is in study 1, *expert raters* compared a total of 462 models constructed by the learners in the course of the instructional program. As expected, a similar pattern of probabilities of change between the different models resulted for the explanatory models. We again found a continuous decrease in the probability of change between the several models constructed by the students while working with the learning environment. Moreover, a comparison of the experimental treatments resulted in a significant effect between the scaffolding-based learners and the self-guided learners (ANOVA, $F = 4.62$, $p < 0.05$; Eta$^2 = 0.13$) immediately after the instructional intervention. Beyond this, the ANOVA showed no further significant differences between the two experimental groups (scaffolding-based vs. self-guided). As the current results are based on a first application of the measurement of change, we used the ANOVA to identify differences between the experimental variations of the groups. In the further development of the measurement of change we used a more complex set of statistical methods (e.g., HLM) to analyze our data.

Unlike the results of the preceding study, the experimental treatments in the second experiment resulted in a significant effect for the *analogy models* (see Figure 3.4).

The results showed a significant difference between measuring points 3_2 and 4_1 (ANOVA, $F = 4.87$, $p < 0.05$; with an effect size of Eta$^2 = 0.14$), where the probability of change in the scaffolding-based group (p$3_2\_4_{1(sb)} = 0.591$) was higher than that in the self-guided group (p$3_2\_4_{1(so)} = 0.288$) due to the instructional intervention.

We can interpret the results of both studies as an indication of semantic sensitivity in the learners with regard to specific cues within the learning environment. The concept of semantic sensitivity was introduced by Anzai and Yokoyama (1984), who argued that individuals working on a learning task immediately encode the information on a task onto a mental model in order to generate a basic understanding of the situational demands. The concept is based on the capability of individuals to focus on cues in the learning environment relevant for the model and to use them to construct a new mental model of the task that results in a more correct or better solution than the preceding model. This argumentation corresponds with the concept of cognitive reconstruction (cf. Dole & Sinatra, 1998) as well as with earlier studies on the construction and revision of models in learning situations (cf. Seel & Dinter, 1995).

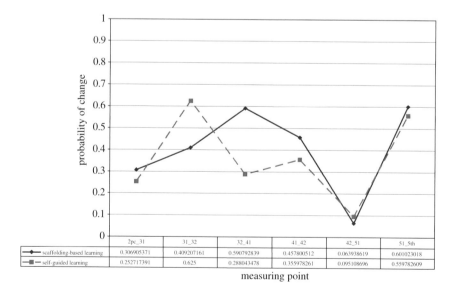

Figure 3.4: Measurement of change for the analogy models of study 2.

Discussion

This chapter focused on the functions of mental models for solving complex problems in several subject matter domains, such as economics, ecology, and geophysics. Mental models are considered an idealized reduction to the relevant attributes of the phenomena to be explained that enable one to express complex and abstract phenomena in concrete terms (Seel, 1991). Instructional psychology defines the development of mental models as well as their external representations as learning-dependent transitions between different states of knowledge on the basis of the learners' interactions with the environment and its significant features. Accordingly, it is possible to distinguish different kinds of model-oriented instructional methods on the basis of divergent conceptions of the autonomy and adaptability of learners. We have applied two comprehensive instructional approaches to influence the construction of models for mastering the complexity of dynamic systems: (1) The cognitive apprenticeship approach, which is used to reconstruct pre-designed conceptual models; and (2) the *MoBuKi* — approach, which is used for discovery learning. The two approaches emphasize relatively complex, semantically rich, computerized laboratory tasks constructed to resemble real-life problems. The approaches differ somewhat in their theoretical goals and methodology; however, the replication studies of the first research program were oriented toward Mayer's (1989) precept that students given model-instruction may be more likely to build mental models of the systems they are studying and to use these models to generate creative solutions to transfer problems, whereas the studies of the second research program emphasized the role of mental models in guided discovery learning and problem-solving about complex systems.

From a cognitive science perspective, complex problem solving, especially in computer-based learning environments, depends to a great extent on the *mental models* subjects are able to construct in order to understand the structure of the system they are provided with and to simulate transformations of this system mentally. Mental models explain the structure and processes of the system, and they thus improve causal understanding (cf. Hale & Barsalou, 1995; Seel, 1991). This means that subjects who are interacting with a complex system construct mental models in order to provide reasons for the invisible structure of the system or for the processes that are running in the system. A suggestion that is interesting for instructional psychology has been made (Greeno, 1989) to the effect that mental models are acquired with significant properties of external situations (such as the learning environment) and the subject's interactions with them. Indeed, the results of the studies reported on in this chapter strongly support this suggestion. This corresponds with the postulation of constructivist learning that the learning environment provided is an important informational resource, which can be used in a strategic manner to extract the information needed to create subjective plausibility and solve learning tasks and problems. Beyond this, our studies also support the assumption that the complexity of the learning environment should reflect the complexity expected for performance in problem-solving. Consequently, tasks are required that enable the learners to explore the environment in dynamic interaction with the context as if they were really there. Furthermore, embedded supports and scaffolds can be provided to assist problem solvers in operating successfully within the learning environment. This corresponds with the current discussion about the failure of the popular movements of constructivist, discovery, problem-based, experiential, and inquiry-based teaching — as well as "learning by design" (Kafai & Ching, 2004; Kolodner et al., 2004). Actually, Kirschner et al. (in press) and Mayer (2004) have made it evident why minimal guidance during instruction cannot work.

Our overall experience is that learning environments such as those used in our studies enable us to focus explicitly on communicating and understanding of problems, that they open up problems for discussion and allow easier resolutions. Our studies support the assertion that carefully designed multimedia programs can support the process of complex problem solving effectively by acting as dynamic intermediaries. However, this is only possible if the programs are designed effectively. Evidently, the cognitive apprenticeship approach is effective when students are provided with model-relevant information to support or facilitate the construction and revision of mental models that imitate the experts' models they are provided with. In comparison with other studies (Casey, 1996; Volet, 1991), the cognitive apprenticeship approach has been shown to be an effective framework for designing model-based learning environments. Moreover, it has proved successful in promoting students' higher order thinking skills as well as in leading them to engage in goal-oriented problem-solving. We can make the same conclusion with regard to the learning environments and their architecture, which we designed to facilitate and improve discovery learning by means of exploratory and analogy models. The model-building kit *MoBuKi* particularly provides students with effective heuristics to develop and apply analogy models to solve complex problems. In terms of research on mental models and their role in instruction, we can suggest that the *MoBuKi* represents a useful "laboratory" — a laboratory in which we can seek to develop a more comprehensive understanding of the ways in which mental models are used in problem-solving about complex systems.

However, there has been remarkably little investigation of complex learning tasks, which may take many hours or even weeks to accomplish. What goes on during that time? Whatever it is, it is slow, effortful, continuous, often unconscious, sensitive, and fragile. There is no magic dose of knowledge in the form of a pill or lecture. It most likely involves a lot of slow, continual exposure to the topic, probably accompanied by several bouts of restructuring the underlying mental representations and reconceptualizing the concepts, plus many hours of accumulating many facts. Accordingly, a central goal of our research is the investigation of the learning-dependent progression of mental models in the course of instruction. The series of quasi-experimental studies we have described focused on the construction and revision of models intended for the explanation of complex phenomena as well as for analogical problem-solving. A special focus in these studies was placed on measuring the stability and change of mental models in the course of learning. The results of the different experiments indicate that learners "respond" adaptively to the learning environment and extract information in order to develop and stabilize a coherent understanding of the complex systems to be explained. However, on the whole the results of the studies show that mental models are strongly situation-dependent and idiosyncratic cognitive artifacts that are changed quickly in accordance with new information. This can be interpreted with the *semantic sensitivity* of the learners with regard to situational demands and new information (cf. Anzai & Yokoyama, 1984).

Although this discussion has provided only a brief view on processes involved in mental modeling, it is possible to conceive of the use of explanatory and analogy models to be essentially one of applying technology to communicate an understanding of problems.

References

Al-Diban, S., & Seel, N. M. (1999). Evaluation als Forschungsaufgabe von Instruktionsdesign — Dargestellt am Beispiel eines multimedialen Lehrprogramms. *Unterrichtswissenschaft, 27*(1), 29−60.

Anderson, J. R. (1983). *The architecture of cognition.* Cambridge, MA: Harvard University Press.

Anzai, Y., & Yokoyama, T. (1984). Internal models in physics problem solving. *Cognition and Instruction, 1,* 397−450.

Bhatta, S. R., & Goel, A. (1997). Learning generic mechanisms for innovative strategies in adaptive design. *The Journal of the Learning Sciences, 6,* 367–396.

Briggs, P. (1990). The role of the user model in learning as an internally and externally directed activity. In: D. Ackermann, & M. J. Tauber (Eds), *Mental models and human-computer interaction 1* (pp. 195−208). Amsterdam: Elsevier.

Brown, D. E., & Clement, J. (1989). Overcoming misconceptions via analogical reasoning: Abstract transfer versus explanatory model construction. *Instructional Science, 18,* 237−261.

Bruner, J. S. (1966). *Toward a theory of instruction.* Cambridge, MA: Harvard University Press.

Buckley, B. C., & Boulter, C. J. (1999). Analysis of representation in model-based teaching and learning in science. In: R. Paton, & I. Neilsen (Eds), *Visual representations and interpretations* (pp. 289−294). London: Springer.

Carlson, H. L. (1991). Learning style and program design in interactive multimedia. *Educational Technology Research and Development, 39*(3), 41−48.

Casey, C. (1996). Incorporating cognitive apprenticeship in multi-media. *Educational Technology Research and Development, 44*(1), 71−84.

Chee, Y. S. (1995). Cognitive apprenticeship and its application to the teaching of Smalltalk in a multimedia interactive learning environment. *Instructional Science, 23,* 133−161.

Collins, A., Brown, J. S., & Newman, S. E. (1989). Cognitive apprenticeship: Teaching the crafts of reading, writing, and mathematics. In: L. B. Resnick (Ed.), *Knowing, learning, and instruction* (pp. 453−494). Hillsdale, NJ: Erlbaum.

Darabi, A. A., Nelson, D. W., & Seel, N. M. (2006). A dynamic mental model approach to examine schema development of a troubleshooting skill: Delayed retention of mental models as a test of schema development. *Technology, Instruction, Cognition, and Learning, 4*(1).

Doerr, H. M. (1996). Integrating the study of trigonometry, vectors, and force through modeling. *School Science and Mathematics, 96,* 407−418.

Dole, J. A., & Sinatra, G. M. (1998). Reconceptualizing change in the cognitive construction of knowledge. *Educational Psychologist, 33*(2/3), 109−128.

Dörner, D. (1976). *Problemlösen als informationsverarbeitung.* Stuttgart: Kohlhammer.

Dörner, D., & Wearing, A. (1995). Complex problem solving: Toward a (computer-simulated) theory. In: P. A. Frensch, & J. Funke (Eds), *Complex problem solving: The European perspective* (pp. 65−99). Hillsdale, NJ: Erlbaum.

Farnham-Diggory, S. (1972). *Cognitive processes in education: A psychological preparation for teaching and curriculum development.* New York: Harper & Row.

Funke, J. (1991). Solving complex problems: Exploration and control of complex systems. In: R. J. Sternberg, & P. A. Frensch (Eds), *Complex problem solving: Principles and mechanisms* (pp. 185−222). Hillsdale, NJ: Erlbaum.

Funke, J., & Frensch, P. A. (1995). Complex problem solving research in North America and Europe: An integrative review. *Foreign Psychology, 5,* 42−47.

Gibbons, A. S. (2001). Model-centered instruction. *Journal of Structural Learning and Intelligent Systems, 14,* 511–540.

Gibbons, A. S. (2003). Model-centered learning and instruction: Comments on Seel (2003). *Technology, Instruction, Cognition and Learning, 1,* 291−299.

Glaser, R., Lesgold, A., & Lajoie, S. (1987). Toward a cognitive theory for the measurement of achievement. In: R. R. Ronning, J. Glover, J. C. Conoley, & J. C. Witt (Eds), *The influence of cognitive psychology on testing and measurement* (pp. 41–85). Hillsdale, NJ: Erlbaum.

Gravemeijer, K., Cobb, P., Bowers, J., & Whitenack, J. (2000). Symbolizing, modeling, and instructional design. In: P. Cobb, E. Yackel, & K. McClain (Eds), *Symbolizing and communicating in mathematics classrooms. Perspectices on discourse, tools, and instructional design* (pp. 225−273). Mahwah, NJ: Erlbaum.

Greeno, J. G. (1989). Situations, mental models, and generative knowledge. In: D. Klahr, & K. Kotovsky (Eds), *Complex information processing* (pp. 285−318). Hillsdale, NJ: Erlbaum.

Hale, C. R., & Barsalou, L. W. (1995). Explanation content and construction during system learning and troubleshooting. *The Journal of the Learning Sciences, 4*, 385−436.

Hammer, D. (1997). Discovery learning and discovery teaching. *Cognition and Instruction, 15*, 485−529.

Holyoak, K. J., & Thagard, P. (1995). *Mental leaps: Analogy in creative thought*. Cambridge, MA: The MIT Press.

Ifenthaler, D., & Seel, N. M. (2005). The measurement of change: Learning-dependent progression of mental models. *Technology, Instruction, Cognition, and Learning, 2*, 321−340.

Jacobson, M. J. (2000). Problem solving about complex systems: Differences between experts and novices. In: B. Fishman, & S. O'Connor-Divelbiss (Eds), *Fourth international conference of the learning sciences* (pp. 14−21). Mahwah, NJ: Erlbaum.

Jenkins, J. J. (1979). Four points to remember: A tetrahedral model of memory experiments. In: L. S. Cermak, & F. I. M. Craik (Eds), *Levels of processing in human memory* (pp. 429−446). Hillsdale, NJ: Erlbaum.

Johnson-Laird, P. N. (1983). *Mental models: Towards a cognitive science of language, inference, and consciousness*. Cambridge: Cambridge University Press.

Johnson-Laird, P. N. (1989). Mental models. In: M. I. Posner (Ed.), *Foundations of cognitive science* (pp. 469−499). Cambridge, MA: The MIT Press.

Kafai, Y. B., & Ching, C. C. (2004). Children as instructional designers: Apprenticing, questioning, and evaluating in the learning science by design project. In: N. M. Seel & S. Dijkstra (Eds), *Curriculum, plans and processes of instructional design: International perspectives* (pp. 115−130). Mahwah, NJ: Erlbaum.

Karplus, R. (1969). *Introductory physics: A model approach*. New York: Benjamins.

Kirschner, P. A., Sweller, J., & Clark, R. E. (in press, for June 2006). Why minimal guidance during instruction does not work: An analysis of the failure of constructivist, discovery, problem-based, experiential, and inquiry-based teaching. *Educational Psychologist, 41*(2).

Kluwe, R. H., & Haider, H. (1990). Modelle zur internen Repräsentation komplexer technischer Systeme. *Sprache & Kognition, 9*(4), 173−192.

Kolodner, J. L., Camp, P. J., Crismond, D., Fasse, B., Gray, J., Holbrook, J., & Ryan, M. (2004). Promoting deep science learning through case-based reasoning: Rituals and practices in learning by design classrooms. In: N. M. Seel, & S. Dijkstra (Eds), *Curriculum, plans and processes of instructional design: International perspectives* (pp. 89−114). Mahwah, NJ: Erlbaum.

Krems, J. F. (1995). Cognitive flexibility and complex problem solving. In: P. A. Frensch, & J. Funke (Eds), *Complex problem solving. The European perspective* (pp. 201−218). Hillsdale, NJ: Erlbaum.

Lesh, R., & Doerr, H. M. (Eds). (2003). *Beyond constructivism. Models and modelling perspectives on mathematics problem solving, learning, and teaching*. Mahwah, NJ: Erlbaum.

Markman, A. B. (1998). *Knowledge representation*. Mahwah, NJ: Erlbaum.

Mayer, R. E. (1989). Models for understanding. *Review of Educational Research, 59*(1), 43−64.

Mayer, R. E. (2004). Should there be a three-strikes rule against pure discovery learning? The case for guided methods of instruction. *American Psychologist, 59*(1), 14−19.

Mayer, R. E., Mathias, A., & Wetzell, K. (2002). Fostering understanding of multimedia messages through pre-training: Evidence for a two-stage theory of mental model construction. *Journal of Experimental Psychology: Applied, 8,* 147−154.

Nair, K. U., & Ramnarayan, S. (2000). Individual differences in need for cognition and complex problem solving. *Journal of Research in Personality, 34,* 305−328.

Norman, D. A. (1983). Some observations on mental models. In: D. Gentner, & A. L. Stevens (Eds), *Mental models* (pp. 7−14). Hillsdale, NJ: Erlbaum.

Penner, D. E. (2001). Cognition, computers, and synthetic science: Building knowledge and meaning through modeling. *Review of Research in Education, 25,* 1−35.

Raudenbush, S. W., Rowan, B., & Cheong, Y. F. (1993). Higher order instructional goals in secondary schools: Class, teacher, and school influences. *American Educational Research Journal, 30,* 523−553.

Resnick, M., & Wilensky, U. (1998). Diving into complexity: Developing probabilistic decentralized thinking through role-playing activities. *The Journal of Learning Sciences, 7,* 153−172.

Rumelhart, D. E., Smolensky, P., McClelland, J. L., & Hinton, G. E. (1986). Schemata and sequential thought processes in PDP models. In: J. L. McClelland, D. E. Rumelhart, & The PDP research group (Eds), *Parallel distributed processing. Explorations in the microstructure of cognition: Vol. 1. Psychological and biological models* (pp. 7−57). Cambridge, MA: MIT Press.

Sasse, M. (1991). How to t(r)ap users' mental models. In: M. J. Tauber, & D. Ackermann (Eds), *Mental models and human–computer interaction 2* (pp. 59−79). Amsterdam: North-Holland.

Schauble, L. (1996). The development of scientific reasoning in knowledge-rich contexts. *Developmental Psychology, 32*(1), 102−119.

Seel, N. M. (1991). *Weltwissen und mentale Modelle.* Göttingen: Hogrefe.

Seel, N. M. (1999). Educational diagnosis of mental models: Assessment problems and technology-based solutions. *Journal of Structural Learning and Intelligent Systems, 14,* 153−185.

Seel, N. M. (2003). Model-centered learning and instruction. *Technology, Instruction, Cognition, and Learning, 1*(1), 59−85.

Seel, N. M. (2005). Designing model-centered learning environments: Hocus-pocus — Or the focus must strictly be on locus. In: J. M. Spector, C. Ohrazda, A. Van Schaak, & D. A. Wiley (Eds), *Innovations in instructional technology: Essays in honor of M. David Merrill* (pp. 65−90). Mahwah, NJ: Erlbaum.

Seel, N. M., Al-Diban, S., & Blumschein, P. (2000). Mental models and instructional planning. In: M. Spector, & T. M. Anderson (Eds), *Integrated and holistic perspectives on learning, instruction and technology: Understanding complexity* (pp. 129−158). Dordrecht, NL: Kluwer.

Seel, N. M., & Dinter, F. R. (1995). Instruction and mental model progression: Learner-dependent effects of teaching strategies on knowledge acquisition and analogical transfer. *Educational Research and Evaluation, 1*(1), 4−35.

Seel, N. M., & Schenk, K. (2003). An evaluation report of multimedia environments as cognitive learning tools. *Evaluation and Program Planning, 26,* 215−224.

Stachowiak, H. (1973). *Allgemeine Modelltheorie.* Wien: Springer.

Stolurow, L. M. (1973). Lernumwelten oder Gelegenheiten zum Nachdenken. In: W. Edelstein, & D. Hopf (Eds), *Bedingungen des Bildungsprozesses. Psychologische und pädagogische Forschungen zum Lehren und Lernen in der Schule* (pp. 351−398). Stuttgart: Klett.

Sweller, J. (1988). Cognitive load during problem solving: Effects on learning. *Cognitive Science, 12,* 257−285.

Volet, S. E. (1991). Modelling and coaching of relevant, metacognitive strategies for enhancing university students' learning. *Learning and Instruction, 1,* 319−336.

Wertheimer, M. (1959). *Productive thinking* (enlarged ed.). New York: Harper & Row.

White, B. (1993). ThinkerTools: Causal models, conceptual change, and science education. *Cognition and Instruction, 10*(1), 1−100.

Young, R. (1983). Surrogates and mappings: Two kinds of conceptual models for interactive devices. In: D. Gentner, & A. L. Stevens (Eds), *Mental models* (pp. 35−52). Hillsdale, NJ: Erlbaum.

Chapter 4

The Social Complexity in Establishing and Sharing Information Resources

Ulrike Cress and Friedrich W. Hesse

Introduction

In traditional educational settings, learning was considered as knowledge transfer from a teacher (who had knowledge) to the students (who had to acquire it). According to this perspective the teachers' task was to present their own knowledge in such a way that students could learn as much as possible. This classical teacher-centered paradigm has changed a lot. We are now aware that learning does not only take place in formal settings like schools, universities or vocational training (Lave & Wenger, 1991); the new learning paradigm refrains from thinking that students learn from omniscient teachers. Instead, we now emphasize that natural settings also provide important learning possibilities where individuals may use very different resources for acquiring knowledge. During childhood as well as during adulthood people learn by observing others or by collaboratively solving complex, real-life problems (Palincsar, 1998). Students actively search for help and information in their environment: they ask others for advice, search for experts and/or seek for further information in the Internet. The more resources people have for acquiring information, the more self-regulated learning can become (Nesbit & Winne, 2003). Consequently, modern instructional design aims to develop learning environments, which provide learners with varied information sources. In order to present natural and complex learning tasks, modern learning environments often support collaboration among the students. For example, they define classes as knowledge communities where students have to exchange information in order to acquire knowledge and build new knowledge (Brown, Collins, & Duguid, 1989; Jonassen, 1999; Scardamalia, 2002; Wenger, 1998).

This perspective of collaborative learning and inter-individual knowledge exchange suggests a further dimension of complexity. It shows that learning is not only complex with regard to cognition, but that learning is also complex with regard to social and interpersonal constructs. The knowledge that is necessary to solve a problem is normally distributed among the group members (Cole & Engestrom, 1993). Group members often need

Handling Complexity in Learning Environments: Theory and Research
Copyright © 2006 by Elsevier Ltd.
All rights of reproduction in any form reserved.
ISBN: 0-08-044986-7

knowledge others have, and individual learning can only take place if this distributed knowledge is exchanged. In this chapter, we focus on situations where individuals exchange knowledge by establishing an information pool, which in turn enables all group members to have access to the pooled information. This information pool serves as a public good (Cress, Barquero, Buder, & Hesse, 2005; Kollock, 1999). This kind of knowledge exchange occurs when people create artefacts, e.g., texts, messages or other kinds of material, which have informational value and which are accessible for all persons in an information pool or repository. Of course, this kind of knowledge exchange is cognitively highly demanding and complex; people have to de-contextualize their knowledge and have to create external representations in order to make the information searchable and transferable to others. Those people needing information have to find and interpret these external representations, have to understand the described concepts and have to apply them to their specific needs and contexts. These *cognitive* demands for contributors and receivers of information are described quite often. Our aim here is to focus on the *social* complexity of this kind of knowledge exchange. We address the sender's perspective and describe how such shared information pools are established, and we ask how motivation leads people to communicate and exchange information in a way that an information pool is generated. In doing this we stress the interactive nature of motivation.

In the first step, we describe three different contexts where a shared information pool is established. In the second step, we develop a theoretical framework, which aims to identify the main social and psychological factors influencing the generation of an information pool. In the third step, we focus on our own experimental approach to consider the generation of information resources in situations, which seem to be the most problematic ones. These are situations where many barriers hinder the exchange of information, and where the establishment of a shared information pool is a social dilemma. We then give a broad overview of our experimental results, describing the effects of some of the factors discussed.

Three Examples of Collaboratively Establishing and Sharing Information Resources

We first describe three different settings where people exchange information and thereby establish a shared information pool. The three examples differ in the motivation people have for exchanging their information, in the role shared pools play, and in the manner in which learning takes place.

Establishing and Sharing Information Resources in Informal Virtual Communities

The first example presents a situation of informal communication where people communicate in topic-specific newsgroups or forums. Newsgroups or forums exist for almost every topic one could think of, and in these settings people often very actively engage in communicating and exchanging information. People with the same hobbies meet virtually in forums about free climbing, marathon running, or collecting stamps. Hobby photographers present their best snapshots, and hobby astronomers show their pictures of meteoroids. In the health sector, newsgroups for almost all known diseases exist. In forums, online doctors give advice to patients and in other newsgroups the patients exchange information among themselves. They communicate about the relevance of symptoms, or tell about their first-hand experiences with a new medication. In other newsgroups, the relatives of patients suffering from the same disease exchange their view, experiences and worries.

It is not really clear if such virtual communities are formed primarily by the need for information exchange, if people mainly search for emotional support by peers, or if they mainly desire to come into contact with people with similar interests (Blanchard & Horan, 1998; Burnett, 2000; Rheingold, 1993). But in any case, people are in a common situation, and their common interest leads them to interact.

The information exchange within such a virtual community is often very informal. People ask each other for advice or for specific information, or they want to tell others about their own experiences. In these communities, the primary goal is not that a shared information pool is generated. The shared information pool emerges as a by-product when all exchanged messages are stored. They build a resource of individual experiences and knowledge, and this resource can be systematically searched by other users. Thus, if one desires to know something specific, it is not necessary to ask the group directly; instead one can also search the pool for it.

Establishing and Sharing Information Resources in the Context of Learning and Knowledge-Building Communities

In the context of learning the generation of shared information repositories is often explicitly intended. The research group around Bereiter and Scardamalia, for example, propagates the use of CSILE (Computer-supported Intentional Learning Environments) or its newer version Knowledge Forum© as a technical tool for knowledge-building communities (Hewitt & Scardamalia, 1998; Scardamalia, Bereiter, McLean, Swallow, & Woodruff, 1989). Both platforms provide a multimedia community space, and learners are instructed to generate texts, comments, questions or answers, and link them to other units of the information space. In this way, a kind of a large hypertext is generated. The main aim of this tool is that learners collaboratively engage in knowledge building. The idea behind the system is a highly constructivist one of "materially-distributed cognition": Artefacts serve as mediators of the distributed cognition; learners generate texts or other kinds of multimedia materials and enter them into the collective system. Other people can interact with these artefacts, provide answers, share their theories about described content, or describe the way they understood a topic. In doing this, the learners invest their individual resources in the collective upgrading of knowledge. Pooling information is not the primary intention of these knowledge-building communities, but the collaborative generation of new knowledge.

Establishing and Sharing Information Resources in the Context of Organizational Knowledge Management

The third example describes the establishment of information resources in organizational learning. The main goal of many knowledge management projects is identifying and saving knowledge which is distributed across the organization and giving all organizational members access to it (Beckman & Liebowitz, 1998). In this context, the generation of an organizational memory or a knowledge base, which contains all kinds of information possibly important for the organization, is central. The main idea is that people enter information into the shared repository so others can make use of it. In a global company, such a database could, for example, be implemented for pooling documents, which the respective branches in different countries can use for similar purposes. So a branch, which is confronted with a specific task, could receive information about the way other departments solved this problem. They perhaps can find appropriate documents, official project descriptions or best practice reports.

In this situation, the primary aim of the organization is to establish a shared resource as public good. In this example, the *pooling* of information is central, whereas in the second example the *building* of knowledge is important.

Theoretical Framework

The three examples describe the diversity of situations where groups share information and establish an information pool. They show how large the differences can be in people's motivation for establishing and sharing information resources. In the following framework, which is summarized in Figure 4.1, we focus on the perspective of a contributor and describe the factors that influence his knowledge-exchange behaviour. We differentiate between three groups of factors: factors that motivate persons to contribute information to a shared information pool, factors that de-motivate persons to do this, and factors that moderate these effects.

Motivating Factors

First, we describe factors that motivate people to establish a shared information resource by contributing information to it. They describe the benefit a person has from doing this. This benefit can lie within the communicative act itself, or it can lie outside that act. The following sections list different motivators, starting with a description of intrinsic motivators, and ending with a description of extrinsic motivators.

Intrinsic motivation   The first example showed that people in newsgroup communication seem to be highly motivated to share information about a variety of issues including their experiences. It is obvious that in this example the reason for sharing information lies within the communicative act itself. Thus, intrinsic motivation is prominent (Deci & Ryan, 2000) and people exchange information because the communicative act is itself a pleasant one. In the most extreme cases, this can even lead to a feeling of flow, which Csikszentmihalyi (1975) described as a feeling of very high personal involvement, where a person is completely absorbed by a challenging task that is perceived to be within the person's capabilities. Virtual communities sometimes seem to lead to such a feeling of flow as suggested by the many people who spend much of their leisure time in virtual communication and sometimes even forget everything around them (Trevino & Webster, 1992). But it is not necessarily the flow that motivates people to exchange information. In most situations, a less extreme form of intrinsic motivation suffices. People, for example, engage in exchanging information simply because this can be challenging and they perceive an increase in

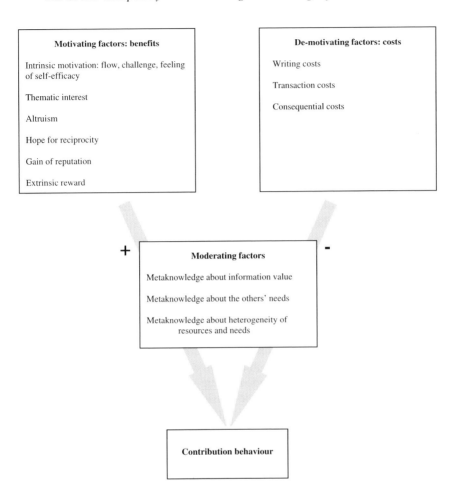

Figure 4.1: Factors influencing people's information-sharing behaviour.

self-efficacy. In newsgroups, this could be the case, if a person has specific expertise and feels able to answer to someone's specific demand that cannot be answered by others. Burnett and Buerkle (2004) found that the greatest number of postings in newsgroups can be categorized as answers to questions. People seem to feel satisfied if they can give advice and help others. This self-efficacy is not only a motivator for information exchange in newsgroups, it is also a motivator in information-exchange situations where a common product is central. In open source communities (Hars & Ou, 2002) where people participate in programming software and in projects like WIKIPEDIA where people engage in commonly writing a global encyclopaedia, people contribute because of their feeling of self-efficacy and because of their high personal involvement in the challenging task.

Thematic interest   Similar to intrinsic motivation is thematic interest (Schiefele, 1991). People motivated by thematic interest participate because they want to know more about a topic, not only because of motivating feelings of competence, self-efficacy or liking the tasks. Thus, the topic itself motivates people to engage in information exchange. Shared thematic interest leads people to debate about a subject in order to reach new insights and to gain new knowledge. This is what is intended by the use of CSILE or Knowledge Forum as described in the second example: In classrooms, such communities are implemented with the goal of awakening pupils' thematic interest. They should get interested in a topic and become curious to know more about it, which should lead them to participate in discussing the topic.

Altruism   If people are intrinsically motivated to share their knowledge then they have an individual benefit from doing it: They like it, it satisfies their individual needs or corresponds with their interests. But what motives occur besides these intrinsic ones? What could motivate people in the third example to contribute information to a shared information pool, even if they share neither common interest nor feel engaged in a highly challenging common task?

One possibility is that people's participation in such situations results from their individual willingness to cooperate. People contribute information to a shared database because they want to help others, for whom this information could be relevant. The role that altruism plays for information exchange in natural settings has not been investigated in detail. In our studies, we confirmed that people with pro-social value orientation contributed significantly more information to a shared database than people with individual orientation or people with competitive motivation (Cress, 2005). However, these personal dispositions explained only a small amount of the variance in the contribution behaviour. Thus, more extrinsic factors should also be considered. In the information-exchange literature, two primary extrinsic sources of motivation are discussed: the hope for reciprocity, and the hope for reputation.

Hope for reciprocity   The reciprocity model is based on Kelley and Thibaut's interdependency theory (Kelley & Thibaut, 1978), which suggests that people act according to the motto: "I help you if you help me, and I withhold help if you act destructively". In experimental studies, Constant, Kiesler, and Sproull (1994) investigated this effect of reciprocity. People had to evaluate a situation, which was described in a vignette. A fictitious person who had once refused to provide a programme now requested for it. People had to evaluate the story from different perspectives. Constant et al. (1994) showed that people behaved in accordance with the reciprocity model, but this effect was moderated by organizational ownership norms. If people had the opinion that products resulting from their work are valued and acknowledged by the organization, then it was more likely that a product was exchanged even if there was no reciprocity.

Connolly and Thorn (1990) consider another aspect of reciprocity in their theory of discretionary databases: the *anticipated reciprocity*. In their model, they assume that people do not contribute to a shared database mainly because they had received information from others in the past, but because they hope to receive information from others in future. Connolly and Thorn state that this "hope for reciprocity" leads to different contribution rates for people with different amounts of information. People who own many or useful pieces of information (for example, experts who have much information, or people who have information which might be highly important) cannot expect that they will receive equally good pieces of information from others. This will reduce their hope of reciprocity, and they will contribute less. In contrast, users who own few or less useful pieces of information (for example, novices or people owning information which could be easily researched by anyone) will contribute many information units so that others will contribute information units of better quality. Connolly and Thorn expected the same effects of this so-called "sender asymmetry" also for "user-asymmetry", which describes a situation where people vary in the interest they have in the information of others. Users who expect that they could benefit greatly from others' information will contribute more than low-benefit users in order to motivate others to do the same. In a laboratory study with small groups using a discretionary database, Connolly and Thorn confirmed their expectations regarding both forms of heterogeneity. Sender asymmetry as well as user asymmetry reduced the contribution rates compared to homogenous groups.

In this context, a study of Bonacich and Schneider (1992) is also instructive. They systematically varied the centrality of small communication networks and showed that peripheral people (who did not have many communication partners, and thus had low chances to receive information for solving a given problem) shared more of their information than people in a central or middle position did. This finding also confirmed the reciprocity model supposing that peripheral people, who had only a reduced chance of receiving information, rely on achieving information by reciprocity. They exchange information in order to motivate their partners to do this as well. This study also found participation to be caused by the hope for reciprocity.

In information exchange in larger groups, there is an inevitable lack of reciprocity. If all users have access to the pool, independently of their own contributions, then there is no possibility of direct reciprocity. A person cannot receive information only through need-based dyads. Instead, when a person contributes information to a shared database then all others have access to this information, and this minimizes a user's feeling of owing the contributor anything. When establishing an information pool as a public good (which means that all group members can benefit from it) then the hope of direct reciprocity is replaced by the hope of a generalized reciprocity. Here the benefit a user receives is not reciprocated by the recipient, but by any other group member (Markus, 1990; Yamagishi & Cook, 1993). This means that in the situation of information exchange through databases a contributor can only have the vague expectation that he or she might receive important information from the person who used his or her contributions. The main problem, which is inherent in public goods is that a contributor may have received information from the public pool independent of his or her own contribution behaviour. So, public goods allow free-riding, and this reduces the motivation to contribute caused by reciprocity expectations. Even so, the hope for reciprocity could still be a motivator for contribution. But the larger the group, the smaller its effect can be, because the less direct and the more generalized the exchange becomes.

Hope for reputation   The larger the group, the less influential is the hope for reciprocity. Another factor becomes more influential: the possibility of gaining reputation. By contributing high-quality information a contributor can gain reputation and visibility within the group. The larger the group is, the more people get to know if somebody made important contributions, or the more influential this person could become. In a field study with academic e-mailing lists, Matzat (2001) found evidence that in the academic community, the opportunity to gain reputation is a strong incentive to actively participate in an online discussion. We assume that the motivation to gain reputation is also high in organizations where people have a personal interest in raising their status. The database software can support this if it allows identifying the contributor of a message. If the software enables obtaining each person's number of contributions, then this activates competitive motives, which enhance participation too. Group-awareness tools, which provide the group with information about each group member's participation behaviour, are often used in virtual communities to stimulate participation and detect free-riders (Lui, Lang, & Kwok, 2002). However, not much systematic investigation about their effects has yet been done.

Extrinsic reward So far we described motivating factors that are closely related to the communicative act itself. But motivators can also be external benefits or rewards that people can obtain. In an educational setting, such external rewards can be grades or different kinds of prizes, in an organizational setting any kind of incentives can serve as rewards. These rewards should motivate people to actively participate because they reinforce this behaviour. But external rewards do not always have a positive and stimulating effect. The self-determination theory of Deci and Ryan provides some evidence that such extrinsic rewards could also undermine the intrinsic motivation, and thus, could cause negative effects instead of the positive ones (Deci, Koestner, & Ryan, 1999). But this undermining effect can only occur when people had been intrinsically motivated. So it could be possible that external rewards are not a good means for motivating people in knowledge building communities, or communities of interest. But in settings where the costs for contribution (see next section) are higher than the individual benefit, extrinsic rewards could be effective to compensate for the costs.

Reward systems seem to be especially promising when the individual reward of a group member depends (at least in part) on the aggregate performance of all group members. Slavin's (1983) meta-analysis of cooperative learning shows that such group rewards, where each person receives the average grade of all group members, are essential to the instructional effectiveness of cooperation in learning groups. In this reward system, each person has an individual stake in maximization of group members' performance because each person's own grade depends on this. Thus, a person helps the others not only because of altruism, but also because of self-interest. But the larger the group is the lower is the possibility that an individual can influence the performance of others. Thus, when shared databases are used in large groups, it seems unrealistic to expect that reward systems in which the individual rewards depend on the group's performance would increase the number of contributions. Consequently, some additional strategies are necessary for larger groups. And here the shared database allows group members to make use of other reward systems because the database software can easily analyse how much each person contributed and how often other group members retrieved each contribution. This information allows integration of two different reward systems: an input-related reward system and a use-related reward system. In the *input-related reward system*, a person gets a reward whenever he or she enters information in the database. This is a kind of direct incentive where a user receives a reward for providing information. In this system, only the number of contributions, but not their quality, is rewarded. Consequently, this reward system implies the risk of getting people to contribute a lot of information, but not necessarily good and useful information. An alternative to the input-related reward system is the *use-related reward system*. Here the amount of external reward a contributor gets depends on the frequency with which other members use his or her contributions. This is a much more indirect kind of reward because when contributors enter information in the database, they do not know exactly how they will be rewarded, since it is unclear how many people will use their contribution. So, there is no certainty that contributions will lead to rewards. Nonetheless, the range of profit is larger because higher rewards are possible if many members use the information. Accordingly, it is in an information provider's own interest to enter information, which is presumably useful to many other people. The use-related reward system should therefore lead to high-quality database entries, which are often used by the members.

De-Motivating Factors

In the previous section, we listed the main motivating factors, and in this section we list the factors, which hinder information exchange. They may cause people to withhold their knowledge and not to contribute it to a shared database. All these de-motivating factors can be described as costs, which arise for a contributor.

Writing costs   A contributor, at a minimum, has to invest time and effort to write the message and enter it into the system. Because in large groups a message can be useful for different people, a contributor should take care to explain the topic with enough detail that people with different backgrounds and different tasks will understand it and can make use of it. This causes much more investment in writing and explaining the information compared to direct face-to-face exchanges between two people. In the example with knowledge-building communities or with open source communities, people do not only have to pool existing information, but they are also expected to build new knowledge. Due to this high demand, a person has to spend much effort for preparing qualitatively high-level contributions.

Transaction costs   Besides these costs related to the informational value of a contribution, another kind of costs arises for the use of the database software: transaction costs for opening the programme and entering the information. Even if this lasts perhaps, only a few minutes, it often interrupts the daily work with which a person is occupied. Additional barriers arise from problems in sending a message to the right address or to the right folder, or with trouble in correcting an entry that might have been misunderstood (faulty mails often cannot be deleted directly by the sender).

The transaction costs depend on the available functions of a computer system and on the concrete situation in which the software is used. High transaction costs are an extreme obstacle for establishing shared information resources (Reid, Malinek, Stott, & Evans, 1996).

Consequential costs   In the long run, consequential costs can also occur for contributors. If a person gives a lot of help, he or she will perhaps be asked for help more and more, which causes further effort. Or if one gives any advice, one will perhaps be made responsible for probable consequences. Other costs occur from the permanence of the messages.

If one enters a question one might feel that everybody will know that he or she needed advice. The fear of negative social return for sending critical or wrong statements could be a high barrier to providing this information (Ardichvili, Page, & Wentling, 2003). In organizational contexts, further social costs arise due to the fact that knowledge is often seen as a kind of power, and sharing it could mean losing this power. Thus, people try to withhold their information in order to maintain their advantage through knowing things others do not know.

Significance of these costs   All these costs together are barriers, which hinder the establishment of a shared information pool. If a person's total costs are higher than all the motivators described in the last section, then the situation is a public-goods dilemma (Dawes, 1980; Ledyard, 1995): One is better off if one does not contribute anything. Because of the shared resource being a public good, one has access to all information, whether one contributes anything or not. Thus, all people possibly can benefit from a contribution, except for the contributor who already owns the information, independently of contributing or withholding it. The contributor has no benefit from contributing, but he or she has to accept the costs. So when a shared information pool is established, everyone individually would be better off if he or she did not contribute anything. But if all people followed this dominant strategy, then there would be no information exchange at all. In this situation, all people would be worse off than if they contributed.

The special features of this information-sharing dilemma, which could lead to a high amount of free-riding in virtual groups, are described by several authors (Cabrera & Cabrera, 2002; Connolly & Thorn, 1990; Cress, 2004; Cress, Barquero, Buder, & Hesse, 2005; Cress & Hesse, 2004; Fulk, Flanagin, Kalman, Monge, & Ryan, 1996; Hollingshead, Fulk, & Monge, 2002). In a laboratory study with an information-exchange dilemma, Connolly and colleagues provide evidence that contribution rates decline as contribution costs increase (Connolly & Thorn, 1990; Connolly, Thorn, & Heminger, 1992). In their experiment, participants took part in a business game and acted as production managers. Each one was responsible for planning the production level of a specific product in a country in order to achieve its worldwide distribution. Each manager had access to useful information on the local economy of one country, information that he or she could contribute to a database available to the other players. Each manager was charged for contributions of information to the database. The contribution charge varied across conditions. The experiment revealed that contribution rates declined sharply with increasing contribution charges. This confirms the results of many experiments with the classical public goods dilemma. The fewer costs people have for cooperative choices (compared to their benefits) the more they will cooperate (for review Ledyard, 1995). This relation also holds true in the information-exchange dilemma.

Moderating Factors

As previously described, the situation of information exchange with shared databases is a social dilemma. The motivating factors mentioned enhance people's tendency to behave cooperatively and to contribute information, while the de-motivating factors strengthen people's tendency to behave uncooperatively and withhold information. However, the influence of both motivators and de-motivators is moderated by several factors, which represent people's knowledge about the distribution of costs and benefits within groups. These factors can be described as different kinds of metaknowledge.

Metaknowledge about information value   Communication via databases often presents a highly anonymous kind of communication. In face-to-face and one-to-one communication settings, a speaker can usually anticipate the needs of the recipient. Through verbal and non-verbal reactions a sender gets feedback on whether the recipient heard and understood the messages, and whether he or she agrees or not. In computer-based many-to-many communication settings, this knowledge is missing (Kiesler, Siegel, & McGuire, 1984). This leads to difficulties in the grounding process, i.e., in creating a common basis for mutual understanding of all people participating in the communication process (Clark & Brennan, 1991). In resource-oriented information exchange, all verbal and non-verbal cues are missing. A person in this kind of exchange probably does not even know who the others are, what information they have or what information they need. So a person cannot be sure that information he or she contributes is valuable for others. It makes the situation even worse if different group members work on different tasks. In this case, they cannot develop an adequate transactive memory describing who is engaged in what task. Transactive memories typically emerge through collaborative learning and working where the group members get informed about what the others know and on which domain they are experts (Moreland, 1999; Moreland, Argote, & Krishnan, 1996; Wegner, 1987). Large groups with members working in parallel normally are not able to develop a reliable transactive memory and thus, cannot know exactly which information others really need. And this in turn lowers the positive effect some motivators have on people's contribution behaviour. People, for example, cannot be altruistic if they do not know the needs of the others; they cannot select which information they should contribute if they do not know which value a piece of information has for others.

Metaknowledge about one's own expertise   Another aspect of a transactive memory is that a group member knows what kind of special expertise he or she has. This metaknowledge would be important for communication via databases, because it can be assumed that one is more willing to enter information into a database if one knows that this information is useful for other people's work. Our experiments described in the next section show that the higher a person's evaluation of their own information, and the higher the expectation their own expertise is useful to others, the higher will be this person's motivation to enter information into a database. This effect is also supported by information sampling theory. With collaborative problem-solving groups, Stasser, Stewart, and Wittenbaum (1995) have shown that metaknowledge about the distribution of expertise across group members increases the communication of non-shared information. If people know about their own expertise and know that the group needs the information they own, they are more willing to communicate their information to the group. But this positive effect of metaknowledge can only apply to situations where people do not have a competitive orientation. With competitive motivation, people would probably be especially likely to withhold the information that they consider to be relevant for others. In such situations, people could make use of their metaknowledge in order to take individual advantage of it.

Metaknowledge about heterogeneity of resources and needs   Another aspect of meta-knowledge deals with the heterogeneity of resources. We mentioned above the assumption that anticipated reciprocity motivates contribution, and we also mentioned the consequent hypothesis that sender asymmetry reduces participation. A person having more or better resources than the others cannot expect to receive information of similar value from others. But other assumptions about an opposite effect could also be made: When people are asked about their fairness concepts for situations with sender asymmetry, then they often apply fairness concepts based on the equity norm. With this norm a situation is perceived as fair if the ratio of individual costs and individual resources is equal across all involved people (Kerr, 1995). This leads to the hypothesis that people with many resources contribute more than those with fewer resources. Several studies confirmed this assumption with various social dilemma games (Marwell & Ames, 1981; Wit, Wilke, & Oppewal, 1992; Van Dijk & Wilke, 1995), while others did not (Rapoport, Bornstein, & Erev, 1989). Apart from the studies of Connolly and Thorn (1990) and Bonacich and Schneider (1992) described before, no other experiments dealing with this question in the information-exchange situations exist. Connolly and Thorn investigated if the number of contributions in the whole group depends on the sender asymmetry, but they did not differentiate between people owning more or fewer resources. Bonacich and Schneider confirmed the model of anticipated reciprocity.

An Experimental Approach for Investigating the Establishment of a Shared Information Pool

In our research, we mainly deal with those problematic situations where the pre-conditions for information exchange are negative. These are mainly situations where people are not motivated to share their information because they fear they will have more costs than personal benefits from contributing information to a shared pool. In these situations, information pooling has all the features of a social dilemma, and thus, a lot of free-riding can be expected. This situation is mainly, but not exclusively, relevant to organizational information pooling as described in the third example. But it plays a role in newsgroups or knowledge building communities, as described in the prior two examples. Also in these settings a high number of lurkers (people reading messages but not contributing any) are observed, and in large groups they even seem to be in the majority. For example, Stegbauer and Rausch (2001) investigated eight mailing lists during a period of 34 months and found that the proportion of lurkers was between 56% and 81%. A study of Gnutella (a widely used file sharing system) showed that 70% of the Gnutella peers did not share any content files and 90% did not answer any queries from other peers (Adar & Hubermann, 2000). Even higher rates of lurking are reported by Matzat (2004) and Zelman and Leydesdorff (1999).

Our primary aim is to investigate systematically the influence of the above-mentioned factors, which are expected to influence people's information sharing behaviour in knowledge-exchange dilemmas. Our experimental research starts from the most negative situation (where people have high transfer costs, no intrinsic motivation to share information, and no metaknowledge) and gradually upgrades the situation by providing people with metaknowledge about their resources and about the needs of others, by lowering their transfer costs, or by providing an extrinsic reward through a bonus compensating for transfer costs. In other experiments, we reduced the anonymity of the group members or made their behaviour identifiable. We also presented information about the cooperativeness of the group members and thus, allowed the creation of descriptive norms and social comparison.

Correlations which exist between people's interests, their pre-knowledge and performance in dealing with real learning material lead to systematic biases. For this reason, we decided to use an artificial and highly controlled setting analogous to those used in experimental social-dilemma research. In these classical studies, people are given resources and have to allocate them to a public or to their private pools. So people are in a decision-making situation, and the payoff for all possible decisions can be exactly described by a payoff function. Compared to such classical social dilemma settings, we use a more complex experimental task where participants first have to work in order to achieve information resources.

In our experiments, the following task is used (for a more detailed description of the task see Cress, 2005; Cress, Barquero, Buder, & Hesse, 2005): Participants are told that they are members of a group of six people simultaneously working at computer terminals at different locations. This team has to calculate the total salaries of fictitious salesmen, and each team member is paid according to the number of salaries he or she manages to calculate. Each salary is composed of two values: a base salary, to be calculated in the first phase, and the total salary, to be calculated in the second phase. In the first phase, a participant earns money for each base salary calculated. After each calculation a person has to decide whether he or she wants to contribute this result to the shared database. But the transfer of this information to the database costs time. Because the first phase is time-limited, the more a participant contributes, the fewer base salaries he or she could calculate, and consequently, the less money he or she earns.

In the second phase, each group member has to calculate the total salaries of as many salesmen as possible. Also in this phase a participant earns money for each total salary calculated. But for the calculation of a salesman's total salary the base salary is needed. If a participant did not calculate it in the first phase, and if this value was not contributed to the database by at least one of the other group members, he or she has to calculate it now (without any payment). By doing this, one loses time. The second phase is also time-limited. Accordingly, during the second phase, the more base salaries the database contains, the more an individual earns. Thus, being cooperative and contributing base salaries to the database in the first phase facilitates the performance of the other group members in the second phase. But in terms of one's own payoff, a participant has no benefit from contributing a base salary to the database because in the second phase each person has the base salaries he or she had calculated in the first phase anyway.

Each experimental session consists of three trials. Each trial starts with an empty database and is divided into the two phases just described. For eliminating group effects the teams are faked. So the participants believe they are part of a real team, but for each person the behaviour of the other group members are simulated in the same way. After the experiment participants are paid according to their individual performance on the three trials.

Experimental Results Revealing the Interplay of the Effects of Benefits, Costs and Metaknowledge

Within this experimental setting we carried out a series of experiments. Our primary aim here is not to describe the experiments and the results in detail, but to provide an overview of results revealing the interplay of the factors described above. The experimental series we will describe deals with the metaknowledge about information value, the metaknowledge about sender asymmetry, and extrinsic reward system.

Metaknowledge About Informational Value

In the first experimental series, we focused on the effect of metaknowledge and its interplay with costs. We introduced metaknowledge about informational value by informing the participants about the importance of their information. For this purpose, we introduced two different kinds of base salaries: In the first phase, on an average every second result was assigned as highly important and the participants knew that in the second phase these results were needed with a higher probability than the less important base salaries. The contribution costs were the same for both kinds of base salaries. In the first study we observed that on an average the participants contributed 58% (SD = 0.34) of the important base salaries they had calculated, but only 31% (SD = 0.29) of the less important base salaries (Cress, 2004). This effect of metaknowledge was very strong — it explained about 41% of the variance — and was replicated in other diverse experiments. In situations where contribution costs for more or less important information were equal, subjects selected their database contributions according to their importance. This reflects that people's decisions to contribute are not only based on consideration of their individual benefit, but also on consideration of the benefit to others. By primarily contributing highly useful information, a contributor individually incurs no higher costs but enables higher benefits for others. With respect to the individual costs, withholding — and thus, avoiding costs — would be more effective for important information as well. But it seems that if one once decides to take on the costs for providing information, then metaknowledge about the importance of information for others ensures that a person contributes mainly those information units, which are useful for others. In this sense, metaknowledge can increase the quality of database contents, as it motivates people to provide mainly information, which is highly relevant for others, and as it reduces the amount of less important or redundant information within the database.

The following experiment has clearly shown that this positive effect of metaknowledge only occurs if people have no higher costs for the provision of important information. In this experiment we compared two experimental groups: In one group the transaction costs for important information and the transaction costs for less important information were the same, in the other group the transaction costs for important information were higher than those for less important information. The results showed that in the group with equal transaction costs for both kinds of information people contributed on average 71% (SD = 0.32) of their important information and 25% (SD = 0.31) of the less important information. This highly significant difference disappeared in the other experimental group (important information units: 32%, SD = 0.32; less important ones: 45%, SD = 0.21). This finding confirms our assumption that metaknowledge is one factor influencing information sharing behaviour, but not the only one. The consideration of a person's own costs and benefits seems to take precedence over the positive influence of metaknowledge about others' needs. If people have metaknowledge they take into account the needs of others, but only if responding to those needs does not create further costs for contribution. This finding also corresponds with a result of another experiment where we compared two conditions; people had metaknowledge about the importance of their information (as described above) or they did not have any such metaknowledge and all the information they had was equally useful for others (Cress, 2004). The contribution rates in the condition without any metaknowledge (50%, SD = 0.34) did not differ significantly from the overall contribution rate in the condition with metaknowledge (54%, SD= 0.30). Thus, providing metaknowledge about the importance of one's own information for others does not generally lead to higher overall contribution rates. Several configurations of experimentation show that metaknowledge about the value of information does not influence how much information is contributed, but it influences which information people select for contribution. In sum, the experiments confirmed the moderating influence of metaknowledge on the effect of costs and benefits.

Metaknowledge About Heterogeneity of Resources

In the second experimental series we studied the effect of another kind of metaknowledge, knowledge about sender asymmetry. For this purpose we compared the contribution rates of people who were made to believe that they had more information than the other half of the group, with the contribution rates of people who were made to believe that they had less information than the other half. The results of these studies were somewhat inconsistent. In one study the contribution rates between both groups in fact differed significantly. People with the conviction of having more information than others also contributed more, a finding in accordance with the equity model. But we could not replicate this result in a later experiment. In the replication attempt, the effect was too small to be statistically significant. In both experiments, we also asked people about their fairness concepts, and in both experiments they stated that it would be more fair if those group members who own more information contributed more. In the second experiment, we observed that this fairness concept did not correspond with people's contribution behaviour. Those people who were made to believe that they owned more information did not behave according to this fairness concept. They contributed only as much as the group, which believed they owned less information. Interestingly, if we asked people about their own participation behaviour, those believing that they had more resources than the others told us that they had also contributed more. So they perceived themselves as acting in accordance with their fairness concept, even if the objective data about their contribution behaviour showed that this was not the case.

Extrinsic Reward Systems

The third experimental series dealt with the effect of an extrinsic reward system. In these experiments, we installed a use-related bonus system where people received a bonus each time one of their own contributions was used by one of the other group members. With this bonus system it was in the interest of each person to contribute primarily information that was useful for others because a contributor only received the bonus if his or her contributions were in fact used by others.

We compared a situation where no extrinsic reward was given with a situation where such a use-related bonus system was installed (Cress, Barquero, Buder, Schwan, & Hesse, 2003). With this bonus a payoff situation was achieved where a person did not derive any individual benefit from withholding information because this bonus was higher than the transfer costs. So the prior dilemma did not exist, because contributing *all* the important base salaries was the most effective strategy. But during the experiment the participants only knew that they would receive a bonus of 10 cents for each use, but they were not explicitly informed that this bonus level was higher than the costs for cooperation. We found a significant main effect of importance and a significant interaction between importance and bonus: Individuals with a bonus system contributed more information of high importance (79%, SD = 0.25) but less information of low importance (19%, SD = 0.27) than those without any extrinsic reward system (56%, SD = 0.35; 30%, SD = 0.30). This interaction indicates that a use-related bonus system could even enhance the positive effect of metaknowledge revealed in the studies of the first experimental series. The use-related bonus system motivated people to select their contributions even more with regard to their importance for others. Thus, although this treatment did not increase the quantity of database contents, it enhanced their quality. In this way, the use-related bonus system could deepen the positive effect of metaknowledge.

In a further study, we compared this positive effect of extrinsic rewards with the effect of a feedback-tool allowing the users to know how often their own contributions were used by others (Cress, 2004). This feedback tool was assumed to increase intrinsic motivation, since it informed a contributor about the relevance of his contributions for others. Thus, this tool was expected to enhance the feeling of self-efficacy without changing the payoff situation. In fact, in our study this feedback tool had no effect. People's contribution behaviour was almost the same with or without this tool. Thus, at least for our environment, the feedback about the use of one's own contributions by others seemed to have only a positive effect, if it was combined with an extrinsic reward.

In all of our experiments where we used an extrinsic reward system, we asked the participants to compare the costs they had to bear for contribution with the individual benefit they achieved through the bonus. Interestingly, we observed in all conditions that the participants systematically underestimated their benefit through the bonus, whereas they overestimated their costs. It seems that people had a systematic bias of interpreting the situation as a social dilemma, even if in fact there was none.

Discussion

Information exchange is often a pre-condition for learning, even though it, of course, cannot guarantee that individuals will learn. In this chapter we focused on situations where people exchange information by establishing a shared information resource. This situation is worth investigating in more detail because it reveals a kind of complexity, which occurs in learning and information-exchange processes in many natural learning settings: social complexity. This social factor is caused by the fact that in such situations it is often the case that some people have information, which others need. Information sharing is far from a simple process, where the group readily transfers information to all the members who need it. Since people have costs for contributions, information exchange becomes a complex public-goods dilemma in which people have individual motives that do not necessarily conform to the needs of the whole group. So, the motivation to share information resources has an interactive character. Because people's individual costs and benefits for contributing information may sometimes stand in direct contradiction to the overall benefit of the group, a high occurrence of free-riding results. But the consideration of their own individual costs and benefits is not the only determinant of people's behaviour when they are faced with such a dilemma. Our experiments showed that people's metaknowledge about the distribution of information across the group members, and their metaknowledge about the needs of others moderates the effects of costs and benefits on their contribution behaviour. If people know that their information units differ in the importance they have for others, then they contribute primarily the important information units. Thus, metaknowledge about the importance of information enhances information exchange in groups. But our experiments also revealed that this consideration of others' needs is limited by the priority of one's own individual benefit. If people have metaknowledge about the importance of their own information for others, they decide to contribute this important information only when it does not cause higher costs than contributing less important information. If individual costs are considered to be too high, people do not respond according to their metaknowledge and contribute as much unimportant as important information.

The experiments additionally showed that external reward systems can make use of people's preference for acting upon individual benefit. A use-related bonus system can enhance the efficacy of information exchange, as it leads to a higher selection of important contributions. Thus, this kind of external reward system allows combining people's motive to maximize their individual benefit with their motive to consider metaknowledge about the needs of others.

These two motivations, maximizing individual benefit and simultaneously considering the other's needs, lead to somewhat inconsistent results when another kind of metaknowledge is brought into focus: if people know that they own quantitatively more information than others, their fairness concepts would require that they contribute more than others, but to do so would be against their own interests. In this dilemma people seem to react in a way that they subjectively have the impression they had contributed more than the others, even if this objectively was not actually the case.

All these findings address settings where costs and benefits arise if people exchange relevant information. So we have to ask if these findings are also valid for educational settings. We assume that there are many similarities between modern learning environments and the kinds of settings we considered. The more collaboration and self-regulation a learning environment allows, the more important such kinds of shared pools become. For example, in the last years CSCL has become very prominent. Here collaboration is central and groups often collaborate by engaging in online discourses or building knowledge communities. Many classrooms, for examples, work with tools like CSILE, Knowledge Forum©, or BSCW (Stahl, 2004). And these tools represent such shared databases we discussed.

In universities, online seminars are becoming more and more common. In these seminars, shared repositories are not only a tool to provide learning material, which students can download (this usage would only mirror the traditional teacher-centred instruction), they are also used as tools for knowledge exchange where students can upload their own papers, summaries, or other relevant material. If these activities are intended by the instructor, all the processes we discussed in this chapter become relevant. The social dilemma perspective explains why in many online seminars people's active participation is so low. What do our results suggest for improving these settings?

It seems to be important that students have knowledge, which is of high value for others, and that they have metaknowledge about this fact. Students should know about the group members' interdependency, they should also know that others need information they have. This means that the instruction should make sure that each student owns information, which is important for others. Students should depend upon one another to achieve a task, and — as our results show — they should be extrinsically rewarded. All these features — interdependency, metaknowledge about it, and rewards — are given, for example, in a Jigsaw task. Here the group's task is structured in a way that each group member is responsible for a unique part of it. The incentive structure should base on the individual scores as well as on the group score, hence each person has a personal interest in participating and providing information for others. So the social-dilemma perspective and the experimental results we presented here confirms the results of a meta-analyses of Slavin (1983). He compared different forms of cooperative learning and found that Jigsaw is superior to other ones.

References

Adar, E., & Hubermann, B. A. (2000). Free riding on Gnutella. *First Monday. 5*(10). Retrieved September 12, 2005, from http://www.firstmonday.dk/issues/issue5_10/adar/

Ardichvili, A., Page, V., & Wentling, T. (2003). Motivation and barriers to participation in virtual knowledge-sharing communities of practice. *Journal of Knowledge Management, 7*(1), 64–77.

Beckman, T., & Liebowitz, J. (1998). *Knowledge organizations: What every manager should know.* Boca Raton: St Lucie Press.

Blanchard, A., & Horan, T. (1998). Virtual communities and social capital. *Social Science Computer Review, 16,* 293–307.

Bonacich, P., & Schneider, S. (1992). Communication networks and collective action. In: W. B. G. Liebrand, D. M. Messick, & H. A. M. Wilke (Eds), *Social dilemmas: Theoretical issues and research findings* (pp. 225–245). Oxford: Pergamon Press.

Brown, J. S., Collins, A., & Duguid, P. (1989). Situated cognition and the culture of learning. *Educational Researcher, 18*(1), 32–42.

Burnett, G. (2000). Information exchange in virtual communities: A typology. *Information Research, 5*(4).

Burnett, G., & Buerkle, H. (2004). Information exchange in virtual communities: A comparative study. *Journal of Computer-Mediated Communication, 9*(2). Retrieved September 12, 2005, from http://www.ascusc.org/jcmc/vol9/issue2/burnett.html

Cabrera, A., & Cabrera, E. F. (2002). Knowledge-sharing dilemmas. *Organization Studies, 23,* 687–710.

Clark, H. H., & Brennan, S. E. (1991). Grounding in communication. In: L. B. Resnick, J. M. Levine, & S. D. Teasley (Eds), *Perspectives on socially shared cognition* (pp. 127–149). Washington: APA.

Cole, M., & Engestrom, Y. (1993). A cultural-historical approach to distributed cognition. In: G. Salomon (Ed.), *Distributed cognitions. Psychological and educational considerations* (pp. 1–46). NY: Cambridge University Press.

Connolly, T., & Thorn, B. K. (1990). Discretionary databases. Theory, data, and implication. In: J. Fulk & C. Steinfield (Eds), *Organizations and communication* (pp. 219–233). Newbury Park, CA: Sage.

Connolly, T., Thorn, B. K., & Heminger, A. (1992). Discretionary databases as social dilemmas. In: W. B. G. Liebrand, D. M. Messick, & H. A. M. Wilke (Eds), *Social dilemmas: Theoretical issues and research findings* (pp. 199–208). Oxford: Pergamon Press.

Constant, D., Kiesler, S., & Sproull, L. (1994). What's mine is ours, or is it? A study of attitudes about information sharing. *Information Systems Research, 5,* 400–422.

Cress, U. (2004). Strategic, metacognitive, and social aspects in resource-oriented knowledge exchange. In: R. Alterman & D. Kirsch (Eds), *Proceedings of the 25th Annual Conference of the Cognitive Science Society.* Mahwah, NJ: Erlbaum. Retrieved September 12, 2005, from http://www.ccm.ua.edu/pdfs/71.pdf

Cress, U. (2005). Ambivalent effect of member portraits in virtual groups. *Journal of Computer-Assisted Learning, 21,* 281–291.

Cress, U., & Hesse, F. W. (2004). Knowledge sharing in groups: Experimental findings of how to overcome a social dilemma. In: Y. Kafai, W. Sandoval, N. Enyedy, A. S. Nixon, & F. Herrera (Eds), *Proceedings of the Sixth International Conference of the Learning Sciences* (pp. 150–157). Mahwah, NJ: Lawrence Erlbaum.

Cress, U., Barquero, B., Buder, J., Sehwan, S., & Hesse, F. W. (2003). Wissensaustausch mittels Datenbanken als Öffentliches-Gut-Dilemma. Die Wirkung von Rückmeldungen und Belohnungen (Knowledge exchange through databases as public-goods dilemma: The effect of feedback and rewards.) *Zeitschrift für Psychologie, 211*(2), 75–85.

Cress, U., Barquero, B., Buder, J., & Hesse, F. W. (2005). Social dilemma in knowledge communication via shared databases. In: R. Bromme, F. W. Hesse, & H. Spada (Eds), *Barriers and biases in computer-mediated knowledge communication — and how they may be overcome* (pp. 143–167). New York: Springer.

Csikszentmihalyi, M. (1975). *Beyond boredom and anxiety.* San Francisco, CA: Jossey-Bass.

Dawes, R. M. (1980). Social dilemmas. *Annual Review of Psychology, 31,* 169–193.

Deci, E. L., & Ryan, R. M. (2000). The "what" and "why" of goal pursuits: Human needs and the self-determination of behavior. *Psychological Bulletin, 125,* 627–668.

Deci, E. L., Koestner, R., & Ryan, R. M. (1999). Meta-analytic review of experiments: Examining the effects of extrinsic rewards on intrinsic motivation. *Psychological Bulletin, 125,* 627–228.

Fulk, J., Flanagin, A. J., Kalman, M. E., Monge, P. R., & Ryan, T. (1996). Connective and communal public goods in interactive communication systems. *Communication Theory, 6,* 60–87.

Hars, A., & Ou, S. (2002). Working for free? Motivations for participating in open source projects. *International Journal of Electronic Communication, 6*(3), 25–39.

Hewitt, J., & Scardamalia, M. (1998). Design principles for distributed knowledge building processes. *Educational Psychology Review, 10*(1), 75–96.

Hollingshead, A. B., Fulk, J., & Monge, P. (2002). Fostering intranet knowledge sharing: An integration of transactive memory and public goods approaches. In: P. Hinds, & S. Kiesler (Eds), *Distributed work* (pp. 335–355). Cambridge, MA: MIT Press.

Jonassen, D. H. (1999). Designing constructivist learning environments. In: C. M. Reigeluth (Ed.), *Instructional-design theories and models* (Vol. 2). Mahwah, NJ: Erlbaum.

Kelley, H. H., & Thibaut, J. (1978). *Interpersonal relations. A theory of interdependence.* New York: Wiley.

Kerr, N. (1995). Norms in social dilemmas. In: D. A. Schroeder (Ed.), *Social dilemmas. Perspectives on individuals and groups.* Westport, CT: Praeger Publishers.

Kiesler, S., Siegel, J., & McGuire, T. W. (1984). Social psychological aspects of computer-mediated communication. *American Psychologist, 39*, 1123–1134.

Kollock, P. (1999). The economies of online cooperation: Gifts and public goods in cyberspace. In: M. Smith, & P. Kollock (Eds), *Communities in cyberspace* (pp. 220–239). London: Routledge.

Lave, J., & Wenger, E. (1991). *Situated learning: Legitimate peripheral participation.* Cambridge: Cambridge University Press.

Ledyard, J. O. (1995). Public goods: A survey of experimental research. In: J. H. Kagel, & A. E. Roth (Eds), *The handbook of experimental economics* (pp. 111–181). Princeton, NJ: Princeton University Press.

Lui, S. M., Lang, K. R., & Kwok, S. H. (2002). Participation incentive mechanisms in peer-to-peer subscription systems. *Proceedings of the 35th Hawaii International Conference on System Sciences, Hawaii.*

Markus, M. L. (1990). Towards a "critical mass" theory of interactive media. In: J. Fulk, & C. Steinfield (Eds), *Organizations and communication.* (pp. 194–218). Newbury Park, CA: Sage.

Marwell, G., & Ames, R. E. (1981). Economists free ride, does anyone else? Experiments on the provision of public goods, IV. *Journal of Public Economics, 15*, 295–310.

Matzat, U. (2001). *Social networks and cooperation in electronic communities: A theoretical-empirical analysis of academic communication and internet discussion groups.* Amsterdam: Thela Publishers.

Matzat, U. (2004). The social embeddedness of academic online groups in offline networks as a norm generating structure: An empirical test of the Coleman model on norm emergence. *Computational & Mathematical Organization Theory, 10*, 205–226.

Moreland, R. L. (1999). Transactive memory: Learning who knows what in work groups and organizations. In: L. L. Thompson, J. M. Levine, & D. M. Messick (Eds), *Shared cognition in organizations. The management of knowledge* (pp. 3–31). London: Erlbaum.

Moreland, R. L., Argote, L., & Krishnan, R. (1996). Socially shared cognition at work: Transactive memory and group performance. In: J. L. Nye, & A. M. Brown (Eds), *What's social about social cognition* (pp. 57–84). Thousand Oaks, CA: Sage.

Nesbit, J. C., & Winne, P. H. (2003). Self-regulated inquiry with network resources. *Canadian Journal of Learning and Technology, 29*(3), 71–92.

Palinscar, A. S. (1998). Social constructivist perspectives on teaching and learning. *Annual Review of Psychology, 49*, 345–375.

Rapoport, A., Bornstein, G., & Erev, I. (1989). Intergroup competition for public goods: Effects of unequal resources and relative group size. *Journal of Personality and Social Psychology, 56*, 748–756.

Reid, F. J. M., Malinek, V., Stott, C. J. T., & Evans, J. B. T. (1996). The messaging threshold in computer-mediated communication. *Ergonomics, 39*, 1017–1037.

Rheingold, H. (1993). *The virtual community.* Reading, MA: Addison-Wesley.

Scardamalia, M. (2002). Collective cognitive responsibility for the advancement of knowledge. In: B. Smith (Ed.), *Liberal education in the knowledge society* (pp. 67–98). Chicago: Open Court.

Scardamalia, M., Bereiter, C., McLean, R., Swallow, J., & Woodruff, E. (1989). Computer-supported intentional learning environments. *Journal of Educational Computer Research, 5*(1), 51–68.

Schiefele, U. (1991). Interest, learning and motivation. *Educational Psychologist, 26*, 299–323.

Slavin, R. E. (1983). When does cooperative learning increase student achievement? *Psychological Bulletin, 94*, 429–445.

Stahl, G. (2004). Groupware goes to school: Adapting BSCW to the classroom. *Journal of Computer Applications in Technology, 19*, 162–174.

Stasser, G., Stewart, D., & Wittenbaum, G. M. (1995). Expert roles and information exchange during discussion: The importance of knowing who knows what. *Journal of Experimental Social Psychology, 31*, 244–265.

Stegbauer, C., & Rausch, A. (2001). Die schweigende Mehrheit — "Lurker" in internetbasierten Diskussionsforen (The silent majority — "Lurkers" on mailing-lists). *Zeitschrift für Soziologie, 30*(1), 48–64.

Trevino, L. K., & Webster, J. (1992). Flow in computer-mediated communication, *Communication Research, 19*(5), 539–573.

Van Dijk, E., & Wilke, H. (1995). Coordination rules in asymmetric social dilemmas: A comparison between public good dilemmas and resource dilemmas. *Journal of Experimental Social Psychology, 31*, 1–27.

Wegner, D. M. (1987). Transactive memory: A contemporary analysis of the group mind. In: G. Mullen, & G. R. Goethals (Eds), *Theories of group behaviour* (pp. 185–208). New York: Springer.

Wenger, E. (1998). *Communities of practice: Learning, meaning, and identity*, Cambridge, UK: Cambridge University Press.

Wit, A., Wilke, H., & Oppewal, H. (1992). Fairness in asymmetric social dilemmas. In: W. B. G. Liebrand, D. M. Messick, & H. A. M. Wilke (Eds), *Social dilemmas* (pp. 183–197). Oxford: Pergamon Press.

Yamagishi, T., & Cook, K. S. (1993). Generalized exchange and social dilemmas. *Social Psychology Quarterly, 56*, 235–248.

Zelman, A., & Leydesdorff, L. (1999). Threaded e-mail messages in self-organization and science & technology studies oriented mailing lists. *Scientometrics, 48*, 316–380.

Chapter 5

The Culture of the Mathematics Classroom: A Complex Determinant of Students' Learning

Fien Depaepe,[1] Erik De Corte and Lieven Verschaffel

Changing Theoretical Perspectives on Mathematics Education

Greeno, Collins and Resnick (1996) distinguish three general perspectives on the nature of mathematical cognition, on how it develops in students' learning activities and how this development can be enhanced by teaching. Each perspective frames the nature of knowing, learning and teaching in a distinctive and complementary way. The perspectives are (1) the behaviourist/empiricist view, (2) the cognitive/rationalist view, and (3) the situative/pragmatist-sociohistoric view. Representative traditions for the first view, according to which knowing is an organized accumulation of associations and skills, are associationism, behaviourism, and connectionism. Gestalt psychology, symbolic information processing, (neo-) Piagetianism and radical constructivism are traditions of research, which Greeno et al. (1996) consider to be branches of the cognitive-rationalist perspective because of their emphasis on the organization of information in cognitive structures and procedures of individual thinkers and learners. Among the traditions that have contributed to the situative/pragmatist-sociohistoric perspective are interactivity theory, ethnography, ecological psychology, socioconstructivism and situated cognition theory. The situative/pragmatist-sociohistoric perspective views knowledge as distributed among people and their environments, including the objects, artefacts, tools, books and communities of which they are a part. In the situated cognition perspective, for instance, knowing and learning mathematics are "both an attribute of groups that carry out cooperative activities and an attribute of individuals who participate in the communities of which they are members" (Greeno et al., 1996, p. 17). In a teaching–learning process, a group or individual with knowledge is attuned to the regularities of activities, which include the constraints and affordances of social practices and of the material and social systems with which they interact.

---

[1]Fien Depaepe is research assistant of the National Fund for Scientific Research — Flanders.

Sfard (1998) suggests a broadly similar contrast between the second and third views, for which she uses, respectively, the terms "acquisitionist" and "participationist". According to this author, the "acquisitionist" group consists of all those (traditional) cognitivist approaches, which explain learning and knowledge in terms of mental entities such as cognitive schemes, tacit models, concept images, or misconceptions, whereas the "participationist" framework embraces all those relatively new theories, which prefer to view learning as a reorganization of activity accompanying the integration of an individual learner with a community of practice. So, the latter framework focuses on the process through which the learner becomes a skilful participant of a given mathematical discourse.

In the late 1980s and 1990s, the cognitivist/rationalist view dominated research in the domain of mathematical education. This view, which draws inspiration from the work of Piaget, gives priority to individual processes occurring in the mathematics classroom and defines learning as an individual activity of re-constructing knowledge, isolated from the historical, social and cultural context in which it is situated. Gradually, the situative/pragmatist-sociohistoric perspective gained influence in the research field of mathematics education. As a result, it became more and more recognized that any activity, thus also any mathematical activity, is historically, socially and culturally situated, and that the meaning of that activity can only be understood if one considers also the context in which it is situated (Evans, 1998). Obviously a major aspect of the context in which mathematics education takes place in schools is the culture of the classroom.

While ethnomathematics, situated cognition and socioconstructivism criticize a purely cognitive psychological perspective that stresses the learner's autonomous learning and cognitive development, they do not take a purely collectivist perspective wherein mathematics learning is only seen as the student's socialization into a pregiven culture and wherein the individual learner is lost (Voigt, 1995). Instead, they value both the individual and social dimensions of mathematics learning. From this viewpoint, mathematics learning is defined as a process of self-organization in which the individual reorganizes his or her activity as he/she interacts with other members of a community (Cobb & Yackel, 1998). According to Lerman (1998, p. 294), it is "a social construction and each person is seen to (re-)create that mathematics for her/himself, with the constraint/perturbation of social interaction as the medium for the development and limitation of those personal creations". So, without overemphasising the influence of the social context, the socioconstructivist, situated cognition and ethnomathematics frameworks typically contend that "these [social and cultural processes] and psychological processes are reflexively related with neither having precedence over the other" (Cobb & Yackel, 1998, p. 175). It should be acknowledged, however, that according to many scholars, this theoretical perspective has not yet succeeded in realizing its ambitious goal of fully integrating both social and psychological perspectives, as it has, in its reaction to previously dominant paradigms, paid too much attention to the former at the expense of the latter (see also Vlassis, 2004).

This chapter intends to outline the impact of the classroom culture on mathematics learning and teaching, and, more particularly, to demonstrate how the emergence and development of the situative/pragmatist-sociohistoric perspective has enriched, and complicated our conceptualization and investigation of mathematical problem solving, learning and teaching. First, we will review some basic insights from this theoretical perspective, which has shown that every mathematical activity is culturally embedded, and that the meaning of any mathematical idea is dependent on the context in which it is used. We will do this by reviewing briefly research from the ethnomathematics of non-Western indigenous societies as well as work that aims at describing the informal, culturally embedded mathematics used in contemporary Western cultures. Evidently, the role of the cultural context of mathematics learning could also be highlighted and investigated through systematic comparisons of mathematical cognitions and achievements between different countries, but, due to space restrictions, we will not discuss this line of comparative research in this chapter (for reviews of this research see De Corte, Greer, & Verschaffel, 1996). Second, we will look at how sociocultural factors influence mathematical learning and cognition by considering aspects of culture and socialization within the microcosm of the mathematics classroom and by investigating how students' knowledge, perspectives, beliefs and values are shaped as a function of their involvement with mathematics in school. In other words, we review the research wherein scholars have started to look at the (typical) mathematics classroom from an anthropological point of view. Third, we will review empirical evidence selectively for the explanatory power of the classroom culture for students' mathematical performance. Finally, we will conclude by summarizing the principal ideas and by stressing the need to go beyond the microculture of the classroom to understand students' learning.

Mathematics as a Cultural Activity

For a long time, it was not questioned that mathematics was a universal and culture-free form of knowledge. According to Bishop (1988), the cultural situatedness of mathematics was ignored because of the confusion between the "universality of truth" of mathematical ideas (i.e., invariant logical principles involved in counting) with the cultural basis of these ideas (i.e., the existence of a great cultural variation in applying these counting principles). During the 1980s, people became more aware of the historical and anthropological research evidence that demonstrated convincingly that mathematics is not culture-free, but culture-bound, and that different sociocultural groups have produced and are practicing different mathematics (Bishop, 1988).

d'Ambrosio (1985) introduced the term "ethnomathematics" to refer to mathematics as practiced, expressed and transmitted within identifiable sociocultural groups. Both parts of this term should be taken in a broad sense (Borba, 1990). "Ethno" should be understood as referring to all possible kinds of sociocultural groups, such as national-tribal societies, labour groups, professional classes and even children of a certain age bracket; and "mathematics" should be understood as encompassing a broad range of human activities, such as ciphering, measuring, classifying, ordering, inferring and modelling. As such, ethnomathematics is a set of knowledge, skills, tools, beliefs and attitudes that is intrinsically linked to a sociocultural group and to its goals, its values and interests, its language, its reality — its "ethnos" (Borba, 1990).

According to the ethnomathematical approach, mathematics is a pancultural phenomenon: It is considered as a cultural product that has evolved in all societies through universal environmental activities like counting, locating, measuring, designing, playing and explaining (Bishop, 1988). Moreover, underlying the distinct ethnomathematics are basic invariant principles, such as the above-mentioned principles underlying counting (Nunes, 1992a, b). But at the same time there are remarkable intercultural differences due to the fact that the mathematical tools, practices and beliefs of distinct sociocultural groups are created in response to circumstances, needs and views unique to each group (Borba, 1990). In this sense, mathematical knowledge is inherently interwoven with the context and the culture in which it is situated. Indeed, the meaning of every mathematical symbol or sign is inherently ambiguous and calls for interpretation; mathematical objects have no absolute meaning but get their meaning from the context in which they are used. The "truth" of the mathematical ideas depends on conventions established by teacher and students during classroom interactions. For instance, in many classes the solution of a mathematical problem is valued as right or wrong depending on whether or not the problem has been solved by means of the procedure or approach being more or less explicitly taught by the teacher. In other classes, the use of untaught solution methods is highly appreciated.

A first and very important line of ethnomathematical research comes from scholars who have analysed the mathematical values, concepts and skills existing in remote, indigenous, non-Western cultures, where no systematic transmission in schools prevails. The decodification of those indigenous mathematics is done using a diversity of ethnographic methodologies, such as carefully analysing typical behaviours and objects, children's games, mythical stories, the language system and so forth, sometimes in combination with traditional psychological tests. Most of this research has been done within Vygotsky's theory about the role of culturally elaborated systems of signs in the development of higher forms of human cognition. As an example, we refer to Saxe's (2005) field studies in a horticultural society, the Oksapmin, in Papua New Guinea. Within that society, counting and numerical representations are mapped onto 27 body parts, resulting in a 27-body-part counting system, characterized by the absence of any base structure (like in a 10-base, a 5-base, or a 2-base number system). The social history of schooling, starting in the 1970s, has led to a gradual shift from the 27-body-part non-base system to more Western base-structured systems. Saxe's study reveals that processes of change result from an interplay between cultural processes (the mastering of various cultural means or instruments) and developmental processes (processes of growth and maturation) in cognition (de Abreu, 2000).

Other ethnomathematical studies involve the documentation and analysis of the informal mathematical practices in Western (sub)cultures that are embedded in specific out-of-school activities and contexts and that may be contrasted with "school mathematics". One of the most representative examples of this kind of ethnomathematical research is the study of Nunes, Schliemann, and Carraher (1993), wherein these researchers compared the solution strategies of Brazilian street vendors (9 to 15-year-old children) in an informal and in a formal test. The informal test was carried out in the children's natural working situation, that is, at street corners or in an open market. The researchers posed successive questions about potential or actual purchases (e.g., I'd like ten coconuts. How much is that?). From all the mathematical problems successfully solved by each subject, a sample was chosen for the formal test, involving the same numbers as in the informal test. The formal test items were presented either as a mathematical operation (e.g., $105 + 105$) or as a word problem (e.g., Mary bought x bananas, each banana cost y; how much did she pay altogether?). This study revealed that children performed very well on problems in out-of-school contexts (i.e., in the street-vending context) compared to their performance on isomorphic school mathematical tasks. Moreover, it was observed that out-of-school activities seemed to elicit informal mathematical reasoning and computation processes invented by the subjects themselves, while students involved in the formal context of the school tended to use — much less successfully — the formal and standardized procedures taught in the mathematics classroom. Similar results were obtained by Lave, Murtaugh, and de la Rocha (1984), who compared shoppers' arithmetic in the supermarket with their performance on a paper-and-pencil arithmetic test, and by de Abreu, Bishop, and Pompeu (1997), who contrasted primary school-children's solutions of mathematics problems embedded in their out-of-school practices with their mathematical performance in the school context. In all these studies, typically mathematical activities, such as counting, ordering, sorting, measuring, weighing and computing were done in radically different ways in informal contexts than as commonly taught in school (De Corte et al., 1996). These research findings have contributed to the criticism that the connection between in and out-of-school mathematical practices is problematically weak (Mottier Lopez, 2005). School mathematics does not sufficiently build on the informal mathematical concepts and skills that children bring to the mathematics lessons. Moreover, school mathematics does not succeed in developing in learners' mathematical knowledge and skills that transfer to out-of-school mathematical activities (De Corte et al., 1996).

The Mathematics Classroom

Another way of looking at how sociocultural factors influence mathematical learning and cognition is to consider aspects of culture and socialization within the microcosm of the mathematics classroom and to investigate how students' learning and performance are shaped as a function of their involvement with mathematics in school (Nickson, 1992). In other words, researchers have started to look at the mathematics classroom culture from an anthropological point of view. In some of these studies, the focus is on how the classroom culture may negatively affect students' mathematical behaviour, learning and thinking. In other studies, it is illustrated how the culture of the mathematics classroom can be used positively as a vehicle for realizing authentic mathematical learning experiences and valuable learning outcomes. A prominent theoretical account of the impact of the mathematics classroom culture on students' mathematical knowledge, perspectives, beliefs and values has been provided by Cobb and associates (Cobb & Yackel, 1996, 1998; Cobb, Stephan, McClain, & Gravemeijer, 2001; McClain & Cobb, 2001). In their framework, an explicit attempt is made to integrate a social and individual perspective on mathematics learning and performance. In this section, this framework will be proposed as an appropriate lens through which one can look at mathematical classroom processes.

Norms and Beliefs as Theoretical Constructs to Describe Mathematics Classroom Processes

Cobb and his associates (Cobb & Yackel, 1996, 1998; Cobb et al., 2001; McClain & Cobb, 2001) describe classroom mathematics cultures in terms of classroom norms and practices on the one hand, and teacher's and students' beliefs, conceptions and activities on the other hand. These groups of concepts reflect the social and psychological perspective underlying socioconstructivism: the social perspective refers to ways of acting, reasoning and arguing that are normative in a classroom community, while the psychological perspective is concerned with the nature of individual students' reasoning, or their particular ways of participating in communal activities (Cobb et al., 2001).

In the social analysis, distinction is made between (a) the classroom social norms, (b) the sociomathematical norms, and (c) the classroom mathematical practices. Classroom social norms are "characteristics of the classroom community and document regularities in classroom activity that are jointly established by the teacher and students" (Cobb et al., 2001, pp. 122–123). For instance, students have to listen to each other; they have to raise their hand before answering. Like classroom social norms, sociomathematical norms are "normative aspects of students' activity that are specific to mathematics" (Cobb et al., 2001, p. 124). What is considered as a "mathematically correct" answer, as a "mathematically different solution method", or as a "mathematically appropriate explanation or justification" are all illustrations of sociomathematical norms. Classroom mathematical practices are defined as "the taken-as-shared mathematical practices established by the classroom community" (Cobb & Yackel, 1998, p. 171). Specific procedures and algorithms that the teacher and students agreed upon to solve certain mathematical problems are typical examples of classroom mathematical practices. Evidently, the social norms, sociomathematical norms and classroom mathematical practices may vary from classroom to classroom.

The psychological perspective of Cobb and associates' framework involves the teacher's and students' beliefs. Cobb and Yackel (1998) distinguish between (a) beliefs about the personal role and the role of others in the mathematics classroom, and the general nature of mathematical activity, (b) specifically mathematical beliefs and values, and (c) mathematical conceptions and activity. The first category refers to "students' interpretations of their own and others' activity" (Cobb & Yackel, 1998, p. 168). Specifically mathematical beliefs and values enable students "to act as increasingly autonomous members of the classroom mathematical community as they participate in the negotiation of sociomathematical norms" (Cobb et al., 2001, p. 124). Mathematical conceptions and activities are seen as acts, "of individual learning in which a student reorganizes his or her mathematical reasoning" (Cobb et al., 2001, p. 125). Beliefs and values are the product of social life, in the sense that individuals constitute a unique belief system by internalizing external constraints of the contexts in which they function (de Abreu et al., 1997).

The psychological and the social perspective result in two different ways of looking at and making sense of what is going on in classrooms. These approaches are not mutually exclusive, but constitute the background from which the other perspective can be understood. Consequently, the theoretical constructs "beliefs" and "norms" are closely and reflexively related: "normative activities of the classroom community emerge and are continually regenerated by the teacher and students as they interpret and respond to each other's actions. Conversely, the teacher's and students' interpretations and actions in the classroom do not exist except as acts of participation in communal classroom practices" (Cobb et al., 2001, p. 119). Similarly, the three above-mentioned aspects of the classroom microculture (i.e., the social norms, sociomathematical norms and classroom mathematical practices) and their psychological counterparts (i.e., the two categories of beliefs and the mathematical interpretations and reasoning) are reflexively related. Indeed, in making their contributions to the establishment of the social norms, students and teachers reorganize their individual beliefs about their own role, others' roles and the general nature of mathematical activity. In their theoretical framework, Cobb and associates do not privilege social norms or individual students' beliefs. They conclude that the social norms and the beliefs of the participants co-evolve in that neither is seen to exist independently of the other. The same applies to the reflexive relation between sociomathematical norms and mathematical beliefs and values, and between classroom mathematical practices and mathematical conceptions and activity (Cobb et al., 2001).

As will be outlined in the next section, negotiation mediates this reflexive process. By negotiating sociomathematical norms, the teacher and students establish a specific mathematical classroom culture; at the same time, the contributors to that negotiation process also reshape their own beliefs during these interactions. In that sense, negotiation is a mediator between culture and cognition.

The interpretative framework of Cobb and his colleagues is certainly helpful in understanding mathematical classroom processes. However, the framework can also be questioned. First, the difference between the social and sociomathematical norms is rather subtle. The possibility that a social norm, as opposed to a sociomathematical norm, might emerge in other subject-matter areas is not sufficient to label it as general or to give it the status of being applicable to different subject-matter domains (Mottier Lopez, 2005). Second, norms and practices are not only a product of the interactions between the teacher and the students, but they are also shaped by larger social institutions (e.g., the school, the Department of Education, ...) that clearly influence the obligatory subject matter, the standards, etc. Therefore, in order to really understand the classroom practices and processes, it is necessary to acknowledge the broader historical, social, cultural and political contexts, which determine, to a certain extent, the social and sociomathematical norms that are negotiated within the classroom (Greer, Verschaffel, & Mukhopadhyay, in press). Third, it seems that the framework of Cobb and his colleagues is especially applicable to describe and analyse classrooms in which an explicit and systematic attempt is made to establish a new classroom culture, rather than for understanding and explaining how an established classroom culture is continuously reconfirmed and/or how different subcultures and countercultures emerge and develop within a (typical) classroom.

Negotiation of Meanings and Norms

A classroom is a place where individuals with distinct sociocultural and educational backgrounds and histories meet and interact with each other. Owing to previous learning experiences in all kinds of in- and out-of-school settings, the teacher and the students have their own expectations about and attitudes towards mathematical learning. Those experiences have coloured the eyes with which individuals look at reality. Individuals' distinct views on classroom mathematical activities result in different framings for those activities, and consequently lead to different interpretations of the classroom situation. In other words, misunderstandings between teacher and students, and among students are common in classroom contexts due to the different ways in which they interpret the inherently ambiguous mathematical objects. Even if they use the same mathematical concepts and terms, the way in which they understand them can be different (Voigt, 1995).

The teacher and students try to eliminate perturbations, by searching for common background knowledge to interpret mathematical ideas, objects and activities. During interactions, they negotiate their background interpretations with each other, by framing the intentionality of the mathematical signs and symbols that are communicated in the classroom (Steinbring, 1998). Through negotiation, new mathematical meanings and new classroom norms emerge as taken-as-shared between the participants. However, the participants can never be sure that their subjective background understandings are consistent. They only interact *as if* they interpret the mathematical topics in the same way (Bauersfeld, 1995). Those taken-as-shared meanings and norms gradually become stabilized mathematical "truths" and accepted norms that further guide the students' and the teacher's behaviour in the classroom, which enables — despite of teacher's and students' different backgrounds of understandings — a smooth functioning of classroom discourse. These norms function implicitly most of the time. Brousseau (1998) introduced the concept "didactical contract" to label this system of norms, rules and expectations that emerge during a never-ending negotiation process. It refers to "a set of interrelated rules and mutual expectations that is negotiated in the mathematics classroom and that dominates the interaction between the teacher and the students during the mathematics lessons as well as the cognitive processes of an individual student when engaged in thinking and problem-solving activities in or related to these lessons" (Verschaffel, Greer & De Corte, 2000, p. 60). The concept is related to the "normative aspects" in the framework of Cobb and associates (Yackel & Cobb, 1996). However, according to Herbst (2003), the didactical contract differs in that it covers not only the immediate context (i.e., the mathematics classroom) but also the broader sociocultural context, whereas Cobb et al.'s notion of classroom norms and practices only addresses the local context of the classroom.

Although the teacher and the students interactively establish new taken-as-shared mathematical meanings and norms through their negotiations, the teacher typically has a stronger influence than the students in establishing the mathematics classroom culture. The teacher is invested with the responsibility and authority for the students' education by society at large (Bishop, 1985). For instance, the teacher's decision to teach certain mathematical topics and not others, to develop certain values rather than others, to accept certain mathematical answers, to decide if students' contributions are appropriate or not reflect the power position of the teacher.

Since teacher beliefs seem to play an essential role in the origin and development of the mathematics classroom culture, and because that culture seems to have an impact on the development of students' beliefs and performances, it seems necessary to modify teachers' beliefs in order to change students' beliefs and behaviour (Mason & Scrivani, 2004). To realize a change in teachers' beliefs, teachers have to become aware of the hidden regularities in their classroom cultures and practices (Voigt, 1998). Often, they only become aware of their own norms and routines when they are confronted with those of other classrooms (Zack, 1999). So, only by making teachers' unconsciously held assumptions and routinely applied practices explicit, can a change in their classroom culture and practice be induced (Ernest, 1998). However, for several reasons, teachers' beliefs, conceptions and activities are resistant to change. First, the teacher is also an agent of a broader social culture (Nickson, 1992). Consequently, the norms and practices that he or she wants to instil will be mediated by the expectations of parents, politicians and the public about what mathematics is. Second, teachers' professional development is often deficient as the opportunities for staff development (e.g., training sessions, workshops) are scarce and mostly on a voluntary basis. Third, the prevailing assessment culture pressures teachers to concentrate on what society finds important (Burkhardt, 2004). Finally, it is also difficult for teachers to change students' beliefs, as students build up their expectations over the years. There exists a great potential for conflict between teachers and students, since not all students will adopt teachers' beliefs in light of their previous educational experience in mathematics (Nickson, 1992). This, among other factors, can give rise to countercultures in the classroom.

The Explanatory Power of the Culture of the Mathematics Classroom

In this section, we will review three categories of studies that document the influence of the culture of the mathematics classroom on students' mathematical thinking and learning. First, a study by Boaler (1998) will be presented concerning the impact of two different approaches to teaching and learning mathematics, namely a process-based approach and a textbook-based approach, on students' mathematical processes and performance. Second, we will review a year-long teaching experiment by McClain and Cobb (2001) that explicitly aimed to promote the establishment of alternative sociomathematical norms in a classroom. Third, studies about the impact of the classroom culture on students' attitude towards the use of real-world knowledge while solving word problems will be discussed.

Impact of the Mathematical Learning Environment: A Process-Based Approach Vs. a Textbook Approach

Boaler (1998) studied approximately 300 students over three years from two different secondary schools (Grades 9−11) who learned mathematics in radically distinct ways. One school taught mathematics in a traditional way, while the other school had recently changed towards a reform-based, process-oriented approach.

The students in the school with the traditional approach were very disciplined and hard working. During interviews with the researcher, students complained about the boring and monotonous math lessons. Many students held the view that mathematics was all about memorizing a vast number of rules and formulas. Furthermore, their beliefs seemed to have many negative implications on their behaviour. For instance, as a consequence of students' assumption that mathematics was all about remembering a rule or method they had used in similar situations, they did not believe that in mathematical situations it was appropriate to try and think themselves about what to do.

In the process-oriented school, the mathematics lessons were organized around open-ended projects, spread over a period of two or three weeks. Students following this approach were expected and stimulated to become independent thinkers who were responsible for their own actions. Contrary to the disciplined nature of the mathematics lessons in the first school, the lessons of the process-based approach were rather chaotic and noisy. During interviews with the researcher, students reported that the mathematics lessons were interesting. They viewed mathematics as solving problems, and as involving active and flexible thinking. Students seemed to act in accordance with the didactical contract: they based their mathematical thinking and behaviour on what they thought was expected of them.

Boaler compared the mathematical performance of students from both schools on a regular mathematics achievement test and on a non-routine application problem wherein students were asked to consider a proposed house, and to decide whether it would pass some local authority design rules. They were given a model and a scale plan of the house, and they had to inspect the angles, calculate areas, volumes, and so on. The mathematics assessed by the written test and by the application task was the same.

The results showed that students at the two schools were equally able to solve the written test, while the scores on the application problem were significantly higher for the process-based than for the traditional school. Boaler concluded that the students in the traditional school had developed inert, procedural knowledge that was difficult to use in anything else than traditional textbook questions. They had not learned to think about problems, and as a consequence they did not know which methods they could use to solve an application task. To the contrary, the students in the process-based approach had acquired the ability to think about different situations, which fostered their performances on the applied tasks too. In conclusion, Boaler found strong evidence for the impact of the context of the mathematics classroom culture and practice on students' mathematical beliefs and performances.

Teaching Experiments Focusing on the Development of Sociomathematical Classroom Norms

Cobb and associates used the interpretative framework described above in a number of teaching experiments in lower primary classrooms that attempted to help and support teachers in radically changing their mathematics teaching practices. These classroom teaching experiments were carried out in close collaboration with the teachers.

Yackel and Cobb (1996) began by doing a post hoc analysis of the classroom situation in order to identify particular social and sociomathematical norms. For instance, they investigated the emergence of the sociomathematical norm of what would count as a "mathematically different answer". Their observations revealed that, on the one hand, students did not know what was considered as a mathematically different solution until the teacher and other students judged that some of their contributions, and not others, were different. On the other hand, the teachers themselves seemed to clarify their own understanding of a mathematically different answer as they interacted with the students. Consequently, Yackel and Cobb concluded that specific sociomathematical norms, such as what is considered as a "mathematically different solution method", emerge during joint activity by a process of implicit negotiation. In a more recent teaching experiment, McClain and Cobb (2001) made more explicit attempts to guide and foster the development of certain sociomathematical norms, and, thus, simultaneously to influence students' mathematics-related beliefs. During a one-year teaching experiment in a first-grade mathematics classroom, they investigated how teachers might proactively support their students' mathematical learning in order to foster the emergence of the type of mathematical disposition advocated in current reform documents relating to mathematics education. More specifically, their intervention aimed at addressing ways of structuring collections of objects that can facilitate the development of strategies for adding and subtracting numbers up to 20, and at establishing an inquiry mathematics culture with young children. One task given to the children was to figure out how many chips were shown there on an overhead projector on which an arrangement of, for instance, five or seven chips was displayed. The objective was to elicit reasoning about the task, and to initiate a shift in pupils from using counting to find the answer towards more sophisticated strategies based on grouping of chips. The results show how, through discussions and interactions focused on the task, the "mathematical difference" sociomathematical norm developed in the classroom. This norm evolved, through re-negotiation, into the norm "what is a more sophisticated solution". Indeed, solutions based on grouping of chips became seen not only as different from, but also as more sophisticated than counting. Similarly, from the "mathematical difference" norm the class derived also the norm of "what counts as an easy, simple or efficient way" to solve a problem: some of the solutions that were accepted as being different were also considered as being easier or more efficient, but others were not.

Suspension of Sense-Making

Since the mid-1990s several scholars have discussed strong cases of unintended and undesirable student learning behaviour and learning outcomes in traditional mathematical classes resulting directly from characteristics of the classroom culture. A major example concerns the suspension of sense-making in children's mathematics problem solving. This concept is used to describe the fact that students often incorrectly neglect their common-sense knowledge and experience about the real world while solving mathematical application problems. Probably the most famous and spectacular example in this regard is the "Captain's problem": "There are 26 sheep and 10 goats on a ship. How old is the captain?" Students, confronted with this problem, seem to be prepared to offer an answer to this unsolvable problem by combining the numbers given in the problem (i.e., $26+10$) to produce an answer (i.e., 36) without being aware of the meaninglessness of the problem and of their solution (Baruk, 1985).

Inspired by this and other examples of striking evidence of suspension of sense-making by students, both Greer (1993) in Northern Ireland and Verschaffel, De Corte, and Lasure (1994) in Flanders carried out an investigation that further demonstrated this phenomenon. In both studies, students were administered in the context of a typical mathematics lesson a paper-and-pencil test using a set of problems including: "Steve has bought 4 planks each 2.5 meters long. How many planks 1 meter long can he saw from these planks?", "John's best time to run 100 meters is 17 seconds. How long will it take him to run 1 kilometer?", "Bruce lives at a distance of 17 km from school and Alice at 8 km from the same school. How far do they live from each other?".

These authors termed each of these items "problematic" (P) in the sense that they require the application of judgment based on real-world knowledge and assumptions rather than the routine application of simple arithmetical operations. Each such P-item was paired with an S-item (for "standard") in which the "obvious" calculation is — they would argue — appropriate. For each item, the students, as well as recording an answer, were invited to comment on the problem and on their response. A response to a P-item was classified as a "realistic reaction" if *either* the answer given indicated that realistic considerations had been taken into account *or* if a comment indicated that the student was aware that the problem was not straightforward. For example, a classification "realistic reaction" for the planks P-item would be given to a student who gave the answer "8" or who made a comment such as "Steve would have a hard time putting together the remaining pieces of 0.5 meters". When a P-item was answered in the predictable routine-based way, they termed it a non-realistic reaction. In both studies, students demonstrated a very strong overall tendency to exclude real-world knowledge and realistic considerations when confronted with the problematic versions of the problem pairs. For instance, in Verschaffel et al.'s (1994) study, only 17% of all reactions to the P-items could be considered as realistic.

These initial studies were replicated in several other countries, using a similar methodology and, to a considerable extent, the same items. The findings were strikingly consistent across many countries. Using the same criteria as in the two initial studies, almost none of the P-items was answered in a realistic fashion by more than a small percentage of students, sometimes to the great surprise and disappointment of these other researcher(s) who had anticipated that the "disastrous" picture of the Irish and Flemish pupils would not apply to their students (for an extensive overview of these replication studies, see Verschaffel et al., 2000).

Based on further research, involving both individual interviews with children who had demonstrated such "non-realistic behaviour" and analyses of typical word problem-solving lessons, the above investigators concluded that it is certainly not a cognitive deficit as such that causes students' general and strong abstention from sense-making when doing arithmetic word problems in a typical school setting, but rather that they are acting — implicitly or explicitly — in accordance with the "rules of the game" of the interactive ritual in which they are involved, or, as others would call it, in accordance with the "didactical contract" (Brousseau, 1998), or the "sociomathematical norms and classroom practices" (Yackel & Cobb, 1996).

The above interpretation of students' non-realistic responses to word problems is in line with Schoenfeld's (1991, p. 340) suggestion that the children who produced such bizarre responses were not irrational but were engaged in sense-making of a different kind:

> Taking the stance of the Western Rationalist in mathematics, I characterized student behaviour … as a violation of sense-making. As I have admonished, however, such behaviour is sense making of the deepest kind. In the context of schooling, such behaviour represents the construction of a set of behaviours that result in praise for good performance, minimal conflict, fitting in socially, etc. What could be more sensible than that? The problem, then, is that the same behaviour that is sensible in one context (schooling as an institution) may violate the protocols of sense-making in another (the culture of mathematics and mathematicians).

This brings us to the question: How do these beliefs about and tactics for the solution of school arithmetic word problem develop in students? It is assumed that this development occurs implicitly, gradually and tacitly through being immersed in the culture of the mathematics classroom in which they engage. Putting it another way, students' strategies and beliefs develop from their perceptions and interpretations of the didactical contract

(Brousseau, 1998) or the sociomathematical norms and classroom practices (Yackel & Cobb, 1996) that determine (explicitly to some extent, but mainly implicitly) how to behave in a mathematics class, how to think, how to communicate with the teacher and so on. More specifically, this enculturation seems to be mainly caused by two aspects of current instructional practice, namely (1) the nature of the problems given and (2) the way in which these problems are conceived and treated by teachers (Verschaffel et al., 2000).

These explanations were further investigated by some researchers. For instance, Reusser and Stebler (1997) found a positive correlation between the percentages of realistic answers students give to P-problems, on the one hand, and the extent to which these children had already been confronted with problematic and atypical mathematical items during previous classroom experiences, on the other hand. Verschaffel, De Corte, and Borghart (1997) investigated (prospective) mathematics teachers' beliefs about the usefulness of realistic considerations while interpreting and solving mathematical problems. They observed that these (prospective) teachers themselves tended to neglect realistic knowledge in their own solution processes of P-items; moreover, they valued non-realistic answers of children to those problems more than realistic answers.

Verschaffel et al. (1998) made an attempt to improve students' mathematical modelling by establishing a powerful learning environment in four fifth-grade classrooms. The cornerstones of the learning environment were: a set of functional, exciting and realistic application problems; a number of varying and powerful instructional techniques; and an appropriate classroom culture, which aims at developing positive beliefs and attitudes towards problem solving. The results of the students involved in the powerful learning environment were compared with the performances of peers involved in traditional mathematics classrooms. Overall, the implementation of the powerful learning environment had a positive effect on students' attitude towards problem solving, their problem-solving performance, their use of heuristic strategies, and their development of metacognitive skills. And, this was not only the case for the mathematically most able children; also children of medium and low ability benefited from the positive effects of the learning environment.

More recently, Mason and Scrivani (2004) tried more systematically to positively influence and systematically assess students' beliefs about mathematics and mathematical learning by changing the classroom-learning environment in line with the basic ideas of the intervention designed by Verschaffel et al. (1998). In two fifth-grade classrooms, a non-traditional classroom culture was elicited through negotiation of new sociomathematical norms. Characteristics of the new classroom culture included: students' active involvement while solving mathematical application problems, stimulating students to engage in cognitive and metacognitive activities, and making students aware that many problems can be interpreted and solved in different ways. The results show that the intervention, spread over a period of three months, had a positive impact on students' beliefs about themselves as math learners and about maths and mathematical problem solving as measured by a beliefs questionnaire, comprising 28 items to be rated on a 5-point Likert scale (e.g., "It is not important to understand a maths problem but it is important to solve it", "Maths problems that take a long time, do not bother me"). Moreover, those students seemed to tumble less in the pitfall of "suspension of sense-making", i.e., they reached significantly higher scores on solving unusual problems than students in the traditional learning environment.

Overall, these studies illustrate, first, that students' mathematical beliefs and performances are influenced by the classroom culture in which their mathematical learning is situated, and, second, that an appropriate classroom culture can be used positively as a vehicle for realizing these valuable learning outcomes and to enhance students' beliefs.

Contributions of these Studies to Our Understanding of Mathematical Learning and Teaching

The above-mentioned studies document how important is it to enrich the cognitive/rationalist perspective with the newer theoretical insights and approaches from the situative/pragmatist-sociohistoric view. What these investigations demonstrate is, first of all, that in the mathematical problem-solving and learning situations, affective and social factors are as much part of students' thinking and learning behaviour as are cognitive factors (Leron & Hazzan, 1997; Schoenfeld, 1991; Vinner, 1997). These additional factors might include, for instance, the need to make sense of and the need to meet expectations of the authority figure involved (e.g., the researcher or the teacher). Or, as Boaler (1999, pp. 264–265) states it: "Within the mathematics classroom, students do not only learn mathematical concepts and procedures; they learn how to interact in the classroom, they learn particular sets of beliefs and practices and they learn the appropriate way to behave in the mathematics classroom". In the above-mentioned studies attempts were made to analyse students' thinking and learning by taking into account such additional "noncognitive" factors. Second, these studies demonstrate that, consequently, when designing new instructional environments for mathematics learning and teaching, the importance of the classroom culture for the enactment of such an instructional sequence cannot be neglected and can certainly not be considered as a simple add-on that has to be considered only after all decisions about the selection and ordering of the instructional tasks, tools and strategies have been made. To implement a reform-based mathematics teaching/learning process, certain social and sociomathematical classroom norms have to be achieved, and this cannot be done separately from the elaboration of the cognitive, content-oriented teaching/learning trajectory (Gravemeijer, 2004).

Conclusion and Discussion

In this chapter, the culture of the mathematics classroom was considered as a strong determinant of students' learning. Indeed, we argued that the classroom culture influences the development of students' beliefs, as well as their mathematical learning and performance. However, it became also clear that the relation between the mathematics classroom culture and students' behaviour and performance is complex and reciprocal. The mathematics classroom culture shapes students' behaviour; students' behaviour together with the teacher's activities in turn influence the culture of the mathematics classroom. The classroom culture is neither pregiven, nor fixed. Instead, the teacher and the students constitute and re-establish it interactively and permanently.

We outlined some studies illustrating that unintended and undesirable student learning behaviour can be negatively affected by the established classroom culture. But other studies revealed that the mathematics classroom culture can also be used positively as a vehicle for realizing a positive attitude towards mathematics and other valuable learning outcomes. However, changing the classroom culture is a very difficult task. Despite a lot of attempts to induce changes in education, there exists a great stability of life in classrooms (van den Berg, 2004; Depaepe et al., 2000[2]). Explanatory for this resistance to change is not only the fact that the norms and practices of the classroom microculture are affected by the culture at the meso- and macrolevel of the educational system, but also that the corresponding beliefs are unconsciously held by the participants (Voigt, 1998). So, a major obstacle for change in school mathematics seems to be the "epistemological obstacle", namely the often hidden existing expectations, ideologies and epistemologies of the teacher and the students (Ernest, 1998). Taking this into account, "we cannot improve the classroom microculture in the same way that we can change the mathematical curriculum or the classroom macroculture characterized by general principles and teaching strategies. Therefore, we should conceptualize the change of a microculture as an evolution rather than as a rearrangement" (Voigt, 1995, p. 164).

Furthermore, although we have stressed the importance of the culture of the mathematics classroom, we are aware that it is, of course, only one determinant of students' mathematical thinking and learning, and but one factor for the enactment of powerful learning environments. To understand students' mathematical thinking and learning, attention for the sociocultural context needs to be complemented with cognitive analyses of students' mental processes, conceptual and strategic difficulties, etc. Accordingly, theorists and developers of powerful learning environments should pay attention to numerous other aspects of such environments, like the selection and sequencing of the instructional tasks, the didactical tools, the instructional techniques, etc., besides the development of an appropriate classroom culture. As argued by several authors, a well-balanced integration of these cognitive-psychological and the socio-constructive perspectives is a hard affair. As a warning against overemphasizing the social aspects of students' learning, Kieran (2001) refers to a study that convincingly demonstrates the great risks of making evaluative statements about the effects of an experimental learning environment on individual students' learning processes and outcomes merely on the basis of group assessments of their learning. The search for a well-balanced and well-integrated synthesis of the individual and social perspective remains one of the greatest challenges for future research (Salomon, 2005).

Finally, we remind the reader that we focused on the microlevel of mathematics education — the culture of the mathematics classroom. We did not take into account how that classroom culture is embedded in the school culture and the broader community. Obviously, the classroom culture is not isolated from these broader cultural influences and

---

[2]In order to explain the resistance to innovation in primary education Depaepe et al. (2000) have referred to the basic patterns that dominate the educational action in the classrooom since the end of the 19th century. In their view, the core structure of pedagogical and didactic practice needs to be sought in the professional aura that teachers assumed over time. Their educative skills relied on the practices and practical experience built up historically and passed down within the school from one generation to the next. It is in this deeply rooted core of educational and child-rearing practices that Depaepe et al. locate the enduring resistance to educational reform: due to the implicit rules of the "grammars" of schooling and educationalizing the internal behaviour at schools remained over years very much time the same.

it can only be fully understood when it is considered in that broader context of what the school and the society intend to accomplish through education (Bruner, 1996).

References

Baruk, S. (1985). *L'âge du capitaine. De l'erreur en mathématiques.* Paris: Editions du Seuil.

Bauersfeld, H. (1995). "Language games" in the mathematics classroom: Their function and their effects. In: P. Cobb, & H. Bauersfeld (Eds), *The emergence of the mathematical meaning: Interaction in classroom cultures* (pp. 271–291). Hove: Erlbaum.

Bishop, A. (1985). The social construction of meaning: A significant development for mathematics education? *For the Learning of Mathematics, 5*(1), 24–28.

Bishop, A. J. (1988). Mathematics education in its cultural context. *Educational Studies in Mathematics, 19,* 179–191.

Boaler, J. (1998). Open and closed mathematics approaches: Student experiences and understandings. *Journal for Research in Mathematics Education, 29*(1), 41–62.

Boaler, J. (1999). Participation, knowledge and beliefs: A community perspective on mathematics learning. *Educational Studies in Mathematics, 40,* 259–281.

Borba, M. C. (1990). Ethnomathematics and education. *For the Learning of Mathematics, 10*(1), 39–42.

Brousseau, G. (1998). Théorie des situations didactiques. Grenoble: La Pensée Sauvage, Éditions.

Bruner, J. (1996). *The culture of education.* Cambridge, MA: Harvard University Press.

Burkhardt, H. (2004). Establishing modelling in the curriculum: Barriers and levers. Paper presented at the study conference of the ICMI study: 14: Applications and modeling in mathematics education, Dortmund, Germany.

Cobb, P., Stephan, M., McClain, K., & Gravemeijer, K. (2001). Participating in classroom mathematical practices. *Journal of the Learning Sciences, 10*(1–2), 113–163.

Cobb, P., & Yackel, E. (1996). Constructivist, emergent, and sociocultural perspectives in the context of developmental research. *Educational Psychologist, 31*(3–4), 175–190.

Cobb, P., & Yackel, E. (1998). A constructivist perspective on the culture of the mathematics classroom. In: F. Seeger, J. Voigt, & U. Waschescio (Eds), *The culture of the mathematics classroom* (pp. 158–190). Cambridge: Cambridge University Press.

d'Ambrosio, U. (1985). Ethnomathematics and its place in the history and pedagogy of mathematics. *For the Learning of Mathematics, 5*(1), 44–48.

de Abreu, G. (2000). Relationships between macro and micro socio-cultural contexts: Implications for the study of interactions in the mathematics classroom. *Educational Studies in Mathematics, 41,* 1–29.

de Abreu, G., Bishop, A., & Pompeu Jr., G. (1997). What children and teachers count as mathematics. In: T. Nunes, & P. Bryant (Eds), *Learning and teaching mathematics: An international perspective* (pp. 233–264). London, UK: Psychology Press.

De Corte, E., Greer, B., & Verschaffel, L. (1996). Mathematics teaching and learning. In: D. C. Berliner, & R. C. Calfee (Eds), *Handbook of educational psychology* (pp. 491–549). New York: Macmillan Library Reference USA.

Depaepe, M., Dams, K., De Vroede, M., Eggermont, B., Lauwers, H., Simon, F., Vandenberghe, R., & Verhoeven, J. (2000). *Order in progress. Everyday educational practice in primary schools —Belgium, 1880–1970.* Leuven: Leuven University Press.

Ernest, P. (1998). The culture of the mathematics classroom and the relations between personal and public knowledge: An epistemological perspective. In: F. Seeger, J. Voigt, & U. Waschescio (Eds), *The culture of the mathematics classroom* (pp. 245–268). Cambridge: Cambridge University Press.

Evans, J. (1998). Problems of transfer of classroom mathematical knowledge to practical situations. In: F. Seeger, J. Voigt, & U. Waschescio (Eds), *The culture of the mathematics classroom* (pp. 269–289). Cambridge: Cambridge University Press.

Gravemeijer, K. (2004). Local instruction theories as means of support for teachers in reform mathematics. *Mathematical Thinking and Learning, 6*(2), 105–128.

Greeno, J. G., Collins, A. M., & Resnick, L. B. (1996). Cognition and learning. In: D. C. Berliner, & R. C. Calfee (Eds), *Handbook of educational psychology* (pp. 15–46). New York: Macmillan.

Greer, B. (1993). The modelling perspective on wor(l)d problems. *Journal of Mathematical Behavior, 12*, 239–250.

Greer, B., Verschaffel, L., & Mukhopadhyay, S. (in press). Modelling for life: Mathematics and children's experience. In: W. Blum, & M. Niss (Eds), *ICMI study 14: Applications and modelling in mathematics education.* Dordrecht: Kluwer.

Herbst, P. G. (2003). Using novel tasks in teaching mathematics: Three tensions affecting the work of the teacher. *American Educational Research Journal, 40*(1), 197–238.

Kieran, C. (2001). The mathematical discourse of 13-year old partnered problem solving and its relation to the mathematics that emerges. *Educational Studies in Mathematics, 46*(1–3), 187–228.

Lave, J., Murtaugh, M., & de la Rocha, O. (1984). The dialectic of arithmetic in grocery shopping. In: B. Rogoff, & J. Lave (Eds), *Everyday cognition: Its development in social context* (pp. 67–94). Cambridge, MA: Harvard University Press.

Lerman, S. (1998). Cultural perspectives on mathematics and mathematics teaching and learning. In: F. Seeger, J. Voigt, & U. Waschescio (Eds), *The culture of the mathematics classroom* (pp. 290–307). Cambridge: Cambridge University Press.

Leron, U., & Hazzan, O. (1997). The world according to Johnny: A coping perspective in mathematics education. *Educational Studies in Mathematics, 32*, 265–292.

Mason, L., & Scrivani, L. (2004). Enhancing students' mathematical beliefs: An intervention study. *Learning and Instruction, 14*, 153–176.

McClain, K., & Cobb, P. (2001). An analysis of development of sociomathematical norms in one first-grade classroom. *Journal for Research in Mathematics Education, 32*, 236–266.

Mottier Lopez, L. (2005). *Co-constitution de la microculture de classe dans une perspective située: Etude d'activités de résolution de problèmes mathématiques en troisième année primaire.* Unpublished doctoral dissertation, Université de Genève, Switserland.

Nickson, M. (1992). The culture of the mathematics classroom: An unknown quantity? In: D. A. Grouws (Ed.), *Handbook of research on mathematics teaching and learning* (pp. 101–114). New York: Macmillan.

Nunes, T. (1992a). Cognitive invariants and cultural variation in mathematical concepts. *International Journal of Behavioral Development, 15*, 433–453.

Nunes, T. (1992b). Ethnomathematics and everyday cognition. In: D. A. Grouws (Ed.), *Handbook of research on mathematics teaching and learning* (pp. 557–574). New York: Macmillan.

Nunes, T., Schliemann, A. D., & Carraher, D. W. (1993). *Street mathematics and school mathematics.* Cambridge: Cambridge University Press.

Reusser, K., & Stebler, R. (1997). Every word problem has a solution: The social rationality of mathematical modeling in schools. *Learning and Instruction, 7*, 309–327.

Salomon, G. (2005). Understanding classroom processes through different methodological approaches: Discussion. Paper presented at the 11th biennial conference of the European association for research on learning and instruction in Nicosia, Cyprus.

Saxe, G. (2005). Cognition in flux: Towards a coordinated treatment of culture and the individual in mathematical thought. In: C. P. Constantinou, D. Demetriou, A. Evagorou, M. Evagorou, A. Kofteros, M. Michael, Chr. Nicolaou, D. Papademetriou, & N. Papadouris (Eds), *11th Biennial Conference, August 23–27, 2005, Nicosia, Cyprus, Abstracts* (p. 651). Nicosia: University of Cyprus.

Schoenfeld, A. (1991). On mathematics as sense-making: An informal attack on the unfortunate divorce of formal and informal mathematics. In: J. F. Voss, D. N. Perkins, & J. W. Segal (Eds), *Informal reasoning and education* (pp. 311–343). Hillsdale, NJ: Erlbaum.

Sfard, A. (1998). On two metaphors for learning and the dangers of choosing just one. *Educational Researcher, 27*(2), 4–13.

Steinbring, H. (1998). Mathematical understanding in classroom interaction: The interrelation of a social and epistemological constraints. In: F. Seeger, J. Voigt, & U. Waschescio (Eds), *The culture of the mathematics classroom* (pp. 344–372). Cambridge: Cambridge University Press.

van den Berg, D. (2004). Sturing en de betekenisgeving door leerkrachten bij innovatieprocessen. In: G. Kelchtermans (Ed.), *De stuurbaarheid van onderwijs: Tussen kunnen en willen, mogen en moeten* (pp. 121–140). Leuven: Universitaire Pers Leuven.

Verschaffel, L., De Corte, E., & Borghart, I. (1997). Pre-service teachers' conceptions and beliefs about the role of real-world knowledge in mathematical modelling of school word problems. *Learning and Instruction, 7,* 339–359.

Verschaffel, L., De Corte, E., & Lasure, S. (1994). Realistic considerations in mathematical modeling of school word problems. *Learning and Instruction, 4,* 273–294.

Verschaffel, L., De Corte, E., Van Vaerenbergh, G., Lasure, S., Bogaerts, H., & Ratinckx, E. (1998). *Leren oplossen van wiskundige contextproblemen in de bovenbouw van de basisschool.* Leuven: Universitaire Pers Leuven.

Verschaffel, L., Greer, B., & De Corte, E. (2000). *Making sense of word problems.* Lisse: Swets & Zeitlinger.

Vinner, S. (1997). The pseudo-conceptual and the pseudo-analytical thought processes in mathematics learning. *Educational Studies in Mathematics, 34,* 97–129.

Vlassis, J. (2004). *Sens et symboles en mathématiques: Etude de l'utilisation du signe moins dans les réductions polynomiales et la résolution d'équations du premier degré à une inconnue.* Thèse non publié. Liège: Université de Liège, Faculté de Psychologie et des Sciences de l'Education.

Voigt, J. (1995). Thematic patterns of interaction and sociomathematical norms. In: P. Cobb, & H. Bauersfeld (Eds), *The emergence of mathematical meaning: Interaction in classroom cultures* (pp. 163–202). Hove: Erlbaum.

Voigt, J. (1998). The culture of the mathematics classroom: Negotiating the mathematical meaning of empirical phenomena. In: F. Seeger, J. Voigt, & U. Waschescio (Eds), *The culture of the mathematics classroom* (pp. 191–220). Cambridge: Cambridge University Press.

Yackel, E., & Cobb, P. (1996). Sociomathematical norms, argumentations and autonomy in mathematics. *Journal for Research in Mathematics Education, 27,* 458–477.

Zack, V. (1999). Everyday and mathematical language in children's argumentation about proof. *Educational Review, 21,* 129–146.

Chapter 6

Scaffolds for Scientific Discovery Learning

Ton de Jong

Introduction

Contemporary learning environments often have an open character and place a great emphasis on learner activities (Lowyck & Elen, 1993). These are also characteristics of inquiry learning environments. In inquiry learning environments, a domain is not directly offered to learners; rather, learners have to induce the characteristics of the domain from experiences or examples. Inquiry learning is often offered in simulation-based (de Jong & Pieters, 2006) or hypermedia environments (Nesbit & Winne, 2003). Since inquiry is a complicated process in which learners may have diverse kinds of problems (de Jong & van Joolingen, 1998), it needs to be combined with guidance for the learner (de Jong, 2005; Mayer, 2004). The most natural way to provide this guidance is to integrate it into the computer-based learning environment by means of cognitive scaffolds. Cognitive scaffolds are tools that enable students to perform processes they would not be able to perform competently without the tool's support. Scaffolds help learners to go just beyond the level of proficiency they have on their own. Vygotsky's concept of the "zone of proximal development" is often used in this regard (Reiser, 2004). Cognitive scaffolds may structure a task, take over parts of a task, or give hints and supporting information for the task. In this respect, cognitive scaffolds bear a resemblance to what have been called mindtools (Jonassen, 2000) and result in what Salomon, Perkins, and Globerson (1991) have labelled an intellectual partnership between the tool and the learner.

   With adequate guidance in the form of cognitive scaffolds, scientific discovery learning can be an effective learning approach in which "intuitive" or "deep" conceptual knowledge can be acquired (Swaak & de Jong, 1996). This chapter presents an overview of computer-based cognitive scaffolds for inquiry learning, linking these scaffolds to specific cognitive hurdles in the inquiry process. An earlier summary was offered by de Jong and van Joolingen (1998), who presented an overview of scientific discovery learning processes, the problems that learners experience in these processes, and cognitive scaffolds to support learners. Recent overviews from a more instructional design perspective have been given by Quintana et al. (2004) and Linn, Bell, and Davis (2004). This chapter starts from the

Handling Complexity in Learning Environments: Theory and Research
Copyright © 2006 by Elsevier Ltd.
All rights of reproduction in any form reserved.
ISBN: 0-08-044986-7

approach based on learning processes used by de Jong and van Joolingen (1998), extends their overview of processes, and looks at recent developments in the field. These recent developments concern new integrated systems for inquiry that contain scaffolds for inquiry, such as Inquiry Island (White et al., 2002), GenScope (Hickey, Kindfield, Horwitz, & Christie, 2003; Hickey & Zuiker, 2003), BGuILE (Reiser et al., 2001), BioWorld (Lajoie, Lavigne, Guerrera, & Munsie, 2001), SimQuest-based environments (van Joolingen & de Jong, 2003), Model-It™ (Jackson, Stratford, Krajcik, & Soloway, 1996a; Stratford, Krajcik, & Soloway, 1998), Co-Lab (van Joolingen, de Jong, Lazonder, Savelsbergh, & Manlove, 2005), and WISE (Linn et al., 2004).

Scaffolds sometimes are defined quite broadly. Hart and Barden-Gabbei (2002) and also Quintana et al. (2004) include as a cognitive scaffold, for example, the use of language that stays close to the students' intuitive concepts. Since this does not directly affect a specified inquiry learning process I would not count this as a cognitive scaffold. In the definition used in this chapter, scaffolds directly support a specific inquiry process either by structuring and/or restricting the operating space of learners or by taking over part of the learning process. A categorization of inquiry learning processes used to organize the overview of scaffolds for inquiry learning will be presented next.

Inquiry Processes

Although there may be some variations, for example, in the way data are gathered (e.g., from experimentation or from data sets), and variations in the complexity of the experimentation (Chinn & Malhotra, 2002), there is a fair consensus about which processes basically comprise inquiry learning. The different classifications in the literature (Friedler, Nachmias, & Linn, 1990; Klahr & Dunbar, 1988; Kuhn, Black, Keselman, & Kaplan, 2000; Njoo & de Jong, 1993; Quintana et al., 2004) differ mainly in their granularity, ranging from very detailed to rather broad, but basically do not differ in the processes that are distinguished. Van Joolingen and de Jong (1997), for example, describe a long series of detailed processes such as "generalizing a variable" and "splitting hypotheses", whereas Quintana et al. (2004) only distinguish "sense making", "process management", and "articulation/reflection", Kuhn (2002) just mentions "inquiry", "analysis", and "inference", and Zhang, Chen, Sun, and Reid (2004) restrict themselves to "interpretation", "experimentation", and "reflection". In this chapter, I follow a set of learning processes introduced in de Jong et al. (2002) that is slightly more extended than the one used by de Jong and Njoo (1992) and de Jong and van Joolingen (1998). This set of learning processes provides a suitable basis for describing scaffolds specific to the learning process. The processes are

- orientation
- hypothesis generation
- experimentation
  - experiment design
  - prediction
  - data interpretation

- drawing a conclusion
- making an evaluation.

In *orientation*, the learner makes a broad analysis of the domain; in *hypothesis generation*, a specific statement (or a set of statements, for example, in the form of a model) about the domain is chosen for consideration; in *experimentation*, a test to investigate the validity of this hypothesis or model is designed and performed, predictions are made and outcomes of the experiments are interpreted; in *conclusion*, a conclusion about the validity of the hypothesis is drawn; and, finally, in *evaluation*, a reflection on the learning process and the domain knowledge acquired is made. Despite the fact that these processes are presented here in a specific and more or less logical sequence, this does not mean that this is necessarily the order in which the processes are carried out by the learner. For example, a learner who has no initial idea about the domain may first perform some experimentation to get a suggestion of what could be present in the domain (Klahr & Dunbar, 1988).

A central and developing "product" in the inquiry learning process is the learner's view of the domain. Figure 6.1 presents a diagrammatic attempt to depict the developing domain view throughout the inquiry process. In this figure, the view of the domain in '*orientation*' has loose ends, relations are not as yet defined, and variables are missing. When a student generates a *hypothesis* (or a proposition) a relation between variables is selected, and an idea (still uncertain) about this relation is formed. Of course, the ideas that are formed in the hypothesis phase are not necessarily constrained to single hypotheses, but may refer to more encompassing parts of the model. In *experimentation*, a move to more manipulable variables is made. When *designing an experiment* the (conceptual variables) from the hypothesis phase are operationalized as variables that can be manipulated. For example, if the hypothesis is about "popularity of websites", this can be operationalized, for example, in the "number of hits per day". In *prediction*, the hypothesis that was stated is translated into observable variables. In *data interpretation*, the outcomes of the experiment are known, and an understanding of the data needs to be reached. For example, students need to think of a relation in terms of a monotonic increasing function or need to identify an interaction between variables from a graph or a table. In stating a *conclusion*, a return is made to the more theoretical level, in which the data that were interpreted are related to the hypothesis and/or model under consideration and decisions on the validity of the original ideas are made.

In Figure 6.1, the process of 'experimentation' is at the level of manipulable (i.e., operationalized) variables, whereas the domain view in the processes of 'orientation', 'hypotheses', and 'conclusion' is at the level of theory. Ideally, a student's view of the domain should go from orientation, through hypotheses to conclusion, resulting in correct and complete knowledge of the domain. In practice, however, after a learning process a student's model often will still have some open ends (an orientation character), unresolved issues (a hypothesis aspect) and some firm ideas (conclusions, albeit occasionally faulty ones). This emphasizes the non-cyclic but iterative character of the inquiry learning process.

The processes mentioned above directly yield knowledge (as is reflected in the developing view of the domain) and de Jong and Njoo (1992) refer to these processes as transformative

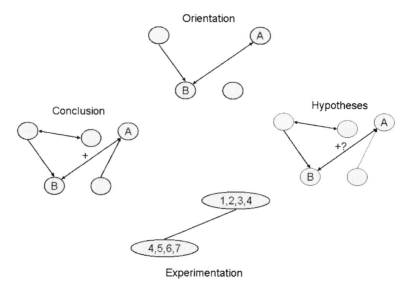

Figure 6.1: A schematic overview of the learner's view of the domain over the
different inquiry processes (ovals are variables, lines represent relations).

inquiry processes. Since inquiry learning is a complex endeavour with a number of activities and iterations, de Jong and Njoo (1992) added the concept of regulation of learning, which comprises processes aimed at planning and monitoring the learning process. Planning may involve the complete cycle of inquiry learning or the formulation of research goals or questions and which experiments to conduct, while monitoring may involve checking whether the initial goals are met, or which experiments are done and which ones still have to be conducted. Together, transformative and regulative processes form the main inquiry learning processes (de Jong & van Joolingen, 1998).

Evaluation takes a special place, located somewhere in between transformative and regulative processes. In evaluation (or reflection) learners re-examine the inquiry process and the results found, try to take a step back and to learn from their experiences. This reflection may concern the inquiry process itself (successful and less-successful actions) as well as the domain discovered (e.g., general domain characteristics). As is the case with all inquiry processes, evaluation activities are not bound to the "natural order" in the cycle, which in the case of "evaluation" would be at the end of the inquiry cycle. In that respect, evaluation activities could influence the inquiry process itself and thus have a "regulative character." However, by evaluation, learners basically acquire higher-level knowledge about the process and the domain knowledge acquired; in this respect, "evaluation" can be seen as a "transformative" process (see de Jong et al., 2005).

The next sections present examples of scaffolds for inquiry learning. The presentation of these scaffolds is organized in line with the inquiry processes outlined above. First, examples of scaffolds for the three processes that are performed on a theoretical level (orientation, hypothesis generation, and conclusion) are presented. The following section will present cognitive scaffolds for experimentation, and then treat scaffolds for regulative processes (planning and monitoring). Finally, a section discusses scaffolds for evaluation. The examples of scaffolds that are given in these sections are meant as an illustration of the possibilities; they are not based on specific selection criteria. Also, some of these scaffolds have not been subject to systematic empirical evaluation of their contribution to the learning process. Some of them are quite recent, while others are part of more comprehensive support in learning environments and cannot be evaluated in isolation. Where evaluation results were available, they are mentioned in the text.

Cognitive Scaffolds for Orientation, Hypothesis Generation, and Conclusion

The three processes that constitute the building of a theoretical model are orientation, hypothesis generation, and conclusion. In *'orientation'* the learner tries to create a global idea of the domain and task at hand. This means that material that is available (background information and the like) is being searched and processed, or experiments are run to explore the variables and relations in a domain. On the basis of these activities, an idea of the domain is formed, variables are identified, tentative ideas of relations between variables are created, and possibly a 'rough' idea of the structure and complexity of the domain is formed. In earlier work (de Jong et al., 2002), we have labelled these incomplete and global ideas "issues". An issue is not a full hypothesis, but a problem statement that guides subsequent experimentation. An example of an issue is: "What is the relation between apothem angle and interior angle" (Lewis, Stern, & Linn, 1993). Issues are distinguished from hypotheses by the lack of a specification of the effect of the input variable(s) on the output variable(s). A *hypothesis* is a tentative specification of the relation between input and output variables. A hypothesis can also have the form of a model or part of a model. As indicated above, according to Klahr and Dunbar (1988) there are two ways to generate a hypothesis; one is from theory and the other is from data (from running experiments). Klahr and Simon (1999) stated that many discoveries do not stem from investigations in which a clear hypothesis was present, but instead stem from investigations that may be regarded as exploratory, focusing on generating hypotheses rather than testing them. In the course of inquiry, learners must reach a *conclusion* and decide to reject or accept hypotheses or models on the basis of data gathered. The variables present in these hypotheses can represent direct measurements of concepts (e.g., percentage increase in the number of people as a measure of the rate of population growth) or they can represent more indirect measurements, or operationalizations of particular concepts (e.g., number of cars sold as an indication of trust in economic developments). In experimentation, a translation from conceptual variables to manipulable and observable variables is made, while in drawing conclusions the reverse route has to be taken. This process often causes problems for learners: apart from accepting or rejecting a hypothesis, learners may also decide, as a conclusion, to refine a hypothesis, on the basis of data that were gathered (see van Joolingen & de Jong, 1997). In refining a hypothesis students may change the nature of the relationship between variables or add a condition to the relationship.

Learners display a number of characteristic problems during these three processes. They do not find the right variables to work with, have trouble stating testable hypotheses, and do not draw the right conclusion from experiments. The last has to do with problems of translating experimental data into more theoretical hypotheses and with the fact that generally people tend to persist in their ideas even when confronted with data that contradict those ideas (Chinn & Brewer, 1993, 2001; Kuhn, Amsel, & O'Loughlin, 1988). There are a number of systems that scaffold learners in the orientation, hypothesis generation, and conclusion processes. These scaffolds then often provide learners with a tool to express their view of the domain, often with an increasing level of specificity that marks the progress through the three different processes.

An example of such an approach can be found in Belvedere. Belvedere is a collaborative learning environment for students to acquire inquiry skills (see, e.g., Suthers, Weiner, Connelly, & Paolucci, 1995; Toth, Suthers, & Lesgold, 2002). In Belvedere, students work with realistic problems, collect data, set hypotheses, etc. A so-called "inquiry diagram" is available to 'explore' the domain under study. This inquiry diagram is a kind of concept mapping tool dedicated to scientific inquiry. The diagram has pre-defined concepts such as "hypothesis" and "data", and also has pre-defined links to connect hypotheses and data. These links indicate whether the data support or conflict with a hypothesis. A similar scaffold is present in the RASHI system (Murray, Bruno, & Woolf, 2003). The inquiry diagram from Belvedere is useful not only for linking data and theory (thus supporting the process of 'conclusion') but is also intended to be used both in the orientation phase when the main variables of the domain are entered in the diagram and in the hypothesis phase when relations are made more specific. Toth et al. (2002) report positive effects on "reasoning scores" for students using the Belvedere inquiry diagram as compared to students who used simple prose to express their view on the domain.

In the Co-Lab system (van Joolingen et al., 2005) the view on the domain is expressed in the form of a model (see Figure 6.2). A graphical modelling tool based on system dynamics is available in Co-Lab (Steed, 1992). This tool can be used to make initial sketches of the domain, to make testable hypotheses as parts of models or complete models, and to create a final model that reflects the students' (Co-Lab is a collaborative environment) final idea of the domain. The Co-lab modelling tool contains facilities to indicate relations between variables at different levels of precision: qualitative and quantitative. In Co-Lab, learners could start with specifying relations between variables in a qualitative way. They can do this by selecting a relation between variables and linking a pre-defined graphical label depicting the relation to it. The transition from qualitative to quantitative models is smooth, which makes the tool suitable for use in the orientation, hypothesis, and conclusion phases. Several ways to support students' construction of models have been explored (Löhner, van Joolingen, & Savelsbergh, 2003).

Hypothesis generation can be supported at several levels of detail. Thinkertools/Inquiry Island environments, for example, present learners with free text blocks to brainstorm about and to present their hypotheses (White et al., 2002). By using sliders, learners can indicate the degree to which they think their hypothesis is "believable", "related to the question they had", and "testable". They also indicate if they have alternative hypotheses. Based on these indications from the learners, an advisor gives general, domain independent, advice on stating hypotheses, such as the advice to go back to the question when the students indicate that the hypothesis is only loosely related to the question. Thinkertools/Inquiry Island has several advisors, each of them related to a specific part of the inquiry cycle.

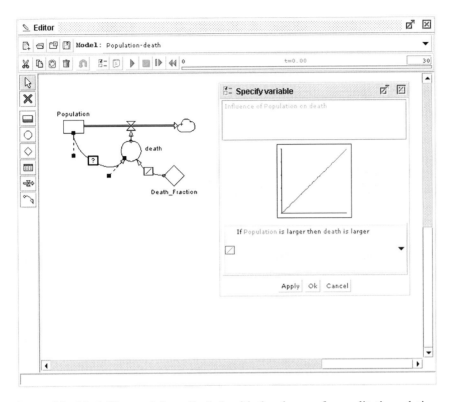

Figure 6.2: Modelling tool from Co-Lab with the chooser for qualitative relations.

A more specific scaffold for hypothesis generation is the so-called hypothesis scratch-pad (Shute & Glaser, 1990; van Joolingen & de Jong, 1991). Van Joolingen and de Jong introduced a scaffold that allowed students to compose hypotheses from separate elements such as variables, relations, and conditions for these phrases. The hypothesis scratchpad of van Joolingen and de Jong appeared to be quite complex for learners to use. Currently (see van Joolingen & de Jong, 2003), a new and simplified version of the original scratchpad has been re-implemented in the SimQuest context (see Figure 6.3). In this new version, learners can compose hypotheses by filling in if-then statements and by selecting variables and relations to fill in the slots. For each hypothesis, they can indicate whether it was tested or not, or whether the data confirmed the hypothesis (for this latter component see the section on the conclusion process). In Model-it (Jackson et al., 1996a ; Stratford et al., 1998) students can also create hypotheses by selecting variables, relations, and characteristics of relations. They do this in a qualitative way quite similar as used in the SimQuest hypothesis scratchpad. In Model-it, these qualitative propositions are interpreted by the computer programme and depicted as graphs, so that students have an immediate graphical view of the hypotheses they have created.

Gijlers and de Jong (submitted) went one step further and provided students working with a SimQuest environment on the physics topic of motion with complete, pre-defined,

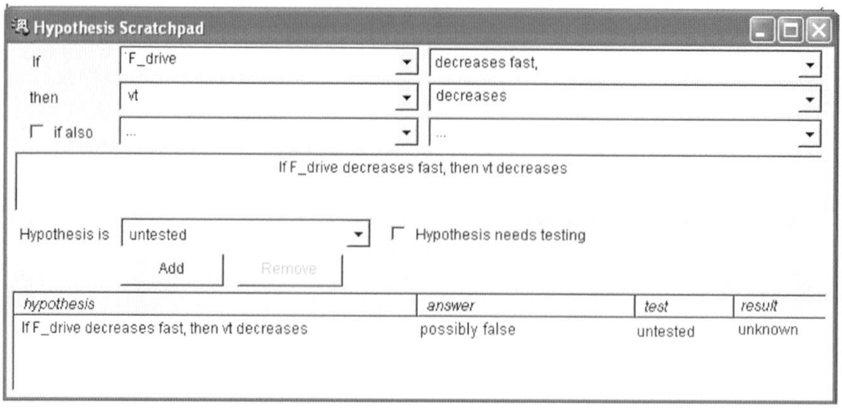

Figure 6.3: Hypothesis scratchpad from SimQuest.

hypotheses. This was inspired by the work of Njoo and de Jong (1993), who found that students could benefit from ready-made hypotheses, and also by a study in which they found that confronting students with each other's propositions could be beneficial for learning (Gijlers & de Jong, 2005). Gijlers and de Jong (submitted) created three experimental groups of collaborating dyads of learners. One control group did not receive specific scaffolds, one group had a shared hypothesis scratchpad (combined with a chat) as in the one from Figure 6.3, and the final group received a large set of propositions about the domain. These last students had to judge these propositions individually, indicating if they were familiar with each proposition, if they thought the proposition to be true, possibly true, possibly false, or false, and, finally, if they wanted to test the proposition or not. When students were coupled in dyads, their individual proposition tables were combined in one shared proposition table as shown in Figure 6.4. If students, who also had a chat function available, together decided to test a proposition, they could click the simulation button. Then they were presented with an assignment that also put the simulation in a state designed to test this specific hypothesis. As an overall result, students in the proposition group outperformed students in the other two groups. In a follow-up study, Gijlers and de Jong (in preparation) compared a group of students who worked with shared proposition tables (as in the previous experiment) with a group of students who also created shared concept maps to get an overall view of the domain. The findings indicated that students in the concept mapping condition performed significantly better than students who had only the shared proposition tables. Further, students in the concept mapping conditions communicated significantly more about the design and outcomes of experiments than students in the shared proposition only condition.

The examples above look upon hypotheses as single statements about a limited set of variables. Hypotheses, however, can also be expressed as models or parts of models, which means that a larger set of variables in their context is taken into account. The concept map as used by Gijlers and de Jong (in preparation) is an example of how a more comprehensive model of the domain might help students in gaining knowledge of the domain.

The drawing of conclusions is often supported by linking evidence and theory. In Bguile (Reiser et al., 2001), a series of inquiry environments in the domain of biology,

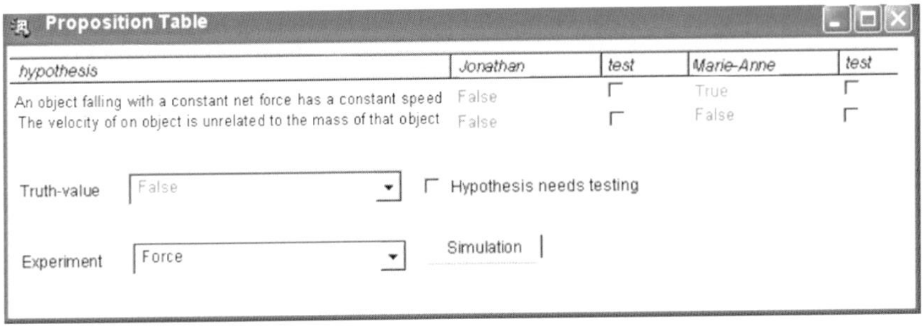

hypothesis	Jonathan	test	Marie-Anne	test
An object falling with a constant net force has a constant speed	False	☐	True	☐
The velocity of on object is unrelated to the mass of that object	False	☐	False	☐

Truth-value [False ▼] ☐ Hypothesis needs testing

Experiment [Force ▼] Simulation |

Figure 6.4: Shared proposition table from a SimQuest application in the physics domain of motion.

learners are offered a scaffold that forces them to directly connect their data and their explanations. The so-called investigation journal gives students the opportunity to link the claims they make with evidence collected in investigations. In Bioworld (Lajoie et al., 2001), an environment for learning how to diagnose a patient's disease, students are also explicitly supported in relating hypotheses and evidence. Students have to find an answer to a patient's (medical) problem. The different sources the students need to solve the problem are represented in the environment. This concerns definitions, medical tests, and symptoms. Experimental data are also available by requesting results from diagnostic tests. The problem statement itself is another source of pertinent information/evidence. As the evidence is collected, it is dynamically displayed in an "evidence palette". Based on this collected evidence, students can adjust a belief meter throughout their problem-solving process to indicate how comfortable they are with a stated diagnosis. Upon completion of the problem, students justify their final diagnosis by constructing a final argument supported by their observations and evidence. In the Knowledge Integration Environments ((KIE), Bell & Linn, 2000), a tool called *Sensemaker* helps students to organize evidence by relating it to the source of evidence and the proposition to which it refers. In addition to Sensemaker, students use another tool called *Mildred* that helps them give explanations for the evidence and relate this to their arguments. This is done by providing students with sentence openers and with domain-specific hints. Similar to the belief meter in BioWorld, students can indicate the usefulness of their evidence on a 6-point scale (e.g., "medium"). From an analysis of explanations developed by students in the domain of "light," Bell and Linn conclude that the tools in KIE indeed help students in their argumentation process.

Veermans, de Jong, and van Joolingen (2000) supported the process of experiment design and the drawing of conclusions by giving hints for designing proper experiments, by analysing the experimentation behaviour of learners, and by providing the students with feedback on the accuracy of their conclusion from the experiment. The studies by Veermans et al. were conducted in a SimQuest context with a simulation on the physics topic of collisions. In their first study (Veermans et al., 2000), students received an assignment that presented a specific situation (e.g., "Try to find out how changing the initial velocity of the green ball (v1) influences the kinetic energy of the ball (Uk1_after) after the collision with the blue ball") and were asked to select a hypothesis from a series of hypotheses offered (e.g., "if v1 increases, then Uk1_after increases"). In this domain, there is an almost one-to-one relation between theoretical and experimental variables, so predictions and hypotheses in this study were very close. After students had selected a hypothesis they conducted experiments and drew a conclusion on the validity of the hypothesis they had selected. After that, the system analysed all the experiments a student had done and composed feedback in relation to the conclusion the student had drawn. Such feedback could, for example, be "If this hypothesis were correct, then the values you observed for Uk1_after in these experiments should match the values that you would expect based on the hypothesis. This is however not the case. This means that there is reason to believe that this hypothesis is not correct" (Veermans et al., 2000, p. 236). Compared to a group of students who received pre-defined feedback that did not take the experimentation history into account, the group with adaptive feedback did not score better on a knowledge post-test, but differences in inquiry processes were found, indicating that the students who received the adaptive feedback used a better inquiry approach (more time on an assignment, more experiments with an assignment, more unique experiments) than the other students. The second study by Veermans et al. focused on the design of experiments and is discussed in the next section.

Cognitive Scaffolds for Experimentation

The basic activities in experimentation are to decide upon which input variables to manipulate and which output variables to inspect, to make predictions about the values of outcome variables, and to create an interpretation of the results of the experiment. A difference may occur here between inquiry environments based on data sets (see, e.g., Winne, 2001) and inquiry environments based on simulations or external labs. If the "data source" for the inquiry process is not an external laboratory or a simulation but an existing data set, there is no direct manipulation of variables. The subprocesses in experimentation then include a selection of variables, an operationalization if necessary, an inspection of the data set, and a prediction of what will be found in other areas of the data set or in the next update of the data set. In this chapter, the focus is on experimentation in simulation or lab-based environments rather than on using data sets.

Experiment Design

One problematic issue here is that in some cases theoretical variables in the hypothesis have to be translated into manipulable and observable variables in the experiment. This can lead to serious problems for learners. Lawson (2002) showed that this is even a problem for pre-service teachers. Smithtown, a simulation-based learning environment in the area of economics, provided students with overviews to relate more abstract and concrete variables (Shute & Glaser, 1990).

It is often found that students design experiments from which they cannot draw conclusions, though in some cases studies show that students do design proper experiments (Kanari & Millar, 2004). There is a range of heuristics that can be used to design good experiments (Baker & Dunbar, 2000), of which the control of variables strategy (CVS,

Chen & Klahr, 1999) also called VOTAT (vary one thing at a time), is the best known (Wilhelm & Beishuizen, 2003). Keselman (2003) had students work with a simulation-based learning environment on a complex domain with multivariable causality (risks of earthquakes). One group of students received extensive practice on manipulating variables and making predictions, while a second group also observed a teacher modelling the design of good experiments. Both groups improved compared to a control group that received no support, but the modelling group improved most on knowledge gained and on skill in designing good experiments. Lin and Lehman (1999) worked with students who learned in a biology simulation-learning environment. They provided students with prompts that aimed to stimulate reflection on the strategies that were used for designing experiments with an emphasis on the control of variables strategies (e.g., "How did you decide that you have enough data to make conclusions", Lin & Lehman, 1999, p. 841). These prompts helped students to understand experiment design principles and resulted in better transfer compared to a group of students who received different types of prompts. Veermans, van Joolingen, and de Jong (2006) compared two simulation-based learning environments on the physics topic of collision. These two environments both hosted a variety of instructional components (model progression, assignments, explanations, monitoring tool) but they differed in offering implicit or explicit heuristics. In the implicit condition the heuristics (including "simplify problem", "VOTAT", "simple values", and "equal increments") were included in the other instructional measures (e.g., in the assignments). This was also the case in the explicit condition, but here the heuristic was also explicitly named and justified. Veermans et al. (2006) found no overall difference between the two conditions on knowledge gained and strategies acquired, but found indications that the explicit condition favoured weak students.

Making Predictions

A prediction is a statement about an expected outcome of an experiment. It differs from a hypothesis in that a hypothesis concerns more theoretical variables and relates to ranges of values ("if acceleration increases, velocity will increase"), whereas a prediction concerns a specific object (instantiated variable) and may refer to a specific outcome (the expected speed of this motorcycle will be 60 mph after 7.8 s). As is the case with hypotheses, learners can be supported in stating predictions by providing them with semi-structured sentences in which they can fill in slots. This is done, for example, in WISE (Slotta, 2004). Students receive sheets with sentences concerning predictions. Learners have only to fill in the dots on these sheets to generate a verifiable prediction. An example of such a sentence is: "with an earthquake of 5 on the Richter scale, the building at my school would … because …." In a study by Lewis et al. (1993), students learning with a simulation on heat and temperature were required to use a notebook to make predictions before running an experiment. In addition, they could also enter their predictions graphically by drawing graphs interactively. These notebook/predictions features were part of a more extensive curriculum change in which more realistic problems and a model of heat flow were also introduced. Overall, the results of the experimental curriculum were positive compared to the traditional curriculum, and informal observations showed that the prediction-making measure was one of the most successful parts of the curriculum reform.

Data Interpretation

Once an experiment has been set up and the chosen values for input variables have been entered, the experiment can be run. This is often done by pressing some kind of "run" button, but sometimes changing values of input variables immediately results in an update of the output variables, often in a graphical way (de Jong et al., 2005). Data that are generated have to be interpreted. Insofar as this means stating the consequences of what has been found for the hypotheses, or generating new hypotheses on the basis of data, this is classified under conclusion. However, numerical data do not always immediately show their meaning. Here, visualizations can help in data interpretation. For example, trends can be recognized in tables, and functions can be recognized in graphs. Making tables and graphs can be considered a higher level of data interpretation; students are often not aware of how to use graphs in inquiry processes (see Lewis et al., 1993).

Data interpretation may also involve the handling of measurement bias. In the case of Co-Lab, for example (van Joolingen et al., 2005), an experiment does not need to take place in a simulation environment, but also can be conducted with other data sources, such as remote or local laboratories. This may have consequences for the processes involved in the experiment. For example, the preparation of the equipment in a local laboratory is a process that is very specific to the situation at hand. There are also more subtle consequences. Compared to a simulation, real experiments house certain threats that normally are not present in a simulated experiment, such as non-calibrated instruments or materials. Kanari and Millar (2004) found that students have considerable trouble dealing with measurement errors. Co-Lab, therefore, has specific features that help students to smooth the data.

Worldwatcher is a software program that contains real data sets acquired by NASA. These data are temperature measurements from all over the world. Worldwatcher visualizes this data with the intention of helping learners understand the complex data. Worldwatcher has a whole set of opportunities for learners to see the data from different angles. Learners can re-group data, compare data from different sources (e.g., compare temperatures in different months), and create overviews, etc. (see Edelson, Gordin, & Pea, 1999). Yet another approach can be found in the BGuILE software Animal Landlord (Smith & Reiser, 1997). In this software program, learners have to analyse data that come from a video and they are asked questions to guide their interpretation of the data.

Cognitive Scaffolds for Regulation of the Inquiry Process

In self-directed inquiry learning, regulation (planning and monitoring) of the inquiry process has to be done by learners themselves.

Planning

The planning of the inquiry process can be supported by making the different steps (orientation, creating a hypothesis, etc.) clear for the students. This gives the student an overview of different steps in the process and helps in planning what to do. Reiser (2004) mentioned the structuring of the task by the learner as one of the main functions of cognitive scaffolds. By structuring a task, the learner is informed of the necessary elements of a task; the operating space of learners is also constrained, making planning and monitoring more feasible processes (de Jong & van Joolingen, 1998). More specific process support can then be given within each of these steps. Njoo and de Jong (1993) successfully provided students with such a structure on paper next to a computer simulation. Such a structure can, however, also be built into the software itself. In Sci-Wise (Shimoda, White, & Frederiksen, 2002) and the follow-up Thinkertools/Inquiry Island (White et al., 2002), for example, the inquiry process is divided into 'questioning', 'hypothesize', 'investigate', 'analyse', 'model', and 'evaluate'. Learners have differently structured tabsheets for each of these tasks and dedicated advisors they can call upon to receive domain independent advice on how to perform a specific inquiry task. From the point of view of regulation, a structure like this helps students recognize and follow the most necessary and essential steps in an inquiry process. In WISE (Slotta, 2004), students are offered different sources of information and sub-problems in a strict sequence. The sources are displayed in multiple representations such as texts, graphs, images, and tables. Students can get an overview of which sub-problems they have already solved and which still have to be done. This environment supports a causal modelling process. If the students answer the different questions, the relations between variables become clear. In this way, students are guided through the inquiry process in a step-by-step manner.

In Co-Lab (van Joolingen et al., 2005), the different steps in the inquiry process are not implemented as separate "windows" or "tabsheets", but are shown in a so-called process coordinator (Manlove, Lazonder, & de Jong, in press). This process coordinator shows the overall structure of the inquiry process, gives explanations of each of the steps, and offers students the opportunity to store information, data, models, etc., in these steps. This online "portfolio" can later be used to generate a report of the inquiry.

Learners can also be supported in their planning process by making specific goals available to them. This is done, for example, in the SimQuest learning environments (van Joolingen & de Jong, 2003). These assignments can be of different types (e.g., specification assignments in which learners are asked to find a certain value), but they all have in common helping the learner to follow specific short-term goals. Evaluations have shown that presenting assignments to learners is effective in increasing knowledge acquisition.

Monitoring

Monitoring what you have done is an important aspect of self-directed learning. Only a few environments give explicit support for keeping track of learner actions. In the SimQuest-learning environments (van Joolingen & de Jong, 2003), a so-called monitoring tool can be included. This tool enables students to save their experiments. This means that the values of input- and output variables are placed in a table with one experiment per row, allowing students to sort the experiments in different ways and to replay an experiment from this monitoring table.

In a similar vein, FILE, an inquiry environment to study experimentation behaviour (Hulshof, Wilhelm, Beishuizen, & van Rijn, 2005) saves and displays all experiment students have done by showing values of input variables and the outcome of the experiment. In Co-Lab (Manlove et al., in press), planning and monitoring are combined so that after having made a plan in terms of subgoals, students can indicate when they have reached a subgoal. In this way they can keep track of their progress. In the KIE environment, self-monitoring prompts are used that go a small step further, asking students to judge what they have learned so far (Davis, 2000, 2004). In this respect, these prompts move in the direction of evaluation prompts (see the next section).

Cognitive Scaffolds for Evaluation

In evaluation, learners observe the inquiry process and the results found, then try to take a step back and to learn from their experiences. This evaluation (or reflection) may concern the inquiry process itself (successful and less-successful actions) as well as the domain discovered (e.g., general domain characteristics). Many learning systems include reflection prompts as part of a set of measures, short questions that ask students to think about their progress and actions (e.g., Lewis et al., 1993). Lajoie et al. (2001) argue that in BioWorld, learners are encouraged to reflect on their process and results by means of the so-called "evidence palette" and the "belief meter". The evidence palette (an overview of all evidence collected for a hypothesis) makes students reflect on their plans and actions, and the belief meter (a measure in which students can indicate how credible their hypothesis is, based on the evidence collected) makes them think about the data collected and screened. In BioWorld, students also have an "argumentation palette" that helps them create a justification for their conclusion. The students' conclusions are compared to an expert conclusion, which helps student reflect on their own argumentation process. As discussed in the preceding section, the KIE (and WISE) environments can use "Checking our Understanding" prompts as well as other more generic reflection prompts to encourage students to monitor their progress and understanding (see Quintana et al., 2004).

A few studies have systematically examined the effect of reflection scaffolds. I have discussed above the study by Lin and Lehman (1999), who found a positive effect of prompts that helped students reflect on their experimentation design. Davis (2000), in the context of the KIE inquiry environment, examined the effects of so-called 'activity' and 'self-monitoring prompts' on project progress and knowledge integration. Activity prompts encouraged students to reflect on content of their activities. An activity prompt may, for example, " ask students to justify their decision or write a scientific explanation of a decision" (Davis, 2000, p. 822). Self-monitoring prompts activated students to state their own planning and monitoring by giving them sentence openers to complete. A sample prompt would be "Pieces of evidence or claims in the article we didn't understand very well included ..." (Davis, 2000, p. 824). Three studies were conducted in the domain of heat and temperature. Two studies compared conditions with different types of reflection prompts, while the third study looked deeper into students' reactions to prompts. Overall, self-monitoring prompts helped more with knowledge integration than activity prompts, although Davis also concludes that similar prompts lead to quite different reactions from different learners.

Zhang et al. (2004) performed a study in which they gave learners the so-called reflective support. This reflective support was support that "... increases learners' self-awareness of the learning processes and prompts their reflective abstraction and integration of their discoveries" (p. 270). The learning environment centred around a simulation on floating and sinking of objects. The treatment consisted of: (a) showing the students their inquiry processes (goals of experiments, predictions, and conclusions); (b) reflection notes that students had to fill in asking them to reflect on the experiment; and (c) a fill-in form after the experiment that asked students to think over the process they had gone through and the discoveries they had made. Students who received this type of evaluation support outperformed students who did not receive this support on a number of performance measures.

Land and Zembal-Saul (2003) examined an inquiry setting about the physics topic of light. Their non-experimental study was an in-depth analysis of videotapes of the learning interactions of two groups of students over a period of time. In the inquiry software, students were prompted to articulate a large number of investigative actions such as their research procedure, evidence, justifications, etc. The overall conclusion of this qualitative study is that reflection prompts help students develop a better understanding of the domain but that the effect of the prompts depends on the students having a sufficient level of prior knowledge.

Moreno and Mayer (2005) conducted three studies with students who learned about botany (characteristics of plants). Students' main assignment was to design plants for certain environmental conditions. Moreno and Mayer manipulated the level of interactivity (students selecting parts of plants in contrast with the parts being selected), guidance (basically corrective vs. explanatory feedback) and reflection (students who were asked to reflect were prompted to give an oral explanation of the choices in plant design). Overall, results showed that reflection helps students in their understanding of the topic, but only for non-interactive environments. Moreno and Mayer (2005) explain this by assuming that the cognitive processes that are elicited by reflection (organizing and integrating) are already elicited by the interactivity in these environments. A further analysis indicated that reflection only fosters learning when it is based on correct information. When the students made choices in plant design themselves, they could have made a wrong design; in such cases reflection does not help.

The prompts described above, though all aimed at stimulating reflection, were quite different in nature. Despite these differences, overall, they result in better knowledge or performance. It is also important to note these studies suggest that reflection only has advantages when there is sufficient knowledge, either through a higher level of prior knowledge (Land & Zembal-Saul, 2003) or gained in the learning process (Moreno & Mayer, 2005).

Discussion

Discovery learning is a way of learning that has strong appeal for many but that has also led to many criticisms. These criticisms often point to the unstructured nature of discovery learning and the highly insecure outcomes. Mayer (2004), for example, discusses classical research in three areas, learning problem solving rules, conservation strategies, and programming concepts. Mayer concludes that pure discovery learning often fails because in discovery learning, students may not be confronted with the to-be-learned material. What is essential, according to Mayer, is that learning takes place only when key learning processes such as selecting, organizing, and integrating knowledge are applied. Pure discovery may leave students in an unclear situation where they want to act but do not have the right information to act upon; expository teaching normally provides students with the right content, but often fails to trigger students to perform as active learners. Guided discovery learning (which we may also term inquiry learning and/or guided scientific discovery learning), if well designed, could take an intermediate position and combine the best of both worlds. Mayer (2004) concluded that guided discovery is indeed the most effective way of teaching compared to pure discovery and expository teaching. Klahr and Nigam (2004) conducted a study in which they compared pure discovery learning with direct instruction. Children around nine years old experimented with wooden ramps down which a ball could roll. Children could vary the steepness, the surface, and the length of the ramp and the type of ball (rubber ball or golf ball), and could observe the influence of their choices on the distance covered by the ball. Klahr and Nigam (2004) assessed children's ability to design proper experiments using a control of variables (CVS) strategy, in which only one variable is changed at a time (see the earlier section on 'experiment design'). In the direct instruction condition, children experimented with the ramps and the balls; additionally, an instructor explained differences between experiments, gave examples of good and bad experiments, and explained the working of CVS. In the pure discovery condition, children only experimented with no instructor feedback at all. Klahr and Nigam (2004) found that subjects in the direct instruction condition dramatically outperformed subjects in the pure discovery condition on a test measuring their ability to design proper (CVS) experiments. A week later, all children had to evaluate two posters on scientific experiments. These posters, made by other children, contained mistakes on CVS. Results showed that children who had mastered CVS in the learning phase outperformed children who did not master CVS on the evaluation of the slides, but that there was no difference between children from the pure discovery or the direct instruction condition. This study by Klahr and Nigam (2004) is interesting from a number of viewpoints. First, it is in line with the study by Mayer (2004) cited above, in that in a pure discovery environment students might easily not encounter the correct knowledge, in this case the CVS strategy. As Klahr and Nigam themselves state " .. in most cases children in discovery situations are more likely than those receiving direct instruction to encounter inconsistent or misleading feedback, encoding errors, causal misattributions, and inadequate practice and elaborations" (Klahr & Nigam, 2004, p. 661). Taking this into account, it is surprising to see that in the pure discovery environment 12 out of 52 children (23%) still mastered the CVS strategy. Second, what Klahr and Nigam call direct instruction could, in terms of Mayer, easily be labelled guided discovery. In fact, in a study by Keselman (2003), students also received training and a model for the CVS strategy similar to the intervention used by Klahr and Nigam, but this was not labelled as direct instruction. As Klahr and Nigam write: "In both conditions, students were actively engaged in the design of their experiments and the physical manipulation of the apparatus" (p. 663). So, children were discovering by doing experiments. Labelling this condition direct instruction, therefore, does not seem to do complete justice to what actually was done by the participants. Both studies (Klahr & Nigam, 2004; Mayer, 2004) emphasize the importance of combining discovery activities with the appropriate guidance.

In this chapter, I have outlined guidance in the form of scaffolds that help create guided discovery environment that should really be effective. In earlier work (de Jong & van Joolingen, 1998) an overview of scaffolds was also presented. Together with the scaffolds presented in this chapter, this offers a wide range of possibilities to support learners. One of the main questions remaining is when a scaffold is necessary and helpful. In this chapter and in de Jong and van Joolingen (1998) a large number of studies evaluating the effectiveness of scaffolds have been mentioned. Overall, the scaffolds presented in this chapter, when evaluation results were present, seem to work well. Still, it is daring to present overall recommendations on the use of scaffolds since conditions differ quite dramatically among the studies presented. These differences concern, for example, the length of the experiment, whether the treatment is part of the real curriculum or is more of a laboratory experiment, the learners (age, prior knowledge, experimentation experience, etc.), the domains, and learning goals (domain knowledge, experimentation strategies). From the studies presented, however, a few general conditions may be deduced that point to factors that may help to increase the effectiveness of inquiry learning environments. These conditions indicate that for introducing inquiry learning with computer simulations effectively, not only should adequate scaffolds be present but also a few other conditions should be met concerning learners, domains, and learning goals.

First, to work proficiently in simulation-based inquiry environments, students should encounter the correct knowledge. This implies that they need to come to the learning environment with adequate prior knowledge that they can use in creating adequate experiments and drawing valid conclusions. Scaffolding must be aimed at helping students reach these correct conclusions. If students do not succeed in drawing the right conclusions themselves, inclusion of facilities that provide them with these conclusions in another way must be considered. Second, inquiry learning might not be suitable for all topics. Especially for learning domain-based procedural skills (e.g., solving long division problems, performing a titration experiment in chemistry) discovery cannot be the starting point. Some modelling and/or direct instruction should be involved. For learning experimentation procedures, inquiry learning environments can be used, but these should then be regarded as experiential learning environments, since the goal is to master the experimentation procedure that is carried out rather than the domain that is the subject of the experimentation (see, for example, Klahr & Nigam, 2004). Finally, it seems advisable to present students with a goal for their inquiry. Currently, inquiry environments are more open regarding the goals to be reached, but recent studies have shown that providing students with a more concrete, but still open, goal (e.g., to create a concept map of the domain (Gijlers & de Jong, in preparation)), a runnable model (Löhner, van Joolingen, Savelsbergh, & van Hout-Wolters, 2005) or instruction for other learners (Vreman-de Olde & de Jong, 2004) helps students in the learning process.

Scaffolds also house a few dangers for learning. Scaffolds aim to enlarge the students' possibilities and help the students enter their "zone of proximal development". This means that scaffolds should be delicately attuned to the level of the students. It also implies that if this is not the case, scaffolds may be bothersome. Bucher and Barden-Gabbei (2002) who studied the functioning of a range of scaffolds in the context of Model-it used in a Biology course in a qualitative non-experimental study, found indications that some of the scaffolds were too restrictive for the level of students involved. A similar conclusion was drawn by Shute (1993). In our SimQuest learning environments we also see that students have the tendency to follow all assignments in the order of presentation (Swaak & de Jong, in press), even if they are free to follow other paths. This may signify that students need to get accustomed to the freedom they have. It also makes clear that there is a need for more "intelligent" scaffolding, where the scaffolds are adapted to the level of the student and may follow a "scaffolding and fading" approach, making the student increasingly responsible during the scientific discovery process.

A new and promising development is found in collaborative scientific discovery learning. The most straightforward way of designing learning environments for collaborative scientific discovery is to let students work together in front of the screen or in class debates with an inquiry environment as is done in a number of WISE cases (Bell, 2004), but computer-regulated collaboration and communication over a distance is also possible (van Joolingen et al., 2005). One of the main learning mechanisms here is that learners may experience conflicts, which they try to resolve through co-construction (Gijlers & de Jong, in preparation, submitted; Tao, 2004). In this case, a partner can function as a scaffold, and discussing alternative hypotheses in collaboration may cause learners to change their beliefs more quickly (Okada & Simon, 1997). This, however, also requires a careful composition of groups (Gijlers & de Jong, 2005; Saleh, Lazonder, & de Jong, 2005), cognitive scaffolds that structure the communication process, and ways to help students when neither of them find the right information in the inquiry environment.

It seems safe to conclude that inquiry learning can be successful, but only when the right conditions are met and only when adequate scaffolds are present. Elen and Lowyck (1998) investigated how student assess the efficiency of instructional approaches. The outcomes of this study show that university students prefer direct instruction that aims at reproduction of the information presented, and that they do not value the use of technology to support the learning process. This outcome can partly be explained by the fact that students are usually assessed on reproduction of information and that they are used to a traditional mode of learning. It may also signify that they have not often been confronted with well-designed and effective simulation-based inquiry environments. Therefore, there is a huge challenge for instructional designers to provide students with these types of environments.

References

Baker, L. M., & Dunbar, K. (2000). Experimental design heuristics for scientific discovery: The use of "baseline" and "known standard" controls. *International Journal of Human-Computer Studies, 53*, 335–349.

Bell, P. (2004). Promoting students' argument construction and collaborative debate in the science classroom. In: M. Linn, E. A. Davis, & P. Bell (Eds), *Internet environments for science education* (pp. 115–143). Mahwah, NJ: Erlbaum.

Bell, P., & Linn, M. (2000). Scientific arguments as learning artifacts: Designing from the web with KIE. *International Journal of Science Education, 22*, 797–817.

Bucher, J. M., & Barden-Gabbei, L. M. (2002). *Strategy use among college students engaged in inquiry-based labs.* Paper presented at the annual meeting of the American Educational Research Association, New Orleans.

Chen, Z., & Klahr, D. (1999). All other things being equal: Acquisition and transfer of the control of variables strategy. *Child Development, 70*, 1098–1120.

Chinn, C. A., & Brewer, W. F. (1993). The role of anomalous data in knowledge acquisition: A theoretical framework and implications for science instruction. *Review of Educational Research, 63*, 1–51.

Chinn, C. A., & Brewer, W. F. (2001). Models of data: A theory of how people evaluate data. *Cognition and Instruction, 19*, 323–393.

Chinn, C. A., & Malhotra, B. A. (2002). Epistemologically authentic inquiry in schools: A theoretical framework for evaluating inquiry tasks. *Science Education, 86*, 175–218.

Davis, E. A. (2000). Scaffolding students' knowledge integration: Prompts for reflection in KIE. *International Journal of Science Education, 22*, 819–837.

Davis, E. A. (2004). Creating critique projects. In: M. Linn, E. A. Davis, & P. Bell (Eds), *Internet environments for science education* (pp. 89–113). Mahwah, NJ: Erlbaum.

de Jong, T. (2005). The guided discovery principle in multimedia learning. In: R. E. Mayer (Ed.), *Cambridge handbook of multimedia learning* (pp. 215–229). Cambridge, UK: Cambridge University Press.

de Jong, T., Beishuizen, J., Hulshof, C. D., Prins, F., van Rijn, H., van Someren, M., Veenman, M., & Wilhelm, P. (2005). Determinants of discovery learning. In: P. Gärdenfors, & P. Johansson (Eds), *Cognition, education and communication technology* (pp. 257–283). Mahwah, NJ: Erlbaum.

de Jong, T., & Njoo, M. (1992). Learning and instruction with computer simulations: Learning processes involved. In: E. de Corte, M. Linn, H. Mandl, & L. Verschaffel (Eds), *Computer-based learning environments and problem solving* (pp. 411–429). Berlin: Springer-Verlag.

de Jong, T., & Pieters, J. M. (2006). The design of powerful learning environments. In: P. A. Alexander, & P. H. Winne (Eds), *Handbook of educational psychology* (2nd ed.). Mahwah, NJ: Erlbaum.

de Jong, T., & van Joolingen, W. R. (1998). Scientific discovery learning with computer simulations of conceptual domains. *Review of Educational Research, 68*, 179–202.

de Jong, T., van Joolingen, W. R., Savelsbergh, E., Lazonder, A., Wilhelm, P., & Ootes, S. (2002). *Co-Lab specifications. Part 1 — Theoretical background*. Enschede, NL: University of Twente.

Edelson, D. C., Gordin, D. N., & Pea, R. D. (1999). Addressing the challenges of inquiry-based learning through technology and curriculum design. *Journal of the Learning Sciences, 8*, 391–450.

Elen, J., & Lowyck, J. (1998). Students' views on the efficiency of instruction: An exploratory survey of the instructional metacognitive knowledge of university freshmen. *Higher Education, 36*, 231–252.

Friedler, Y., Nachmias, R., & Linn, M. C. (1990). Learning scientific reasoning skills in microcomputer-based laboratories. *Journal of Research in Science Teaching, 27*, 173–191.

Gijlers, H., & de Jong, T. (2005). The relation between prior knowledge and students' collaborative discovery learning processes. *Journal of Research in Science Teaching, 42*, 264–282.

Gijlers, H., & de Jong, T. (in preparation). Facilitating collaborative inquiry learning with shared concept maps and proposition tables.

Gijlers, H., & de Jong, T. (submitted). Sharing and confronting propositions in collaborative scientific discovery learning.

Hart, A. H., & Barden-Gabbei, L. M. (2002). Student learning practices when using computer simulation software imbedded with simulations. Paper presented at the annual meeting of the American Educational Research Association, April New Orleans.

Hickey, D. T., Kindfield, A. C. H., Horwitz, P., & Christie, M. A. (2003). Integrating curriculum, instruction, assessment, and evaluation in a technology-supported genetics environment. *American Educational Research Journal, 40*, 495–538.

Hickey, D. T., & Zuiker, S. (2003). A new perspective for evaluating innovative science learning environments. *Science Education, 87*, 539–563.

Hulshof, C. D., Wilhelm, P., Beishuizen, J. J., & van Rijn, H. (2005). FILE: A tool for the study of inquiry learning. *Computers in Human Behavior, 21*, 945–956.

Jackson, S., Stratford, S., Krajcik, J., & Soloway, E. (1996a). Making dynamic modeling accessible to pre-college science students. *Interactive Learning Environments, 4*, 233–257.

Jackson, S., Stratford, S. J., Krajcik, J., & Soloway, E. (1996b). A learner-centred tool for students building models. *Communications of the ACM, 39*, 48–49.

Jonassen, D. H. (2000). *Mindtools for schools*. New York: Macmillan.

Kanari, Z., & Millar, R. (2004). Reasoning from data: How students collect and interpret data in science investigations. *Journal of Research in Science Teaching, 41*, 748–769.

Keselman, A. (2003). Supporting inquiry learning by promoting normative understanding of multivariable causality. *Journal of Research in Science Teaching, 40*, 898–921.

Klahr, D., & Dunbar, K. (1988). Dual space search during scientific reasoning. *Cognitive Science, 12*, 1–48.

Klahr, D., & Nigam, M. (2004). The equivalence of learning paths in early science instruction: Effects of direct instruction and discovery learning. *Psychological Science, 15*, 661–668.

Klahr, D., & Simon, H. A. (1999). Studies of scientific discovery: Complementary approaches and convergent findings. *Psychological Bulletin, 125*, 524–543.

Kuhn, D. (2002). What is scientific thinking and how does it develop? In: U. Goswami (Ed.), *Handbook of childhood cognitive development* (pp. 371–393). Oxford, UK: Blackwell.

Kuhn, D., Amsel, E., & O'Loughlin, M. (1988). *The development of scientific thinking skills*. San Diego, CA: Academic Press.

Kuhn, D., Black, J., Keselman, A., & Kaplan, D. (2000). The development of cognitive skills to support inquiry learning. *Cognition and Instruction, 18*, 495–523.

Lajoie, S. P., Lavigne, N. C., Guerrera, C., & Munsie, S. D. (2001). Constructing knowledge in the context of Bioworld. *Instructional Science, 29*, 155–186.

Land, S. M., & Zembal-Saul, C. (2003). Scaffolding reflection and articulation of scientific explanations in a data-rich, project-based learning environment: An investigation of progress portfolio. *Educational Technology Research & Development, 51*(4), 67–86.

Lawson, A. E. (2002). Sound and faulty arguments generated by pre-service biology teachers when testing hypotheses involving unobservable entities. *Journal of Research in Science Teaching, 39*, 237–252.

Lewis, E. L., Stern, J. L., & Linn, M. C. (1993). The effect of computer simulations on introductory thermodynamics understanding. *Educational Technology, 33*, 45–58.

Lin, X., & Lehman, J. D. (1999). Supporting learning of variable control in a computer-based biology environment: Effects of prompting college students to reflect on their own thinking. *Journal of Research in Science Teaching, 36*, 837–858.

Linn, M. C., Bell, P., & Davis, E. A. (2004). Specific design principles: Elaborating the scaffolded knowledge integration framework. In: M. Linn, E. A. Davis, & P. Bell (Eds), *Internet environments for science education* (pp. 315–341). Mahwah, NJ: Erlbaum.

Linn, M. C., Davis, E. A., & Bell, P. (Eds). (2004). *Internet environments for science education*. Mahwah, NJ: Erlbaum.

Löhner, S., van Joolingen, W. R., & Savelsbergh, E. R. (2003). The effect of external representation on constructing computer models of complex phenomena. *Instructional Science, 31*, 395–418.

Löhner, S., van Joolingen, W. R., Savelsbergh, E. R., & van Hout-Wolters, B. (2005). Students' reasoning during modelling in an inquiry learning environment. *Computers in Human Behavior, 21*, 441–461.

Lowyck, J., & Elen, J. (1993). Transitions in the theoretical foundation of instructional design. In: T. M. Duffy, J. Lowyck, & D. H. Jonassen (Eds), *Designing environments for constructive learning* (pp. 213–229). Berlin: Springer-Verlag.

Manlove, S., Lazonder, A. W., & de Jong, T. (in press). Regulative support for collaborative scientific inquiry learning. *Journal of Computer Assisted Learning.*

Mayer, R. E. (2004). Should there be a three-strikes rule against pure discovery learning? *American Psychologist, 59*, 14–19.

Moreno, R., & Mayer, R. E. (2005). Role of guidance, reflection, and interactivity in an agent-based multimedia game. *Journal of Educational Psychology, 97*, 117–128.

Murray, T., Bruno, M., & Woolf, B. (2003). A coached learning environment for case-based inquiry learning in human biology. Paper presented at the E-Learn 2003, November, Phoenix.

Nesbit, J. C., & Winne, P. H. (2003). Self-regulated learning with networked resources. *Canadian Journal of Learning and Technology, 29*, 71–92.

Njoo, M., & de Jong, T. (1993). Exploratory learning with a computer simulation for control theory: Learning processes and instructional support. *Journal of Research in Science Teaching, 30*, 821–844.

Okada, T., & Simon, H. A. (1997). Collaborative discovery in a scientific domain. *Cognitive Science, 21*, 109–146.

Quintana, C., Reiser, B. J., Davis, E. A., Krajcik, J., Fretz, E., Duncan, R. G., Kyza, E., Edelson, D., & Soloway, E. (2004). A scaffolding design framework for software to support science inquiry. *The Journal of the Learning Sciences, 13*, 337–387.

Reiser, B. J. (2004). Scaffolding complex learning: The mechanisms of structuring and problematizing student work. *The Journal of the Learning Sciences, 13*, 273–304.

Reiser, B. J., Tabak, I., Sandoval, W. A., Smith, B., Steinmuller, F., & Leone, T. J. (2001). BGuILE: Strategic and conceptual scaffolds for scientific inquiry in biology classrooms. In: S. M. Carver, & D. Klahr (Eds), *Cognition and instruction: Twenty-five years of progress* (pp. 263–305). Mahwah, NJ: Erlbaum.

Saleh, M., Lazonder, A. W., & de Jong, T. (2005). Effects of within-class ability grouping on social interaction, achievement, and motivation. *Instructional Science, 33*, 105–119.

Salomon, G., Perkins, D., & Globerson, T. (1991). Partners in cognition: Extending human intelligence with intelligent technologies. *Educational Researcher, 20*, 2–9.

Shimoda, T. A., White, B. Y., & Frederiksen, J. (2002). Student goal orientation in learning inquiry skills with modifiable advisors. *Science Education, 88*, 244–263.

Shute, V. J. (1993). A comparison of learning environments: All that glitters. In: S. P. Lajoie, & S. J. Derry (Eds), *Computers as cognitive tools* (pp. 47–74). Hillsdale, NJ: Erlbaum.

Shute, V. J., & Glaser, R. (1990). A large-scale evaluation of an intelligent discovery world: Smithtown. *Interactive Learning Environments, 1*, 51–77.

Slotta, J. (2004). The web-based inquiry science environment (WISE): Scaffolding knowledge integration in the science classroom. In: M. Linn, E. A. Davis, & P. Bell (Eds), *Internet environments for science education* (pp. 203–233). Mahwah, NJ: Erlbaum.

Smith, B. K., & Reiser, B. J. (1997). What should a wildebeest say? Interactive nature films for high school classrooms. Paper presented at the ACM Multimedia, Seattle.

Steed, M. (1992). Stella, a simulation construction kit: Cognitive process and educational implications. *Journal of Computers in Mathematics and Science Teaching, 11*, 39–52.

Stratford, S. J., Krajcik, J., & Soloway, E. (1998). Secondary students' dynamic modelling processes: Analyzing, reasoning about, synthesizing and testing models of stream ecosystems. *Journal of Science Education and Technology, 7*, 215–234.

Suthers, D., Weiner, A., Connelly, J., & Paolucci, M. (1995). Belvedere: Engaging students in critical discussion of science and public policy issues. Paper presented at the AI&Ed 95, the 7th world conference on artificial intelligence in education, Washington, DC.

Swaak, J., & de Jong, T. (1996). Measuring intuitive knowledge in science: The development of the what-if test. *Studies in Educational Evaluation, 22*, 341–362.

Swaak, J., & de Jong, T. (in press). Order or no order. System vs. learner control in sequencing simulation based scientific discovery learning. In: F. E. Ritter, E. Lehtinen, T. O'Shea, & J. Nerb (Eds), *In order to learn: How ordering effects in machine learning illuminate human learning and vice versa.* New York: Oxford University Press.

Tao, P. K. (2004). Developing understanding of image formation by lenses through collaborative learning mediated by multimedia computer-assisted learning programs. *International Journal of Science Education, 26*, 1171–1197.

Toth, E. E., Suthers, D. D., & Lesgold, A. M. (2002). "Mapping to know": The effects of representational guidance and reflective assessment on scientific inquiry. *Science Education, 86*, 264–286.

van Joolingen, W. R., & de Jong, T. (1991). Supporting hypothesis generation by learners exploring an interactive computer simulation. *Instructional Science, 20*, 389–404.

van Joolingen, W. R., & de Jong, T. (1997). An extended dual search space model of learning with computer simulations. *Instructional Science, 25*, 307–346.

van Joolingen, W. R., & de Jong, T. (2003). SimQuest: Authoring educational simulations. In: T. Murray, S. Blessing, & S. Ainsworth (Eds), *Authoring tools for advanced technology educational software: Toward cost-effective production of adaptive, interactive, and intelligent educational software* (pp. 1–31). Dordrecht: Kluwer Academic Publishers.

van Joolingen, W. R., de Jong, T., Lazonder, A. W., Savelsbergh, E., & Manlove, S. (2005). Co-Lab: Research and development of an on-line learning environment for collaborative scientific discovery learning. *Computers in Human Behavior, 21*, 671–688.

Veermans, K. H., de Jong, T., & van Joolingen, W. R. (2000). Promoting self directed learning in simulation based discovery learning environments through intelligent support. *Interactive Learning Environments, 8*, 229–255.

Veermans, K. H., van Joolingen, W. R., & de Jong, T. (2006). Use of heuristics to facilitate scientific discovery learning in a simulation learning environment in a physics domain. *International Journal of Science Education, 28*, 341–361.

Vreman-de Olde, C., & de Jong, T. (2004). Student-generated assignments about electrical circuits in a computer simulation. *International Journal of Science Education, 26*, 859–873.

White, B. Y., Frederiksen, J., Frederiksen, T., Eslinger, E., Loper, S., & Collins, A. (2002). Inquiry island: Affordances of a multi-agent environment for scientific inquiry and reflective learning. Paper presented at the fifth international conference of the learning sciences (ICLS).

Wilhelm, P., & Beishuizen, J. J. (2003). Content effects in self-directed inductive learning. *Learning & Instruction, 13*, 381–402.

Winne, P. H. (2001). Self-regulated learning viewed from models of information processing. In: B. J. Zimmerman, & D. H. Schunk (Eds), *Self-regulated learning and academic achievement: Theoretical perspectives* (2nd ed., pp. 153–189). Hillsdale, NJ: Erlbaum.

Zhang, J., Chen, Q., Sun, Y., & Reid, D. J. (2004). Triple scheme of learning support design for scientific discovery learning based on computer simulation: Experimental research. *Journal of Computer Assisted Learning, 20*, 269–282.

Chapter 7

Coping with Complexity in Multimedia Learning

Richard E. Mayer

Introduction

How can we help people understand cause-and-effect explanations of how complex systems work, such as how the human respiratory system works, how lightning storms develop, or how an electric motor works? Multimedia learning environments have the potential to help people understand how complex systems work. However, a major challenge for instructional designers is to provide explanations of complex systems that capture the system's complexity without overwhelming the learner. This chapter is based on the premise that the design of multimedia instruction for complex systems should be consistent with cognitive science theories of how people learn and with the empirical research based on multimedia learning.

In this chapter, I explore seven theory-grounded and research-based techniques for coping with complexity in multimedia learning as suggested by Mayer (2001) and by Mayer and Moreno (2003): off-loading (presenting words in spoken form rather than printed form), segmenting (allowing learners to control the pace of presentation), pretraining (providing pretraining in the names and characteristics of system components), weeding (eliminating extraneous material), signaling (adding cues for how to process the material), aligning (placing printed words near corresponding parts of graphics), and synchronizing (presenting corresponding narration and animation simultaneously). I summarize the empirical evidence for each technique and relate each technique to a cognitive theory of multimedia learning.

Consider the following scenario. You want to know how an electric motor works so you go to a computer, and click on the entry for "electric motor" in a multimedia encyclopedia. On the screen, a window of scrollable text appears which provides a short definition on a bright orange background with the encyclopedia's logo and pictures of various machines that use electric motors. Some of the words are underlined, indicating that you can click on them and at the bottom is a list of underlined terms such as "how it works";

when you click on one of the underlined words another window appears containing a definition or explanation of the word you clicked on, again on a brightly colored background with a logo and small pictures around the perimeter, and again you can click on the underlined words. Back on the first window, there are icons representing a speaker, a picture, and a movie. If you click on the speaker icon, the computer reads the text to you in machine-like voice. If you click on the picture icon, a window opens displaying a series of photos. If you click on the movie icon, an animation is presented in yet another window. Before too long the screen is covered with windows, you are overwhelmed, and not much learning has occurred.

This is an example of what we have called a *cognitive overload situation* (Mayer & Moreno, 2003; Mayer, 2005b,c) in which the amount of cognitive processing required by a multimedia presentation exceeds the cognitive processing capacity of the learner. Cognitive overload occurs when "the processing demands evoked by the learning task ... exceed the processing capacity of the cognitive system" (Mayer & Moreno, 2003, p. 44). Avoiding or minimizing the potential for cognitive overload is a crucial challenge for instructional designers. In short, instructional designers must be sensitive to the complexity of the instructional scenario, where complexity is defined as the amount of cognitive processing required.[1]

The complexity of instructional messages can come from two sources — the need for essential processing and the need for extraneous processing. Essential processing involves making sense of the essential material in the lesson and depends on the material's intrinsic difficulty. Extraneous processing involves cognitive processing that is not aimed at making sense of the material in the lesson, but rather depends on the way that the material is presented. It follows that there are two ways of coping with complexity in multimedia learning (1) managing complexity when it is unavoidable, using what we call techniques for managing essential processing (Mayer, 2005b) and (2) reducing complexity when it is avoidable, using what we call techniques for reducing extraneous processing (Mayer, 2005c).

According to the cognitive theory of multimedia learning (Mayer, 2001, 2005a) — summarized in Figure 7.1 — meaningful learning occurs when the learner engages in a

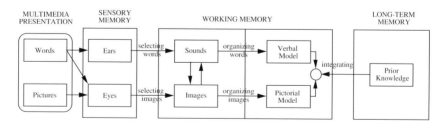

Figure 7.1: Cognitive theory of multimedia learning.

---

[1] The amount of cognitive processing required in a learning task can be called cognitive load. A discussion of techniques for measuring cognitive load (or "the amount of cognitive processing required") is beyond the scope of this paper, but is a crucial issue in coping with complexity.

series of cognitive processes that include paying attention to relevant words from the verbal part of a multimedia lesson, paying attention to relevant images from the pictorial part of a multimedia lesson, mentally organizing the words into a verbal mental representation, mentally organizing the images into a pictorial mental representation, and integrating the two representations with each other and with prior knowledge. These processes require cognitive capacity, so meaningful learning is enhanced by techniques for managing and reducing complexity.

Managing Essential Processing by Managing Complexity

In some situations — which can be called *intrinsic overload scenarios* — the complexity of the learning task is attributable to the inherent complexity of the to-be-learned material. In short, the *essential processing* (Mayer & Moreno, 2003; Mayer, 2005a) or *intrinsic load* (Sweller, 1999, 2005) demanded by the to-be-learned material exceeds the processing capacity of the learner. Three methods for managing essential processing are off-loading, segmenting, and pretraining.

Off-Loading

Consider an annotated animation of how an electric motor works presented at a fast pace, with sentences printed on the screen to describe the events depicted in the animation. There are many interacting parts — the negative terminal of the battery, the positive terminal of the battery, the wire between the negative terminal and the top of the commutator, the wire between the positive terminal and the bottom of the commutator, the commutator, the wire loop, the top magnet and the bottom magnet — as well as interacting invisible forces — such as the magnetic field and the flow of electrons. Learners — especially those who are not familiar with electronics — may be overwhelmed by the challenge of viewing the animation while reading the sentences. When they look at the animation they cannot read the words and when they read the words they cannot view the animation. In short, the visual channel can become overloaded. Learners are unable to pay attention to all of the essential printed words and images, as indicated by the select words and select images arrows in Figure 7.1.

What can be done to manage the complexity of this cognitive overload scenario? One solution is *off-loading* the words from the visual channel to the verbal channel by presenting the words in spoken form rather than printed form. In this way, the learner can process the animation in the visual channel and process the words in the verbal channel. Mayer (2001, 2005b) refers to this as the *modality principle*: People learn more deeply from multimedia lessons when words are presented in spoken form rather than printed form.

Does off-loading improve learner understanding as measured by tests of problem-solving transfer? Mayer (2005b) reviewed 21 published comparisons between learning with graphics and spoken words versus learning with graphics and printed words (Jeung, Chandler, & Sweller, 1997, Experiments 1, 2, & 3; Mayer & Moreno, 1998, Experiments 1 & 2; Mayer & Moreno, 1999, Experiments 1 & 2; Kalyuga, Chandler, & Sweller, 2000, Experiment 1; O'Neil et al., 2000, Experiment 1; Moreno, Mayer, Spires, & Lester, 2001, Experiments 1, 4a, 4b, 5a, & 5b; Craig, Gholson, & Driscoll, 2002, Experiment 2; Moreno & Mayer, 2002,

Experiments 1a, 1b, 1c, 2a, & 2b; Mayer, Dow, & Mayer, 2003, Experiment 1). In all 21 comparisons, people who learned from graphics and spoken words performed better on tests of problem-solving transfer than did people who learned from graphics and printed words. The median effect size (based on Cohen's *d*) favoring spoken over printed words was 0.97, which is considered to be a large effect. These results — summarized in the top row of Table 7.1 — confirm that off-loading can be an effective technique for managing complexity.

Segmenting

Although off-loading can be an effective method for managing complexity, in some cases additional methods may be needed. Even when multimedia material is presented as a narrated animation, the learner may not be able to keep up with the pace of the presentation. In this type of cognitive overload, the learner is not able to pay attention to all of the fast-paced information to be processed in the visual channel and/or verbal channel.

What can be done to manage the complexity of this cognitive overload situation? Segmenting is a technique in which a narrated animation is broken down into meaningful segments, with the learner able to initiate the next segment by carrying out some simple action such as clicking on a "CONTINUE" button. For example, instead of a continuous 3-min presentation of a narrated animation explaining how an electric motor works, a segmented presentation contains short segments lasting about 15 seconds in which the learner can click on a button to go on to the next segment. Segmenting allows learners to control the pace of presentation, and thereby manage the complexity inherent in the material. Learners can complete all needed processing of one segment before moving on to the next. The segmenting principle is that people learn more deeply when a multimedia lesson is presented in learner-paced segments rather than as a continuous unit.

Does segmenting improve learning? Mayer (2005b) reviewed three published comparisons of people who learned from a continuous narrated animation and those who learned from a segmented narrated animation (Mayer & Chandler, 2001, Experiment 2; Mayer et al., 2003, Experiments 2a & 2b). In all three comparisons, the segmented group performed better on subsequent problem-solving transfer tests than did continuous groups, yielding a median effect size (*d*) of 0.98. Overall, these results — summarized in the second row of Table 7.1 — provide encouraging preliminary evidence that segmenting can be used to help manage complexity in multimedia lessons.

Pretraining

Sometimes segmenting of a narrated animation is not possible or feasible, and sometimes, additional means are needed to manage the inherent complexity of the material. For example, in processing a multimedia lesson on how an electric motor works, a learner must mentally build component models — a representation of each part, its name, its location, and what states it can be in — and a causal model — a representation of how a change in one part affects a change in another part and so on. The learner may devote so much cognitive capacity to remembering the name, location, and states of each part (i.e., building component models) that the learner has insufficient capacity left to build a causal chain of how the electric motor works (i.e., building a causal model).

Table 7.1: Seven ways to cope with complexity in multimedia learning.

Technique	Description	Principle	Effect size*	Number of comparisons*
Off-loading	Present words in spoken form rather than printed form	Modality	0.97	21 of 21
Segmenting	Allow learners to control the pace of presentation	Segmenting	0.98	3 of 3
Pretraining	Provide pretraining in the names and characteristics of system components	Pretraining	0.92	7 of 7
Weeding	Eliminate extraneous material	Coherence	1.32	10 of 11
Signaling	Add cues for how to process the material	Signaling	0.60	3 of 3
Aligning	Place printed words near corresponding parts of graphics	Spatial contiguity	1.11	8 of 8
Synchronizing	Present corresponding narration and animation simultaneously	Temporal contiguity	1.31	8 of 8

*Data based on Mayer (2005b,c).

How can we help the learner manage the inherent complexity in this cognitive overload situation? Having prior knowledge is the classic way to manage complexity, because the learner's existing knowledge can be used to organize the incoming information (Kalyuga, 2005). If you already are familiar with the names and characteristics of the key parts of the system, you can focus your cognitive processing on how the parts interact — that is, on building a cause-and-effect chain. Although the development of component models takes time, it may be possible to provide focused pretraining on the names, locations, and characteristics of the key components in a to-be-learned causal system. The *pretraining principle* (Mayer, 2001, 2005b; Mayer & Moreno, 2003) is that people learn more deeply from a multimedia message when they know the names and characteristics of the main concepts. For example, pretraining for a lesson on electric motors could focus on students learning the names, location, and possible states of each part, such as positive terminal, negative terminal, wire, commutator, wire loop, top magnet, and bottom magnet. Then, when presented with a narrated animation of how an electric motor works the learner could allocate more cognitive capacity to learning cause-and-effect connections.

Does pretraining improve student understanding of a narrated animation explaining how something works? Mayer (2005b) reviewed seven published comparisons of learning from graphics and words with or without pretraining (Pollock, Chandler, & Sweller, 2002, Experiments 1 & 3; Mayer, Mathias, & Wetzell, 2002, Experiments 1, 2, & 3; Mayer, Mautone, & Prothero, 2002, Experiments 2 & 3). In all comparisons, people who received pretraining performed better on subsequent problem-solving transfer tests than did people who learned without pretraining. The median effect size (*d*) favoring the pretraining group was 0.92, which is considered to be a large effect. These results are summarized in the third row of Table 7.1. Overall, there is consistent evidence supporting the role of pretraining in managing complexity that is inherent in multimedia lessons.

Reducing Extraneous Processing by Reducing Complexity

So far, I have investigated how to manage complexity that is inherent in the instructional materials by using off-loading, segmenting, or pretraining. In this section, I investigate how to reduce complexity when the instructional materials are poorly designed. In an *extraneous overload scenario*, the processing demands attributable to intrinsic processing (needed for making sense of the material) and extraneous processing (needed because of the inefficient way the material is presented) exceed the cognitive capacity of the learner. The remedy for this overload situation is to redesign the presentation format in a way that reduces or eliminates the need for extraneous processing. In short, when the multimedia lesson is complex because it requires extraneous processing, the solution is to redesign the lesson in ways that reduce the need for extraneous processing. Four techniques for reducing extraneous processing are weeding, signaling, aligning, and synchronizing.

Weeding

Consider a situation in which a learner is viewing a narrated animation about how electric motors work. The lesson contains extraneous graphics, such as pictures of devices that use electric motors and video clips of an assembly line producing electric motors, extraneous words, such as narration about the lives of the inventor and descriptions of how the parts are mined, and extraneous sounds, such as background music. Alternatively, consider a textbook lesson containing printed text and illustrations. In this case, the lesson contains extraneous graphics, such as photos of various electric motors and background colored designs, and extraneous words, such as stories about the lives of inventors and descriptions of how the parts are mined. Learners may allocate so much cognitive capacity to processing extraneous material that they do not have sufficient capacity remaining to process the essential material. As a result, they are not able to deeply understand how an electric motor works. Although designers may intend for extraneous material to promote learner interest, the extraneous material may instead make deep learning less likely to occur.

A straightforward solution to the problem of having too much extraneous material in a multimedia presentation is to eliminate the extraneous material. We call this method *weeding* (Mayer & Moreno, 2003; Mayer, 2005c). For example, in a multimedia lesson on how an electric motor works, weeding involves deleting extraneous video clips, pictures, stories, and background music that are not directly supportive of the instructional goal. The *coherence principle* is that people learn more deeply from a multimedia presentation when extraneous material is excluded rather than included (Mayer, 2001, 2005c).

Does weeding work? Mayer (2005c) reviewed 11 published comparisons of a group that received a concise multimedia lesson versus a group that received an expanded multimedia lesson containing extraneous background music, video clips, photos, or words (Mayer et al., 1996, Experiments 1, 2, & 3; Harp & Mayer, 1997, Experiment 1; Harp & Mayer, 1998, Experiments 1, 2, 3, & 4; Moreno & Mayer, 2000, Experiments 1, & 2; Mayer, Heiser, & Lonn, 2001, Experiment 3). In 10 of the 11 comparisons, people performed better on problem-solving transfer tests when the extraneous material was eliminated, yielding a median effect size of $d = 1.32$. As summarized in the fourth row of Table 7.1, these results demonstrate the efficacy of weeding as technique for reducing complexity.

Signaling

When weeding is not feasible, signaling is an alternative way to focus the learner's attention on essential rather than extraneous material. Signaling involves placing cues in printed or spoken text that directs the learner's attention to the essential material. Signaling includes presenting an outline at the start of a section, adding headings that are based on the outline, underlining key phrases, and inserting pointer words such as "first ... second ... third" or "because of this". When the text is spoken, the headings, key phrases, and pointer words can be pronounced with a deeper voice for emphasis. The *signaling principle* is that people learn more deeply from a multimedia lesson when cues are added that highlight the organization of the essential material (Mayer, 2001, 2005c).

Does signaling of multimedia material improve learning? There is some preliminary evidence that signaling can improve problem-solving transfer performance both with illustrated text (Harp & Mayer, 1998, Experiment 3a) and narrated animation (Mautone & Mayer, 2001, Experiments 3a & 3b). In three of three comparisons, students who received signaled multimedia presentations performed better on tests of problem-solving transfer than did students who received non-signaled multimedia presentations. The median effect size was $d = 0.60$, which is considered to be a medium effect. Overall, although there is some promising preliminary evidence (summarized in the fifth row of Table 7.1), more research is needed to determine the consistency and strength of signaling effects in multimedia learning.

Aligning

In the previous two scenarios, complexity resulted from extraneous material in a multimedia lesson, and the remedy was to remove the extraneous material (i.e., by weeding) or highlight the essential material (i.e., by signaling). Alternatively, in some book-based or computer-based presentations complexity is created because poor organization forces learners to engage in extraneous cognitive processing. For example, consider the situation in which a learner is reading a book-based lesson containing text on one page and corresponding illustrations on the next page. When the learner reads about an action, he or she must scan the next page to find the corresponding part of the illustration. This scanning activity takes up precious cognitive processing resources, leaving less capacity for the learner to make sense of the material.

How can we reduce the complexity of this scenario? Mayer and Moreno (2003; Mayer, 2005c) recommend using a technique called *aligning* — placing text next to the corresponding portion of a graphic. Aligning is based on the *spatial contiguity principle*: People learn more deeply when corresponding words and graphics are presented near rather than far from each other on the page or screen (Mayer, 2001, 2005c). For example, if the text says "electrons flow from the negative terminal through the wire to the commutator", these words should be placed within a graphic next to the negative terminal, wire, and commutator. Aligning is intended to reduce the demands on the learner to engage in extraneous cognitive processing such as finding the portion of the illustration that corresponds to a portion of the text.

Does aligning improve learner understanding? Mayer (2005c) reviewed eight published comparisons of groups who learned from multimedia presentations in which the words and graphics were or were not aligned (Mayer, 1989, Experiment 2; Sweller, Chandler, Tierney, & Cooper, 1990, Experiment 1; Chandler & Sweller, 1991, Experiment 1; Mayer, Steinhoff, Bower, & Mars, 1995, Experiments 1, 2, & 3; Tindall-Ford, Chandler, & Sweller, 1997, Experiment 1; Moreno & Mayer, 1999, Experiment 1). In all of the eight comparisons, students who received aligned lessons performed better on problem-solving transfer tests than did students who received non-aligned lessons. The median effect size was $d = 1.11$, which is considered to be large. Overall, as summarized in the sixth line of Table 7.1, it appears that aligning can be a successful technique for reducing complexity and thereby increasing opportunities for deep learning.

Synchronizing

In the previous section, complexity was created by spatially separating corresponding words and graphics. In this section, I consider a situation in which corresponding words and graphics are separated in time — that is, the words are presented before or after their corresponding graphic. For example, imagine a computer-based scenario in which the learner clicks on a "text" icon to hear or read about how an electric motor works, and then clicks on a "movie" icon to see an animation depicting the workings of an electric motor. Although the learner receives two presentations of the explanation — one in words and one in pictures — they are separated in time. Temporal separation of corresponding words and pictures creates complexity because learners must try to mentally hold one representation in working memory (such as "the electrons flow from the negative terminal through the wire to the commutator") until the corresponding representation is presented (such as an animation depicting electron flow). If cognitive resources are needed to maintain representations in working memory, less capacity is available to engage in the essential processing that leads to deep understanding.

How can we reduce the complexity caused by temporal separation of corresponding words and pictures? Synchronizing involves presenting corresponding words and pictures at the same time. For example, while the narrator says "the electrons flow from the negative terminal through the wire to the commutator", the animation depicts this electron flow. In this way, the learner is better able to build a mental connection between the pictorial and verbal representations of the event — thus enabling the cognitive process called *integration* in Figure 7.1. Synchronizing is based on the *temporal contiguity principle* (Mayer, 2001, 2005c): People learn more deeply from a multimedia lesson when corresponding animation and narration are presented simultaneously rather than successively.

What does the research have to say about the effectiveness of synchronizing? Mayer (2005c) reviewed eight published comparisons of groups that received multimedia lessons containing concurrent animation and narration or successive animation and narration (Mayer & Anderson, 1991, Experiments 1 & 2a; Mayer & Anderson, 1992, Experiments 1 & 2; Mayer & Sims, 1994, Experiments 1 & 2; Mayer, Moreno, Boire, & Vagge, 1999, Experiments 1 & 2). In eight out of eight comparisons, the concurrent group performed better on tests of problem-solving transfer than did the successive group, yielding a median effect size of $d = 1.31$, which is considered to be large. Overall, as summarized in the bottom line of Table 7.1, synchronizing can be an effective way to reduce complexity.

Summary

The complexity of multimedia instructional messages derives from two sources (1) complexity that is inherent in the material and therefore requires essential cognitive processing and (2) complexity that is caused by cognitively insensitive instructional design and therefore requires extraneous cognitive processing. In this chapter, I have proposed three techniques to manage essential cognitive processing in scenarios where complexity is inherent in the material (off-loading, segmenting, and pretraining) and I have proposed four techniques to reduce extraneous cognitive processing in scenarios where complexity is caused by cognitively insensitive instructional design (weeding, signaling, aligning, and synchronizing). Table 7.1 summarizes each of the seven ways to address the problem of complexity in multimedia learning.

Some important directions for future research include developing valid and reliable measures of cognitive load, investigating whether the techniques summarized in this chapter also apply to more authentic learning environments (e.g., learning in schools), and determining the role of individual differences (e.g., prior knowledge and verbalizer/visualizer learning style). In summary, a major challenge in the field of instructional design is to develop research-based techniques for coping with complexity.

References

Chandler, P., & Sweller, J. (1991). Cognitive load theory and the format of instruction. *Cognition and Instruction, 8*, 293–332.

Craig, S. D., Gholson, B., & Driscoll, D. M. (2002). Animated pedagogical agents in multimedia educational environments: Effects of agent properties, picture features, and redundancy. *Journal of Educational Psychology, 94*, 428–434.

Harp, S. F., & Mayer, R. E. (1997). The role of interest in learning from scientific text and illustrations: On the distinction between emotional interest and cognitive interest. *Journal of Educational Psychology, 89*, 92–102.

Harp, S. F., & Mayer, R. E. (1998). How seductive details do their damage: A theory of cognitive interest in science learning. *Journal of Educational Psychology, 90*, 414–434.

Jeung, H., Chandler, P., & Sweller, J. (1997). The role of visual indicators in dual sensory mode instruction. *Educational Psychology, 17*, 329–343.

Kalyuga, S. (2005). The prior knowledge principle in multimedia learning. In: R. E. Mayer (Ed.), *Cambridge handbook of multimedia learning* (pp. 325–338). New York: Cambridge University Press.

Kalyuga, S., Chandler, P., & Sweller, J. (2000). Incorporating learner experience into the design of multimedia instruction. *Journal of Educational Psychology, 92*, 126–136.

Mautone, P. D., & Mayer, R. E. (2001). Signaling as a cognitive guide in multimedia learning. *Journal of Educational Psychology, 93*, 377–389.

Mayer, R. E. (1989). Systematic thinking fostered by illustrations in scientific text. *Journal of Educational Psychology, 81*, 240–246.

Mayer, R. E. (2001). *Multimedia learning.* New York: Cambridge University Press.

Mayer, R. E. (2005a). Cognitive theory of multimedia learning. In: R. E. Mayer (Ed.), *Cambridge handbook of multimedia learning* (pp. 31–48). New York: Cambridge University Press.

Mayer, R. E. (2005b). Principles for managing essential processing in multimedia learning: Segmenting, pretraining, and modality principles. In: R. E. Mayer (Ed.), *Cambridge handbook of multimedia learning* (pp. 169–182). New York: Cambridge University Press.

Mayer, R. E. (2005c). Principles for reducing extraneous processing in multimedia learning: Coherence, redundancy, spatial contiguity, and temporal contiguity principles. In: R. E. Mayer (Ed.), *Cambridge handbook of multimedia learning* (pp. 183–200). New York: Cambridge University Press.

Mayer, R. E., & Anderson, R. B. (1991). Animations need narrations: An experimental test of a dual-coding hypothesis. *Journal of Educational Psychology, 83*, 484-490.

Mayer, R. E., & Anderson, R. B. (1992). The instructive animation: Helping students build connections between words and pictures in multimedia learning. *Journal of Educational Psychology, 84*, 444–452.

Mayer, R. E., Bove, W., Bryman, A., Mars, R., & Tapangco, L. (1996). When less is more: Meaningful learning from visual and verbal summaries of science textbook lessons. *Journal of Educational Psychology, 88*, 64–73.

Mayer, R. E., & Chandler, P. (2001). When learning is just a click away: Does simple user interaction foster deeper understanding of multimedia messages? *Journal of Educational Psychology, 93*, 390–397.

Mayer, R. E., Dow, G., & Mayer, S. (2003). Multimedia learning in an interactive self-explaining environment: What works in the design of agent-based microworlds? *Journal of Educational Psychology*, *95*, 806–813.

Mayer, R. E., Heiser, H., & Lonn, S. (2001). Cognitive constraints on multimedia learning: When presenting more material results in less understanding. *Journal of Educational Psychology*, *93*, 187–198.

Mayer, R. E., Mathias, A., & Wetzell, K. (2002). Fostering understanding of multimedia messages through pre-training: Evidence for a two-stage theory of mental model construction. *Journal of Experimental Psychology: Applied*, *8*, 147–154.

Mayer, R. E., Mautone, P., & Prothero, W. (2002). Pictorial aids for learning by doing in a multi-media geology simulation game. *Journal of Educational Psychology*, *94*, 171–185.

Mayer, R. E., & Moreno, R. (1998). A split-attention effect in multimedia learning: Evidence for dual processing systems in working memory. *Journal of Educational Psychology*, *90*, 312–320.

Mayer, R. E., & Moreno, R. (1999). Cognitive principles of multimedia learning: The role of modality and contiguity. *Journal of Educational Psychology*, *91*, 358–368.

Mayer, R. E., & Moreno, R. (2003). Nine ways to reduce cognitive load in multimedia learning. *Educational Psychologist*, *38*, 43–52.

Mayer, R. E., Moreno, R., Boire, M., & Vagge, S. (1999). Maximizing constructivist learning from multimedia communications by minimizing cognitive load. *Journal of Educational Psychology*, *91*, 638–643.

Mayer, R. E., & Sims, V. K. (1994). For whom is a picture worth a thousand words? Extensions of a dual-coding theory of multimedia learning? *Journal of Educational Psychology*, *86*, 389–401.

Mayer, R. E., Steinhoff, K., Bower, G., & Mars, R. (1995). A generative theory of textbook design: Using annotated illustrations to foster meaningful learning of science text. *Educational Technology Research and Development*, *43*, 31–43.

Moreno, R., & Mayer, R. E. (1999). Cognitive principles of multimedia learning: The role of modality and contiguity. *Journal of Educational Psychology*, *91*, 358–368.

Moreno, R., & Mayer, R. E. (2000). A coherence effect in multimedia learning: The case for minimizing irrelevant sounds in the design of multimedia messages. *Journal of Educational Psychology*, *92*, 117–125.

Moreno, R., & Mayer, R. E. (2002). Learning science in virtual reality multimedia environments: Role of methods and media. *Journal of Educational Psychology*, *94*, 598–610.

Moreno, R., Mayer, R. E., Spires, H., & Lester, J. (2001). The case for social agency in computer-based teaching: Do students learn more deeply when they interact with animated pedagogical agents? *Cognition and Instruction*, *19*, 177–214.

O'Neil, H. F., Mayer, R. E., Herl, H. E., Niemi, C., Olin, K., & Thurman, R. A. (2000). Instructional strategies for virtual aviation training environments. In: H. F. O'Neil, & D. H. Andrews (Eds), *Aircrew training and assessment* (pp. 105–130). Mahwah, NJ: Lawrence Erlbaum.

Pollock, E., Chandler, P., & Sweller, J. (2002). Assimilating complex information. *Learning and Instruction*, *12*, 61–86.

Sweller, J. (1999). *Instructional design in technical areas*. Camberwell, Australia: ACER Press.

Sweller, J. (2005). Implications of cognitive load theory for multimedia learning. In: R. E. Mayer (Ed.), *Cambridge handbook of multimedia learning* (pp. 19–30). New York: Cambridge University Press.

Sweller, J., Chandler, P., Tierney, P., & Cooper, M. (1990). Cognitive load and selective attention as factors in the structuring of technical material. *Journal of Experimental Psychology: General*, *119*, 176–192.

Tindall-Ford, S., Chandler, P., & Sweller, J. (1997). When two sensory modalities are better than one. *Journal of Experimental Psychology: Applied*, *3*, 257–287.

Chapter 8

Collaboration Load

Pierre Dillenbourg and Mireille Bétrancourt[1]

Introduction

This chapter addresses the notion of complexity in collaborative learning, especially computer-supported collaborative learning (CSCL). Collaborative learning may simply be the joint use of learning materials such as textbooks or drill-and-practice software. However, due to its socio-constructivist roots, CSCL research often addresses group learning in complex environments. Most empirical studies that investigate collaborative problem solving CSCL environments include a problem space and a social interaction space such as chat, forums and argumentation tools. The problem space can be a computerized environment such as a microworld, a simulation or an alternative such as paper readings, field trips or a physical experiment. Hence, learning in a CSCL environment adds to the complexity of computer-based constructivist environments with the complexity of computer-mediated communication. While these two spaces have often been computationally separated (two different windows on the screen), recent CSCL environments integrate them computationally, for instance, by relating utterances to task objects (Zahn, Barquero, & Schwan, 2004).

The interaction with any computerized learning environment imposes an additional cognitive load, especially at the beginning of its use, as proposed by Sweller (this volume, Chapter 1) and de Jong (this volume, Chapter 6) and others. In CSCL, this 'computer interaction' related load is combined with the 'social interaction' load or collaborative load (that is, the need to manage interactions with the other group members). On one hand, this increased load may interfere negatively with learning processes, consuming some of the individuals' cognitive resources. On the other hand, it may be beneficial to learning: Cognitive load increases in-group learning because additional cognitive mechanisms are triggered by collaborative interactions. Those mechanisms (e.g., explanation, argumentation) may generate the learning effects that are expected in collaborative situations. In

[1]The studies partly reported here were conducted with P. Jermann, N. Nova, C. Rebetez, M. Sangin, D. Traum, T. Wherle, J. Goslin and Y. Bourquin. They were partly funded by two grants from the Swiss National Science Foundation.

other words, collaboration load has advantages and drawbacks. The question of collaboration load is a particular instance of a trade-off that exists in any learning situation; there is no learning without some cognitive load, but there is no learning with too much cognitive load either. In light of the latter, this contribution begins with a short review of this trade-off as it has been investigated in learning in general (see section on Cognitive Load and Learning).

The question of collaboration load and its effect on learning has been largely unexplored. We do not report on results of empirical studies that were specifically targeted to measure collaboration load, instead this paper addresses three main questions.

1. What constitutes collaboration load? Which mechanisms triggered during collaborative learning more often than during individual learning contribute to increase cognitive load? Is it the need to verbalize one's own thoughts? Is it the effort to understand one's teammates and, more globally, to construct a shared understanding of the task at hand? Is it the need to maintain some kind of representation of a partner's goals, knowledge and actions? While collaboration enables division of labour does it decrease cognitive load? Some of the factors that come into play when estimating cognitive load will be disentangled in the section on what constitutes cognitive load.
2. Do CSCL environments influence collaboration load? Different media have an impact on the cost factors. Which interface features and tool functionalities increase or decrease the different costs factors (verbalization, grounding, modelling, …)? Reviewing all the features of human–computer interaction that have an effect on collaboration load would be beyond the scope of this paper. However, some tool features (e.g., persistency of information, mutual awareness) that were revealed by empirical studies conducted with CSCL environments will be illustrated. These studies were not designed for measuring collaboration load, but nonetheless provide insights on this topic.
3. What are the implications for CSCL designers? Collaboration load is not an intrinsic feature of CSCL environments but depends on specific features of the CSCL environments. Based on this insight, some properties that designers may use to 'tune' the collaboration load induced by a specific environment will be described.

We are unable to provide definite answers to any of the questions above. This contribution does, however, explore these questions, disentangle factors and raise sub-questions that could initiate further research in this arena.

Cognitive Load and Learning

Students use the same brain when they learn alone or in groups. For these reasons, our analysis of cognitive load in collaborative learning is first situated within a more general debate on the cognitive load involved in learning.

For many years, there has been a discrepancy between the psychological and the educational perspective on the cognitive load factors in a learning task. Since the dawn of the constructivist approach in the 1960s, educational scientists have believed that conceptual learning occurs only if the learning task requires learners to engage in intensive cognitive processes. Conceptual learning, also known as 'deep learning', is characterized by the transformation of a learner's cognitive structures in a way that the acquired knowledge, procedures or schemata could be used in other situations or domains (De Corte, 2003). In contrast, surface learning, or rote memorization, enables the learner to apply the learned schema only to similar situations. Whereas exercises to improve surface learning are quite well known and used in educational situations, methods that improve conceptual learning are still under experimental investigation. Learning at a conceptual level means tremendous changes in the learners' cognitive schemes or conceptions. Learning tasks and practices that engage learners in rich and complex interactions with the learning environment, such as inquiry learning or discovery learning, have been shown to be situations in which deep learning can occur (Schnotz, Vosniadou, & Carretero, 1999). Yet, collaborative learning belongs to the pedagogical practices that generate a rather heavy cognitive load.

Some psychologists claim that learning can only occur if the cognitive resources required to process a learning task are maintained below a 'reasonable' level such as the current view of the cognitive system as described in Baddeley's model (Baddeley, 1997, 2000). In this view, the cognitive system consists of two processing components: a long-term memory (LTM) in which knowledge is stored permanently and a working memory that processes the information sent by the perceptual system on the basis of the knowledge stored in LTM. Many experimental results confirmed the assumption that working memory is limited in capacity (Baddeley, 1997; Cowan, 2001). The consequences of cognitive processing limitations on learning have been formalized and extensively investigated by the tenets of Cognitive Load Theory (Paas, Renkl, & Sweller, 2004; Sweller, 1988). According to the Cognitive Load Theory, deep learning is described as the acquisition of cognitive schemata that enable categorizing the problem, choosing the correct procedures to apply and regulating problem solving. The construction of such schemata is cognitively demanding. Consequently, the processing of the learning task itself competes with the construction of cognitive schemata if the learning task is too demanding. A large body of research has investigated the effect of the format of instruction on learning. For example, it was demonstrated that multimedia instructional materials in which mutually referring verbal and graphic information are displayed separately on the page are detrimental to learning compared to material in which graphic and verbal information is spatially integrated (Sweller, Chandler, Tierney, & Cooper, 1990). According to the authors, the separated display forced learners to repeatedly shift their attention from one source to the other and thus increased the cognitive resources that should be dedicated to mentally integrating the two sources of information. The cognitive overload induced by the 'split-attention effect' would explain the learning impairment. Principles for designing effective instructional material have been derived from this research and are still the object of thorough investigation (Mayer & Moreno, 2002; Sweller, 2003).

Expertise can tremendously increase the processing capacities of working memory (Ericsson & Kintsch, 1995). When dealing with new elements that have not been previously learned, there is no schema in LTM that can indicate how the elements should be processed and all the burden falls on the working memory. Conversely, for well-learned material and activity, schemas stored in LTM control the coordination and the combination of elements, allowing huge amounts of information to be processed in working memory (Sweller, 2003). As a consequence, some instructional guidelines that have been proven effective for novice learners are not applicable for more advanced learners. For example,

Kalyuga, Chandler, and Sweller (2000) showed that the modality effect, according to which it is better to present verbal information in auditory mode when the material also involves graphical information, could be reverted by expertise. While novice learners benefited more from the audio-visual material compared with the visual-only material, this advantage disappeared after a few training sessions. As expertise increased, a visual-only presentation was superior to an audio-visual presentation, particularly when the text information was removed (graphic presentation only). Guidance provided by text information was necessary for novices but was redundant for experts who had a schema available to process the material.

Intrinsic and Extrinsic Load

Current developments in Cognitive Load Theory consider two sources of load when learners have to process instructional material in order to achieve a learning task (Paas et al., 2004; Sweller, 2003):

– Intrinsic load refers to the load required to process the instructional task. It is related to the complexity of the content itself and particularly to the degree of interactivity between elements, which impacts the number of elements that must be held in working memory simultaneously;
– Extrinsic load refers to two sub-categories of load:
  – Germane load promotes the construction of the cognitive schema, which is the ultimate goal of deep learning;
  – Extraneous load refers to the additional load that is influenced by the format of instruction (material presentation or structure of the learning task) and that does not contribute to learning.

Deep learning can occur only if cognitive resources are sufficient to cover the processing requirements. In other words, cognitive overload may explain why some learning situations fail to induce deep learning. Extraneous load should therefore be reduced to a minimum through adequate presentation formats and learning tasks.

These educational and psychological views on cognitive load in learning seem contradictory; educational scientists aim to design cognitively demanding learning tasks, psychologists seek to minimize the cognitive resources engaged in the learning task. The 'goal-free effect' (Sweller, van Merriënboer, & Paas, 1998) is an excellent example of this tension; deep learning is improved when learners are not provided with the final goal but only with intermediate goals. While this seems contradictory to the self-monitored approach that claims that explicitly stating learning objectives increases learning outcomes (Tourneur, 1975), the two perspectives may not be as contradictory as they appear at first sight. First, the notion of germane load, recently taken into consideration by the cognitive load model, acknowledges that cognitive load can be beneficial to learning, provided that this load is allocated to the construction of cognitive schemata rather than to the processing of extraneous information. In subjective workload assessment instruments such as the NASA Task Load index (TLX; Hart & Staveland, 1988) or the Subjective Workload Assessment Technique (SWAT; Reid & Nygren, 1988), cognitive load refers not only to the cognitive effort but also to frustration and stress. Effort is not always painful or unpleasant. Effort can be an excellent motivator to proceed, as the sensation of 'flow' in game situations and can be turned to a learning motor. In computer supported learning, microworlds and discovery-based learning environments do sometimes create a level of motivation that sustains a positive learning experience despite a very high cognitive load (Rieber, 1996).

Measurement of Cognitive Load

As useful as it can be to provide instructional guidelines, the cognitive load model raises difficulties regarding its assessment. In most studies, cognitive load is assessed by self-reporting indicators and as a relative measure to distinguish between conditions. Gerjets, Sheiter, and Catrambone (2004) used a self-reporting scale adapted from the NASA-TLX to investigate the processing of multimedia instructional materials. They found no clues in the cognitive load estimation to understand the results. More complex indicators, based on both subjective evaluation and performance (scores, time) were identified to constitute a reliable estimate of the mental efficiency of instructional methods (Paas, Tuovinen, Tabbers, & van Gerven, 2003; Rubio, Diaz, Martin, & Puente, 2004). Physiological measures (e.g., heartrate, electro-dermal reactions, pupil dilatation, blinking, neuro-imaging techniques) can be regarded as more direct evidence for cognitive load, but they are difficult, if not impossible, to apply in ecological learning situations. Less indirect than learning outcomes or subjective evaluation, but easier to handle in a deep-learning situation, the dual-task paradigm has scarcely been used in instructional studies (Brünken, Steinbacher, Plass, & Leutner, 2002), The dual-task methodology consists of measuring how reaction times to a secondary task vary over different treatment conditions in the primary task. The dual-task paradigm can effectively distinguish between load in different sensory modalities (auditory vs. spatial, e.g., Brünken, Plaas, & Leutner, 2004) or processing modes (verbal vs. visual, e.g., Gyselink, Ehrlich, Cornoldi, de Beni, & Dubois, 2000). However, the methodological challenge remains to design 'pure' secondary tasks: spatial tasks often involving visual processing and conversely. With neuro-imaging techniques on monkeys, Koch (2004) showed that when a spatial task is performed, even if it does not involve visual perception (e.g., spatial localization in the dark), visual areas in the brain are activated. Verbal material may involve auditory load by way of the auditory loop even when presented in written mode. As a consequence, the effect of instructional formats on secondary tasks may be confusing and does not necessarily address well-established findings in instructional design (Brünken et al., 2004). Finally, one should keep in mind that the maximal-cognitive load varies across people, time and context. Working memory-processing capacity depends on the level of expertise (Ericsson & Kintsch, 1995), individual ability (Gyselink et al., 2000), metacognitive processes (Valcke, 2002) and level of involvement in the task. It is therefore difficult to discriminate between a cognitive load level that is manageable and beneficial to learning and the overload level that is detrimental to learning.

In addition to methodological difficulty, a more fundamental issue is being able to measure the desired variable. In subjective evaluation, do the students express workload or cognitive load? Workload is the student's perception of his or her amount of work. It is quite different from the cognitive load that refers to the limited capacity of working memory. Actually, these two concepts are easily differentiated at the theoretical level, but more difficult to dissociate at the empirical level. As discussed earlier, measures of cognitive load in instructional design studies often involve self-evaluation scales or questionnaires. In this case, we wonder if students are able to distinctively perceive their workload and their cognitive load, as will be explored later on. Further, no method to date permits identifying the 'nature' of the cognitive load that is being measured. How can we identify extraneous cognitive load as a separate entity from germane cognitive load?

Minimal vs. Optimal Collaborative Load?

The notion of collaborative effort has been addressed in the study of dialogue. Clark and Wilkes-Gibbs (1986) analysed the effort necessary for two people to understand each other. They stressed that what is important is not individual effort by the receiver of a communicative act, but the overall 'least collaborative effort'. Thereby, they mean that the cost of producing a perfect utterance may be higher than the cost of repairing the problems that arise. For instance, subjects are less careful about adapting utterances to their partner when they know they can provide feedback on their understanding (Schober, 1993).

The notion of least effort fits with the economy of discussion in everyday life situations, when partners naturally minimize efforts to reach mutual understanding. This also holds for two students who have to work together. However, studies of collaborative learning reveal that collaboration leads to learning if peers are engaged in intensive interactions such as argumentation or explanation. What produces learning is the 'effort after shared meaning' (Schwartz, 1995). For instance CSCL designers deliberately form pairs with conflicting opinions, because this conflict-solving situation will require peers to produce a higher effort to build a shared solution. In other words, we face the same argument on the status of cognitive load in learning in groups as in learning individually.

We hence need to discriminate between the positive and negative effects of cognitive load, the latter being implicit in the term 'overload'. Misunderstandings increase the effort of knowledge elicitation and may hence be positive for learning. In contrast, too many misunderstandings would of course spoil collaboration. We therefore use the notion of *optimal collaborative effort* (Dillenbourg, Traum, & Schneider, 1996) that is the equivalent of the notion of 'germane load': The interactions that enable students to co-construct knowledge are not effortless; they require some effort. For instance, Webb (1991) discriminated two levels of elaboration in explanations: the low elaborated explanations were not predictive of learning gains while elaborated explanations, which have a higher cost, led to learning gains. The goal of the CSCL designer is to tune this collaboration load within an acceptable range, i.e., above a floor threshold below which too few cognitive processes are triggered but below a ceiling threshold (overload) above which collaboration becomes painful or unmanageable. Any collaboration load that goes beyond the optimal collaborative effort, makes collaboration unnecessarily difficult, and could be associated to extraneous cognitive load.

What Constitutes Collaboration Load?

We now attempt to disentangle the different factors that impact on collaboration load. First, we address the load reduction that may be produced by the division of labour and then we review mechanisms that increase cognitive load: the verbalization of thoughts, the construction of a shared understanding and the maintenance of a representation of the other team members. The ideal collaborative learning situation would minimize extraneous load (by load reduction mechanisms) and generate germane load through rich social interactions.

The Benefits of Division of Labour

The benefits of division of labour have been illustrated in situations where the task regulation could be performed by a subject other than the one carrying out the task operations. Even though group members act together on a task, one partner often takes responsibility for the low-level aspects of the task while the other focuses on strategic aspects (Miyake, 1986). Blaye, Light, Joiner, and Sheldon (1991) showed that this mutual regulation was progressively internalized as self-regulation skills. The division between cognitive and metacognitive layers of the task may lead to an individual offload; the cognitive load of mutual regulation (A does the task and B monitors A) can be hypothesized to be lower than the cognitive load of self-regulation (A does the task plus A regulates A).

Some pedagogical methods for group learning use division of labour for reducing cognitive load. When students have to learn about complex issues, a common collaborative script is to ask them to adopt controversial roles. For instance, student A plays the role of an engineer who designs a new product, while B is a financial manager and C is the lawyer. Each student has to handle his or her own set of arguments, detecting when they are relevant. If one student would have to conduct the same reasoning individually, he/she would need to handle multiple sets of arguments, i.e., checking for each argument produced if there is an existing counter-argument. This recursive self-refutation process is expected to induce a higher cognitive load than mutual argumentation.

This task/meta division occurs in collaborative sessions rather than in cooperative settings: When team members split the task into independent subtasks, it does not change the cognitive load, but only the workload. If, instead of writing a full report, I have to write half of it, the cognitive load of writing a sentence at a given time remains the same, what changes is the time I will spend on the whole report.

In order to measure the increase/decrease of cognitive load in collaborative situations, we compared the level of cognitive load in a learning task concerning individuals and pairs (Rebetez, Sangin, Bétrancourt, Dillenbourg, 2004). Pairs reported a lower cognitive effort than individuals. The students were asked to study some multimedia material together; a situation that afforded no division of labour. The explanation of the perception of a lower load has to be explained by a lower workload or by other factors. One may be the 'social facilitation effect' (Michaels, Blommel, Brocato, Linkous, & Rowe, 1982), which explains performance increases by the mere presence of others, despite any interaction. Social facilitation may impact on the subjective feeling of effort but not on the very notion of cognitive load.

The Cost of Verbalization

Even if our own reasoning is structured by language, turning ideas into sentences consists of an additional process that is not free of charge. Verbalizing one's thoughts requires a metacognitive activity that can be harmful to the task performance particularly for procedural and automatic tasks. Biemiller and Meichenbaum (1992) showed that students who found a task cognitively demanding had few resources left for following their 'think aloud' instructions. Verbalization implies reflective mechanisms (being aware of one's own knowledge) plus giving voice to internal reasoning. Pure verbalization is cognitively demanding because of the necessity to apply discourse linearization processes (Levelt, 1989). For instance, during a highly automated task, verbalization induces a cognitive overload that is perceptible through pauses, hesitations and slowing down of the task achievement (Hoc & Leplat, 1983). In addition, it has been shown that thinking-aloud methods, often used in expertise modelling and usability studies, change the task itself. Verbalization during the course of action induces more planning than when the action is performed regularly (Ericsson & Simon, 1980).

Since verbalization induces some cognitive load, it raises the same argument described above. Is it beneficial or detrimental to learning? Webb (1989, 1991) found that the effects of verbalization depend on the degree of elaboration of the explanation produced during collaborative learning. This effect may be related to the 'self-explanation-effect', which refers to learners learning more from examples when they are asked to explain these examples to themselves (Chi, Bassok, Lewis, Reimann, & Glaser, 1989). The learning situation typically entailed both declarative and procedural knowledge that the learner should acquire in order to be capable of solving application and transfer problems. Using a thinking-aloud protocol, the studies showed that the difference between good and poor learners could be explained by quantitative and qualitative differences in the explanation produced. For example, not only did good learners produce more self-explanations during examples studying, but they also tried to find out how each piece of information was derived from the other. The self-explanation effect is not due to a simple externalization process but rather to deep cognitive processing, consisting of drawing inferences from the example and the conceptual knowledge already acquired (Van Lehn, Jones, & Chi, 1992). These cognitive effects of explanations do not come for free, they reflect intense cognitive processing and the load necessary to construct an explanation. Since collaborative learning induces, although not systematically, the need to explain to each other usually in order to make joint decisions, one can infer that at least the same load as self-explanation is incurred.

The Cost of Grounding

Dialogue is of course more than verbalization. The construction of a mutual understanding or grounding (Clark & Brennan, 1991) requires additional mechanisms; when *A* tells something to *B*, *B* listens and interprets what *A* says, *A* monitors what *B* has understood what *A* meant while *B* provides *A* with some cues of his (or her) understanding (i.e., backchannel). *A* may repair his/her utterances on the basis of this backchannel or *A* may tailor his/her utterances to what he/she expects *B* to understand (audience design). This formal analysis of dialogue seems to indicate a huge cognitive load, much higher than what we experience in daily conversations. Actually, we use a range of default reasoning mechanisms (e.g., *A* agrees with me unless he/she explicitly disagrees) that reduces the cognitive load of everyday dialogue. We nonetheless experience this load in specific situations where communication is made difficult by the channel (e.g., bad phone conversation), the content (a complex domain), a difference of referential background (e.g., cultural differences), etc.

Among the different sub-processes of grounding, let us focus on the process of tailoring utterances to the receiver. Mechanisms of 'audience design' (Lockridge & Brennan, 2002) are salient, for instance, if one compares explaining how to reach an address to a foreigner vs. to somebody who knows the city well. Horton and Gerrig (2005) explored the memory demands induced by the 'audience design' mechanisms. Their experiment shows that audience design was more likely to occur in conditions where the subjects received some help for remembering what the listener had seen before. In other words, audience design contributes to cognitive load.

One could expect that explaining to somebody else generates a higher cognitive load (and hence higher learning outcomes) than self-explanation since explaining to someone else requires both the mechanisms of audience design and of constructing an explanation (self-explanation). We explored this hypothesis with different levels of interactivity in the explanation process (no listener, silent listener, interactive listener), but we found no clear evidence that explaining to someone is more or less effective than self-explanation (Ploetzner, Dillenbourg, Praier, & Traum, 1999). Does it mean that there is no pure self-explanation? Put more directly, any self-explanation experiment actually includes a listener. Although the experimenter does not directly interact with the subject, the subject knows that the experiment will listen to the recording later on. Conversely, does the absence of clear effects mean that the additional cognitive mechanisms involved in dialogue (but not in self-explanation) are not cognitively demanding enough? It is only for the sake of disentangling mechanisms that we dissociated the effort that A makes to be understood by B and the effort that B makes to understand A; mutual understanding is of course a joint effort where both the emitter and listener contribute. The process of constructing a shared understanding is referred to in psycholinguistics as the grounding process. Clark and Brennan (1991) studied how the cost of grounding varies from one medium to another, where the concept of 'cost' covers both cognitive load and physical workload. They discriminate several sub-costs: the production costs refer to the effort for articulating or typing the message; the formulation costs refer to how easy is it to decide exactly what to say; the reception costs are concerned with the effort necessary for listening to or reading the message, including attention and waiting time; the understanding costs are those necessary for interpreting the message in context; the start-up costs refer to how partners initiate a conversation; the delay costs are those necessary for making the receiver wait during formulation. This set of factors also includes the asynchrony costs (for instance, not being able to tell what is being responded to), the speaker change costs, the fault costs and the repair costs. Each of these factors varies with the medium, not only globally (e.g., chat vs. voice) but also in a very specific way (two different chat systems may vary the costs). A study by Dillenbourg and Traum (in press) (see below) provides more details on the cost of grounding across different media.

The sum of these costs corresponds to the global effort required to build a shared understanding. For instance, in a remote audio-conferencing environment, the lack of visual cues requires devoting more attention to turn taking than in face-to-face conversation. Another example is that, in face-to-face dialogue, misunderstandings can be detected even before an utterance is completed by the emitter, while in chat environments, the receiver does not see the utterance until it is completed and sent. Computer-mediated communication may induce high costs. The relationship between these costs and cognitive load is not simple. Some of these costs may slow down dialogue or increase the physical load, but not necessarily increase the cognitive load. Nevertheless, taken together, these costs increase the complexity of the learning task for novice users who have to simultaneously learn the domain and the communication environment (Hron & Friedrich, 2003). This extraneous load concerns not only the usability of the tool but also the acquisition of specific conversation rules. For instance, chat users will learn that adding "[…]" at the end of a turn means that the message will continue in the next turn ('delay costs').

Common sense tells us that these extrinsic costs will quickly decrease as learners become familiar with the system. This is only true if the system is used on a regular basis. Actually, most empirical research on complex CSCL environments consists of short duration experiments in which this decrease cannot be rigorously assessed. Most long-term experiments tend to use more standard environments, such as forums.

Finally, some of the factors that increase extraneous load may not be detrimental for some learning tasks. For instance, the time one apparently wastes typing sentences in web-based forums is also a time that can be used for reflection. Learners benefit from having more time to reflect on their answers. In other words, any equation such as "the closer to face-to-face, the lower the cognitive load" would fail to account for the very adaptive nature of humans and the cognitive off-load generated by some software features (Dillenbourg, 2005).

The Cost of Modelling

The construction of a shared understanding requires that each partner build some representation of the other partners' beliefs, knowledge or goals. We refer to this process as *mutual modelling*, a facet of intersubjectivity (Bromme, 2000; Wertsch, 1985). By using the term 'model', we do not intend to imply this is a detailed or explicit representation of the partner. Simply stated, if *A* wants to (dis-)agree with *B*, *A* needs some representation of *B*'s position; if *A* wants to repair *B*'s misunderstanding, *A* needs some representation of what *B* understood. Mutual modelling is, like the grounding process, very functional with its degree of precision dependant on the task. For instance, the gourding criterion is extremely high when two pilots are discussing the track where their aircraft should land, but is much lower if they are chatting about the last party they went to.

This mutual model is not constructed in a vacuum but is based on initial representations. Common grounds are initialized by the assumptions people make about their partners from cues such as their community membership (age, culture, profession, ...) and from co-presence (e.g., common grounds include any event A and B attended together) (Clark & Marshall, 1981). Several scholars studied how this initial model imparts on communication, namely because it can easily be manipulated. For instance, Slugoski, Lalljee, Lamb, and Ginsburg (1993) told some participants that their partners (played by an experimenter) received the same information as the participants themselves and told other participants that their partners received a different piece of information. They observed that the participants adapted their explanation to their partners by focusing on items that this fake partner was supposed to ignore. The mutual modelling part can be seen as the diagnosis part (or 'communality assessment' — Horton & Gerrig, 2005) of the audience design process; *A* needs some information about *B* to tailor his/her explanation to *B*. Similarly, Brennan (1991) showed that the participants used different initial strategies in forming queries depending on who they were told their partner was. Other simpler inference mechanisms such as default reasoning rules (e.g., *B* agrees with me unless he disagrees) are developed according to the conversational context.

In summary, the need for modelling a peer's knowledge ranges from global clichés to detailed information. Subsequently, the mechanisms for modelling range from default assumptions to elaborated inferences. Hence, the cognitive load and the benefits of the mutual modelling process will be very different in various collaborative contexts. We nonetheless hypothesize that when triggered, the mechanisms for monitoring how one's partner understands the task contribute to deepening one's own understanding. Mutual modelling is some kind of "thinking in stereo", that looks at the knowledge from two different angles.

Do Computerized Environments Influence Collaboration Load?

We did not conduct studies that specifically aimed at measuring collaboration load. However, over the last years, we carried out experiments on CSCL environments that provided us with some preliminary elements for understanding collaboration load.

Cumulating Load from Learning Material and Collaboration

This research project originated from a study of Schnotz, Böckeler and Gzrondziel (1999) who found evidence for the collaboration load assumption. In the first experiment, individual learners had to study a hypertext explaining time zones on earth with either interactive and animated graphics (simulations) or static graphics. They found that learners studying individually with the interactive graphics performed better than learners studying with static graphics when answering factual questions, but not when answering comprehension questions. One hypothesis was that learners with the animated graphics condition looked at the simulation passively, whereas learners with the static graphics condition mentally performed the time zone simulation. The tendency of subjects to 'underprocess' animated learning content has been found in other studies and is referred to as the 'underwhelming' effect of animated graphics (Lowe, 2004). In a second experiment, learners were grouped in pairs to study the same instructional material. Pairs learning with the animated material had poorer performance to both kinds of questions than pairs with the static graphics condition. According to Schnotz et al. (1999), learners in pairs did not benefit from the simulation because they had to allocate cognitive resources to co-ordinate their learning with the peer, in addition to process the visual display. The authors inferred that the sum of the load induced by visually complex graphics and the load involved by managing the collaboration could lead to cognitive overload and hence impair the learning process. As complementary evidence for this explanation, the subjects reported that they had less peace to think deeply in the collaborative condition. However, because the two studies were distinct experiments, no direct statistical comparison was possible between the individual and collaborative situations regarding performance.

An alternative explanation of Schnotz et al. (1999) results is that pairs could not benefit from the dynamic graphics since they could not base their shared understanding on a stable graphic representation. Since animations display rapid and transient information, they do not provide external support to the referring objects. Deictic gestures are key mechanisms in the construction of common grounds. By inhibiting them, animated pictures might also inhibit the most interesting interactions of collaborative learning, leaving pairs with only the drawbacks. Since the persistency of representation is essential for grounding (see next section), displaying permanent static snapshots of the critical steps of the animation while it is running would be a good way to ensure persistency of the depiction in addition to the dynamic visualization of the phenomenon.

We carried out an experiment to investigate this hypothesis, using a factorial design with three factors: visualization (static or animated); permanence (presence of static snapshots or not); and learning situation (individual or collaborative) (Rebetez et al., 2004). The participants had to study two animations explaining astronomic and geologic phenomena. In all conditions, then they had to answer retention and transfer questions individually. Retention questions involved recalling information that was provided in the instructional material whereas transfer questions required learners to draw inferences from the material by mentally simulating the phenomenon. Describing our results in a detailed way goes beyond the scope of this chapter. However we found three interesting results that pertain to the notion of collaboration load.

First, in the individual situation, the animated visualization improved performance compared with static graphics for retention questions only, with no differences found on transfer questions. In contrast, in the collaborative situation the animated visualization was beneficial both for retention and transfer questions, compared with static graphics. Second, a series of five scales adapted from the NASA-TLX was used as a self-reporting measure of cognitive load (cognitive effort, time pressure, mental demand, performance satisfaction and frustration). Learners in pairs reported significantly less cognitive effort than learners in individual situations. The other scales pertaining to cognitive load followed the same trend but not significantly (see Figure 8.1). In other words, not only did pairs have better performance than individual learners but they also evaluated their cognitive load as lower than individual learners. These two results contradict Schnotz's et al. (1999) 'collaboration load' hypothesis.

Our third main result is also intriguing. When static snapshots were provided alongside the graphics, performance increased for individuals but decreased for pairs. This is surprising since these snapshots aimed at supporting grounding mechanisms during group discussions. Our tentative explanation is that this condition produced a "split-interaction effect". This effect appears when collaborative learning is impaired by interference between the two concurrent modes of interaction; on the one hand, the interactions between the users and the system, and on the other hand, the interactions among users. These results are even more surprising if one considers that the difference of interactivity between the two conditions was limited to being allowed to view snapshots or not and that those who were allowed to do so, did not do it very frequently. Actually, the observed effects are not as much due to a lack of cognitive resources as to a split-attention effect between interacting with the simulation and interacting with the peer.

This hypothesis relies on recent results (Wilson & Peruch, 2002) indicating that the users' focus of attention is more influential on learning achievement than users' physical interaction with the material. In two first experiments, the authors compared learners who actively explored a virtual spatial environment to learners who just looked at someone exploring for them. Surprisingly, results showed that active and passive learners were not

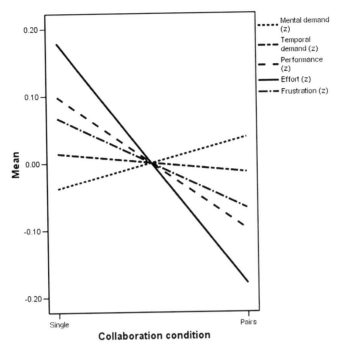

Figure 8.1: Self-reported five-scale measure of cognitive load in pairs (right) and individual (left) learning situations (using Z scores for the sake of comparison).

systematically different regarding their learning of the environment (including navigation measures). In a third experiment, Wilson and Peruch (2002) added instructions for active and passive learners: In one condition, learners were told to pay attention to objects in the environment and in another condition, they were told to pay attention to the spatial layout. Again the active or passive factor did not yield any consistent difference, but the instructions had a significant effect on the remembering of objects or layout accordingly. The authors proposed that cognitive interactivity is determined by the focus of attention and is not heavily affected by behavioral interactivity. This might explain why, in our study, the snapshots caused a split-interaction effect in the collaborative condition even if learners did not interact heavily with the device. The snapshots would have attracted learners' attention, creating cognitive interactivity, which affected their processing even though there was hardly any physical interaction.

Grounding across Different Media

A second study (Dillenbourg & Traum, in press) revealed that the medium features that influence collaboration load are not those one initially expects. For instance, studies showed that collaborating with a video-conferencing system is not necessarily more effective than with an audio-conferencing system. A chat (synchronous text-based communication) enforcing turn taking rules and similar to face-to-face meetings is not more effective than a chat with its idiosyncratic turn taking habits, etc. (Dillenbourg, 2005). The reported study aimed at analysing the grounding mechanisms in a multimodal collaborative environment (Dillenbourg & Traum, in press). Twenty pairs of participants had to solve an enigma problem using a chat and a whiteboard (drawing software that allows joint construction and editing of graphical representations). We estimated the grounding effort by counting the rate of acknowledgement, i.e., the ratio between the number of acknowledged interactions and the total number of interactions. In typed interactions, peers acknowledged 41% of the utterances of their partners, on average. The rate for the spoken conversation pairs, however, was 90%. This comparison is slightly awkward since the acknowledgement rate is dependent on the way speech is segmented into utterances. Nevertheless, this difference tells us something about the cost of grounding in a chat environment. Because this cost is high, subjects are selective about the type of information that justifies a grounding act. This difference of acknowledgement concerns the physical workload (the time and effort for typing) rather than the cognitive load (the resources used to acknowledge). Two other findings are more relevant for the appraisal of collaboration load.

First, the rate of acknowledgement was 26% for information that subjects simply retrieved from the game and transmitted to each other (hereafter 'facts'), for instance "Hans is the barman", while the rate of acknowledgement was 46% for the information they inferred from the situations (hereafter 'inferences') such as "Hans had a motive to kill Lisa". Syntactically, a sentence such as "Hans is the barman" is identical to "Hans is the killer". What is different is the role of such a sentence in the joint problem solving process, namely the probability of disagreement. Inferences such as "X has a good reason to kill" are personal interpretations of facts and hence more likely to be points of disagreement. If the acknowledgement rate of such utterances varies, it implies that grounding is sensitive to the status of these utterances within the problem-solving process. These findings contribute discriminating the grounding mechanisms at the utterance level and grounding at the knowledge level (Dillenbourg & Traum, in press). In terms of collaboration load, the latter matters more than the former. The cognitive load necessary to remember what the partner knows, what he agreed upon or what he might disagree with — the process of mutual modelling — has already been discussed. In a sentence such as "He is really suspicious", the mutual modelling required for grounding at the utterance level (what does my partner refers to by "He"?) is less demanding than the mutual modelling required for grounding at the knowledge level (What does he mean by "really suspicious"?).

Second, we expected the whiteboard to be used to clarify the participants' verbal interactions in the chat, in the same way we draw a schema on a napkin for explaining what we mean. This experiment revealed the opposite relationship; the whiteboard was the central place of interaction, and the chat interactions were mostly accessory to it. The chat was mostly used to ground short notes posted on the whiteboard and to discuss non-persistent information, namely the strategy (e.g., "let's do this now"). The whiteboard was used for gathering all important information and for organizing it (namely, structuring information by suspects and discarding suspects proved to be innocent) (see Figure 8.2). In other words, the pairs jointly maintained a representation of the state of the problem on the whiteboard. The whiteboard was used as (external) working memory, i.e., the place to store a (shared) representation of the problem state. As the notion of cognitive load is intrinsically related to the limits of our working memory, the notion of collaboration load should

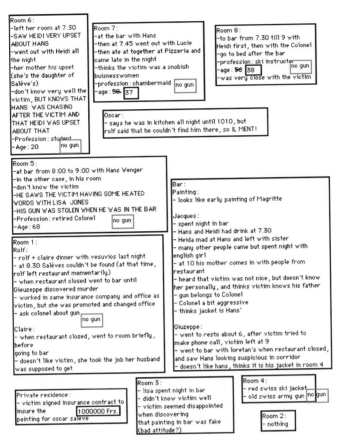

Figure 8.2: Group working memory: Constructing shared and persistent representation of the problem state.

be related to the capacity of maintaining this shared-working memory. However, the effect of such external-working memory on individual cognitive load is complex; it is not because pairs share a physical representation of the problem state that they do not also build a mental representation that remains subject to the limitations of working memory. This relationship between external group memories and collaboration is further discussed in the conclusion.

Supporting Mutual Modelling

This third study was directed at investigating mutual modelling mechanisms. The collaborative task was a game called SpaceMiners (Figure 8.3) (Nova, Wehrle, Goslin, Bourquin, & Dillenbourg, 2003). This 3D game involves two players in space missions where they have to launch drones in order to collect asteroids full of minerals and bring them to space stations. The drones' direction is modified by the planet's gravity and by some objects that the teams drop in space. The teams' task is to collect the largest amount of minerals located in asteroids and to bring them to the space station on the left.

We measured mutual modelling by interrupting group activity at 3 pre-defined points in time and by asking them to select from a list what they would do next and what they think their partner would do next. The accuracy of mutual modelling was estimated by the overlap between what *A* says (s)he will do and what *B* says *A* will do (hereafter MM-rate). We manipulated the degree of mutual modelling by using the availability of so-called awareness tools (Gutwin & Greenberg, 1998) as the independent variable. These tools are software components that inform users, within multi-users environments, of what the other users are doing, where they are located, what they are looking at, and so forth. The awareness tools implemented in SpaceMiners informed *A* about what *B* was looking at and where *B* was going to set some objects.

The awareness tools led to higher group performance, which is consistent with previous findings (Gutwin & Greenberg, 1998), but did not improve the accuracy of the mutual model; pairs with the awareness tools did not obtain a higher MM-rate than pairs without awareness tools. However, a two-way analysis of variance conducted on contrasted groups (post-hoc split) showed that pairs in the awareness condition who spent more time using the awareness tools reached higher levels of mutual modelling than the others.

A fourth study led to contradictory results (Nova, Girardin, & Dillenbourg, in press). Teams of 3 subjects had to walk across our university campus in order to find a virtual object. Each of them carried a laptop (a tablet PC) displaying a map of the campus, their own position and a proximity sensor (telling them how far the object to be found is). In the first condition, the subjects had an awareness tool; they could see the position of their teammates on the map. In the second condition, they had no awareness tool. In both conditions, they could also draw annotations on the map. The performance of the groups (the length of the path of each group member before finding the object) was equivalent in both conditions. We measured mutual modelling by asking the subjects to draw their own path and the path of their partners on a paper map of the campus. The groups without the awareness tool drew more accurate paths than the groups with the awareness tool. The explanation is that the lack of the awareness tool led them to draw more annotations on the map, annotations that constituted a more explicit act of mutual information.

In summary, the awareness tool partly off-loaded groups with the burden of mutual modelling, which led to more accurate and to less accurate mutual models in the third and fourth studies, respectively. These results illustrate our earlier discussion on the relationship between learning outcomes and cognitive/collaboration load and our notion of 'optimal collaborative effort'. Reducing load is not always more effective; some collaborative load is part of the natural mechanisms that makes collaboration produce learning.

How Can CSCL Designers Tune Collaboration Load?

These four studies show that there is no intrinsic cognitive load to collaborative situations in general because there are many ways of collaborating, multiplied by many ways for supporting collaboration in computerized environments. The cognitive load depends on the nature of the task, on the composition of the group, on the features of CSCL environments and on the interactions among these three factors. Hence, the key issue is how to design a CSCL environment in a way that increases or decreases extraneous collaboration load. Research in human–computer interaction has devoted a lot of attention to the cognitive load induced by any interface. We do not address these general issues of interface design here, but focus on factors that specifically concern the cognitive load of CSCL environments. Empirical studies have not yet provided us with a set of rules that designers should apply. Instead, we describe the design space, i.e., the features that designers should consider when thinking in terms of collaboration load.

– As mentioned earlier, CSCL environments vary by the extent to which each team member is informed of what the others are doing. The design of shared editors was based on the WYSIWIS principle: What you see is what I see; all group users have the same view (Stefik, Bobrow, Foster, Lanning, & Tatar, 1987). This principle must be relaxed when the group includes many members or when the task is so complex that group members have to work on different parts of the task. In these cases, users need different views. In order to sustain group coordination, designers created 'awareness tools' (Gutwin & Greenberg, 1998), that were already addressed in the chapter. A key question in the design of environments for collaborative problem solving is: Which elements of information should be provided by the awareness tools in order to decrease extraneous collaboration load but without inhibiting the mutual modelling process that is necessary for learning? This question is similar to the one a teacher asks when he decides that his students could use their pocket calculators in order to off-load some parts of the computation while not affecting notions they are supposed to learn.

– Another feature of CSCL environments that we mentioned earlier is the persistency of display; jointly constructed schemata, when they are persistent, partly off-load memory by providing group members with a shared representation of the problem state. This is not basically different from face-to-face collaborative settings where group members draw a schema on paper or construct an artefact together. However, an interesting difference is that a shared representation contains its own history. Some environments may colour objects according to the author or will fade out colours with time. Other environments enable the user to 'undo' a certain number of recent changes or even to scroll back in the history of previous problem states. This history results from a combination of automatic and explicit "save as" recordings. We have no empirical data regarding how much this history off-loads the metacognitive processes of the team (perceiving their own strategy, identifying loops, errors, …) but it certainly extends the group memory.

– Many CSCL environments record the history of interactions, which is another instance of the persistency principle. This history may be a flat list of interactions as in a chat environment, a WIKI or a blog. It may reflect the structure of conversation as in "threaded" environments (Reyes & Tchounikine, 2003) or even the rhetorical structure of the argument (as in Belvedere — Suthers et al., 2001). The interface reifies the dialogue to the group members themselves. It can be argued that the LTM off-load generated by an interaction history may indeed increase working memory load. Searching through a long list of messages is intensive. However, all chat users know how useful it is to scroll up a few lines to clarify an utterance. We saw in the experiment mentioned on grounding that even novice chat users were able to participate in multiple parallel synchronous conversations because the tool partly off-loads the need to memorize the conversational context for each interlocutor. In a CSCL environment, the communication among team members becomes a substance that both the system and team members may process. One research direction is to improve the analysis of this substance by the system (Barros & Verdejo, 2000; Constantino-González, Suthers, & Icaza, 2001; Inaba & Okamoto, 1996). Another research direction is to provide group members with some graphical representation of their interaction histories and let them interpret these representations. We refer to these representations as *group mirrors* (Dillenbourg et al., 2002; Jermann, 2004; Zumbach, Mühlenbrock, Jansen, Reimann, & Hoppe, 2002). Jermann (2004) investigated the hypothesis that these mirrors would off-load the process of self-regulation. The task given to the pairs was to tune the lights of several crossroads to optimize the flow of cars through a city. In the first set of experiments, he observed that the most effective pairs were those who discussed their options before tuning the lights. In such a dynamic system, a simple approach by trial-and-error leads to low performance. Therefore, this information was encompassed into a group mirror i.e., a software component that provides users with the ratio between their number of interactions and their number of actions (see Figure 8.3). Experiments show that pairs do interact differently when provided with this feedback, although this difference does not lead to higher group performance. The question here is whether the cognitive load reduction provided by the external regulation is higher than the new cognitive load induced by reading and interpreting the group mirror.

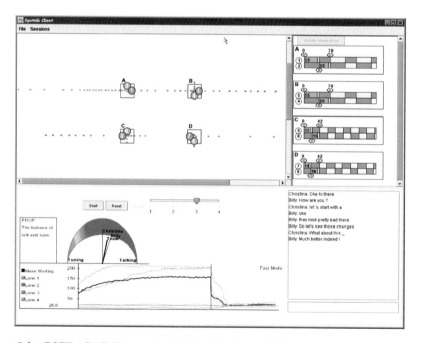

Figure 8.3: COTRAS (Collaborative Traffic Simulator). The group mirror is the red-green meter with 3 arrows, one for each user and one for the group (Jermann, 2004).

– Another feature of a CSCL environment is the use of semi-structured communication interfaces, as illustrated in Figure 8.4, which is usually a text-based communication tool embedded into a series of interface items (Baker & Lund; 1996; Soller, 2002; Suthers et al., 2001; Veerman & Treasure-Jones, 1999). These tools partly off-load the physical load of typing utterances by offering predefined speech act buttons (e.g., "I agree"). The purpose of these interfaces overall is to favour the emergence of specific interaction patterns. This may also support the grounding mechanisms by making explicit which utterance is being acknowledged, which object is being referred to or which type of speech act is being uttered (Reyes & Tchounikine, 2003). Do these tools off-load the students working memory? This is certainly not the case at the beginning. Dialogue moves are usually performed in an implicit way. Forcing students to express their next dialogue move constitutes another example that increases cognitive load, which is didactically suitable but may nevertheless be detrimental to collaborative learning.

The features we listed refer mainly to software tools. Another trend in CSCL research concerns the design and experimentation of 'scripts'. *A collaboration script* (Aronson, Blaney, Sikes, Stephan, & Snapp, 1978; O'Donnell & Dansereau, 1992) is a set of instructions prescribing how the group members should interact, how they should collaborate and/or how they should solve the problem. The collaboration process is not left open but structured as a sequence of phases. Each phase corresponds to a specific task where group members have a specific role to play. A well-known script is the 'reciprocal teaching'

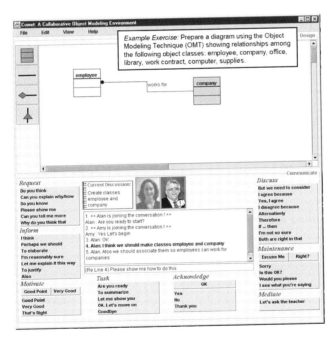

Figure 8.4: Example of semi-structured interface; buttons in the bottom part offer pre-defined communication acts and sentence openers (Soller, 2002).

approach set up by Palincsar and Brown (1984). One peer reads a paragraph of text and the other questions him/her about his/her understanding. The roles are shifted for the next paragraph. We developed and investigated several scripts (Dillenbourg & Jermann, in press), such as the ArgueGraph scripts aimed at raising conflict solving interactions among group members or the ConceptGrid script, a JIGSAW-like script, aimed at triggering explanations. Do scripts increase or decrease collaboration load? Any script has to be "played", i.e., the student has to remember what, when, how to do, etc., which increases the load. However, some scripts may reduce cognitive load since they reduce the need for mutual modelling; when roles are clearly defined, the learner may play his or her role and spend less energy for a close coordination with other roles. Actually, the scripts we designed deliberately increase the collaboration load. In order to trigger argumentation, the ArgueGraph script forms pairs with student having conflicting opinions, i.e., it increases the effort necessary to reach consensus. The ConceptGrid script provides groups of four students with four different subsets of knowledge, thereby increasing the explanation effort they have to engage in to build a concept grid. Scripts are ways for designers to tune the collaboration load.

Conclusion: Group Cognitive Load

The discussion so far focused on the load that collaboration imposes on individuals. A distributed cognition theories (Pea, 1993; Hutchins, 1995; Salomon, 1993) perspective would be to consider the cognitive load for the group as a whole. This alternative was briefly mentioned in section on 'Cognitive Load and Learning' when we discussed that at jointly constructed representations play the group level the role that working memory plays at the individual level; maintaining and updating representations of the state of the problem. This distributed cognition viewpoint also concerns the mutual modelling process. It may be the case that team members do not build a representation of their partners' mental states but instead a representation of the interaction process at the group level. Instead of modelling who knows what, who does what, who said what, the team members could maintain a representation of what the team knows, did or said. We refer to this as the *group model* instead of the mutual model.

These two visions of teams, as collections of individuals or as larger units, have been opposed for the sake of argument, but the real challenge is to understand how they articulate with each other. Let us take a simple example; a knot in my handkerchief to remind me to buy bread is expected to off-load my memory. Actually, the situation is slightly more complex; I still have to remember that this knot means "buy bread". In our study, peers co-constructed a visual and physical representation of the task that included information beyond the capacity of working memory. However, they still needed, in order to take decisions, some mental representations of this external representation (e.g., a guy with a red cross meant "this person is not guilty" for many teams). We know that information may stay in the working memory for longer periods by using an articulatory loop (repeating it) or using knowledge structures in LTM (Ericsson & Kintsch, 1995). It may be that the shared visual representation plays a similar role, providing group members with a continuous reactivation of the elements to be maintained in working memory.

The notion of memory at the group level is different from the notion of working memory of individuals. It has a physical counterpart (usually some artefact), it has a larger capacity and it is more visual than audible. In other words, group memory could be conceived as the equivalent, at the group scale, of the concept of long-term working memory at the individual scale. It extends individual and collective cognitive capacities by offloading, organizing and updating information available to the group. In this context, collaboration load could be defined as the effort engaged in by team members to co-construct a long-term working memory by incrementally grounding the role of each piece of information with respect to the problem solving process.

Acknowledgements

The author thanks Gaëlle Molinari and the anonymous chapter reviewers for their help in shaping this chapter.

References

Aronson, E., Blaney, N., Sikes, J., Stephan, G., & Snapp, M. (1978). *The jigsaw classroom*. Beverly Hills, CA: Sage.

Baddeley, A. (1997). *Human memory: Theory and practice*. London: Erlbaum.

Baddeley, A. (2000). The episodic buffer: A new component of working memory? *Trends in Cognitive Sciences, 4*, 417–423.

Baker, M. J., & Lund, K. (1996). Flexibly structuring the interaction in a CSCL environment. In: P. Brna, A. Paiva, & J. Self (Eds), Proceedings of the European conference on artificial intelligence in education, Lisbon, Portugal (pp. 401–407), September–October.

Barros, B., & Verdejo, F. (2000). Analysing student interaction processes in order to improve collaboration: The DEGREE approach. *Journal of Artificial Intelligence in Education, 11*, 211–241.

Biemiller, A., & Meichenbaum, D. (1992). The nature and nurture of the self-directed learner. *Educational Leadership, 50*(2), 75–80.

Blaye, A., Light, P., Joiner, R., & Sheldon, S. (1991). Collaboration as a facilitator of planning and problem solving on a computer based task. *British Journal of Psychology, 9*, 471–483.

Brennan, S. E. (1991). Conversation with and through computers. *User Modeling and User-Adapted Interaction, 1*, 67–86.

Bromme, R. (2000). Beyond one's own perspective: The psychology of cognitive interdisciplinarity. In: P. Weingart, & N. Stehr (Eds), *Practicing interdisciplinarity* (pp. 115–133). Toronto: Toronto University Press.

Brünken, R., Plass, J. L., & Leutner, D. (2004). Assessment of cognitive load in mutlimedia learning with dual-task methodology: Auditory load and modality effect. *Instructional Science, 32*, 115–132.

Brünken, R., Steinbacher, S., Plass, J. L., & Leutner, D. (2002). Assessment of cognitive load in multimedia learning using dual-task methodology. *Experimental Psychology, 49*, 1–12.

Chi, M. T. H., Bassok, M., Lewis, M. W., Reimann, P., & Glaser, R. (1989). Self-explanations: How students study and use examples in learning to solve problems. *Cognitive Science, 13*, 145–182.

Clark, H. H., & Brennan S. E. (1991). Grounding in communication. In: L. Resnick, J. Levine, & S. Teasley (Eds), *Perspectives on socially shared cognition* (pp. 127–149). Hyattsville, MD: American Psychological Association.

Clark, H. H., & Marshall, C. R. (1981). Definite reference and mutual knowledge. In: A. K. Joshi, B. L. Webber, & I. A. Sag (Eds), *Elements of discourse understanding* (pp. 10–63). Cambridge: Cambridge University Press.

Clark, H. H., & Wilkes-Gibbs, D. (1986). Referring as a collaborative process. *Cognition, 22*, 1–39.

Constantino-Gonzáles, M. A., Suthers, D., & Icaza, J. (2001). Designing and evaluating a collaboration coach: Knowledge and reasoning. In: J. D. Moore, C. L. Redfield, & W. L. Johnson (Eds), *Artificial intelligence in education: AI-ED in the wired and wireless future*, 10th international conference on artificial intelligence in education. Amsterdam: IOS Press (pp. 176–187).

Cowan, N. (2001). The magical number 4 in short-term memory: A reconsideration of mental storage capacity. *Behavioral and Brain Sciences, 24*, 87–114.

De Corte, E. (2003). Designing learning environment that foster the productive use of acquired knowledge and skills. In: E. De Corte, L. Verschaffel, N. Entwistle, & J. van Merriënboer (Eds), *Unravelling basic components and dimensions of powerful learning environments* (pp. 21–33). Amsterdam: Pergamon.

Dillenbourg, P. (2005). Designing biases that augment socio-cognitive interactions. In: R. Bromme, F. Hesse, & H. Spada (Eds), *Barriers and biases in computer-mediated knowledge communication and how they may be overcome* (Computer-Supported Collaborative Learning Series, pp. 243–264). Dordrecht, NL: Kluwer.

Dillenbourg, P., & Jermann, P. (in press). SWISH: A model for designing CSCL scripts. In: F. Fischer, H. Mandl, J. Haake, & I. Kollar (Eds), *Scripting computer-supported collaborative learning – Cognitive, computational, and educational perspectives* (Computer-Supported Collaborative Learning Series). Dordrecht, NL: Kluwer

Dillenbourg, P., Ott, D., Wehrle, T., Bourquin, Y., Jermann, P., Corti, D., & Salo, P. (2002). The socio-cognitive functions of community mirrors. In: F. Flückiger, C. Jutz, P. Schulz, & L. Cantoni (Eds), *Proceedings of the 4th international conference on new educational environments*, Lugano, May.

Dillenbourg, P., & Traum, D. (in press). The complementarity of a whiteboard and a chat in building a shared solution. *Journal of Learning Sciences.*

Dillenbourg, P., Traum, D., & Schneider D. (1996). Grounding in multi-modal task oriented collaboration. In: *Proceedings of the European conference on artificial intelligence in education* (pp. 415–425). Lisbon, Portugal, September.

Ericsson, K. A., & Kintsch, W. (1995). Long-term working memory. *Psychological Review, 102,* 211–245.

Ericsson, K. A., & Simon, H. A. (1980). Verbal reports as data. *Psychological Review, 87,* 215–251.

Gerjets, P., Scheiter, K., & Catrambone, R. (2004). Designing instructional examples to reduce intrinsic cognitive load: Molar versus modular presentation of solution procedures. *Instructional Science, 32,* 33–58.

Gutwin, C., & Greenberg, S. (1998). *The effects of workspace awareness on the usability of real-time distributed groupware.* Research Report 98-632-23. Department of Computer Science, University of Calgary, Alberta, Canada.

Gyselink, V., Ehrlich, M.-F., Cornoldi, C., de Beni R., & Dubois, V. (2000). Visuospatial working memory in learning from multimedia systems. *Journal of Computer Assisted Learning, 16,* 166–176.

Hart, S. G., & Staveland, L. E. (1988). Development of NASA-TLX (task load index): Results of experimental and theoretical research. In: P. A. Hancock, & N. Meshkati (Eds), *Human mental workload* (pp. 139–183). Amsterdam: North Holland.

Hoc, J. M., & Leplat, J. (1983). Evolution of different modalities of verbalization. *International Journal of Man–Machine Studies, 19,* 283–306.

Horton, W. S., & Gerrig, R. J. (2005). The impact of memory demands on audience design during language production. *Cognition, 96,* 127–142.

Hron, A., & Friedrich, H. F. (2003). A review of web-based collaborative learning: Factors beyond technology. *Journal of Computer Assisted Learning, 19,* 70–79.

Hutchins, E. (1995). How a cockpit remembers its speeds. *Cognitive Science, 19,* 265–288.

Inaba, A., & Okamoto, T. (1996). Development of the intelligent discussion support system for collaborative learning. *Proceedings of Ed-Telecom'96,* Boston (pp. 494–503), June.

Jermann, P. (2004). *Computer support for interaction regulation in collaborative problem-solving.* Unpublished doctoral thesis. Faculté de Psychologie et des Sciences de l'Éducation de l'Université de Genève, Switzerland.

Kalyuga, S., Chandler, P., & Sweller, J. (2000). Incorporating learner experience into the design of multimedia instruction. *Journal of Educational Psychology, 92,* 126–136.

Koch, C. (2004). *The quest for consciousness: a neurobiological approach.* Englewood, CO: Roberts & Company.

Levelt, J. M. W. (1989). *Speaking: From intention to articulation.* Cambridge, MA: The MIT Press.

Lockridge C. B., & Brennan, S. E. (2002). Addressees' needs influence speakers' early syntactic choices. *Psychonomic Bulletin & Review, 9,* 550–557.

Lowe, R. K. (2004). Interrogation of a dynamic visualization during learning. *Learning and Instruction, 14,* 257–274.

Mayer, R. E., & Moreno, R. (2002). Aids to computer-based multimedia learning. *Learning and Instruction, 12,* 107–119.

Michaels, J. W., Blommel, J. M., Brocato, R. M., Linkous, R. A., & Rowe, J. S. (1982). Social facilitation and inhibition in a natural setting. *Replications in Social Psychology, 2,* 21–24.

Miyake, N. (1986). Constructive interaction and the iterative process of understanding. *Cognitive Science, 10,* 151–177.

Nova, N., Girardin, F., & Dillenbourg, P. (2005). 'Location is not enough!': An empirical study of location-awareness in mobile collaboration. *Proceedings of the third IEEE International Workshop on Wireless and Mobile Technologies in Education,* November 28–30, 2005 (pp. 21–28). Tokushima, Japan. IEEE Press: Los Alamitos, California.

Nova N., Wehrle, T., Goslin, J., Bourquin, Y., & Dillenbourg, P. (2003). The impacts of awareness tools on mutual modelling in a collaborative video-game. *Proceedings of the 9th international workshop on groupware,* Autrans, France, September.

O'Donnell, A. M., & Dansereau, D. F. (1992). Scripted cooperation in student dyads: A method for analyzing and enhancing academic learning and performance. In: R. Hertz-Lazarowitz, & N. Miller (Eds), *Interaction in cooperative groups: The theoretical anatomy of group learning* (pp. 120–141). London: Cambridge University Press.

Paas, F., Renkl, A., & Sweller, J. (Eds). (2004). *Advances in cognitive load theory: Methodology and instructional design. Instructional Science, 32*(Special issue).

Paas, F., Tuovinen, J. E., Tabbers, H., & Van Gerven, P. W. M. (2003). Cognitive load measurement as a means to advance cognitive load theory. *Educational Psychologist, 38*(1), 63–71.

Palincsar, A. S., & Brown A. L. (1984). Reciprocal teaching of comprehension-fostering and comprehension-monitoring activities. *Cognition and Instruction, 1,* 117–175.

Pea, R. (1993). Practices of distributed intelligence and designs for education. In: G. Salomon (Ed.), *Distributed cognitions. Psychological and educational considerations* (pp. 47–87). Cambridge, UK: Cambridge University Press.

Ploetzner, R., Dillenbourg P., Praier M., & Traum D. (1999). Learning by explaining to oneself and to others. In: P. Dillenbourg (Ed.), *Collaborative-learning: Cognitive and computational approaches* (pp. 103–121). Oxford: Elsevier.

Rebetez, C., Sangin, M., Bétrancourt, M., & Dillenbourg, P. (2004). Effects of collaboration in the context of learning from animations, *Proceedings of the EARLI SIG meeting on comprehension of texts and graphics: Basic and applied issues,* Valencia, Spain (pp. 187–192), September.

Reid, G. B., & Nygren, T. E. (1988). The subjective workload assessment technique: A scaling procedure for measuring mental workload. In: P. A. Hancock, & N. Meshkati (Eds), *Human mental workload* (pp. 185–218). Amsterdam: North Holland.

Reyes, P., & Tchounikine, P. (2003). Supporting emergence of threaded learning conversations through augmenting interactional and sequantial coherence. *International conference on computer supported collaborative learning* (CSCL, best Ph.D. student paper award), Bergen, Norway, pp. 83–92.

Rieber, L. P. (1996). Seriously considering play: Designing interactive learning environments based on the blending of microworlds, simulations, and games. *Educational Technology Research & Development, 44,* 43–58.

Rubio, S., Diaz, E., Martin, J., & Puente, J. M. (2004). Evaluation of subjective mental workload: A comparison of SWAT, NASA TLX and Workload Profile methods. *Applied Psychology: An International Review, 53,* 61–86.

Salomon, G. (1993). No distribution without individual's cognition: A dynamic interactional view. In: G. Salomon (Ed.), *Distributed cognitions. Psychological and educational considerations* (pp. 111–138). Cambridge, MA: Cambridge University Press.

Schober, M. F. (1993). Spatial perspective-taking in conversation. *Cognition, 47,* 1–24.

Schnotz, W., Böckeler, J., & Grzondziel, H. (1999). Individual and co-operative learning with interactive animated pictures. *European Journal of Psychology of Education, 14,* 245–265.

Schnotz, W., Vosniadou, S., & Carretero, M. (Eds) (1999). *New perspectives on conceptual change.* Oxford: Elsevier.

Schwartz, D. L. (1995). The emergence of abstract dyad representations in dyad problem solving. *The Journal of the Learning Sciences, 4,* 321–354.

Slugoski, B. R., Lalljee, M., Lamb, R., & Ginsburg, G. P. (1993). Attribution in conversational context: Effect of mutual knowledge on explanation giving. *European Journal of Social Psychology, 23,* 219–238.

Soller, A. (2002). Computational analysis of knowledge sharing in collaborative distance learning. Unpublished doctoral dissertation, University of Pittsburgh, PA.

Stefik, M., Bobrow, D, G., Foster, G., Lanning, S., & Tatar, D. (1987). WYSIWIS Revised: Early experiences with multiuser interfaces. *ACM Transactions on Office Information Systems, 5,* 147–167.

Suthers, D., Connelly, J., Lesgold, A., Paolucci, M., Toth, E., Toth, J., & Weiner, A. (2001). Representational and advisory guidance for students learning scientific inquiry. In: K. D. Forbus, & P. J. Feltovich (Eds), *Smart machines in education: The coming revolution in educational technology* (pp. 7–35). Menlo Park, CA: AAAI/The M.I.T. Press.

Sweller, J. (1988). Cognitive load during problem solving: Effects on learning. *Cognitive Science, 12,* 257–285.

Sweller, J. (2003). Evolution of human cognitive architecture. In: B. H. Ross (Ed.), *The psychology of learning and motivation* (Vol. 43, pp. 215–266). New York: Academic Press.

Sweller, J., Chandler, P., Tierney, P., & Cooper, M. (1990). Cognitive load and selective attention as factors in the structuring of technical material. *Journal of Experimental Psychology: General, 119,* 176–192.

Sweller, J., van Merriënboer, J. J. G., & Paas, F. (1998). Cognitive architecture and instructional design. *Educational Psychology Review, 10,* 251–295.

Tourneur, Y. (1975). *Recherche en éducation: effets des objectifs dans l'apprentissage.* Direction Générale de l'Organisation de L'Enseignement, Bruxelles, Belgique.

Valcke, M. (2002). Cognitive load: Updating the theory? *Learning and Instruction, 12,* 147–154.

Van Lehn, K., Jones, R. M., & Chi, M. T. H. (1992). A model of the self-explanation effect. *Journal of the Learning Sciences, 2,* 1–59.

Veerman, A. L., & Treasure-Jones, T. (1999). Software for problem solving through collaborative argumentation. In: P. Poirier, & J. Andriessen (Eds), *Foundations of argumentative test processing* (pp. 203–230). Amsterdam: Amsterdam University Press.

Webb, N. M. (1989). Peer interaction and learning in small groups. *International Journal of Educational Research, 13,* 21–40.

Webb, N. M. (1991). Task related verbal interaction and mathematical learning in small groups. *Research in Mathematics Education, 22,* 366–389.

Wertsch, J. V. (1985). Adult–child interaction as a source of self-regulation in children. In: S. R. Yussen (Ed.), *The growth of reflection in children* (pp. 69–97). Madison, WI: Academic Press.

Wilson, P.N., & Peruch, P. (2002). The influence of interactivity and attention on spatial learning in a desktop virtual environment. *Current Psychology of Cognition, 21,* 601–633.

Zahn, C., Barquero, B., & Schwan, S. (2004). Learning with hyperlinked videos – design criteria and efficient strategies of using audiovisual hypermedia. *Learning and Instruction, 14,* 275–291.

Zumbach, J., Mühlenbrock, M., Jansen, M., Reimann, P., & Hoppe, H. U. (2002). Multi-dimensional tracking in virtual learning teams: An exploratory study. In: G. Stahl (Ed.), *Computer support for collaborative learning: Foundations for a CSCL community* (pp. 650–651). Mahwah, NJ: Erlbaum.

Chapter 9

Balancing Support for Student Learning

Jan D. Vermunt

Introduction

Contemporary learning environments tend to be complex for many learners (Elen & Clark, this volume, Introduction). Dealing with authentic tasks that call for active and self-regulated learning poses demands on learners, which are far more demanding than in past decades. However, since these tasks and forms of learning are typical for what students encounter after they graduate from school, it is argued that current instructional methods prepare students better for lifelong learning and working than traditional methods (Bolhuis, 2003).

In contemporary conceptions of teaching, the quality of student learning is emphasised. This is especially the case in educational research and practice in the Netherlands, but also in many other European countries (e.g., Lonka & Lindblom-Ylänne, 1996; Entwistle, McCune, & Hounsell, 2003). One reason for this change is epistemological in nature: the quality of knowledge gained by active knowledge construction is supposed to be better (more accessible, coherent, usable) than knowledge acquired by the passive intake of knowledge (Lowyck & Elen, 1993; Simons, Van der Linden, & Duffy, 2000). A second reason is societal in nature: frequent changes in work, technology, and society make it more necessary than before for people to keep acquiring new knowledge after their school career. It is obvious that they should learn at school the knowledge and skills needed for this lifelong process of learning (Boekaerts, 1997).

From an epistemological perspective, it is important that teaching is aimed at fostering learning processes characterised by active knowledge construction. From a societal point of view, it is important that education takes care that students learn to self-initiate such types of learning. In this way, students acquire a disposition to keep acquiring new knowledge actively and independently after their formal education has ended. Learning to learn has increasingly become a major educational goal. This calls for teaching theories and instructional design models that are specifically aimed at promoting complex learning-to-learn processes in students.

Handling Complexity in Learning Environments: Theory and Research
Copyright © 2006 by Elsevier Ltd.
All rights of reproduction in any form reserved.
ISBN: 0-08-044986-7

In this chapter a crucial question is addressed: how to provide support in order to help students cope with complexity? First, a theoretical model on balancing support for various forms of student learning will be presented. Empirical research pertaining to the model will be discussed. The case of secondary school reform in the Netherlands will then be discussed in relation to the model. Finally, implications for theory, practice, and further research will be inferred.

A Model of Balancing Support to Student Learning

Learning and Teaching Functions

An important question addressed in previous research within the knowledge-construction tradition was about the nature of the learning activities that students use to construct their knowledge. A review of the literature (Vermunt & Verloop, 1999) indicated that, in general, three types of these learning and thinking activities were discerned: cognitive, affective, and regulative activities (see, for example, Wagner & McCombs, 1995). In a series of empirical studies, both qualitative and quantitative in nature, Vermunt (1996, 1998) investigated how students employed these activities during their normal studying behaviour, and how the use of these activities was related to internal and external sources of control. The results indicated that three main cognitive processing strategies could be discerned: (a) a deep processing strategy that combines the learning activities 'relating', 'structuring', and 'critical processing'; (b) a stepwise processing strategy, consisting of the learning activities 'analysing' and 'memorising'; and (c) a concrete processing strategy, with 'concretising' and 'applying' as major learning activities. With regard to regulation strategies, it was found that the distinguishing dimension was internal versus external control of learning processes. Three main strategies were also consistently observed with respect to control: (a) a self-regulated strategy, in which the students perform most regulation activities themselves; (b) an externally regulated strategy, in which students let their learning process be regulated by teachers, books, etc.; and (c) lack of regulation, manifested when students are unable to regulate their learning processes themselves, and experience insufficient support of external regulation as provided by teachers and the learning environment in general (Vermunt, 1996, 1998).

The use of these processing and regulation strategies was consistently associated with students' conceptions of learning and their learning orientations. Vermunt and Vermetten (2004) use the term 'learning pattern' as a superordinate concept in which the cognitive and affective processing of subject matter, the metacognitive regulation of learning, conceptions of learning, and learning orientations are united. In several studies (e.g., Vermunt, 1998; Boyle, Duffy, & Dunleavy, 2003), four such patterns were found: undirected, reproduction-directed, meaning-directed, and application-directed learning. Research conducted by Vermetten, Vermunt, and Lodewijks (1999) showed that learning patterns are not immutable and that their development can be influenced by instructional features.

Categories that are very similar to those found in the literature on learning activities show up in the literature on teaching activities. For example, Rosenshine and Stevens (1986) give the following examples of good teaching activities: explaining relationships within the subject matter, giving examples, planning the learning process, monitoring students' progress, and motivating students. It seems that learning and teaching activities can be described with the same terms (Shuell, 1996; Simons, 1997). Hence, one can speak of *teaching/learning functions*. Shuell (1996) uses the term *learning functions* to refer to the functions that need to be fulfiled for high-quality learning to take place and that can be executed either by the learner or by the teacher. These learning functions can be divided into processing, affective, and regulation functions; a feature that parallels the distinction between cognitive, affective, and metacognitive (regulative) learning activities. *Teaching functions* refer to those functions, which promote high-quality student learning. The processing functions of teaching concern presenting and clarifying the subject matter. The affective functions refer to creating and maintaining a positive motivational and emotional climate for learners. The regulation functions are aimed at steering students' learning processes. Different teaching strategies can be distinguished based on their influence on the thinking activities students use to learn. They can be placed on a dimensional axis ranging from strongly externally regulated to shared regulation to loosely externally regulated (see also Biggs, 1996). Strong external regulation means taking over learning and thinking activities from students, shared regulation means activating those activities, and loose external regulation means capitalising on the same learning and thinking activities. In the case of loose external regulation, the need for student-regulation of learning is high. These teaching strategies, or more general instructional strategies, constitute different levels of external regulation, and therefore also of the degree of control students are expected to exert over their own learning.

The Interplay between Self-Regulation and External Regulation of Learning

Teaching and learning strategies are not always compatible. Between students' self-regulation and teachers' external regulation of learning processes, complex interplays may take place. *Congruence* occurs when students' learning strategies and teachers' teaching strategies are compatible; *friction* occurs when this is not the case. From the viewpoint of influence on the learning and thinking activities students employ, *constructive and destructive* frictions may be discerned. Constructive frictions represent a challenge for students to increase their skill in learning or thinking strategies. These may be necessary to make students willing to change and to stimulate them to develop skill in the use of learning and thinking activities they are not inclined to use on their own. Destructive frictions may cause a decrease in learning or thinking skills. Here, existing learning and thinking skills are not called upon or potential skills are not developed. The outcomes of congruence are denoted as mathemagenic effects. Destructive friction results in interference phenomena, also called mathemathantic effects (Lohman, 1986; Clark, 1990; Janssen, 1996). These occur when a teaching strategy has negative effects on students' learning process or learning outcomes, or if teaching gives rise to, or maintains, misconceptions (e.g., Schoenfeld, 1988).

As is the case with external regulation of learning processes, the degree of self-regulation of learning of which students are capable can be represented by a continuum ranging from very little to very high, with all intermediate positions possible. For the same reason of clarity that made us single out three positions on the teacher-regulation continuum, we will discuss three positions on the self-regulation continuum. The first is that students master a learning activity well and use it skilfully and on their own initiative (high degree of self-regulation). In the second case, students master a learning activity only to a limited extent, or they master it well but do not use it spontaneously, in the right situations or sufficiently skillfully in the subject domain (intermediate degree). In the last case, they neither master nor use a particular learning activity (low degree).

In Table 9.1, possible interactions between self-regulation and external regulation of learning processes are presented. On the diagonal, there is congruence between these two modes of control. For example, if students are not able to regulate their own learning and the teacher does it for them, teaching and learning strategies are balanced for that moment. The majority of cells, six out of nine, represent friction between teaching and learning. Some of these are destructive in nature; for example, when students who are capable of self-regulated learning have a teacher who prescribes the way they should learn in detail. Others are constructive, in the sense that they challenge students to try new ways of learning and thinking.

The scheme depicted in Table 9.1 can be understood at various levels of specificity. At a general level, 'degree of self-regulation of learning' signifies students' general capability to self-regulate their learning processes. This refers to their skill in employing the total set of learning activities. At a more specific level, it refers to students' skill in a particular learning strategy, represented by a subset of learning activities. For example, students may be good at the self-regulated use of relating, structuring, and critical processing activities (deep processing strategy), but far less skilled in concretising and applying activities (concrete processing strategy). At the most specific level, the scheme may refer to students' skill in the self-regulated use of one particular learning activity, e.g., 'planning', or 'selecting', or 'motivating'.

Strong External Regulation

Under strong external regulation, the instructional agent (teacher, book, course materials, computer, etc.) conducts the learning activities and so there is little stimulation for students to engage in these activities themselves. An example would be that the teacher explains all similarities and differences between two theories, models, or practical experiences, so that students do not have to search for these relations themselves. If the teacher utilises a strong teacher-regulated form of instruction, congruence between learning and teaching occurs when students do not master a particular learning activity. This is the case, for instance,

Table 9.1: Interplay between three levels of external regulation and three levels of self-regulation of learning processes.

Degree of self-regulation of learning	Degree of external regulation of learning		
	Strong	Shared	Loose
High	Destructive friction	Destructive friction	Congruence
Intermediate	Destructive friction	Congruence	Constructive friction
Low	Congruence	Constructive friction	Destructive friction

when students are not looking for relations within the subject matter and the teacher explains these relations, or when students are not motivated and the teacher employs strategies to enhance their motivation.

Friction between a strongly controlling teaching strategy and students' learning strategies may be expected to occur when students master and use a learning strategy well (Hamaker, 1986). This is the case, for example, if students are capable of self-regulating their learning process in a particular domain but the teacher or textbook prescribes in detail what, how, and in what order the student should learn. In this case, a decrease in the learning or thinking skill may take place for the students, which is caused by a lack of application. Clark (1990), for example, traced studies in which ineffective instruction actually interfered with learning. On the basis of a review of these studies, he concluded that these mathemathantic effects occur when the instructional agent tries to take over learning strategies from students and when this agent tries to impose system control over student control, in those cases in which students are able to perform these functions themselves. Entwistle (1992) also warns against the interfering effects of taking over too many learning activities from students. For example, according to Entwistle, detailed handouts that are assumed to foster student learning may instead cause dependence. Students begin to think that reproducing the information as provided by the teacher is all that is expected of them. Lindblom-Ylänne (1999) found that many medical students, who studied in a traditional curriculum, doubted whether that type of curriculum was suited to become a competent doctor. They felt that the traditional learning environment forced them into a reproductive way of studying that did not suit them, which led to many doubts among these students about whether to continue their studies.

Friction also occurs with this teaching strategy when students master a learning activity to an intermediate extent. In this case, students are hindered in further developing their skill. This is the case, for example, when students who are in the process of developing skill in self-diagnostic regulation activities enter a learning environment in which these diagnostic functions are taken over by the teacher. Shuell (1996) warns that care should be taken to prevent students from becoming dependent on the instructional strategies employed by the teacher for learning new material and skills. Both types of frictions are of a destructive nature (see Table 9.1).

The most common form of traditional teaching is one in which strong external regulation is dominant. This type of teaching prevailed in many secondary schools in the Netherlands. In this instructional model, the subject matter is determined mainly by instructional agents (government agencies, parents, school officials, and teachers), and it is explained and clarified in lectures. Sometimes there is individual or small group work in which the subject matter is deepened, problems are clarified, feedback on assignments is given, etc. Frequently, there are test periods in which the subjects of the past period are assessed. The subject matter, learning objectives, study resources, criteria for the learning outcomes, assessment, and feedback are all not in the hands of the students, but in the hands of the instructional agents. Students only choose their approaches to studying (see Vermunt, 2003).

In summary, a strong external regulation strategy may be necessary if students are unable to employ particular learning activities that are important for the material to be learned. If a student fails to see the relations between two theories and the teacher or textbook explains these relations, the student learns these relations and experiences a gain in knowledge. If the teacher continues substituting this learning function, however, students are not stimulated to develop their expertise in self-regulated use of the learning activity. There is no gain in the skill of employing the learning activity for self-regulated knowledge construction. If, however, the teacher not only explains the relations between two theories, but also explains how he or she came to see those relations, or shows the act of 'relating' the theories *in vivo* by thinking aloud, this substituting strategy may well serve a modelling function.

Shared Regulation

Under shared regulation, the instructional agent stimulates students to conduct a certain learning activity themselves. For example, a teacher can give students the assignment of thinking about relations between two theories, models, or practical experiences themselves.

When the teacher uses a shared-regulation form of instruction, congruence between learning and teaching occurs when the students master a learning activity to an intermediate degree. An example of this is that students do not process the subject matter critically on their own initiative, but are nevertheless stimulated by a group discussion to draw their own conclusions and to form personal judgments (Lonka & Ahola, 1995).

In this shared-control strategy, constructive friction will take place if students do not master learning or thinking activities in the subject domain at hand. For example, the teacher asks the students to think of examples, while they are not used to doing so. These constructive frictions represent situations in which students are unable to use a particular learning activity independently, but are able to do so with the guidance of an expert. Lindblom-Ylänne (1999), for example, describes the transition from a traditional to a more activating, process-oriented curriculum in the Faculty of Psychology at the University of Helsinki. Many students experienced a friction between the way of studying they were used to and the more self-regulated way of studying that was expected from them in the new curriculum. The changes were not so abrupt, however, that students gave up. Most of them realised that later in their studies and professional life this independence was also expected from them, and they developed their way of learning to be more self-regulated.

Destructive friction may be expected if students master learning or thinking activities well and use them spontaneously in the right situations. One can imagine that students who are capable of the self-regulated use of particular learning activities get irritated and off-balance if the teacher continually stimulates them to employ these learning activities (e.g., Lohman, 1986). This is a situation, however, that is quite common in higher education. For example, in higher vocational education, students' learning styles are often application-directed in nature. This means that learning activities like concretising and applying are learner-initiated: students do not have to be stimulated to think about the applicability of what they learn. However, many teachers in higher vocational education have an application-oriented way of teaching: they give many tasks, questions, and assignments in which students are asked for possible examples and applications of what they learn. It seems superfluous to stimulate students to employ learning activities they use on their own initiative. In these situations, other learning activities, like structuring concepts, relating theories, critical processing of ideas, are often excluded from the learning process: students do not use them on their own initiative, and teachers do not stimulate students to use them.

An example of a teaching method in which shared regulation is dominant is problem-based learning (PBL). In PBL, students work at trying to understand and explain problems in small groups of about 10 persons (the tutorial group). The starting point for the learning process is a problem: a short description of a phenomenon about which students should acquire knowledge. The problem-based way of working is systematically structured into seven steps, the 'seven jump' (Bouhuijs & Gijselaers, 1993): (1) clarifying terms and concepts that are not readily understood; (2) defining the problem; (3) analysing the problem; (4) summarising the various explanations of the problem into a coherent model; (5) formulating learning objectives; (6) individual study activities outside the group; and (7) report and synthesise the newly acquired information. In the tutorial group, students analyse the problem and formulate learning objectives: questions to which they should find an answer through individual study. After a period of individual study, the students meet again and report what they have learned about the problem. Unclear matters are then clarified and the acquired information is discussed, critically evaluated, and integrated. During their work in the tutorial group, the students are guided by a tutor, whose main task is to facilitate the learning and group processes (Barrows & Tamblyn, 1980; Schmidt & Moust, 1998). Tutorial groups meet twice weekly for sessions of two hours. During the first hour of such a meeting, students try to understand and explain the problem discussed previously and report what they have found when studying the literature (step 7). During the second hour, students discuss a new problem and formulate learning objectives for individual study with regard to this new problem (steps 1–5). Besides these tutorial groups, students also attend practicals, skills trainings, and a few lectures. At the end of a block period, that typically lasts between five and eight weeks, the block test is administered, after which a new block period starts with another theme.

In sum, from the viewpoint of development as a learner, the shared-control strategy is best suited for those situations in which students have already acquired some skill in employing a particular learning activity, but have a need for further skill development. Furthermore, it is well suited to challenging students to try new forms of learning in which they cannot utilise learning activities they are familiar with (e.g., memorising). It is less suited for situations in which students have already acquired expertise in the self-regulated use of particular learning activities.

Loose External Regulation

Under loose external regulation, the instructional agent assumes that students will conduct proper learning activities on their own accord. For example, when a teacher does not pay attention to similarities and differences between two theories, models, or practical experiences, he leaves it to the students whether they will look for these or not. When the teacher uses a loose teacher-regulated form of instruction, congruence between learning and teaching occurs if students master a learning strategy well and use it on their own initiative and in the right situations (Simons, 1993). This is the case, for example, when teachers do not undertake any activities to regulate students' learning processes during their independent studying of texts, and students have the necessary regulatory skills at their disposal. Another example is a teacher who knows that students, in a certain domain, are capable of generating concrete examples, and therefore does not provide any of these.

Friction may be expected when students do not master the learning or thinking strategies that are called for. This is the case when the teacher relies on self-regulated strategies but students are incapable of performing them. Students may want to use an externally regulated strategy but do not receive sufficient support for doing so. Ertmer, Newby, and MacDougall (1996) documented such a phenomenon in the differential reactions to a case-based instructional approach for students differing in self-regulatory skills. If the degree of students' self-regulation is inadequate and the teacher-regulation is deficient, the lack of regulation presents a threat to learning. Mayer (2004) reviews research on pure discovery learning and argues that often it does not help students to learn. If students do not master the learning or thinking activities on which the teacher relies, there is destructive friction. This was often the case in traditional university education in the Netherlands. Students in Dutch secondary education were often taken by the hands by their teachers and received homework from lesson to lesson. When they arrived after their final exams and the summer holidays at the university, they were told that in nine months the examinations would take place, that these would cover thousands of pages of course materials, and that there were weekly lectures in which the subject matter would be explained. The distance between what these beginning students were used to in terms of way of learning, and the self-regulated way of learning that was expected from them in the new environment, was for large groups of students a gap too large to bridge, which led to high rates of attrition in the first year of study. If students master a strategy to some extent, there may be constructive friction.

An example of a teaching/learning method in which loose teacher-regulation is dominant is self-directed specialisation learning. In the later years of studies in higher education, forms of self-directed specialisation learning are applied that are individually supervised. A well-known example is the Master Thesis in the form of a report of empirical, literature, or resources research (Vermunt, 2003). By then, students have acquired the common, basic knowledge base of the discipline and then specialise in certain aspects of it, often based on individual interests. Sometimes also two or three students work together on such a project, when there are students with shared interests. Typically, projects like these usually have a somewhat longer duration (three to six months), and knowledge acquisition about the specific subject is often part of the project. One or two staff members function as supervisors. Students write a research proposal in which the research problem, goals, activities, resources to be used, the project outcomes intended, and the way of supervision are described. In essence, this comes down to a study task or project assignment that the students formulate for themselves. This proposal is discussed with the supervisors, and based on their comments students revise the proposal before executing it. Further supervision is often tailor-made, depending, for example, on the research phase the student is in, the difficulty level of the project and the need for supervision, or the degree of self-regulation a student is capable of. After finishing the research report, it is evaluated based on criteria that were formulated beforehand. Sometimes process criteria are also included in the evaluation.

In sum, this loose teacher-regulation strategy seems appropriate when students are proficient in the use of particular learning activities, or when they are on their way to getting proficient. It allows the teacher to pay attention to other learning functions than to those the students already master sufficiently for the domain at hand. It is not suitable in situations where students' skill in regulation of learning is low, either in general or with respect to particularly important learning activities.

Process-Oriented Teaching — from External Regulation to Self-Regulation of Learning Processes

If the goal of teaching is not only to achieve gains in knowledge or understanding of subject matter, but also improvement in the ability to self-regulate knowledge construction, one has to look for ways of combining the strong points of the relationships between teaching and learning described above. Central issues, then, become the development from teacher-regulated to student-regulated learning and balancing support to the needs of different learners.

In case of congruence, self-regulation and teacher-regulation of learning are in balance. In the long run, however, this might imply a standstill in students' development of independent learning strategies. From this perspective, especially constructive frictions are of interest. Herewith, the teacher challenges students to use those learning and thinking strategies that they do not master well yet or that they do not use on their own accord. Constructive frictions are comparable to what Vygotsky (1978) called the zone of proximal development.

Learning to learn and think independently we can now interpret as a shift from a strong, via a shared, to a loose teacher-regulation, under concurrent training in independent learning and thinking strategies to come from a low, via an intermediate, to a high degree of self-regulation (Palincsar & Brown, 1989). In Table 9.1, it can also be seen that this is dependent on the starting level of students' degree of self-regulation they are capable of (see Vermunt & Verloop, 1999 for a more elaborate discussion of the interplay between teaching and learning).

Destructive frictions often take place. Teachers and designers of instruction, for instance, frequently have the tendency to take over as many learning and thinking activities from students as possible (Bednar, Cunningham, Duffy, & Perry, 1991; Sternberg & Horvath, 1995). *Process-oriented teaching* tries to promote congruence and constructive friction, and to avoid destructive friction. The aim is to teach domain-specific knowledge and the learning and thinking strategies that students need to construct, change, and utilise their knowledge of the subject domain, in coherence. The emphasis is on a gradual transfer of learning functions from teachers to students. In terms of development in students' learning styles, process-oriented teaching aims at stimulating the development of meaning and application-directed learning styles, and discouraging undirected and reproduction-directed ways of learning. The main tasks for teachers in this view are initiating, supporting, and influencing the thinking processes that students use to learn (Simons, 1993). Elsewhere, principles of process-oriented teaching are discussed more extensively (e.g., Volet, McGill, & Pears, 1995; Vermunt & Verschaffel, 2000).

Process-oriented teaching is aimed at the integrated teaching of learning and thinking strategies, on the one hand, and domain-specific knowledge, on the other. It is an instructional model in which learners are taught to employ suitable learning and thinking activities to construct, change, and utilise their knowledge of a particular subject domain. This type of teaching is called process-oriented teaching because it focuses on learners' processes of knowledge construction and utilisation. The emphasis is on a gradual transfer of control over thinking and learning processes from the teacher and/or other instructional agents to students. The underlying regulation conception assumes that it is impossible, but also undesirable, to carry out the learning processes for students and to exert maximum control over them. The main teacher tasks in this conception are initiating and supporting the thinking activities that students employ in their learning (Simons, 1997).

For example, in the renewal of the teacher education programme of Leiden University, the development of a coherent system of study tasks was central (Vermunt & Lowyck, 2000). Study tasks were conceptualised as a kind of learning plans and included the following elements: (1) learning objectives; (2) learning activities; (3) learning resources (literature, websites, CD-ROMs, DVDs, experts, etc.); (4) intended learning outcomes (e.g., an essay, a lesson plan, reflection report); and (5) assessment criteria and the forms of feedback on achievement. The principle of decreasing regulation or control was operationalised so that in the study tasks required of students at the beginning of their teacher education programme many of the elements mentioned above were filled out by the teacher educator. As the programme progressed, students had to fill out ever more elements of these study tasks. For example, in the tasks 'Research Methods' at about the halfway mark in the programme, the formulation of the learning objectives and the assessment of the learning outcomes were still mostly in the hands of the teacher educator. The choice of the learning activities, study sources, and intended learning outcomes, was done by student teacher and teacher educator together in mutual agreement, in which the teacher educator helped the student to come to a good formulation. In the study task 'Research project' that students did more towards the end of the programme, they were totally responsible for the learning activities and study sources, while learning activities and learning outcomes aimed at were determined in mutual consultation. Assessment and feedback were more shared at this point than with the former study task, since students now also evaluated and argued in their report the extent to which the research contributed to their professional development as a teacher. In other words, the elements of the study tasks were fixed in a 'format'; and in the course of the programme, students got ever more responsibility in filing in the elements. In every study task a so-called 'regulation matrix' was included, that made transparent the way of regulation in this particular study task and the responsibilities for both student teacher and teacher educator (see Table 9.2).

Table 9.2: An example of decreasing external regulation in two study tasks: 'Research methods' (A) and 'Research project' (B).

Elements of study task	Degree of external regulation of learning		
	Strong	**Shared**	**Loose**
Learning objectives	A	B	
Learning activities		A	B
Study sources		A	B
Learning outcomes aimed at		AB	
Assessment and feedback	A	B	

Ten Cate, Snell, Mann, and Vermunt (2004) developed this idea into a learning-oriented teaching (LOT) model for medical education. This model is focused on tracing and supporting the learning process. One of the main characteristics of the model is the amount of support medical students need.

Balancing Support to Different Learners

A main implication of the model outlined above is that learners may need different kind of support, depending on their skill in self-regulated learning in general or in the use of certain learning activities in particular. The intention is to foster constructive friction and to avoid destructive friction between student-regulation and teacher-regulation of student learning. Hence, what is a good support strategy for one learner may not be a good support strategy for another. In individual computer-supported learning, this principle is relatively easy to handle. However, as class size increases and the heterogeneity among the students is high, it becomes more difficult.

In one of our own educational psychology courses, in which students discussed articles while organised into thematic working groups, we had the following assignment:

1. "Rank order the following learning activities to the degree you are good at them: memorising, concretising, relating, structuring, applying, critical processing, analysing, selecting. (These learning activities had been briefly described.)
2. Think of an assignment for yourself to activate that learning activity you are least good in when studying the literature for next week".

A student, for example, for whom 'critical processing' had ended at the bottom of the rank order, should make a task for himself as follows: "Think of three arguments in favour and against the position that Bednar takes in the debate about objectivism versus constructivism".

This assignment had several advantages. First, students were encouraged to think about their strong and weak sides as a learner. A groupwise inventory by the teacher of the most and least used learning activities yielded, in a simple way, insight into the strong and weak sides of the group as a whole. The students went about studying the articles with different assignments (different support), while the teacher only had to think of one. The subject matter itself was the same for everybody, while the way in which the studying of the subject matter was supported differed for students with different learning patterns. Students were stimulated to develop their weak sides.

The Case of New Learning: Secondary School Reforms in the Netherlands

Simons et al. (2000) advocate the view that graduates should foremost have acquired skills that enable them to keep learning throughout their lives, to think independently, to work together, and to regulate their own learning and thinking. They describe this 'new learning' in terms of new learning outcomes, new types of learning processes, and new teaching methods that are both demanded by today's society and stressed by contemporary constructivist learning theories.

Recently, many institutes for secondary education in the Netherlands began to experiment with new forms of teaching and learning. At the same time, a lively debate has started about the value of 'new' and 'old' approaches to teaching and learning. In the Spring of 2005, there was a boom of newspaper publications in the Netherlands about this new learning. Although the educational innovations that are meant by this term vary, they are all innovations in which learners have more to say about the regulation of their learning. Learners have more freedom of choice and responsibility and there is a greater call on their own initiative (see, for example, De Kock, Sleegers, & Voeten, 2004).

The underlying line of reasoning is as follows: students are often no longer motivated by standard education. If we want to stimulate their intrinsic motivation, we have to connect more closely with what they want to learn, and to what they find interesting. By letting them choose more about what, when, where, and how they learn, we promote more motivated and meaningful learning, the joy in learning and going to school with pleasure (see, for example, Giessen & Schöttelndreier, 2005).

Research on the way people learn indeed shows direct relationships between intrinsic motivation (personal interest), a conception of learning in which learning is viewed as constructing own knowledge and insights, self-regulation of one's learning processes, and deep processing of subject matter. And also between extrinsic motivation, a conception of learning in which learning is seen as the intake of knowledge from others, external regulation of one's learning processes, and surface processing of subject matter (Vermunt & Vermetten, 2004).

The central issue in the discussion is the issue of regulation and direction: who determines what, when, how, with what goal, etc. is learned: the learner or the teacher? It is about freedom versus structure, and student-regulation versus teacher-regulation of learning. But even more important than this general issue is the question to what aspects of the learning process this freedom of choice refers to. It is especially in this matter that the various forms of teaching and variants of new learning differ from each other.

What can be chosen about learning? In our view, some important dimensions are:

• What is learned?
• Why is something learned and with what objective?
• At what moment is something learned?
• Where is something learned?
• How is something learned?
• With whom is something learned?
• What sources may be used to learn something?
• What criteria should the learning outcomes meet?
• Who assesses whether the topic is learned well enough?

Even in the most traditional forms of teaching, students have something to say about how they learn something, and where and when they do their homework. That is about the limit of their freedom of choice. In full autodidactic learning, students determine all aspects of their learning as described above. They become their own teacher. All other forms of teaching lie in between these two extremes.

In various forms of new learning students get, for example, freedom of choice (and the other side of the coin, responsibility) for choosing their learning objectives, determining their learning activities, consulting sources, and documenting their learning outcomes. For example, students get assignments but freedom of choice about when they want to work on them. They get regular 'challenges', in which they can show what they have learned. There is a 'student-follow-yourself' system, or 'portfolio-boxes in which you can put things of which you are proud'. All forms of new learning and teaching put more emphasis on cooperative learning than traditional teaching (De Kock et al., 2004). Or, as students say it in their own words: "you get more understanding from learning and doing yourself", "you learn better from other students", "you remember better because you recognize it", "what is fun and interesting you do not forget so soon" (KPC Group, 2005).

The various variants differ in the degree of structure and freedom they offer to the students. Mostly, the final or programme goals are fixed, only the road that leads to them is changed. The more extreme variants go into the direction of autodidactic learning, in which pupils can, for example, decide themselves whether they are ready for learning to read.

With this development in teaching to students between 12 and 18 years, a development has arrived that we saw earlier in the teaching of 18+ and 12− years. In this sense it is a rather logical development. For example, in the last five years higher vocational education in the Netherlands massively switched to what is called competency-based teaching. Key concepts include self-regulated learning, personal development plans, self-evaluation, authentic tasks and tests, portfolios, and so on (HAN, 2003).

A striking fact is that many of the 'new' or 'natural' approaches to learning and teaching for secondary education, show many characteristics of teaching methods that are used in higher education already on a rather broad base (competency-based learning, PBL, project-centred learning, practice-based learning, assignment-based teaching). For example, the approach to teaching developed for pre-university secondary education at several schools, shows many characteristics of PBL as already used for more than 30 years at the University of Maastricht. In many forms of new learning and teaching for pre-professional education, such as practice-based approaches to learning and teaching, we recognise forms of project-centred learning as used already some time at various universities and institutes of higher vocational education. Under the flag of new learning, we also see many examples of dual forms of teaching, in which learning from professional practice is combined with learning at school, especially in vocational education. In this type of teaching, personal development plans are often used that are deduced from the competence profile of a profession, and portfolio's with which learners can document their learning progress.

Does new learning yield better learning outcomes than 'traditional', or 'regular' forms of learning and teaching? Van der Werf (2005) argued that this was not the case. She, however, looked mainly at learning outcomes on traditional tests. The comparison could not be made with regard to skills of self-regulated learning, being able to make choices with regard to what, when, how, and with what goal to learn, and so on. Traditional teaching was not directed at the learning of these skills and therefore these were not assessed. The same holds for skills related to cooperative learning.

The situation recalls the early period of PBL at the University of Maastricht some 30 years ago. Only a few people outside Maastricht then believed that PBL was a proper way to educate good doctors. Comparative research in which medical students from both PBL and traditional curricula had to answer factual questions, showed that there was no difference in factual knowledge between students from the new and old medical curricula (Norman & Schmidt, 1992). On other types of learning outcomes, especially in the area of skills, PBL-students were in the advantage. Recent reviews on comparisons between PBL curricula and traditional curricula confirm these outcomes (e.g., Dochy, Segers, Van den Bossche, & Gijbels, 2003; Gijbels, Dochy, Van den Bossche, & Segers, 2005).

Learning only those topics that one likes does not prepare a pupil well for a life full of learning, and can be at odds with the demands that society poses for graduates. After all, from the business community, society, and professional groups demands are also posed as to what skills graduates should possess. What a doctor should know and be able to do is described rather specifically. When someone has pain in the throat and goes to the doctor, it must not be the case that the doctor did not find the throat interesting enough to learn about. The exclusive right to determine curricula resides not only with the students, but also with schools, who share a societal responsibility for appropriate educational outcomes.

It is often underestimated what it means for teachers when their school switches to new learning. They get new roles, their beliefs about good teaching might not coincide with those behind the innovation, and new capabilities are expected. Even more than for students a switch to new learning means that new learning processes are expected from teachers. This includes new roles and accompanying capabilities like tutor, coach, mentor, constructor of assignments, skills trainer, portfolio coach, cooperation coach, project coach, assessor, diagnostician, challenger, model, activator, monitor, reflector, evaluator, competency assessor, professional growth consultant, educational developer, information and communication technologist, authentic assessment constructor, block coordinator, and so on. In the new structure, for example, they must help learners to formulate good questions, encourage their curiosity, keep an overview over students' development, and keep their mouth shut when students are finding out something.

For teachers all this is not a piece of cake. They not only get different teaching roles to fulfil, but it touches upon their identity as a teacher. For example, it may be very hard for teachers to get used to working in a room where different groups of learners and teachers are working simultaneously. Being the king or queen in one's own classroom is in the past. Also, the role of tutor, helping students to learn multiple subjects is not easy and resembles the dilemma of the general practitioner: when is one's own help sufficient, and when is a referral to a specialist (for example, the Math subject teacher) necessary? Of course, there is a big difference between schools that start as a new school with this new learning concept and existing schools that do so. In the first case, the school can start with a team of teachers who all believe in the new concept; in the second case, all teachers will have to get convinced of the value of the concept.

Discussion and Conclusions

Of course, we do not have to be afraid of these new forms of learning and teaching. PBL, for example, is a rather structured teaching method in which learners may and must decide more than in traditional teaching, but in which the tutor keeps an eye on whether students do not get outside of the bandwidth of their freedom of choice. PBL and project-centered teaching are widely used teaching methods in higher education today. Besides, other methods have been developed and still others are being developed. That is only beneficial for the freedom of choice of parents and students.

The positive thing is that the distance between the school world and the real-life world of children in secondary education is made smaller. Experiments with new forms of learning and teaching are emerging. This should, however, be accompanied by thorough research on the outcomes of these types of teaching. Cooperation between universities and schools might lead to simultaneous research and development of new forms of learning and teaching. To this end, research should focus on the way students learn, the way teachers teach, the interplay between these two, and the necessary professional development of teachers.

Preparing for lifelong learning means that students must learn to regulate all aspects of their learning processes themselves. After they have left school, there is no one who tells them what and how to learn (Boekaerts, 1997). Therefore, in our view it is very important that

1. there is a structure in the school curriculum in which forms of teaching, learning and assessment, tasks and assignments systematically and gradually require more self-regulation of students, and in which students are taught how they can learn ever more independently. We consider a gradual increase in self-regulated learning better than a sudden immersion. Elsewhere (Vermunt, 2003), we have explored what teaching methods are suited for this new learning and how these can be sequenced in such a way that there is a robust build-up. Students also have to *learn* to plan, pose own objectives, formulate learning questions, monitor their progress, search for solutions when they do not succeed, etc.
2. differences between students are taken into account with regard to the degree with which they are able to learn independently and the support and guidance they need to do so. We consider it very important that a student's abilities with regard to self-regulated learning are assessed, and that independence is built-up from that point. Abandoning traditional didactic teaching as the dominant form gives the teacher more freedom to take differences between individuals and groups of students into account and adapt support and guidance accordingly.
3. there is some variation in forms of learning and teaching. For new, difficult subject matter it may be best that the teacher takes up the reins for a moment. On the other hand, a project with much freedom of choice may be very motivating even in the first years (Kirschner, 2000). Nothing is more lethal to motivation than a succession of merely project-centred learning, PBL, assignment-based teaching, frontal traditional teaching, or whatever other kind of teaching.

The theoretical perspective outlined in this chapter calls for further research and theory development. Many questions remain to be solved. From the above perspective, future research should be directed at the further development of a teaching and learning theory that puts learning processes into the focus of attention. Research should be directed, for example, at the way teachers use the various teaching strategies and what learning functions these strategies address. Moreover, too little is known about relations between craft knowledge and professional orientations of teachers on the one hand, and the way in which they deal with learning functions on the other. We need to know more about congruence and friction between learning and teaching strategies, the way in which different levels of self-regulation and external regulation of learning processes operate upon one another and whether this interplay occurs differently in different kinds of learning environments. Forthcoming research should also be directed at the way the transition of teacher-regulation to student-regulation of learning processes can be concretely realised in different learning environments.

References

Barrows, H. S., & Tamblyn, R. M. (1980). *Problem-based learning: An approach to medical education*. New York: Springer.

Bednar, A. K., Cunningham, D., Duffy, T. M., & Perry, J. D. (1991). Theory into practice: How do we link. In: G. J. Anglin (Ed.), *Instructional technology: Past, present and future* (pp. 88−101). Englewood, CO: Libraries Unlimited.

Biggs, J. (1996). Enhancing teaching through constructive alignment. *Higher Education, 32,* 347–364.

Boekaerts, M. (1997). Self-regulated learning: A new concept embraced by researchers, policy makers, educators, teachers, and students. *Learning and Instruction, 7,* 161–186.

Bolhuis, S. (2003). Towards process-oriented teaching for self-directed lifelong learning: A multidimensional perspective. *Learning and Instruction, 13,* 327–347.

Bouhuijs, P. A. J., & Gijselaers, W. H. (1993). Course construction in problem-based learning. In: P. A. J. Bouhuijs, H. G. Schmidt, & H. Van Berkel (Eds), *Problem-based learning as an educational strategy* (pp. 79–90). Maastricht: Network Publications.

Boyle, A. B., Duffy, T., & Dunleavy, K. (2003). Learning styles and academic outcome: The validity and utility of Vermunt's Inventory of Learning Styles in a British higher education setting. *British Journal of Educational Psychology, 73,* 263–290.

Clark, R. E. (1990). When teaching kills learning: Research on mathemathantics. In: H. Mandl, E. De Corte, S. N. Bennett, & H. F. Friedrich (Eds), *Learning and instruction: European research in an international context* (Vol. 2.2, pp. 1–22). Oxford: Pergamon.

De Kock, A., Sleegers, P., & Voeten, M. J. M. (2004). New learning and the classification of learning environments in secondary education. *Review of Educational Research, 74,* 141–170.

Dochy, F., Segers, M., Van den Bossche, P., & Gijbels, D. (2003). Effects of problem-based learning: A meta-analysis. *Learning and Instruction, 13,* 533–568.

Entwistle, N. (1992). *The impact of teaching on learning outcomes in higher education — A literature review.* Edinburgh: University of Edinburgh, Centre for Research on Learning and Instruction.

Entwistle, N., McCune, V., & Hounsell, J. (2003). Investigating ways of enhancing university teaching-learning environments: Measuring students' approaches to studying and perceptions of teaching. In: E. De Corte, L. Verschaffel, N. Entwistle, & J. van Merriënboer (Eds), *Powerful learning environments: Unravelling basic components and dimensions* (pp. 89–107). Oxford: Pergamon.

Ertmer, P. A., Newby, T. J., & MacDougall, M. (1996). Students' responses and approaches to case-based instruction: The role of reflective self-regulation. *American Educational Research Journal, 33,* 719–752.

Giessen, P., & Schöttelndreier, M. (2005). Nieuw leren is hard leren [New learning is hard learning]. *De Volkskrant,* 5 March, p. 29.

Gijbels, D., Dochy, F., Van den Bossche, P., & Segers, M. (2005). Effects of problem-based learning: A meta-analysis from the angle of assessment. *Review of Educational Research, 75,* 27–61.

Hamaker, C. (1986). The effects of adjunct questions on prose learning. *Review of Educational Research, 56,* 212–242.

HAN (2003). *Chassis voor het onderwijs — Onderwijskundig en organisatorisch kader voor de bacheloropleidingen* [Chassis for teaching — Educational and organisational framework for the bachelor programmes]. The Netherlands: Arnhem and Nijmegen University for Professional Education.

Janssen, P. J. (1996). Studaxology: The expertise students need to be effective in higher education. *Higher Education, 31*, 117–141.

Kirschner, P. (2000). *The inevitable duality of higher education: Cooperative higher education.* Inaugural address, University of Maastricht, The Netherlands.

KPC Group. (2005). *Het nieuwe leren implementeren* [Implementing new learning]. DVD.'s Hertogenbosch: KPC Group.

Lindblom-Ylänne, S. (1999). *Studying in a traditional medical curriculum — Study success, orientations to studying and problems that arise.* Doctoral dissertation, Faculty of Medicine, University of Helsinki, Finland.

Lohman, D. F. (1986). Predicting mathemathantic effects in the teaching of higher order skills. *Educational Psychologist, 21*, 191–208.

Lonka, K., & Ahola, K. (1995). Activating instruction — How to foster study and thinking skills in higher education. *European Journal of Psychology of Education, 10*, 351–368.

Lonka, K., & Lindblom-Ylänne, S. (1996). Epistemologies, conceptions of learning, and study practices in medicine and psychology. *Higher Education, 31*, 5–24.

Lowyck, J., & Elen, J. (1993). Transitions in the theoretical foundation of instructional design. In: T. M. Duffy, J. Lowyck, & D. H. Jonassen (Eds), *Designing environments for constructive learning* (pp. 213–230). New York: Springer.

Mayer, R. E. (2004). Should there be a three-strike rule against pure discovery learning? The case for guided methods of instruction. *American Psychologist, 59*, 14–19.

Norman, G. R., & Schmidt, H. G. (1992). The psychological basis of problem-based learning: A review of the evidence. *Academic Medicine, 67*, 557–565.

Palincsar, A. S., & Brown, A. L. (1989). Classroom dialogues to promote self-regulated comprehension. In: J. Brophy (Ed.), *Advances in research on teaching* (Vol. 1, pp. 35–67). Greenwich, CO: JAI Press.

Rosenshine, B., & Stevens, R. (1986). Teaching functions. In: M. C. Wittrock (Ed.), *Handbook of research on teaching* (3rd ed., pp. 376–391). New York: MacMillan.

Schmidt, H. G., & Moust, J. H. C. (1998). *Probleemgestuurd onderwijs: Praktijk en theorie* [Problem-based learning: Practice and theory]. Groningen: Wolters-Noordhoff.

Schoenfeld, A. H. (1988). When good teaching leads to bad results: The disaster of "well-taught" mathematics courses. *Educational Psychologist, 23*, 145–166.

Shuell, T. J. (1996). Teaching and learning in a classroom context. In: D. C. Berliner, & R. C. Calfee (Eds), *Handbook of educational psychology* (pp. 726–764). New York: Simon & Schuster Macmillan.

Simons, P. R. J. (1993). Constructive learning: The role of the learner. In: T. M. Duffy, J. Lowyck, & D. H. Jonassen (Eds), *Designing environments for constructive learning* (pp. 291–314). New York: Springer.

Simons, P. R. J. (1997). From romanticism to practice in learning. *Lifelong Learning in Europe, 1*, 8–15.

Simons, P. R. J., Van der Linden, J., & Duffy, T. (2000). New learning: Three ways to learn in a new balance. In: R. J. Simons, J. van der Linden, & T. Duffy (Eds), *New learning* (pp. 1–20). Dordrecht: Kluwer.

Sternberg, R. J., & Horvath, J. A. (1995). A prototype view of expert teaching. *Educational Researcher, 24*(6), 9–17.

Ten Cate, O., Snell, L., Mann, K., & Vermunt, J. (2004). Orienting teaching towards the learning process. *Academic Medicine, 79*, 219–228.

Van der Werf, G. (2005). *Leren in het Studiehuis. Consumeren, construeren of engageren?* [Learning in the study house. Consuming, constructing, or engaging?] Inaugural address, University of Groningen, the Netherlands.

Vermetten, Y. J., Vermunt, J. D., & Lodewijks, H. G. (1999). A longitudinal perspective on learning strategies in higher education — different viewpoints towards development. *British Journal of Educational Psychology, 69*, 221–242.

Vermunt, J. D. (1996). Metacognitive, cognitive and affective aspects of learning styles and strategies: A phenomenographic analysis. *Higher Education, 31*, 25–50.

Vermunt, J. D. (1998). The regulation of constructive learning processes. *British Journal of Educational Psychology, 68*, 149–171.

Vermunt, J. D. (2003). The power of learning environments and the quality of student learning. In: E. De Corte, L. Verschaffel, N. Entwistle, & J. van Merriënboer (Eds), *Powerful learning environments: Unravelling basic components and dimensions* (pp. 109–124). Oxford: Pergamon.

Vermunt, J., & Lowyck, J. (2000). Leeractiviteiten en procesgericht onderwijs [Learning activities and process-oriented teaching]. In: G. ten Dam, H. van Hout, C. Terlouw, & J. Willems (Eds), *Onderwijskunde hoger onderwijs — Handboek voor docenten* [Educational science for higher education — handbook for teachers] (pp. 30–55). Assen: Van Gorcum.

Vermunt, J. D., & Verloop, N. (1999). Congruence and friction between learning and teaching. *Learning and Instruction, 9*, 257–280.

Vermunt, J. D., & Vermetten, Y. J. (2004). Patterns in student learning: Relationships between learning strategies, conceptions of learning, and learning orientations. *Educational Psychology Review, 16*, 359–384.

Vermunt, J., & Verschaffel, L. (2000). Process-oriented teaching. In: R. J. Simons, J. van der Linden, & T. Duffy (Eds), *New learning* (pp. 209–225). Dordrecht: Kluwer.

Volet, S., McGill, T., & Pears, H. (1995). Implementing process-based instruction in regular university teaching: Conceptual, methodological and practical issues. *European Journal of Psychology of Education, 10*, 385–400.

Vygotsky, L. S. (1978). *Mind in society: The development of higher psychological processes.* Cambridge, MA: Harvard University Press.

Wagner, E. D., & McCombs, B. L. (1995). Learner-centred psychological principles in practice: Designs for distance education. *Educational Technology, 35*(3), 32–35.

Chapter 10

The Use of Instructional Interventions: Lean Learning Environments as a Solution for a Design Problem

Jan Elen and Geraldine Clarebout

Introduction

Instruction in general, and instructional design in particular, assumes that learning is enhanced through means of well-targeted support. In an instructional setting, support is offered and learners may benefit from it. Gagné, Briggs, and Wager (1988) clearly expressed it as follows: "Instruction is a human undertaking whose purpose is to help people learn. Although learning may happen without any instruction, the effects of instruction on learning are often beneficial and easy to observe" (p. 3). Review studies illustrate the validity of this assumption by stipulating the conditions in terms of the learner, the task, and the context characteristics under which a specific kind of support can be called functional. Dillon and Gabbard (1998), for example, specified the conditions under which hypermedia can be beneficial for learner comprehension; de Jong and van Joolingen (1998) analyzed the power of computer simulations for science learning, and Atkinson, Derry, Renkl, and Wortham (2000) derived principles to use worked examples in instructional settings. In all these cases an instructional intervention was regarded as functional when learners learned more or learned more efficiently when adequately using the instructional intervention. This is also reflected in the term 'scaffold', which is often used to refer to tools, strategies, or guides that support students learning. Scaffolds aim to support learners in attaining a higher level of understanding, one that would not be reached if students worked individually, or without support devices (Brush & Saye, 2001; Hannafin, Land, & Oliver, 1999).

Different kinds of support made available in instructional settings are not always effective or beneficial (Clark & Estes, 2002). Support is only beneficial when functional and adequately used by the learners (e.g., Rothkopf, 1971; Winne, 1982). Unfortunately, evidence is growing that learners often use support inadequately or not at all, and in many cases not as intended by the instructional designers (e.g., Aleven, Stahl, Schworm, Fischer, & Wallace, 2003; Clarebout & Elen, 2006; Elen & Louw, submitted; Perkins, 1985).

Learners seem to make wrong or inappropriate decisions when selecting among support alternatives and regularly use support in an inaccurate manner or in a way not intended by the teacher or designer. André's (1979) study is illustrative: in this study, pre-questions were inserted as examples of interesting test items, but students used these pre-questions to assess the importance of the information elements and thus to determine what should be studied. More recently, Greene and Land (2000) provided students with questions during their problem-solving process to encourage deep-level processing. Their results revealed that students responded to these questions with surface-level cognitive activities.

At the very least, such learners' actions reduce the beneficial effects of support. At worst, mathemathantic effects (Clark, 1990) or expertise reversal effects (Kalyuga, Ayres, Chandler, & Sweller, 2003) are observed in which scaffolding hampers learning.

This chapter analyzes the phenomenon of non-use and/or inadequate use as an additional perspective to the issue of dealing with complexity in learning environments. More specifically, situations are analyzed in which learners do not optimally benefit from support opportunities in an instructional environment because they do not use the provided support at all, or because they do not use it as intended by the instructional designer or teacher. This analysis aims to identify those situations in which the non-use or inadequate use of instructional interventions can be considered problematic. This identification of problematic occurrences of non-use and/or inadequate use may help in the development of solutions.

Conceptual Clarifications

To clarify the discussion of the non-use and/or inadequate use of instructional interventions, the following conceptual distinctions are made: (a) *learning task* refers to what the learner has to learn with a given set of learning materials, (b) *support* refers to all those elements that are deliberately integrated into or added to the learning task in view of fostering learning, and (c) *learning environment* is an encompassing term referring to both the learning task and the support. A second major distinction, based on primary outcome goals, is to be made between two types of environments used in educational settings: learning environments and task environments. Whereas the acquisition of knowledge, skills, and/or attitudes is the main goal of learning environments, the execution of a performance task is the primary goal of task environments. It will be clear that performance tasks can also be part of learning environments and, similarly, that task environments may be presented to students with a collateral effect in mind, i.e., the acquisition of general or specific problem-solving skills.

Support, or other instructional interventions, may be embedded in learning tasks. For instance, the application of a specific sequencing strategy may embody learning support (Aly, Willems, & Elen, 2004). Support or instructional interventions can also be added to the learning task. Support *per se* is therefore non-embedded. For instance, specific advice on how to handle a problem-solving environment may be added to such a task environment in order to scaffold its use by learners (e.g., Clarebout & Elen, 2004). Whether support is integrated into or added to the learning or performance task is an important distinction from the perspective of the use of that support. In the case of embeddedness, support can hardly be avoided once the learner engages in the learning task, since the task includes the support. Of course, support can still be used more or less adequately, as was the case in a study by Greene and Land (2000). Further, in cases where instructional interventions are added to the task and, are thus easily identifiable, students may either ignore the support or use it more or less adequately. This was illustrated in Brush and Saye's (2001) study. They provided students with conceptual scaffolds in a history problem, namely guides and journal entries to complete. Results showed that few groups did use scaffolds, and those groups that used them did so very superficially.

Different Positions

The literature displays a variety of positions on the description and assessment of the non-use and/or inadequate use of instructional interventions. Merrill, Drake, Lacy, Pratt, and the ID2-Research Group (1996) take a very clear and straightforward position. They exclude the problem by definition. For them, "students are persons who submit themselves to the acquisition of specific knowledge and skill from instruction; learners are persons who construct their own meaning from their experiences. All of us are learners, but only those who submit themselves to deliberate instructional situations are students" (p. 6). This quote seems to imply that the non-use or inadequate use of instructional interventions indicates that 'learners' want to remain 'learners' and do not want to become 'students'. The radically formulated position implies that in a learning environment all instructional interventions have a transparent functionality and transparency. Non-use and/or inadequate use is then the result of a (not necessarily deliberate) decision made by the students.

Jonassen, Hernandez-Serrano, and Choi (2000) formulated a highly critical reaction to this position. They claim that the above definition of a student reflects a purely 'transmissive model of education' in which students must accept an external authority and commit themselves to that authority and its instructions. These authors argue that such a 'transmissive model' has at least two shortcomings. First "the transmissive model of instruction is not a generalizable model and does not account for all learning and instruction" (p. 105). Second, the model "fails to account for students who may be highly motivated but who fail to see the relevance of submitting to a process which might seem unlikely to them to lead to the understanding or enlightenment they seek" (p. 105). Jonassen et al. argue in favor of a constructivist approach, which in their view enables the accommodation of students who do and do not want to be submissive.

A more balanced view, and from a very different background can be found in Goodyear (2000). He claims that for a very long time instructional theory assumed the availability of a 'compliant learner'. He argues that — in view of designing environments for lifelong learning — 'the decline of the compliant learner' is to be seriously considered. He states: "By this I mean that it is becoming increasingly difficult to imagine that we can design learning technology systems around an assumption that they will be used by learners in the ways we prescribe" (p. 3). He illustrates this statement by referring to the poor effectiveness of multiple technology-based educational innovations. Goodyear argues that "Many of the core ideas, theories and methods in the field of educational technology, and especially in areas like ISD or instructional design, have origins which were heavily shaped by reasonable assumptions about a compliant learner" (p. 5). Examples of this sort of training include military or high-risk training. Goodyear specifies that given the current state of affairs and the fact that many target persons have multiple affiliations and responsibilities; the assumption of a compliant learner has become problematic. He argues in favor of considering learners to be 'autonomous'. Goodyear is not alone in using the notion of compliance when it comes to the use of instructional support. Todorovich, Wirth, Zhang, Tillman, and Fleming (2004) use a similar construct when they elaborate a 'compliance ratio'. The compliance ratio is the total amount of time needed to perform a task, divided by the amount of time allocated by the teacher. A compliant student is then a student who performs a task exactly as prescribed by a teacher and within the allocated time.

The views held by these three groups of authors illustrate that (a) the non-use or inadequate use of instructional interventions is referred to while using very different concepts, and (b) there is no apparent agreement as to the assessment of the phenomenon. While some authors restrict instructional settings to situations in which instructional interventions are adequately used by students, authors at the opposite side of the spectrum seem to negate the phenomenon by relying on students' independent or autonomous learning skills. Both extremes seem to neglect the simple observation that learners regularly do not acquire contextually relevant competencies or skills because they do not exploit the theoretical potential of learning environments. Or, as stated by Perkins (1985), both extremes seem to neglect that students may not grasp all learning opportunities made available to them.

The fourth perspective is offered by Winne (1985b, in press). Winne argues that for a learning environment to be effective, learners and the learning environment must be calibrated. Calibration implies a given state of optimal mutual adaptation, and refers to processes engaged in by the learner in order to continuously establish this mutual adaptation (Winne, 2004). Calibration is also more restrictively used as a term to refer to the accuracy of one's beliefs about potential functioning (Klassen, 2002). In this more technical sense, learners are calibrated to a task when there is a good match between confidence about their performance and their actual performance. Poorly calibrated students are typically overconfident with difficult tasks and underconfident with easy tasks (Stone, 2000). Both authors suggest that 100% calibration may not always be optimal. Students may be more motivated to work on a task when they are to some extent overconfident. In this definition of calibration, knowledge monitoring, as part of self-regulative or metacognitive activities (Tobias & Everson, 1996, 2002), determines the extent of calibration (Stone, 2000).

This brief overview of the literature reveals that students regularly do not or inadequately use support in learning environments, regardless of the type of support. The following specific observations can be made:

- Especially in 'instructional settings' students may not use or inadequately use instructional interventions. Instructional settings refer to goal-oriented situations in which learners are presented with an environment that contains deliberately inserted or integrated elements of support.
- The occurrence of non-use or inadequate use of instructional interventions has different levels of probability depending on the context and nature of the support (e.g., embedded versus non-embedded).
- The quality (use versus adequacy of use) of the phenomenon is mainly dependent upon the nature of the support.

Additionally, there is little agreement about the problematic nature of the phenomenon; it is questioned whether the assumption of a compliant learner itself should not be replaced by the notion of an autonomous or adaptive learner.

The Lack of Adequate Use of Instructional Interventions: When Is it a Problem, Who Is to Blame, and What Can Be Done?

In this section, the lack of adequate use of instructional interventions is theoretically and formally analyzed from an instructional design perspective. Figure 10.1 presents an overview of the analysis by considering the distinction between learning and task environments.

As previously mentioned instructional interventions can be embedded or added non-embedded. The literature clearly shows that in the case of embedded devices students' inadequate use prevails, while in the case of non-embedded devices problems with both non-use and inadequate use can be observed. Greene and Land (2000) for instance, argued about the poor effects of a metacognitive tool by referring to the students' poor use of the tool.

The inadequate use of embedded instructional interventions is problematic only when the adequate use of the intervention results in positive learning effects. When adequate use of the intervention does not generate positive learning effects, the functionality itself of the intervention is to be questioned. From an instructional design perspective one may even argue that extraneous cognitive load is inadvertently induced by the insertion of a

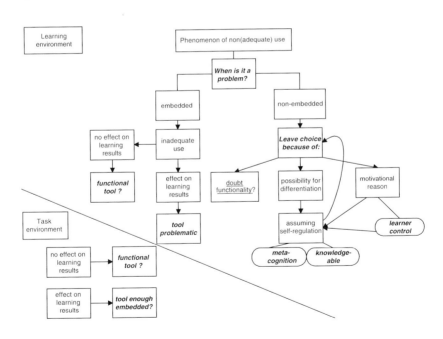

Figure 10.1: The problematic nature of non-use or inadequate use of instructional interventions.

non-functional or dysfunctional device. Carrier and her colleagues (Carrier, Davidson, Higson, & Williams, 1984; Carrier, Davidson, Williams, & Kalweit, 1986), revealed that students who used a practice tool did not perform better than students not using this tool. Evidently, the benefit of integrating this tool into the learning environment can be questioned. At the same time, one may wonder about the 'quality' of the device when the device is functional (i.e., adequate use results in better learning) but used inadequately. In such a situation, the design of the environment was erroneous either by not considering differences between students, or by only considering a restricted set of student variables. For instance, Greene and Land (2000) discuss the relevance of considering students' ability to grasp the potential of specific scaffolds (support devices). They point out that an underestimation of this variable has resulted in inserting scaffolds that induced students to only superficially process the information. A better design may result if students' knowledge about instructional interventions (Lowyck, Elen, & Clarebout, 2004) and their skills to handle these interventions were considered. Oliver and Hannafin (2000) indicate that both aspects are necessary. They state that knowing how to use a support device — although necessary — does not guarantee that students will know when and why to employ this device.

A different situation occurs in the case of non-embedded devices. In the case of non-embedded support devices, the students can choose whether or not to use the device. In this situation, the use or non-use of the interventions is at stake, rather than the adequacy of the use. Designers may decide to give students the choice to use or not use a device for at least three reasons. First, designers may be unsure about the functionality of the device. Rather than inducing the learner to use the device, use or non-use is left up to the learner. While a clear benefit cannot be shown, it is predicted that the tool may benefit and certainly will not harm individual students. In such cases, especially given the doubts about the functionality of the device, non-use or inadequate can hardly be regarded as problematic. Moreover, the choice presented to students may create a problem of extraneous overload (see literature on seductive details; e.g., Harp & Mayer, 1998). Designers may also be confronted with a heterogeneous target group. Some devices may be functional for subgroup A but less functional for subgroup B, while a different set of instructional interventions is expected to be functional for subgroup B but not for subgroup A. The study of Ross, Rakow, and Bush (1980), for instance, revealed that an environment becomes more effective when the amount of support is matched to students' prior knowledge. In order to handle differences among students, Veerman, de Jong, and van Joolingen (2000) suggest use of an intelligent support system. The designer may also decide to present learners with the choice to use an intervention by considering research on learner control, which suggests that the provision of choice may increase feelings of self-efficacy and hence contribute to motivation. Carrier, Davidson, and Williams (1985), for example, found that high ability students performed better when they selected a high number of elaborations. High ability students forced to process the same high amount of elaborations performed worse. In this study, the choice option seemed to have increased students' motivation and, hence, their performance.

When dealing with a diverse group of students or in cases where students' motivation needs to be supported, designers basically assume that learners will be able to choose the instructional intervention that is most beneficial to them. More technically, given the choice between potentially functional instructional interventions, designers assume that students have the necessary self-regulating skills. It is assumed that students are sufficiently knowledgeable about the functionality of instructional interventions presented and can decide what device to use considering their own learning process. If the designer does not make this assumption then either the choice between potentially functional interventions should not be offered or the nature of the device itself should be altered. Unfortunately, while designers often assume learners to have the necessary self-regulation skills, this assumption often proves to be wrong. Chapelle and Mizuno (1989) illustrated this point. They revealed that students do not always make use of optimal strategies, and hence, instructors should not expect that all learners can assess their own learning needs. Confronted with relatively low self-regulating skills of the learners, the designer may (a) decide to provide learner control for less crucial features of the environment, (b) change the device in order to embed it more strongly, or (c) more directly induce its use. A suggestion of such a feature can be found in Schnackenberg and Sullivan (2000). In their study, a full-minus and a lean-plus group were compared. Students in the lean-plus group tend to not request additional instruction, while students in the full-minus group tend not to bypass instruction. Providing control over bypassing instruction seems a less crucial factor over student perceptions of control, and does not seem to have an influence on performance. In this study, the full-minus group performed as well as a group that received all instruction without the possibility of bypass. Similar results were found by Hicken, Sullivan, and Klein (1992) who concluded that learners rely on default choices made by instructors. In line with Kinzie, Sullivan, and Berdel (1988), they suggest that not actual but perceived control over instructional events motivates students.

Logically, the non-use of instructional devices in a choice context is only problematic if a device is clearly functional for a specific learner confronted with a specific learning task. The presence of this kind of problem might be an indication that designers have insufficiently considered a possible lack of students' self-regulation skills.

If a task environment is presented to the learner and a device is not used, the question about the functionality of the intervention must be raised. When the functionality of the device is not evident, the need for its inclusion could be seriously doubted. If the device is essential but not used, it should be questioned whether it is made sufficiently clear to the student that using the tool is indeed an integral part of the task. In other words, it should be questioned whether the device was sufficiently embedded in the task.

In conclusion, this analysis reveals that the adequate use of instructional interventions is primarily a design problem that relates to the unclear or unproven functionality of specific instructional devices and/or difficulties in considering learner characteristics in the design that are related to learning in the particular instructional setting.

Design Implications

The analysis presented raises two main design issues. The first issue relates to what design decision to take when there is no or insufficient evidence about the context-, task-, or learner-specific functionality of an intervention. The second issue pertains to what learner variables to consider in order to ensure the use of theoretically functional instructional interventions.

In the case of doubt about the tool's functionality, the designer has to decide whether or not to include the intervention. The problem varies in seriousness with growing doubts or increased certainty. Assuming that instructional interventions might not be harmful, designers may decide to include the intervention in various settings with a conceived functionality of 50% in order to maximize learning opportunities. Added or non-embedded instructional interventions seem advisable only when learners are high self-regulators, that is, only when learners can be assumed to be able and willing to decide correctly about the use of instructional interventions. In such a situation, the designer may assume that these learners will make adequate decisions. If learners are not highly self-regulated the probability that the instructional intervention will be functional decreases. With an estimated functionality of 50% and only average self-regulators, the actual probability of the instructional intervention is reduced to 25%. With low self-regulators, the probability is 0.

However, when instructional interventions are embedded a different strategy is advisable, since a 50% probability of functionality implies an equally large probability of dysfunctionality. The instructional intervention may actually increase the processing load and therefore make the task more demanding. This may result in mathemathantic effects as illustrated by Ross et al. (1980) and by de Jong, de Hoog, and de Vries (1993).

This reasoning results in the conclusion that adding instructional interventions to the environment requires (a) ample evidence about the functionality of the instructional intervention or (b) the assumption that learners are highly self-regulated.

Luckily, instructional research has resulted in insights about the context-specific functionality of at least some instructional interventions. At the same time, the adequate use of even functional instructional interventions is not guaranteed because learners may not know why and/or how to profit from the opportunities provided by the instructional interventions. This may relate to a fundamental instructional design problem. In designing a learning environment, the designer analyzes a learning goal and the members of the target group. Based on these analyses, an environment consisting of a series of instructional interventions is designed. In doing so, the designer changes the learning task. The task is no longer limited to reaching the learning goal but to reaching it within a specific setting. As indicated by de Jong and his colleagues (de Jong et al., 1993; van Joolingen & de Jong, 1991) support offered should be considered as an additional learning task for the learner. This aspect needs more consideration in the design process itself.

This insight has already been endorsed in educational innovation. In the case of major instructional innovations, the need for training students (and teachers) to deal with new expectations and requirements has been acknowledged (e.g., Gräsel, Fischer, & Mandl, 2000). Such training may precede the actual confrontation with the learning environment or may be integrated in it through direct advice on the use of particular interventions or feedback on the use of interventions. This reasoning suggests that because the learning task is changed by embedding it in an instructional setting, it is not sufficient to consider task-related motivation and knowledge; context-related motivation and knowledge also require attention. This has already been acknowledged in the literature on the introduction of information and communication technology (ICT) into instruction.

The preceding analysis reveals two things: First, in case of doubt about the instructional intervention's functionality, a designer should choose to add the intervention only when learners are highly self-regulated. A lean version of the learning environment seems advisable when the instructional intervention is embedded or when doubts exist about the self-regulation skills of the students. Second, the designer may also consider the changes to the learning task and the knowledge and motivation of learners toward this learning context. Therefore, what makes learners knowledgeable and motivated to use a series of instructional interventions, requires research attention. Instructional knowledgeability refers to knowing one's way around in an instructional setting or learning environment. Instructional motivation refers to the extent of a knowledgeable learner's willingness to seize the affordances for learning included in the learning environment.

In the remainder of this contribution, an attempt is made to identify factors that contribute to this instructional motivation and knowledgeability. Then, various approaches for handling the phenomenon in learning environments are discussed.

Instructional Motivation and Knowledgeability

A review of the literature suggests a variety of factors have been posited to contribute to a motivated and knowledgeable use of instructional interventions. These factors must be considered when designing *a priori* or integrated 'training' on learning within a specific context. We distinguish between cognitive, metacognitive, motivational and affective variables, although it is clear that these variables constitute a complex rather than factors with direct and unique impacts. Moreover, this discussion is presented with awareness of the problems related to categorizing and labeling variables.

The first set of factors is *cognitive* in nature. In general, cognitive factors relate to knowledge about the instructional interventions themselves (see also Oliver & Hannafin, 2000). Problems may arise when (a) the instructional intervention is unfamiliar to students (e.g., students do not know what a concept map is), (b) potential purposes of the use of the intervention are not known by the student (e.g., students do not know that a concept map can be used for structuring ideas), and/or (c) the student does not know how to use the intervention generally or in the specific context of use (e.g., students do not have the skills to construct a concept map). Given the lack of knowledge or the presence of misconceptions, instructional interventions may go unnoticed (e.g., learners may not notice the presence of keywords in an instructional text), may be ignored (e.g., learners may not know the meaning of a button and therefore not use it) or may be used inappropriately (e.g., students may view diagrams as decorations rather than treat them as instructional devices).

The second set of factors is *metacognitive or regulative* in nature, referring to knowledgeability. Metacognitive factors that affect the use of instructional interventions pertain to learners' knowledge about the context-specific relationships between instructional interventions and learning, and to the ability to use the instructional intervention to foster learning (Elen, Lowyck, & Proost, 1996). Examples include the conceived and/or perceived functionality of instructional interventions. Winne (1985a), for instance, concluded that students must correctly perceive the intentions behind the instructional cues in order to use them adequately. Similarly, Marek, Griggs, and Christopher (1999) revealed that students' conceptions of a given adjunct aid may influence its use. Respondents in this study were disinclined to use adjunct aids since these aids required a more elaborate study pattern. From a similar perspective, Lowyck et al. (2004) analyzed the moderating effect of instructional conceptions. These authors argue that instructional conceptions in interaction with learning environments result in perceptions of the environment, which in turn affects the learning processes. Within the context of metacognitive factors, adaptive help-seeking as part of self-regulating strategies should also be mentioned. By adaptive help-seeking, Newman (2002) refers to the ability to judge one's own learning with respect to asking for help to learn 'independently'. By extension, adaptive help-seeking may also refer to the ability to look for help from the instructional interventions. Adaptive help-seeking may increase the probability that instructional interventions are used when needed. Adaptive help-seeking, however, does not guarantee that the interventions are used appropriately.

Motivational variables also affect the use of instructional interventions. Könings, Brand-Gruwel, and van Merriënboer (2005) refer to the self-efficacy tradition when discussing the use of instructional interventions as part of the broader category of learning activities. They point out that "According to the Self-Efficacy Theory of Bandura (1977), students form outcome expectations, referring to expectations about the usefulness of certain learning activities for reaching goals. Additionally, they have efficacy expectations: beliefs about the own ability to perform those learning activities. Both outcome expectations and efficacy expectancies must be positive, before a student will put forth effort to reach the educational goals." It is to be expected that instructional interventions will be used only if a learner is willing to expend effort for the task. In line with Bandura, it can be postulated that the probability of use of instructional interventions will increase when both outcome and efficacy expectations are positive. A similar suggestion is made in the literature on the avoidance of help-seeking. Ryan, Gheen, and Midgely (1998) argue that students with low self-efficacy may be less inclined to seek help. These students are more likely to believe that others will think that their need for help indicates a lack of ability. Students with high self-efficacy on the other hand, are more likely to seek and secure the necessary help. When encountering a failure or difficulty, these students do not worry about whether others will attribute this to their lack of ability. The literature (Ryan, Pintrich, & Midgley, 2001) on help-seeking additionally suggests that some students may deliberately avoid help, or more specifically, abstain from using instructional interventions. These students know that they need help, but still avoid it for practical concerns (e.g., asking for help is not practical, or too cumbersome; there are norms against asking for help) as well as psychosocial concerns (desire for autonomy, threat to competence). The use of instructional interventions may likewise be affected by different goal orientations. Ryan et al. (2001) and Newman (1998) have argued that a mastery goal orientation increases the probability for requesting help, whereas a performance goal orientation seems to be linked to asking for the right answer.

In the *affective* category, a number of variables can be found that pertain to the emotional reactions toward instructional interventions. In general terms, the literature on the use of technology is an example as it illustrates how affective variables have an impact on the use and hence, the effect of technology (e.g., Proost, Elen, & Lowyck, 1997). Research (e.g., Elen & Clarebout, 2001) has shown that people may feel threatened if induced to use technology and this feeling may reduce the use of that intervention as intended.

Suggested Solutions

The phenomenon of non-use or inadequate use of instructional interventions is an interactive one (Elen & Clarebout, 2005). Various authors have already discussed how the phenomenon could be dealt with in the learning environment. Three different groups of solutions have been proposed.

The first group of answers to the phenomenon of non-use or inadequate use of instructional interventions does not regard this phenomenon as problematic. Different responses in this group all reject the problematic nature of the phenomenon and claim that it might be an artifact of a 'traditional approach to teaching and instruction'. It is not the case that a learner lacks instructional motivation or is not instructionally knowledgeable; but rather that the learner is not submissive or compliant because he or she knows, within the specific context, better than any instructional designer/teacher what is important to learn and how this can be best accomplished. In other words, the observation that students do not use and/or do not use the interventions as intended is taken as the starting point in order to argue in favor of rich, open, and/or multiple inclusive learning environments. In our analysis, it has been argued that this is only the case when learners are highly self-regulated, a point now repeatedly made in the literature (Kirschner, Sweller, & Clark, in press; Mayer, 2004).

In rich environments, learners can pursue their own learning goals through support devices that suit them best. From this perspective, Goodyear (2000) calls for a 'user-centered educational technology'. He stresses that there is a "need to prioritize the development of technological support for the real-world activities in which our client learners engage" (p. 5). Goodyear builds on insights from cognitive psychology and instructional design. He argues in favor of using these insights to support the learners' actual activities. By focusing on lifelong learners, Goodyear proposes embedding instruction into the instruments and tools used by learners. Goodyear seems to argue that the phenomenon of inadequate or non-use is an artifact of irrelevant, inauthentic learning tasks. In other words, Goodyear argues that learners may have to be trained to use the interventions and that authentic tasks may motivate learners to use the interventions. Entwistle and Walker (2002) focus on the instructional setting. They stress the need for considering individual differences. They call not only for powerful learning environments but for multiple inclusive environments. Multiple inclusive environments comprise a variety of support in order to serve a diversified target group. Entwistle and Walker (2002) assume that support will be used as intended if readily available, adapted to the specific learner and linked to actual tasks. Entwistle and Walker seem to suggest that not only the learning task, but also its contextual embedding must be considered in the design. In its most radical form, representatives of this first group call for co-designing the learning environment (see Lowyck & Pöysä, 2001). Because learners know best what their learning environment should look like, it is up to them to design their learning environment in close collaboration with the instructor or instructional designer. These authors argue in favor of an immersive approach on how to learn to use the instructional interventions.

A different solution is presented by a number of authors who react against the 'naïve' assumption of high self-regulation skills and who are far more skeptical about students' instructional motivation and knowledgeability. By considering the generally negative outcomes from research on discovery learning (see Mayer, 2004) and learner control (Friend

& Cole, 1990; Large, 1996; Williams, 1996), an argument is made in favor of embedding support in the learning task. A classical example is the idea of Skinner (1968) to introduce teaching machines. While the ideas of Skinner rest on a behaviorist understanding of learning, cognitive findings also stress the need to structure learning tasks, embed support and then gradually withdraw that support. The 4C/ID-model of van Merriënboer (1997) remains the most elaborate example of a cognitive instructional design model that calls for deliberately structuring learning tasks and sub-tasks in order to increase the effectiveness of the learning environment.

The third group of authors has suggested that the problem might be resolved by adding information about the instructional interventions to the learning environment. Lowyck and Elen (1994) called this the double-exposure strategy. It is expected that by informing students about the functionality of the instructional interventions, their use will be optimized. The proposed solution is in line with ideas generated for instructions on consumer products. Taylor and Bower (2004) found that the intention to comply with product instructions is enhanced when people are told how compliance will lead to the desired outcome. The kind of information needed and when to deliver it are a subject of continued debate. The use of pedagogical agents is one of the possibilities. These agents can provide support adapted to the learning paths of the learners (Johnson, Rickel, & Lester, 2000), and explain instructional interventions when students fail to use potentially helpful supports. Therefore, when a more innovative set of instructional interventions is provided, some initial training seems advisable. The most typical example probably relates to the use of technology. It is self-evident that students must know how to handle the technology in order to benefit from the educational use of ICT.

The basic assumption underlying this third group of solutions is that instructional support will be adequately used if adequate information is provided about the nature and the importance of the learning task as well as about the importance, and the beneficial nature of instructional support. By doing so, this third group mainly addresses cognitive and metacognitive sources of the phenomenon.

Discussion and Conclusions

The phenomenon of non-use or inadequate use of instructional interventions raises a number of serious instructional design problems and highlights basic features of learning in instructional settings. Our analysis first highlighted that in some situations non-use or inadequate use of instructional interventions may not be problematic. This is especially the case when doubts exist about the functionality of the instructional intervention. In general, the analysis results in the advice not to embed instructional interventions in which functionality is not evident in order to avoid overload. It has been argued that adding an intervention is only indicated when learners are highly self-regulated. The analysis therefore results in the advice to confront complexity by reducing it in order to provide a lean learning environment.

When functional interventions are underused or inappropriately used, a different design problem arises. In such cases, the problem pertains to a fundamental observation: by supporting learners in executing a learning task, that task is changed. Hence, it is essential that sufficient attention be paid to the motivation and knowledge of a learner not only to execute a task but also to do so in a specific context. It is up to the designer to ensure that learners are sufficiently knowledgeable and motivated to use the interventions. It has been shown that various strategies can be used to ensure this. In the case of pervasive innovations, some initial training might be needed. In other cases, a more integrated approach might be followed by including advice and/or feedback in the environment itself. The analysis reveals that the attention of the designer cannot be limited to the domain of the learning task. Knowledge about the instructional interventions and about the relationship between the intervention and learning, as well as the motivation for learning within the learning environment needs to be considered during the design process. A step must be added to the design process. Once a design decision has been made, the reflective question about the use of that intervention by the learner needs to be raised. This clearly results in a closer relationship between design and development, as these questions are recursive.

Whereas the first line of reasoning highlights the benefits of lean learning environments, the second describes the need for elaboration in the environment. In order to address complexity for the student, it is clear that both arguments must be considered: The less lean the environment, the more elements will have to be added to support learners to deal with all the elements. The leaner the environment becomes, the more elegant it will become as well.

References

Aleven, V., Stahl, E., Schworm, S., Fischer, F., & Wallace, R. (2003). Help seeking and help design in interactive learning environments. *Review of Educational Research, 73*, 277–320.

Aly, M., Willems, G., & Elen, J. (2004). Instructional multimedia programs in orthodontic training: The need for sequencing models. *Orthodontics: The Journal for Professional Development and Clinical Skills, 1*, 293–300.

André, T. (1979). Does answering higher-level questions while reading facilitate productive learning? *Review of Educational Research, 49*, 280–318.

Atkinson, R. K., Derry, S. J., Renkl, A., & Wortham, D. (2000). Learning from examples: Instructional principles from the worked examples research. *Review of Educational Research, 70*, 181–214.

Bandura, A. (1977). *Social learning theory*. New York: General Learning Press.

Brush, T., & Saye, J. (2001). The use of embedded scaffolds with hypermedia-supported student-centered learning. *Journal of Educational Multimedia and Hypermedia, 10*, 333–356.

Carrier, C., Davidson, G., Higson, V., & Williams, M. (1984). Selection of options by field independent and field dependent children in a computer-based concept lesson. *Journal of Computer-Based Instruction, 11*, 49–54.

Carrier, C., Davidson, G., & Williams, M. (1985). The selection of instructional options in a computer-based co-ordinate concept lesson. *Educational Communication and Technology Journal, 33*, 199–212.

Carrier, C., Davidson, G., Williams, M., & Kalweit, C. (1986). Instructional options and encouragement effects in micro-computer concept lesson. *Journal of Educational Research, 79*, 222–229.

Chapelle, C., & Mizuno, S. (1989). Students' strategies with learner-controlled CALL. *Calico Journal, 7*(2), 25–47.

Clarebout, G., & Elen, J. (2006). Tool use in computer-based learning environments: Towards a research framework. *Computers in Human Behavior, 22*(3), 389–411.

Clarebout, G., & Elen, J. (2004). STUWAWA: Studying tool use with and without agents. In: L. Cantoni, & C. McLoughlin (Eds), *Proceedings of ED-media 2004. World conference on educational multimedia, hypermedia, & telecommunications* (pp. 747–752). Norfolk, VA: AACE.

Clark, R. E. (1990). When teaching kills learning: Research on mathemathantics. In: H. Mandl, E. De Corte, N. Bennett, & H. F. Friedrich (Eds), *Learning and instruction* (Vol. 2.2, pp. 1–22). New York: Pergamon Press.

Clark, R. E., & Estes, F. (2002). *Turning research into results. A guide to selecting the right performance solutions.* Atlanta, GA: CEP Press.

de Jong, T., de Hoog, R., & de Vries, F. (1993). Coping with complex environments: The effects of providing overviews and a transparent interface on learning with a computer simulation. *International Journal of Man-Machine Studies, 39*, 621–639.

de Jong, T., & van Joolingen, W. R. (1998). Scientific discovery learning with computer simulations of conceptual domains. *Review of Educational Research, 68*, 179–201.

Dillon, A., & Gabbard, R. (1998). Hypermedia as an educational technology: A review of the quantitative research literature on learner comprehension, control, and style. *Review of Educational Research, 68*, 322–349.

Elen, J., & Clarebout, G. (2001). An invasion in the classroom: Influence of an ill-structured innovation on instructional and epistemological beliefs. *Learning Environments Research, 4*, 87–105.

Elen, J., & Clarebout, G. (2005). Touching the limits of instructional design. *Educational Technology, 45*(5), 44–47.

Elen, J., & Louw, P. (submitted). The impact of instructional conceptions on the use of adjunct aids. *Educational Technology Research and Development.*

Elen, J., Lowyck, J., & Proost, K. (1996). Design of telematic learning environments: A cognitive mediational view. *Educational Research and Evaluation*: *An International Journal on Theory and Practice, 2*, 213–230.

Entwistle, N. J., & Walker, P. (2002). Strategic alertness and expanded awareness within sophisticated conceptions of teaching. In: N. Hativa, & P. Goodyear (Eds), *Teacher thinking, beliefs and knowledge in higher education* (pp. 15–40). Dordrecht, NL: Kluwer Academic Publishers.

Friend, C. L., & Cole, C. L. (1990). Learner control in computer-based instruction: A current literature review. *Educational Technology, 30*(11), 47–49.

Gagné, R. M., Briggs, L. J., & Wager, W. W. (1988). *Principles of instructional design* (3rd ed.). New York: Holt, Rinehart and Winston.

Goodyear, P. (2000). Environments for lifelong learning. Ergonomics, architecture and educational design. In: J. M. Spector, & T. M. Anderson (Eds), *Integrated and holistic perspectives on learning, instruction and technology* (pp. 1–18). Dordrecht, NL: Kluwer Academic Publishers.

Gräsel, C., Fischer, F., & Mandl, H. (2000). The use of additional information in problem-oriented learning environments. *Learning Environment Research, 3*, 287–325.

Greene, B. A., & Land, S. M. (2000). A qualitative analysis of scaffolding use in a resource-based learning environment involving the world wide web. *Journal of Educational Computing Research, 23*, 151–179.

Hannafin, M., Land, S., & Oliver, K. (1999). Open learning environments: Foundation, methods and models. In: C. M. Reigeluth (Ed.), *Instructional design theories and models. A new paradigm of instructional theory* (Vol. 2, pp. 115–140). Mahwah, NJ: Erlbaum.

Harp, S. F., & Mayer, R. E. (1998). How seductive details do their damage: A theory of cognitive interest in science teaching. *Journal of Educational Psychology, 90*, 414–434.

Hicken, S., Sullivan, H., & Klein, J. (1992). Learner control modes and incentive variations in computer-delivered instruction. *Educational Technology Research and Development, 40*, 15–26.

Johnson, W. L., Rickel, J. W., & Lester, J. C. (2000). Animated pedagogical agents. Face-to-face interaction in interactive learning environments. *International Journal of Artificial Intelligence in Education, 11*, 47–78.

Jonassen, D. H., Hernandez-Serrano, J., & Choi, I. (2000). Integrating constructivism and learning technologies. In: J. M. Spector, & T. M. Anderson (Eds), *Integrated and holistic perspectives on learning, instruction and technology* (pp. 103–128). Dordrecht, NL: Kluwer Academic Publishers.

Kalyuga, S., Ayers, P., Chandler, P., & Sweller, J. (2003). The expertise reversal effect. *Educational Psychologist, 38*, 23–31.

Kinzie, M. B., Sullivan, H. J., & Berdel, R. L. (1988). Learner control and achievement in science computer-assisted instruction. *Journal of Educational Psychology, 80*, 299–303.

Kirschner, P., Sweller, J., & Clark, R. E. (in press). Why minimal guidance during instruction does not work: An analysis of the failure of constructivist, discovery, problem-based, experiential, and inquiry-based teaching. *Educational Psychologist, 41*(2).

Klassen, R. (2002). A question of calibration: A review of the self-efficacy beliefs of students with learning disabilities. *Learning Disability Quarterly, 25*, 88–102.

Könings, K. D., Brand-Gruwel, S., & van Merriënboer, J. (2005). Towards more powerful learning environments through combining the perspectives of designers, teachers and students. *British Journal of Educational Psychology, 75*(4), 645–660.

Large, A. (1996). Hypertext instructional program and learner control: A research review. *Education for Information, 14*, 95–106.

Lowyck, J., & Elen, J. (1994). *Student's instructional metacognition in learning environments* (Internal Report). Leuven, BE: CIP&T.

Lowyck, J., Elen, J., & Clarebout, G. (2004). Instructional conceptions: Analysis from an instructional design perspective. *International Journal of Educational Research, 41*(6), 429–444.

Lowyck, J., & Pöysö, J. (2001). Design of collaborative learning environments. *Computers in Human Behavior, 17*, 507–516.

Marek, P., Griggs, R. A., & Christopher, A. N. (1999). Pedagogical aids in textbooks: Do students' perceptions justify their prevalence? *Teaching of Psychology, 26*, 11–19.

Mayer, R. E. (2004). Should there be a three-strikes rule against pure discovery learning? The case for guide methods of instruction. *American Psychologist, 59*(1), 14–19.

Merrill, M. D., Drake, L., Lacy, M., Pratt, J., & the ID2 Research Group. (1996). Reclaiming instructional design. *Educational Technology, 36*(5), 5–7.

Newman, R. S. (1998). Students' help seeking during problem solving: Influences of personal and contextual achievement goals. *Journal of Educational Psychology, 90*, 644–658.

Newman, R. S. (2002). How self-regulated learners cope with academic difficulty: The role of adaptive help seeking. *Theory into Practice, 41*(2), 132–138.

Oliver, K. M., & Hannafin, M. J. (2000). Student management of web-based hypermedia resources during open-ended problem solving. *The Journal of Educational Research, 94*, 75–92.

Perkins, D. N. (1985). The fingertip effect: How information-processing technology changes thinking. *Educational Researcher, 14*(7), 11–17.

Proost, K., Elen, J., & Lowyck, J. (1997). Effects of gender on perceptions and preferences for telematic learning environments. *Journal of Research on Computing in Education, 29*, 370–384.

Ross, S. M., Rakow, E. A., & Bush, A. J. (1980). Instructional adaptation for self-managed learning systems. *Journal of Educational Psychology, 72*, 312–320.

Rothkopf, E. Z. (1971). The concept of mathemagenic activities. *Review of Educational Research, 40*, 325–336.

Ryan, A. M., Gheen, M. H., & Midgely, C. (1998). Why do students avoid asking for help? An examination of the interplay among students' academic self-efficacy, teachers' social-emotional role, and the classroom goal structure. *Journal of Educational Psychology, 90*, 528–535.

Ryan, A. M., Pintrich, P. R., & Midgley, C. (2001). Avoiding seeking help in the classroom: Who and why? *Educational Psychology Review, 13*(2), 93–113.

Schnackenberg, H. L., & Sullivan, H. J. (2000). Learner control over full and lean computer-based instruction under differing ability level. *Educational Technology Research and Development, 48*(2), 19–35.

Skinner, B. F. (1968). *The technology of teaching.* New York: Appleton-Century-Crofts.

Stone, N. J. (2000). Exploring the relationship between calibration and self-regulated learning. *Educational Psychology Review, 12*, 437–475.

Taylor, V. A., & Bower, A. B. (2004). Improving product instruction compliance: "If you tell me why, I might comply". *Psychology & Marketing, 21*, 229–245.

Tobias, S., & Everson, H. T. (1996). *Assessing metacognitive knowledge monitoring* (College Board Report No. 96-11). New York: College Entrance Examination Board.

Tobias, S., & Everson, T. H. (2002). *Knowing what you know and what you don't: Further research on metacognitive knowledge monitoring* (College Board Report No. 2002–3). New York: College Entrance Examination Board.

Todorovich, J. R., Wirth, C. K., Zhang, J. J., Tillman, M. D., & Fleming, D. S. (2004). Measuring student compliance in elementary physical education. *Teaching Elementary Physical Education, 15*(4), 28–30.

Van Joolingen, W. R., & de Jong, T. (1991). Supporting hypothesis generation by learners exploring an interactive computer simulation. *Instructional Science, 20*, 389–404.

Van Merriënboer, J. J. (1997). *Training complex cognitive skills: A four component instructional deisgn model for technical training.* Englewood Cliffs, NJ: Educational Technology.

Veerman, K., de Jong, T., & van Joolingen, W. R. (2000). Promoting self-directed learning in simulation-based discovery learning environments through intelligent support. *Interactive Learning Environments, 8*(1), 1–27.

Williams, M. D. (1996). Learner-control and instructional technology. In: D. H. Jonassen (Ed.), *Handbook of research for educational communications and technology* (pp. 957–983). New York: Macmillan Library.

Winne, P. H. (1982). Minimizing the black box problem to enhance the validity of theories about instructional effects. *Instructional Science, 11*, 13–28.

Winne, P. H. (1985a). Cognitive processing in the classroom. In: T. Husen, & T. N. Postlethwaite (Eds), *International encyclopaedia of education: Research and studies* (pp. 795–808). Oxford, UK: Pergamon Press.

Winne, P. H. (1985b). Steps toward promoting cognitive achievements. *The Elementary School Journal, 85*, 673–693.

Winne, P. (2004) Students' calibration of knowledge and learning processes: Implications for designing powerful software learning environments. *International Journal of Educational Research, 41*(6), 461–488.

Chapter 11

Performance Assessment and Learning Task Selection in Environments for Complex Learning

Jeroen J. G. van Merriënboer, Dominique Sluijsmans, Gemma Corbalan, Slava Kalyuga, Fred Paas and Colin Tattersall

Introduction

Recent instructional theories tend to focus on authentic learning tasks that are based on real-life experiences as the driving force for complex learning (Merrill, 2002; Van Merriënboer & Kirschner, 2001). The general assumption is that providing learners with authentic "whole" tasks helps them to integrate the knowledge, skills, and attitudes necessary for effective task performance; gives them the opportunity to learn to coordinate qualitatively different constituent skills that make up this performance, and eventually enables them to transfer what is learned to their daily life or work settings. This assumption forms the basis of several educational approaches, such as the case method, project-based education, problem-based learning, and competence-based education.

At the same time, there is a wish to expand the flexibility of education to better adapt it to the needs of individual learners and to improve its efficiency. A flexible curriculum is defined as a curriculum in which not all learners receive the same sequence of learning tasks (i.e., one educational programme for all), but in which each learner receives his or her *own* sequence of learning tasks that is dynamically adapted to individual needs, progress, and preferences (i.e., a tailored educational programme for each student). Assessment is critical to the selection of a suitable next learning task. At one extreme, the system (teacher, eLearning application) assesses a learner's progress and selects the next learning task for the student to work on. At the other extreme, the self-regulated learner continuously self-assesses his or her progress and selects the next learning task from all available tasks. But as a rule, learning task selection is a shared responsibility of the system and the learner, where the responsibility of the learners may increase as they further develop the self-regulation skills that are necessary to select suitable learning tasks, including self-assessment skills, orienting skills (what could I learn from this task?), planning skills (how much time and effort would I need to invest in this task?), monitoring skills (did I learn enough to stop working on this task?), and so on.

The central question we will try to answer in this chapter is how the dynamic adaptation of learning tasks can best be achieved. First, a brief description is given of the four-component instructional design model (4C/ID-model), which uses authentic learning tasks as the basic building blocks of an educational programme. For the dynamic selection of learning tasks, critical factors in this model are the available *support* for each task and the task *difficulty*. Second, the key role of assessment leading to task selection is discussed. It is argued that performance measures alone are not a sufficient basis for task selection, and may be improved by taking into account the time and effort that students invest in reaching this performance. Furthermore, rich learning tasks aim at the integration of knowledge, skills, and attitudes and therefore need to be assessed on many qualitatively different aspects, requiring a mix of measurement instruments. Protocol portfolio scoring (PPS; Straetmans, Sluijsmans, Bolhuis, & van Merriënboer, 2003) offers a method to combine the findings of different instruments for task selection. Third, different models for the dynamic selection of learning tasks with a particular level of support and a particular level of difficulty are discussed. The final section presents the main conclusions and directions for future research.

The 4C/ID-Model

Van Merriënboer's 4C/ID-model (Van Merriënboer, 1997; Van Merriënboer, Clark, & de Croock, 2002a) describes how learning tasks fulfil the role of a *framework* for an integrated curriculum (see Figure 11.1; the "circles" represent learning tasks). Three requirements on this framework are that (1) learning tasks are organized in easy-to-difficult categories or task classes (the dotted boxes around sets of learning tasks), (2) learners receive full support for the first learning task in each task class after which support is gradually reduced to none for the last learning task, and (3) learning tasks provide a high variability of practice.

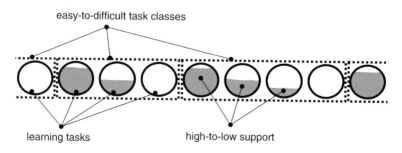

Figure 11.1: A sequence of learning tasks, organized in easy-to-difficult task classes and with fading support in each task class.

First, it is clearly impossible to use very difficult learning tasks at the start of a curriculum or educational programme because this would yield excessive cognitive load for the learners, with negative effects on learning, performance, and motivation (Sweller, Van Merriënboer, & Paas, 1998; Van Merriënboer, Kirschner, & Kester, 2003; Van Merriënboer & Sweller, 2005). The common solution is to let learners start their work on relatively easy learning tasks and progress towards more difficult tasks. In a whole-task approach, the coordination and integration of constituent skills (e.g., routine aspects, problem-solving aspects, attitudinal aspects) is stressed from the very beginning, so that learners quickly develop a holistic vision of the task that is gradually embellished during training. This is akin to the "global before local skills" principle in cognitive apprenticeship (Collins, Brown, & Newman, 1989) or the "zoom lens metaphor" in Reigeluth's (1999) elaboration theory. There are categories of learning tasks or *task classes*, each of which represents a version of the task with a particular level of difficulty (the dotted boxes in Figure 11.1). Learning tasks within a particular task class are equivalent in the sense that they can be performed using the same body of knowledge. A more difficult task class requires more knowledge or more embellished knowledge for effective performance than the preceding, easier task classes.

Second, when learners start to work on a new, more difficult task class, it is essential to give them support for performing the tasks. Support may be fully integrated with the learning tasks by providing — a part of — an acceptable solution to the learners, as is done in a case study or in a completion task where the learner must complete a partially given solution, or it may be separated from the task and take the form of guidance, as is done by a process worksheet that guides the learner through the process of performing the task by giving hints and directions. The support always diminishes in a process of "scaffolding" as learners acquire more expertise (see the filling of the circles in Figure 11.1). One powerful approach to scaffolding, for instance, is known as the "completion strategy". In this strategy, learners start with fully worked examples or case studies that confront them not only with a given problem state and a desired goal state, but also with an example solution. Questions and evaluation assignments stimulate the learners to reflect on the strong and weak points of the given solution. Studying worked examples focuses learners' attention on problem states and associated solution steps and so enables them to induce generalized solutions or schemata. Then, learners may proceed to work on completion tasks that present a given state, a goal state, and a *partial* solution that must be completed. There is still considerable support, because the given part of the solution provides direction to the problem-solving process. Finally, learners receive conventional tasks without support — only then are they required to construct complete solutions. When learners are able to perform conventional tasks independently up to pre-specified standards, they may proceed to the next task class. Several studies showed strong positive effects on learning for the completion strategy (Renkl & Atkinson, 2003; Van Merriënboer & de Croock, 1992).

Third, the complete set of tasks students work on should display a high "variability of practice", that is, the learning tasks should differ from each other on all dimensions on which tasks also differ in the real world. This is typically reached by designing learning tasks in such a way that they differ with regard to their embedded assessments, the context or situation in which the task is performed, the way the task is presented, the saliency of defining characteristics, and so forth. This enables learners to abstract away from details and to construct general cognitive schemata that allow for transfer of learning to daily life or future work settings (Paas & Van Merriënboer, 1994a).

In a flexible curriculum, professional competencies, which are examples of complex skills, are not coupled to separate modules or courses but gradually developed through work on learning tasks. It should be possible to take differences between students into account when suitable tasks are selected. Some students have skills acquired elsewhere that should be taken into account, and some students are better able to acquire new complex skills and therefore need less practice and coaching than other students. In the 4C/ID-framework described above, this means that for each individual student it should be possible at any given point in time to select the best task class to work on (i.e., the optimal *difficulty* of the next task), and to select within this task class a learning task with an optimal level of *support*. Thus, a high-ability student may quickly proceed from task class to task class and mainly work on tasks with little support, while a low-ability student may need many more tasks to complete the programme, progress slowly from task class to task class, and work mainly on tasks with sizeable support. This dynamic approach to task selection requires a continuous assessment of learners' progress.

Assessment

The dynamic process of task selection is based on the continuous assessment of the level of expertise of individual learners. Well-designed assessments must be valid, reliable, and fair as they form the basis for making sound decisions about the learning trajectory of students. In learning environments that are oriented towards integrated objectives, performance assessments focus on the ability to use combinations of acquired skills, knowledge, and attitudes. They often require learners to apply these combinations in a real-life context. Outcomes of a learner's performance are analysed, whereby a decision is made based on the demonstrated level of proficiency. Decisions are then made about the level of achievement attained by comparing student performance to pre-specified standards. For dynamic task selection, several dimensions need to be included in the assessment of performance. First, the 4C/ID-model indicates that in addition to performance, the amount of effort that a student invests to reach this level of performance may be important. Second, complex task performance should be assessed on sometimes many qualitatively different aspects (e.g., a multitude of routine, problem-solving, and attitudinal aspects of behaviour), which is made possible by PPS.

Mental Effort and Efficiency

Models for dynamic task selection typically take learners' performance as their input, defined in terms of the number of correctly answered test items, the number of errors, or speed. However, the 4C/ID-model stresses that other dimensions, such as cognitive load, are at least equally important for the assessment of prior knowledge, which is simply defined as the learner's initial level of expertise, and expertise as it further develops during training. Cognitive load is a multidimensional construct. First, it includes intrinsic load, which originates from the interaction between task characteristics (e.g., task complexity, task format) and learner characteristics (e.g., prior knowledge, age, spatial ability) and so yields an *a priori* estimate of cognitive load. Second, it includes extraneous load, which is caused by processes that do not directly contribute to learning (e.g., integrating different information sources, searching for relevant information). Third, it includes germane load, which genuine learning processes pose on the cognitive system. The total load is reflected in a measurement of *mental effort*, which refers to the cognitive capacity that is actually allocated to accommodate the demands imposed by the learning task (Paas & Van Merriënboer, 1993, 1994b). It yields important information that is not necessarily reflected in load and performance measures, because the voluntary investment of cognitive resources is taken into account. For instance, it is quite feasible for two persons to attain the same performance levels with one person working through a very laborious process to arrive at the correct solution, whereas the other person reaches the same solution with a minimum of effort. While both people demonstrate identical performance, "expertise" may be argued to be lower for the person who exerts substantial effort than for the person who performs the task with minimum effort — and the optimal next learning task for the first person is likely to be less difficult, and/or contain more support, than the optimal next task for the second person.

Thus, an appropriate assessment of expertise should include measures of mental effort and performance. Paas, Tuovinen, Tabbers, and van Gerven (2003) discuss different measurement techniques for mental effort, including rating scales, secondary task methods, and psychophysiological measures. On the basis of a comprehensive review of about 30 studies, they conclude that "… the use of rating scales to measure mental effort remains popular, because they are easy to use; do not interfere with primary task performance; are inexpensive; can detect small variations in workload; are reliable, and provide decent convergent, construct, and discriminate validity" (p. 68). Hambleton, Jaeger, Plake, and Mills (2000) discuss several methods for the measurement of complex task performance, which assess and weigh different aspects of behaviour. One such method, the PPS, is discussed in the next section.

A final step in the assessment of expertise is the difficult task of combining a student's mental effort and performance measures, because a meaningful interpretation of a certain level of invested effort can only be given in the context of its associated performance and vice versa. Paas and Van Merriënboer (1993; see also Paas et al., 2003) developed a computational approach to combine measures of mental effort with measures of associated performance to compare the *mental efficiency* associated with instructional conditions — under the assumption that learners' behaviour in a particular condition is more efficient if their performance is higher than might be expected on the basis of their invested mental effort or, equivalently, if their invested mental effort is lower than might be expected on the basis of their performance. Using this approach, high task performance associated with low effort is called high mental efficiency, whereas low task performance with high effort is called low mental efficiency. It should be stressed that mental efficiency is a *relative* construct, because an efficiency of zero does not refer to the zero point of a measurement scale, but to the relationship between performance and mental effort. Nevertheless, it is believed to be a stronger basis for task selection than performance alone.

Protocol Portfolio Scoring

PPS (Straetmans et al., 2003) allows for systematic and continuous monitoring of a student's progress on different aspects of performance. For example, if student doctors learn to examine patients they should be assessed for one-and-the-same learning task on routine aspects (e.g., auscultation), problem-solving aspects (e.g., diagnosing), and attitudinal aspects (e.g., friendly approach). According to the 4C/ID-model, assessments on learning tasks within the same task class, which may be supported or unsupported, will typically be used to decide on the level of support for the next learning task; assessments on unsupported learning tasks only will typically be used to decide on a possible shift to a more difficult task class.

In Table 11.1, an example is given of the formative use of PPS for the selection of new learning tasks. A first requirement of PPS is that a range of learning tasks with different embedded assessment methods (e.g., tasks with multiple-choice tests, tasks with situational judgment tests, tasks with work-sample tests, tasks with a performance-on-the-job assessment etc.; see the column labelled *Task Type* in Table 11.1) is used to gather reliable and valid information about a learner's performance. Each assessment method has a weak link in the quality chain that links the performance of the learner to the conclusion about the professional competency in a particular context. Therefore, it is important to choose for a mix of assessment methods that covers all the quality aspects (Straetmans & Sanders, 2001).

Educational programmes designed according to the 4C/ID-model always specify the standards for routine, problem-solving, and attitudinal aspects of performance. This satisfies the second requirement of PPS, namely, that one pre-specified set of standards for acceptable performance is available to assess a student on each learning task (see the top row in Table 11.1, where performance is judged on eight aspects). Usually, content experts determine the standards for all relevant aspects of behaviour. Standards may pertain to *criteria*, which specify minimum requirements in terms of accuracy, speed, productivity, and so forth; *values*, which indicate that the task must be performed according to appropriate rules, regulations or conventions, and *attitudes*, which often refer to the way other persons should be approached. In PPS, assessment is always criterion-referenced because the learner's current level of expertise is compared with intended outcomes rather than with peer students.

To illustrate PPS, an overview of a fictitious portfolio of one task class with six learning tasks is presented in Table 11.1. The assessment methods embedded in the — supported (e.g., worked examples and completion problems) and unsupported (e.g., conventional problems) — tasks in each task class are on the vertical dimension, and the assessment standards for the different aspects of performance are on the horizontal dimension. Table 11.1 indicates that at each point in time, when the assessment results of a new learning task are added to the scoring system, decisions can be based on a "horizontal evaluation" and a "vertical evaluation". The horizontal evaluation indicates to which degree the standards are met for a student's *overall* performance; it reflects the student's level of mastery of the whole complex skill or professional competency. The vertical evaluation indicates the degree to which the standards are met for *one particular aspect* of a student's performance, as assessed with various assessment tools on a range of learning tasks. It reflects the student's level of mastery of only one aspect of the complex skill.

PPS in combination with a dedicated computer programme provides a sound basis for task selection. With regard to the desired level of support, the horizontal evaluation of learning tasks within the same task class is of critical importance. Support decreases when horizontal evaluation results improve, support increases when horizontal evaluation results degrade, and no more support is provided when horizontal evaluation results are above the standard.

Table 11.1: Overview of a fictitious protocol portfolio scoring.

Task class	Task	Task type[a]	Assessor		Vertical standards (for 8 aspects)								Horizontal standards (over scored aspects)		
					4.7	3.5	2.5	3.5	3.5	3.5	4.0	4.5	Horizontal standard[b]	Mean score	Decision[c]
					Score per aspect (maximum score = 6 for each aspect)										
1	1.1	WOE-MCT	HK		3	2	3	3	4	2	2	3			
			Mean Score		3.0	2.0	3.0	3.0	4.0	2.0	2.0	3.0	3.74	3.0	–
			Decision		–	–	+	–	+	–	–	–			
1	1.2	COM-SJT	GS		5	2	1	3	3	4	2	3			
			Mean score		4.0	2.0	2.0	3.0	3.5	3.0	2.0	3.0	3.71	2.8	–
			Decision		–	–	–	–	+	–	–	–			
1	1.3	WOE-WST	GS		6	5	5	5	6	6	6	5			
			Mean score		4.7	3.5	3.0	4.0	4.0	4.0	4.0	4.0	3.71	3.8	+
			Decision		+	+	+	+	+	+	+	–			
1	1.4	CON-POJ	SA[d]		3	4	2	4	4	3	3	4			
			Mean score		4.3	3.7	2.5	4.0	4.0	4.0	3.7	4.0	3.71	3.7	–
			Decision		–	+	+	+	+	+	–	–			
1	1.5	COM-WST	HK		5	4	4	6	6	5	6	4			
			Mean score		4.3	4.0	3.3	4.3	4.4	4.3	4.3	4.3	3.71	4.0	+
			Decision		–	+	+	+	+	+	+	–			
1	1.6	COM-POJ	AH		5	4	6	5	5	6	6	5			
			Mean score		4.4	4.0	3.8	4.5	4.5	4.6	4.6	4.6	3.71	4.3	+
			Decision		–	+	+	+	+	+	+	+			

(*Continued*)

Table 11.1: (*Continued*).

Task class	Task	Task type[a]	Assessor	Vertical standards (for 8 aspects) — Score per aspect (maximum score = 6 for each aspect)								Horizontal standards (over scored aspects)		
				4.7	**3.5**	**2.5**	**3.5**	**3.5**	**3.5**	**4.0**	**4.5**	Horizontal standard[b]	Mean score	Decision[c]
2	2.1	WOP-MCT	PA[d]	2	5		3	3	5		4			
			Mean score	2.0	5.0		3.0	3.0	5.0		4.0	3.9	3.7	
			Decision	–	+		–	–	+		–			–

Et cetera...

[a] WOE-MCT, worked-out example combined with multiple-choice test; COM-SJT, completion assignment combined with a situational judgement test; WOE-WST, worked-out example combined with a work sample test; CON-POJ, conventional task combined with a performance-on-the-job assessment, COM-WST, completion assignment combined with work sample test; CON-POJ, conventional task combined with performance-on-the-job assessment, and WOP-MCT, worked-out example with process support combined with multiple-choice tst.

[b] Mean of the measured vertical standards.

[c] –, performance below standard thus vary support; +, performance above standard thus withdraw support.

[d] SA, self-assessment; PA, peer assessment.

Furthermore, vertical evaluation results indicate which aspects of performance should be emphasized or de-emphasized in the next learning task (because they are not yet mastered, or they are already mastered by the student, respectively). With regard to the desired level of difficulty, the horizontal evaluation of unsupported tasks is of critical importance: The learner progresses to a next task class or difficulty level only when evaluation results for unsupported tasks are above the standard. This process repeats itself until the student successfully performs the conventional, unsupported tasks in the most difficult task class.

Research on Models for Dynamic Task Selection

Salden, Paas, and van Merriënboer (2006; see also van Merriënboer & Luursema, 1996) discuss the value of the 4C/ID-model for adaptive eLearning, with a focus on the dynamic selection of learning tasks. They describe adaptive eLearning as a straightforward two-step cycle: (1) assessment of a learner's expertise, for example, in terms of efficiency, PPS, or a combination of both, and (2) task selection. Previous studies selected *either* tasks with a particular level of support *or* tasks with a particular level of difficulty. For example, van Merriënboer, Schuurman, de Croock, and Paas (2002b) report a study on teaching computer programming in which three groups of participants received learning tasks with support, no support, or adaptive support. For a transfer test that was performed after the training, the proportion of correctly used programming concepts was higher for the adaptive support group than for the support and no-support groups. Another set of studies was concerned with the difficulty of selected learning tasks rather than the given level of support. In the domain of air traffic control, Camp, Paas, Rikers, and van Merriënboer (2001) and Salden, Paas, Broers, and van Merriënboer (2004) compared the effectiveness of a fixed easy-to-difficult sequence of learning tasks with dynamic task selection based on the relative measure of mental efficiency described before: the higher the mental efficiency, the more difficult the next learning task. In both studies, dynamic task selection yielded more efficient transfer test performance than the use of a fixed sequence of tasks.

In this section, we focus exclusively on studies and models that adapt *both* the level of support *and* the level of difficulty of learning tasks to the level of expertise of individual learners. We distinguish three types of models. In system-controlled models, some educational agent (teacher, eLearning application) selects the optimal learning task, for a particular student, from all available tasks. In shared-responsibility models, some educational agent selects a suitable subset of learning tasks, for a particular student, from all available tasks, after which the student makes a final selection from this subset. Thus, there is partial system control (i.e., selecting the subset) and partial student control (i.e., selecting the final task). In advisory models, an educational agent may or may not select a suitable subset of tasks, but the student is advised on his or her selection of the next task from this subset to work on.

System-Controlled Models for Task Selection

Kalyuga and Sweller (2005) conducted a study in the domain of algebra in which both the level of difficulty and the given support for the next task were adapted to the mental efficiency of the learner. A 9-point self-rating scale was used to measure mental effort and a rapid assessment test was used to measure performance. This test asked students to indicate their first step towards the solution of a complex task. High correlations (up to 0.92) were found between performance on rapid assessment tests and traditional performance tests that required complete solutions of corresponding tasks (Kalyuga & Sweller, 2004). *Cognitive efficiency* (E) was defined as a combined measure for monitoring learners' progress during instruction and real-time adaptation of learning tasks to changing levels of expertise. It is simply defined as $E = P/R$, where R is the mental effort rating and P the performance measure on the same task. This indicator has the same general features as mental efficiency defined by Paas and van Merriënboer (1993), in that it is higher if similar levels of performance are reached with less effort or, alternatively, higher levels of performance are reached with the same mental effort. Students were presented with tasks at different levels of difficulty, and for each level a critical level of cognitive efficiency (Ecr) was arbitrarily defined as the maximum performance score (which was different per difficulty level) divided by the maximum mental effort score (which was always 9). Cognitive efficiency is positive if $E > E$cr and negative if $E < E$cr. The rationale for this definition is that if someone invests maximum mental effort in a task but does not display the maximum level of performance, his or her expertise should be regarded as suboptimal. On the other hand, if someone performs at the maximum level with less than a maximum mental effort, his or her expertise should be regarded as optimal.

In the adaptive group, learners were presented with algebra tasks at three different difficulty levels. If their cognitive efficiency was negative for tasks at the lowest level, they continued with the study of worked examples; if their cognitive efficiency was positive for tasks at the lowest level but negative for tasks at the second level, they continued with simple completion tasks; if their cognitive efficiency was positive for tasks at the lowest and second level but negative for tasks at the third level, they continued with difficult completion tasks, and, finally, if their cognitive efficiency was positive for tasks at all three levels, they continued with conventional problems. Similar adaptive methods were applied when students were working on the worked examples, completion tasks, or conventional problems (see Figure 11.2). Each student in the adaptive condition was paired to a student in the control condition, who served as a yoked control. Kalyuga and Sweller (2005) report higher gains in algebraic skills from pre-test to post-test and higher gains in cognitive efficiency for the adaptive group than for the control group. Thus, in agreement with studies that adapted either support or difficulty, adaptive learning was also found to be superior to non-adaptive learning when both support and difficulty were adapted in an integrated fashion.

Shared-Responsibility Models for Task Selection

System-controlled models as discussed in the previous section have at least two disadvantages: (1) the lack of any freedom of choice over tasks may negatively affect learners' motivation, and (2) students have no opportunity to learn how to select their own learning tasks and plan their own learning, whereas the development of self-regulation skills is seen to be important. With regard to the first point, research points out that *some* freedom of choice indeed has positive effects on motivation, but *too much* freedom may lead to stress, high mental effort, and demotivation (Iyengar & Lepper, 2000; Schwartz, 2004). Thus, a

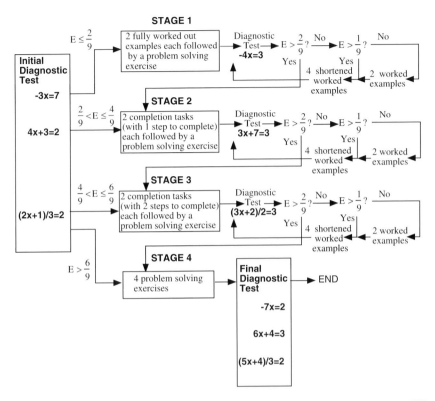

Figure 11.2: Selection algorithm governing the selection of learning tasks with different levels of difficulty (stages 1–4) and support (worked examples, completion tasks, and conventional tasks/problem-solving exercises) (Adapted from Kalyuga and Sweller, 2005).

shared-responsibility model in which the system makes a pre-selection of suitable tasks, and the student makes the final selection, is expected to be superior to a completely student-controlled model in which the learner has to select one task from a very large set of available tasks. With regard to the second point, a gradual transfer of responsibility over task selection from the system to the student, as his or her self-regulation skills further develop, may be desirable.

A first pilot study has been conducted to compare a system-controlled model with a shared-responsibility model on motivation/interest and learning outcomes. Students were working in an electronic learning environment (see Figure 11.3a) that presented learning tasks in the domain of dietetics. A simulator called "body weight" (see Figure 11.3b) enabled students to execute required actions to perform the learning tasks. For instance, it allowed students to study how particular changes in someone's diet or daily physical exercises affected his or her body weight over time. The learning tasks were selected from a database containing tasks that differed from each other with regard to difficulty, amount of support, and other task features. Five levels of difficulty, or task classes, were distinguished. Within each task class there were five levels of learner support, which can be ordered from

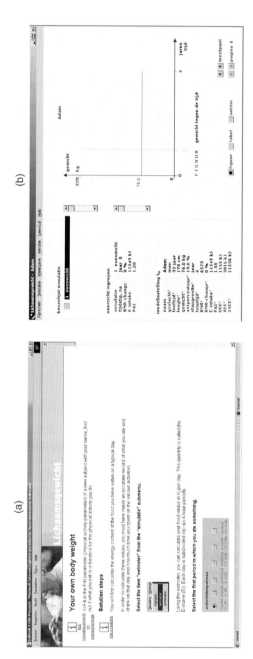

Figure 11.3: The learning environment, showing part of a learning task (a) and the simulator used to perform the task (b).

high to low: (1) worked examples with "process support" or how-to instructions; (b) worked examples with "product support" or exemplary screen dumps; (c) completion tasks with a small part to complete; (d) completion tasks with a large part to complete, and (e) conventional tasks without support. Thus, there were 25 ordered categories of tasks (least difficult with five decreasing support levels, more difficult with five decreasing support levels, and so forth). In each of those 25 categories, tasks had equal difficulty and equal support but yet differed from each other on several features that also differ in the real world (e.g., dealing with different persons with different body weights, sex, age, diets, smoking habits, physical exercise patterns, cultural backgrounds, etc.).

As in the study of Kalyuga and Sweller (2005), each learning task was selected on the basis of a combination of individual performance and mental effort scores. Performance was assessed for each learning task by (a) scores on multiple-choice questions, and (b) accuracy scores for using the simulator, after which the combined score was transformed into a 7-point scale. A 7-point rating scale was also used to measure mental effort. Performance and mental effort reports determined the appropriate difficulty level and/or the appropriate amount of learner support within the current difficulty level. Table 11.2 shows the task-selection algorithm. Mental effort scores (ME) are subtracted from performance (P) scores in the formula: $P - ME$. That is, the higher the performance is, and the lower the invested mental effort is (e.g., a score of 5 on performance and 2 on mental effort), the easier the next task is for the student. In that case the students will jump forward 3 steps ($5 - 2 = +3$), that is, the level of support will decrease 3 levels. Only after a student has properly completed a conventional task at a particular difficulty level, will the system allow him or her to progress to the next difficulty level. In the system-controlled condition, the system selects the optimum level of difficulty and support and then randomly selects one learning task to present to the student from the appropriate category. In the shared-responsibility condition, the system also selects the optimum level of difficulty and support, but now the student is given the possibility to choose one task from the subset of appropriate learning tasks (i.e., tasks with equal difficulty and support but dealing with different persons with different characteristics). The — partial — learner control in the shared-responsibility condition is expected to be more appealing and motivating for students and so increase learning outcomes.

Table 11.2:   Task-selection algorithm indicating jump sizes between learning tasks.

Mental effort	Performance						
	1 0%	2 16.66%	3 33.33%	4 50%	5 66.66%	6 83.33%	7 100%
1	0	0	0	+3	+4	+5	+5
2	0	0	0	+2	+3	+4	+5
3	−2	−1	0	+1	+2	+3	+4
4	−3	−2	−1	0	+1	+2	+3
5	−4	−3	−2	−1	0	+1	+2
6	−5	−4	−3	−2	0	0	0
7	−5	−5	−4	−3	0	0	0

Results of this pilot study show that students in the shared-responsibility group ($n = 13$) achieved somewhat higher performance scores ($M = 59.4$; $SD = 13.70$) than students in the system-controlled group ($n = 12$; $M = 55.5$; $SD = 17.86$; $t(23) = -0.62$). Students in the shared-responsibility group reported lower invested mental effort ($M = 3.70$; $SD = 1.08$) than students in the system-controlled group ($M = 4.11$; $SD = 1.15$; $t(23) = 0.94$). And students in the shared-responsibility group showed higher mental efficiency ($M = 0.21$; $SD = 1.12$) than students in the system-controlled group ($M = -0.23$; $SD = 1.12$; $t(23) = -0.90$). While all observed effects are in the expected direction, the differences are not statistically significant. A possible explanation for the lack of significant differences might be the small amount of only three tasks that students could choose from in the shared-responsibility condition. Future studies will provide students with much more freedom of choice.

Motivation was measured with items from the interest/enjoyment subscale of the intrinsic motivation inventory (IMI; Tsigilis & Theodosiou, 2003). The IMI is a multidimensional measurement instrument for intrinsic motivation and self-regulation. The interest/enjoyment subscale is considered to be the most important self-report measure of intrinsic motivation, which is in turn expected to positively influence learning outcomes. On the items of this subscale (7-point rating scales) filled out after the course, students in the shared-responsibility condition reported a marginally significant higher interest in the training ($M = 2.77$; $SD = 0.95$) than students in the system-controlled condition ($M = 2.05$; $SD = 0.88$; $t(19) = -1.807$, $p < 0.10$). These preliminary results indicate an advantage of adding partial learner control to a system that adapts both the difficulty and the level of support of the learning tasks.

Follow-up studies will differ from the current study in three ways. First, the present study compared two highly adaptive conditions, which adapted both the amount of support and the level of difficulty of learning tasks to the individual learner and thus only differed with regard to learner control over tasks with different features. In future studies, non-adaptive conditions will be included to increase the difference between conditions. Second, the amount of tasks to choose from was very small in the present study: Learners could only choose from three tasks with different features. Future studies will drastically increase the number of tasks to choose from in the shared-responsibility condition. Finally, future studies will not only give learners control over task features, but also over the level of support and task difficulty. Giving learners control over more aspects of the learning tasks may, under particular conditions, further increase their interest and motivation. Such studies may also progressively increase learner control as their level of expertise increases; for instance, first give students only control over selecting task features with a given difficulty and support (as in the presented study), then give them control over task features and the amount of learner support, and finally give them control over task features, support, as well as task difficulty.

Advisory Models for Task Selection

Shared-responsibility models make it possible to give students an optimal level of control over task selection. This level of student control will typically be higher towards the end of an educational programme than in its beginning, because students gradually develop the self-regulation skills that are necessary for the independent selection of learning tasks. In a sense, this increased level of student control or, vice versa, decreased level of system control, is similar to increasing the difficulty of learning tasks in the course of an educational programme. Advice may be given to students to help them deal with a higher level of student control over task selection, just like support is given to students to help them deal with learning tasks with a higher difficulty level. Well-designed advisory models provide guidance to students for their process of task selection, and promote the learning of self-regulation skills that enable this process. Three types of models may be distinguished: procedural models, social models, and metacognitive models.

Procedural advisory models basically provide students with the same rules or algorithms that could be applied to implement system control. These may include rules to compute efficiency on the basis of performance and invested time and/or effort, rules to decide on the desired level of support for a next learning task based on PPS, and rules to decide when to continue to a next task class or difficulty level based on the performance and/or invested time and effort for conventional learning tasks. Procedural models provide straightforward advice and may, for instance, be implemented as a kind of product comparison sheet for consumers that provide some basic data (e.g., maximum price, preference for a particular brand, minimum requirements, etc.) in order to receive advice for a particular purchase. In our case, students have to specify some basic data from their portfolio, such as the level of expertise for different aspects of behaviour, the overall level of expertise for a particular professional competency, and the features of learning tasks already worked on, to enable a comparison of all available learning tasks. The student is then advised to select the most suitable task. While the rules that were used to reach this advice may be explicated and explained to the students, in principle, learners may "thoughtlessly" apply the procedural model to select a new learning task. Furthermore, due to their algorithmic nature, procedural advisory models are highly specific and will be difficult to transfer to other learning domains and educational settings.

Social advisory models apply self-organization principles to open an additional channel of advice for learners when sequencing learning tasks (Koper et al., 2005; Tattersall et al., 2005). The approach revolves around a continuous process of collecting, processing, and presenting data on the paths taken by all different learners using the learning tasks. This process sets up a feedback loop in which the progress of previous, successful learners is fed back to learners facing a similar sequencing choice ("other learners successfully reached the goal you are striving to attain by proceeding this way"). The learner is then able to use this recommendation in the task-selection process. With this technology, sequences of tasks emerge as a result of indirect social navigation (Höök, Benyon, & Munro, 2003). The feedback loop can be influenced to favour more efficient paths (those which have led previous learners to faster attainment of required levels of performance), more attractive paths (those which have been more highly rated by previous learners), and so on. The recommendations have an advisory nature, and are not intended to push all learners down a single path as quickly as possible. Rather, the approach aims to allow learners to make informed choices concerning steps on their learning journey, based on actual rather than predicted learner behaviour. In contrast to procedural models, social models apply a very general approach that is applicable over many learning domains and educational settings. But the used feedback principles are not very helpful for students to improve their own self-regulation skills.

Finally, *metacognitive* advisory models explicitly help students to apply cognitive strategies for assessing their own performance and keeping the scores, for interpreting horizontal and vertical evaluation results from their PPS, for matching evaluation results with the qualities of available learning tasks, for making an informed selection from those tasks, for planning their own work on those learning tasks, and so forth. First, a metacognitive model provides heuristic "rules of thumb" rather than algorithmic rules. This forces students to reflect on their application and may facilitate transfer to other learning domains and educational settings. Second, a metacognitive model takes explicated strategies rather than feedback principles as a basis. This may help students to develop cognitive strategies for regulating their own learning. Based on these two assumptions, it may be argued (Kicken, Brand-Gruwel, & van Merriënboer, 2005) that a metacognitive advisory model is more effective than a procedural or social model for the development of self-regulation skills and, in particular, task-selection skills.

Discussion

In this chapter, we discussed different models for increasing the flexibility of educational programmes that use rich learning tasks as the framework of the curriculum. Such programmes can be designed with the 4C/ID-model, which organizes learning tasks in easy-to-difficult task classes, provides support for the tasks early in a task class but decreases support to none at the end of a task class, and ensures that learning tasks differ on those aspects that also differ in the real world (i.e., variability of practice). Performance assessments, either made by the teacher, students themselves, or their peers are the basis for all dynamic task-selection models. Well-designed assessments take performance as well as the costs (effort, time) for reaching this performance into account, and enable the measurement of the many qualitatively different aspects that can be distinguished in complex behaviours. System-controlled models select the next task with an optimal level of support and difficulty for an individual student; shared-responsibility models select a subset of tasks from all available tasks after which the student makes a final selection, and advisory models also give the student advice on the process of task selection. Social and metacognitive advisory models best meet the desire to develop self-regulated learners.

Models for dynamic task selection are central to the design of environments for complex learning. Rich learning tasks are used in those environments to stimulate the integration of skills, knowledge, and attitudes. But learners' performance on those tasks will greatly differ and make the effects of the environment on learning and learning outcomes highly unpredictable. Continuous assessment of learner progress and dynamic selection of learning tasks is therefore a *sine qua non* for effective, efficient, and appealing environments for complex learning. Without continuous assessment and real-time adaptation, many low-ability learners are doomed to fail. Furthermore, complex learning is not only aiming at the development of complex first-order skills or professional competencies, but also at the development of higher-order skills such as self-regulation and metacognition. Obviously, self-regulation skills can only be trained if learners are given some control over particular aspects of their learning environment. And the selection of learning tasks is in our view the most central control aspect because these tasks are the driving force for complex learning. Theoretical implications and directions for future research on task selection and complex learning pertain to measurement and assessment, learning task characteristics, and different task-selection models.

With regard to measurement and assessment, the efficiency method needs further theoretical and empirical validation with regard to including other costs than mental effort (e.g., time on task) in the computation of efficiency (see Tuovinen & Paas, 2004), including not only one overall performance measure but also scores on different aspects of performance. The protocol for scoring student portfolios as described in this chapter focused on formative assessment leading to task selection. It should be noted that additional operations are needed if PPS is used for *summative* assessment. Then, only unsupported, conventional tasks are taken into account and, to compute a criterion-referenced score for students, the obtained scores for a particular task class should be adjusted with a correction factor that is lower for an easy task class and higher for a more difficult task class. Finally, more research is needed on the role of self- and peer-assessment leading to task selection. Teachers and learners interpret relevant aspects of task performance and learning tasks differently (see Bjork, 1999), which may lead to undesirable differences in the learning effectiveness of teacher-, peer-, and learner-controlled task selection. In short, it is critical to change the dominating assessment culture from "being assessed on what-you-know" to "assessing yourself on what-you-are-able-to-do", because the latter provides a better basis for task selection and facilitates complex learning.

Second, with regard to learning task characteristics, a first question pertains to the complex relationship between difficulty and support. If a learner's performance or efficiency is suboptimal, should we present a next task that is equally difficult as the previous one but with *more* support; should we present a next task that is *less* difficult than the previous one but with the *same* level of support; or should we vary *both* the available level of support and its difficulty? The 4C/ID-model prescribes varying only the support until the learner can perform the task without any support, according to relevant standards and criteria, and only then to continue with more difficult learning tasks (i.e., progress to a next task class). However, strong empirical support for this claim is yet missing. Another question pertains to the implementation of variability of practice. It is assumed that the complete set of selected learning tasks should contain tasks that differ from each other with regard to embedded assessment methods, the context in which the task is performed, the saliency of defining characteristics, and so forth. It is often assumed that sufficient variability on that dimension in the complete set of available learning tasks also ensures enough variability in the set of selected tasks for each individual learner. But under some circumstances, it may be desirable to make explicit decisions on particular characteristics (e.g., the type of assessment applied, the performance context) of a next learning task. Although, there are still several questions left with regard to the characteristics of to-be-selected learning tasks, the results of the studies presented in this chapter clearly show that the dynamic adaptation of learning tasks to the individual needs of learners is preferable to the use of a fixed, non-adaptive sequence of learning tasks.

Third and last, with regard to different models and approaches it may be expected that advisory models will become more and more important in the field of education. The development of self-regulation skills and higher-order skills is increasingly seen as an important goal of education, and this includes the individual ability to select learning tasks that best help to reach educational and personal goals. The question is not if new learning tasks should be selected by the teacher (or another intelligent agent) or by the student, but how teachers can select learning tasks for students who are not yet able to do this, how they can help students to take more and more responsibility for selecting their own learning tasks, and how they can help students with this by giving proper advice and providing guidance. Advisory models try to answer precisely those questions. Such models assume a shared responsibility over task selection with increasing student control and decreasing advice, as students are becoming better self-regulated learners. An important question for future research is how different approaches such as providing information from social feedback loops and giving metacognitive support can best be combined to develop optimal advice. In short, learners should be given control over those aspects of the learning environment they can already handle, they should be given advice on those aspects they cannot fully handle yet, and they should not be given control over aspects beyond their current capabilities.

The practical implications of the reported work are straightforward and far-reaching. In their search for flexible forms of student-controlled "education on demand", many schools and institutes in Higher Professional Education are currently moving to a "supermarket model", in which students have total freedom to select any learning task or course they like, at any point in time. This model may work well for self-regulated high-ability learners, who are well able to self -assess their level of professional performance and use these results to select their own learning tasks. But it may have disastrous effects for the majority of students who have not yet developed such self-regulation skills. We hope that shared-responsibility models and, in particular, advisory models that are based on sound research may help schools to increase the flexibility of their educational programmes while at the same time maintaining their high quality.

References

Bjork, R. A. (1999). Assessing our own competence: Heuristics and illusions. In: D. Gohper, & A. Koriat (Eds), *Attention and performance XVII. Cognitive regulation of performance: Interaction of theory and application* (pp. 435-459). Cambridge, MA: MIT Press.

Camp, G., Paas, F., Rikers, R., & van Merriënboer, J. J. G. (2001). Dynamic problem selection in air traffic control training: A comparison between performance, mental effort and mental efficiency. *Computers in Human Behavior, 17*, 575–595.

Collins, A., Brown, J. S., & Newman, S. E. (1989). Cognitive apprenticeship: Teaching the craft of reading, writing and mathematics. In: L. B. Resnick (Ed.), *Knowing, learning, and instruction: Essays in honor of Robert Glaser* (pp. 453–493). Hillsdale, NJ: Erlbaum.

Hambleton, R. K., Jaeger, R. M., Plake, B. S., & Mills, C. (2000). Setting performance standards on complex educational assessments. *Applied Psychological Measurement, 24*, 355–366.

Höök, K., Benyon, D., & Munro, A. J. (Eds). (2003). *Designing information spaces: The social navigation approach*. Heidelberg, Germany: Springer.

Iyengar, S. S., & Lepper, M. R. (2000). When choice is demotivating: Can one desire too much of a good thing? *Journal of Personality & Social Psychology, 79*, 995–1006.

Kalyuga, S., & Sweller, J. (2004). Measuring knowledge to optimize cognitive load factors during instruction. *Journal of Educational Psychology, 96*, 558–568.

Kalyuga, S., & Sweller, J. (2005). Rapid dynamic assessment of expertise to optimize the efficiency of e-learning. *Educational Technology, Research and Development*, *53*(3), 83–93.

Kicken, W., Brand-Gruwel, S., & van Merriënboer, J. J. G. (2005). *Advisering bij het kiezen van leertaken: Veilig op weg naar vraaggestuurd onderwijs* [Advice on the selection of learning tasks: A safe approach to education on-demand]. Paper presented at the OnderwijsResearchDagen (ORD), May 30–June 1, Gent, Belgium.

Koper, R., Giesbers, B., van Rosmalen, P., Sloep, P., van Bruggen, J., Tattersall, C., Vogten, H., & Brouns, F. (2005). A design model for lifelong learning networks. *Interactive Learning Environments*, *13*(1–2), 71–92.

Merrill, M. D. (2002). First principles of instructional design. *Educational Technology, Research and Development*, *50*, 43–59.

Paas, F., & van Merriënboer, J. J. G. (1993). The efficiency of instructional conditions: An approach to combine mental effort and performance measures. *Human Factors*, *35*, 737–743.

Paas, F., & van Merriënboer, J. J. G. (1994a). Variability of worked examples and transfer of geometrical problem-solving skills: A cognitive load approach. *Journal of Educational Psychology*, *86*, 122–133.

Paas, F., & van Merriënboer, J. J. G. (1994b). Instructional control of cognitive load in the training of complex cognitive tasks. *Educational Psychology Review*, *6*, 51–71.

Paas, F., Tuovinen, J. E., Tabbers, H., & van Gerven, P. (2003). Cognitive load measurement as a means to advance cognitive load theory. *Educational Psychologist*, *38*, 63–71.

Reigeluth, C. M. (1999). The elaboration theory: Guidance for scope and sequence decisions. In: C. M. Reigeluth (Ed.), *Instructional design theories and models: A new paradigm of instructional theory* (Vol. 2, pp. 424–453). Mahwah, NJ: Erlbaum.

Renkl, A., & Atkinson, R. K. (2003). Structuring the transition from example study to problem solving in cognitive skill acquisition: A cognitive load perspective. *Educational Psychologist*, *38*, 15–22.

Salden, R. J. C. M., Paas, F., Broers, N. J., & van Merriënboer, J. J. G. (2004). Mental effort and performance as determinants for the dynamic selection of learning tasks in air traffic control training. *Instructional Science*, *32*(1–2), 153–172.

Salden, R. J. C. M., Paas, F., & van Merriënboer, J. J. G. (2006). A comparison of approaches to learning task selection in the training of complex cognitive skills. *Computers in Human Behavior*, *22*(3), 321–333.

Schwartz, B. (2004). *The paradox of choice: Why more is less*. New York: Harper Collins Publishers.

Straetmans, G., & Sanders, P. F. (2001). *Beoordelen van competenties van leraren* [Assessing competencies of teachers]. Utrecht, The Netherlands: EPS.

Straetmans, G., Sluijsmans, D., Bolhuis, B., & van Merriënboer, J. J. G. (2003). Integratie van instructie en assessment in competentiegericht onderwijs [Integration of instruction and assessment in competence based education]. *Tijdschrift voor Hoger Onderwijs*, *3*, 171–197.

Sweller, J., van Merriënboer, J. J. G., & Paas, F. (1998). Cognitive architecture and instructional design. *Educational Psychology Review*, *10*, 251–296.

Tattersall, C., Manderveld, J., van den Berg, B., van Es, R., Janssen, J., & Koper, R. (2005). Self organising wayfinding support for lifelong learners. *Education and Information Technologies*, *10*(1–2), 111–123.

Tsigilis, N., & Theodosiou, A. (2003). Temporal stability of the intrinsic motivation inventory. *Perceptual and Motor Skills*, *97*, 271–280.

Tuovinen, J., & Paas, F. (2004). Exploring multidimensional approaches to the efficiency of instructional conditions. *Instructional Science, 32*, 133–152.

Van Merriënboer, J. J. G. (1997). *Training complex cognitive skills*. Englewood Cliffs, NJ: Educational Technology Publications.

Van Merriënboer, J. J. G., Clark, R. E., & de Croock, M. B. M. (2002a). Blueprints for complex learning: The 4C/ID-model. *Educational Technology, Research and Development, 50*(2), 39–64.

Van Merriënboer, J. J. G., & de Croock, M. B. M. (1992). Strategies for computer-based programming instruction: Program completion vs. program generation. *Journal of Educational Computing Research, 8,* 365–394.

Van Merriënboer, J. J. G., & Kirschner, P. A. (2001). Three worlds of instructional design: State of the art and future directions. *Instructional Science, 29,* 429–441.

Van Merriënboer, J. J. G., Kirschner, P. A., & Kester, L. (2003). Taking the load off a learner's mind: Instructional design for complex learning. *Educational Psychologist, 38,* 5–13.

Van Merriënboer, J. J. G., & Luursema, J. J. (1996). Implementing instructional models in computer-based learning environments: A case study in problem selection. In T. T. Liao (Ed.), *Advanced educational technology: Research issues and future potential* (pp. 184–206). Berlin: Springer Verlag.

Van Merriënboer, J. J. G., Schuurman, J. G., de Croock, M. B. M., & Paas, F. (2002b). Redirecting learners' attention during training: Effects on cognitive load, transfer test performance and training efficiency. *Learning and Instruction, 12,* 11–37.

Van Merriënboer, J. J. G., & Sweller, J. (2005). Cognitive load theory and complex learning: Recent developments and future directions. *Educational Psychology Review, 17*(2), 147–177.

Chapter 12

Meeting Challenges to Researching Learning from Instruction by Increasing the Complexity of Research

Philip H. Winne[1]

Aims of the Chapter

The theme of this book is complexity and various manifestations of complexity that arise in the context of theorizing about and researching core issues in the learning sciences. My dictionary (*Encarta World English Dictionary*, 1999) provides two definitions of complexity:

1. The condition of being difficult to understand, or being made up of many interrelated things.
2. Any one of the interrelated problems or difficulties involved in a complicated matter (often used in the plural).

It is old news that (a) cognition and learning have proven difficult to understand and (b) hosts of interrelated factors have been implicated in modeling cognition and learning. Indeed, these complexities of cognition and learning are, in part, why learning scientists are attracted to wrestle with the topics of their scholarship. Yet, I believe a fair number of learning scientists would have expected that science would be more advanced than it is. What is it about the complexity of learning from instruction that has prevented a quicker route to a general, powerful, and elegant theory?

In this chapter, several issues are identified that bear on this question. I begin by painting a landscape of select models of cognition and learning that, in my judgment, characterizes a broad scope of empirical research on learning and instruction, two of the main topics investigated under the umbrella of the learning sciences. My purpose is neither to provide a thorough report about any one model nor to comprehensively portray a sector of the field. Rather, I intend to provide a representative backdrop for a subsequent analysis.

[1]Support for this work was provided by grants to Philip H. Winne from the Social Sciences and Humanities Research Council of Canada (410-2002-1787 and 512-2003-1012), the Canada Research Chair program, and Simon Fraser University.

After presenting these sketches, they are analyzed in terms of three critical issues researchers face when abstract models are examined using empirical data: model misspecification, focus, and grain size. Issues of model misspecification arise in relation to the first definition of complexity previously quoted. The second definition of complexity poses challenges about focus and grain size. These three issues are critical to examining the nature of learning and learning from instruction.

Having critiqued models that describe how learning occurs, I try to pull theory and research up by its bootstraps. How can researchers address the challenges of model misspecification, focus and grain size to achieve sharper views about cognition and learning? Several suggestions are offered.

Modeling Cognitive Elements of Learning and Instruction

Research on Teaching Effects (and Effectiveness)

Gage's *Handbook of Research on Teaching* (1963) marshaled in one volume of slightly more than 1200 pages an extraordinary and wide-ranging survey of theoretical and empirical work in educational psychology. The architecture of the *Handbook* reflected emerging trends in this field and, in my view, exerted enormous influence on the shape of the field that developed over the next 2–3 decades of scholarship.

In particular, the *Handbook* had three substantial influences. First, experimental research methods, presented influentially in Campbell and Stanley's (1963) chapter, "Experimental and Quasi-Experimental Designs for Research on Teaching", was cleaved from observational research methodologies that were so effectively described in Medley and Mitzel's (1963) chapter, "Measuring Classroom Behavior by Systematic Observation". Second, several chapters, notably "Social Interaction in the Classroom" by Withall and Lewis (1963) and "The Social Background of Teaching" by Charters (1963), made powerful cases for a claim that context variables were important in accounting for how teaching variables affected and correlated with students' development of knowledge and motivation. Third, although this trend had been maturing for the entire 20th century (see Corno, 2001), the *Handbook* reinforced conceptions that learning (and teaching) varied by the subject matter being studied. Learning in reading was held different from learning in social studies from learning in science.

What model or models of cognition and learning prevailed in the chapters of the *Handbook*? In simplest form (see also Gage, 1972; Mitzel, 1957) the model included four categories of variables. First, contextual variables described the situation within which teaching and learning unfolded. These included the social environment of a school and its teachers and students, teachers' personalities, group climate, and so on. For lack of a better label, the second category is labeled task variables. Task variables differentiated epistemological features of subject areas like mathematics, composition, and social studies and the kinds of manipulations students performed on information within these domains: solving (mathematics problems), generating (rhetorical structures for purposes of communicating), analyzing (political arguments), and so on. Third, learner variables referred to properties such as intelligence and its possible component factors, interest, and motivation.

Fourth, interaction variables also referred to how, particularly in verbal channels, teachers communicated to students information about the subject matter and the students' engagements with it, and how students reciprocally communicated with teachers.

The basic framework for models arising from this general, four-variable architecture of teaching effects was that context variables and learner variables each affected interaction variables which, in turn, affected task variables. Task variables were directly responsible for learning.

Cognitive Models of Learning from Instruction

Contemporary with developments in research on teaching and teaching effects, another large thrust of research in the field of learning and instruction harvested a different scientific crop, one that grew from an emphasis on studying cognition (see Di Vesta, 1987). Roots of this work reach deeply into two philosophical traditions. One originated at least as early as Aristotle's model of associations and an empiricist view that knowledge is achieved by copying into mind the (or some sample of) qualities in an objective world. The other arose from a Platonic epistemology and rationalist principles. Learning, viewed through Platonic lenses, meant knowing the world imperfectly because qualities of the world always are filtered through and even distorted by the lens of human perception. To compensate, learners actively interpret, reason, and apply various mental heuristics in striving to render more accurate or, alternatively, useful re-presentations of information about the world. Recently, sociocultural cognitive models have arisen that cast the sense of usefulness in terms of value in and for social interaction.

Writing nearly 20 years ago, Di Vesta (1987) used the phrase "contextualist–constructivist" to characterize cognitive models of learning and instruction, a description that is apt today. By the contextual part of this description, Di Vesta referred to a multipart characterization of context in terms of (at least): attributes of materials to be learned, properties about how these materials were presented, the learner's characteristics and goals, and features of the task or test by which the learner demonstrates knowledge or applies skills. One robust and widely influential model in this tradition was Jenkins' (1978) tetrahedral model. Its four categories of interacting variables were learner characteristics, learner activities, instructional variables, and criterial task.

By the constructivist part of his phrase, Di Vesta referred to qualitative features of how learners interact with information presented during instructional activities. According to the constructivist tenet, learners do not just observe raw data, cognitively operate on it and, as a result, transform that information into nearly exact copies of knowledge. Instead, learners use the knowledge they have to interpret information presented for learning. Using information from these two sources, they assemble or construct a personal version of the raw data that is textured and elaborated by what they knew before. *Ipso facto*, learning is unique for each learner except in the statistically unlikely (and, possibly logically necessary) case in which two learners bring identical knowledge to learning activities.

Within the contextualist–constructivist collage, a prevalent part of modeling how students learn has been to list cognitive operations that transform information into knowledge and, in some cases, knowledge into skill. Consequently, the field now has an encyclopedia of cognitive operations. To mention just a few examples: maintenance rehearsal as distinct from elaborative rehearsal (e.g., Craik & Lockhart, 1972), visuo-spatial processing (e.g., Baddeley, 1986), means-ends analysis (e.g., Newell & Simon, 1972), and metacognitive monitoring (e.g., Flavell, 1979).

While the contextualist–constructivist view of learning easily qualifies as complex, it pointed to cognitive operations as *the* cause of learning (or as the reason learning did not materialize). Variance in learning arose because information processed differed, cognitive operations applied to information differed, or both. Like models of teaching effects briefly sketched in the preceding section, context unquestionably mattered. The way context matters is that contextual factors — of all their various sorts — afford or constrain cognitive operations that are triggered when a learner constructs knowledge and skills. Presumably, though, whenever the same cognitive operations are applied in the same context, the results should be identical.

Self-Regulated Learning Models: Learning to Change Learning from Instruction

The models of teaching effects and of learner cognition were actively taken up and each was seminal. Research conducted under their auspices generated findings that were practically valuable and theoretically informing. Notwithstanding these benefits, research investigations too often failed to detect the cause–effect or correlational relations that were predicted on the basis of these models. One explanation for some of these "nonfindings" was that random events overwhelmed the theoretically predicted relationships; that noise drowned signal. Another explanation, however, was at hand but was challenging to grasp.

In 1960, as the cognitive revolution was marshaling its forces, Miller, Galanter, and Pribram published a landmark book called *Plans and the Structure of Behavior*. In addressing many issues about cognition, their book is perhaps most remembered for forwarding the test-operate-test-exit or TOTE cycle as a general description about how organisms, including students, interacted with their environments. The TOTE is elegant in its simplicity: A learner tests the current state of learning. If it fails to meet standards, the learner operates on the environment — either by physically interacting with it and/or cognitively operating on information in working memory — to effect a change. The result of these operations is tested. If the result is judged satisfactory, the learner exits this cycle of engagement and proceeds to the next. If the result of a test is not satisfactory, further operations are applied, their results tested, and so on until a threshold is reached where marginal returns by further operating at this state of a task are judged too small. Then, the learner exits this cycle of engagement and proceeds to the next.

I interpret that researchers who worked in the framework of cognitive models of learning from instruction assumed the link between tests and operations in TOTEs — between some factor of instructional design and the cognitive operations learners were theorized to apply in this context — was deterministic; that is (a) products always are caused by specific operations and (b) a product theoretically could be accurately predicted by a researcher (or a learner) given the right information and enough information about context.

What if this assumption about determinacy is wrong or, at least, not utterly determined? In particular, what if learners are constructive, not only in forming knowledge out of information presented during instruction and prior knowledge, but also in forming understandings about how to engage cognitively with information in the context of factors comprising their teacher's instructional design (Winne, 1982; Winne & Marx, 1977)? If learners varied in their perceptions about how to participate in learning from teaching, this would override simple, direct relations between factors of instruction and measures of instructional outcomes.

Indeed, learners do vary in their interpretations about the meanings they ascribe to various features of instructional design that researchers (and teachers) intend to guide learners about how they should engage in learning (Winne, 1983b; Winne & Marx, 1982). Moreover, learners *choose* among perceptions they construct about tasks, about their teacher's interactions with them, and about evaluations of their performance.

This elaborated sense of what Di Vesta (1987) described as the constructivist facet of cognitive models has now become widely accepted: Learners are agents. In a context of widely ranging and different perceptions about external factors (e.g., the availability of feedback, resources that can be consulted during learning) and about internal factors (self-efficacy, domain knowledge), they set courses for learning as they make decisions in four phases of self-regulated learning (Winne & Hadwin, 1998; Winne, 2001):

1. constructing descriptions of learning tasks,
2. choosing what goals they pursue and devising plans for reaching those goals,
3. metacognitively monitoring (à la TOTE cycles) how learning unfolds as they apply chosen cognitive operations that construct products, and
4. adapting elements in any or all of the foregoing circumstances when quantitative factors (e.g., time, number correct, frequency of feedback) and qualitative features (e.g., effort, satisfaction, interest) of engagements in learning do not meet their standards of success.

Models of self-regulated learning have an important corollary. No matter what steps teachers and experimenters take to control factors in an instructional design, with their intent to make an instructional experience explicit and identical across learners, self-regulating agentic learners may vary in which cognitive operations they apply to learn. Variance in *how* learners engage with factors of the "same" instructional design — be it a treatment in an experiment or a lesson in a classroom — may have significantly different effects on their achievement. In other words, variance in outcome variables can arise because learners are self-regulating. By exercising self-regulation, each learner constructs a context for learning that may differ from what an instructional designer intended. Moreover, the contexts learners construct almost surely differ.

Three Challenges to Models: Misspecification, Focus, and Granularity

The literature of the learning sciences is replete with descriptions of methodological challenges to developing and testing valid theories about the variables that describe learning. A reasonably thorough survey can be found in the second edition of the *Handbook of Educational Psychology* (Alexander & Winne, 2006). Among all these, three particular challenges have not yet received sufficient address: misspecification, focus, and granularity.

Misspecification

Many models in the learning sciences (and science, in general) are misspecified, which manifests as three kinds of flaws in particular. First, the model cannot avoid omitting some factors that really matter in a "natural" process and, thus, relations that would involve these factors also are necessarily omitted. Second, the model includes some factors that are superfluous and, therefore, relations involving these factors are also superfluous. Third, the model includes some inaccuracy in its estimate of weights or probabilities that qualify relationships among factors.

These three flaws of model misspecification are one reason why empirical research is essential in the learning sciences. The purposes of empirical research are not only to test models and generate information for updating models. Empirical researchers also must be alert for and sensitive to opportunities to examine observations in ways that suggest changes to models that reduce misspecification. Changes to models may be small modifications or they may be large-scale revisions — evolutions and revolutions, if you will (Lakatos, 1978). Lessening the misspecification of factors in models in both conceptual and statistical senses is extraordinarily challenging. It is possible that models may never be complete and that modeling may never be finished.

Focus

The term focus refers to a challenge that arises because factors in models are interrelated or, from a statistical point of view, covary. When two factors covary, researchers are prompted to ask several questions: How much do they covary and why do they covary? Should a researcher focus on one of these two factors as the cause of the other? Or, does a third distal factor play the role of a common cause of both proximal factors such that there is no causal relation between the two "focal" variables? Is the relation between proximal factors unidirectional over time such that factor A causes factor B to take on new values or qualities but not vice versa? Or, is the relationship reciprocal such that each factor can cause the other to vary over time in a pattern A→ B → new A → new B …? Or, is the relationship spurious because there is only one factor that successively receives recursively generated input, continuously "updating" itself over time in ways that seem to suggest different factors rather than one underlying factor?

Granularity

Granularity or grain size is an issue with respect to the "level of detail" at which learning science should examine factors in models of cognition and learning and data that reflect elements in models (see Winne, Jamieson-Noel, & Muis, 2002). The issue of what is appropriate grain size arises often in considering cognitive events. First, what is an event? An event is an operation or process, such as searching memory, that generates a product, such as a proposition. Consider one apparently simple cognitive event — retrieving a proposition from long-term memory about the chemical composition of table salt (NaCl). Is this retrieval event characterized by binary qualities? For instance, is retrieval attempted or not? Is retrieval successful or not? Alternatively, is a retrieval event comprised of scientifically separable component events? For example, when a learner searches for a proposition in long-term memory, is the scope of search and the criterion (or criteria) used to determine when to stop searching affected by factors such as feeling of knowing (see Winne, 2004)? Assuming information in long-term memory exists in an associative network and that activating any particular node in the network spreads activation to associated nodes (see Winne, 2001, for a simple description) is a retrieval event one that really unfolds as a series of component events — stages of retrieval, if you will — that are delimited by each traversal of a node in long-term memory? If this latter conjecture is true, what is lost by integrating these several events and modeling a "whole" retrieval event in binary terms?

How Three Models of Learning and Cognition Succumb to Challenges of Modeling

In many ways, the three broad categories of models sampled in the preceding sections — teaching effects, cognition, and self-regulated learning — are representative of successive attempts in the learning sciences to conquer the challenges of misspecification, focus, and granularity. Yet, however much one model may gain on its predecessor, all three models wrestle with and, in some ways, lose these challenges.

Failing to Meet Challenges of Model Misspecification

Models developed under the banner of research on teaching effects recognized that a large number and wide variety of factors influenced outcomes beyond just the ways teachers interacted with students. But extensive lists of contextual, task, teacher and learner variables led to an unsolvable problem. If each of these variables influences students' development of knowledge, skills, motivation, and capabilities for future learning, there are too many factors to consider. A compelling example is the exceptionally thorough review of research on teaching effects by Dunkin and Biddle (1974). They listed hundreds of variables that research had found to affect students' achievement. Each of the variables they identified was a main effect, that is, an effect independent of the effects of other variables. On considering possibilities that at least some of these variables might interact with others, the list suffers combinatorial explosion — literally millions of possibilities need to be given account. As Cronbach (1975) so eloquently wrote, "Every second-order interaction is moderated by third-order interactions, which in turn are moderated by higher-order interactions. Once we attend to interactions, we enter a hall of mirrors that extends to infinity" (p. 119). Therefore, whenever any one variable is omitted from a model, the model runs the risk of being misspecified.

Temporal successors to the model of teacher effects, represented, for example, by Jenkins' tetrahedral (1978) model and by Winne and Hadwin's (1998) model of self-regulated learning, do not fare better in this regard. These models likewise suffer the infinitely long hall of mirrors concerning interactions.

The field of learning sciences, in my view, has not dedicated enough effort to decreasing model misspecification by taking a path to root out superfluous variables. Researchers gain recognition based on new findings but not by replicating prior ones. Unlike many other sciences, a single demonstration of an effect has not served as an invitation for others to try to replicate it in their labs or local schools. It is extremely rare that journal editors publish replications. Nor does the literature include very many studies about any kind of model or variable that report no statistically detectable relation among variables named in the study's hypotheses. In my experience, journal editors have rejected such articles citing grounds that such findings are "nonfindings." This denies Popper's (1963) logic or, if one is not a fan of that logical system, at least it begs the question of type I errors (errors in committing to rejecting a null hypothesis when, in fact, the finding is merely an extreme but random occurrence in a world where the null hypothesis is true). In this condition, yesterday's variables of interest fade away for lack of curiosity in the research community or lack of interest by funding agencies. They do not disappear because they have been scientifically proven to have nil effect. As a consequence, newer research is misspecified if it simply ignores variables that history has proven to affect an outcome, even if only weakly, are misspecified.

The final kind of model misspecification described earlier is inaccuracy in assigning weights or probabilities to relations among variables in models. In this respect, the learning sciences can be chided for making very little use at all of methodologies and quantitative analyses that afford opportunities to estimate weights describing "how much" one variable influences another. On the other hand, the measurement scales for data in our field rarely justify applying arithmetic operations (addition, subtraction, multiplication, and division). Nonetheless, sums of item scores on measures such as knowledge or motivation serve as our data. A mathematically more justified approach is to estimate an ability parameter using any of the family of Rasch or item response theory methodologies (Michell, 1997). Were this done more regularly, quantitative methods that generate weights for quantifying relationships between variables would be more appropriate. Until then, research that is guided by the three families of models sketched here run afoul of misspecification because they fail to estimate the degree of these relationships with accuracy.

In sum, all three families of models have not fared well with respect to conquering challenges of model misspecification. As a consequence, unnecessary complexity besets educational psychology.

Failing to Meet Challenges of Sharpened Focus

As noted earlier, the challenge of selecting a focus for research arises because factors are not causally independent of one another, because they are aggregates that share components, or because they covary statistically. Research generated from all three families of models sketched here has not overcome this challenge.

On first consideration, there seems to be a simple and powerful rejoinder to my assertion. All the researcher needs to do is partial variance from the variable of interest using any of several widely available and well-known statistical methods. Multiple regression, principal components analysis, canonical correlation, or loglinear analysis are examples. Using such methods to partial variance and thereby sharpen focus in research has a long history as a preferred methodology, likely arising from Yule's (1897) classic paper on multiple and partial correlation and Spearman's (1904) use of factor analysis to sharpen focus in studies of intelligence.

These quantitative methods share a fatal flaw. It is not that their mathematical formulation is wrong. Rather, the flaw concerns how researchers interpret results generated by these methods (Winne, 1983a, b). In brief, quantitative methods that partial variance from a focal predictor variable (or a set of predictor variables) are applied with the intention of purifying the variable so it does not statistically covary with another (or a set of other) predictor variable(s). The methods can be described as follows: Using the data describing participants in a study, build a linear model of the focal variable using the predictor variable(s) one wants to partial out of the focal variable. Then, use the pattern coefficients of this linear model and the data to estimate the value of the focal predictor variable for each participant in the study. Finally, subtract from the obtained value of the focal variable the value of the focal variable estimated on the basis of this statistical model. In statistical terms, the result is a score on the focal variable that is residualized on the basis of the nonfocal variable(s).

Researchers applying this method almost always fail to use precise language when writing about the residualized focal variable. If the focal variable's residuals are correlated with other variables outside the set of variables on which it has been residualized, these correlations will not have the same values as correlations between the unresidualized variable and those other variables (except if the correlation between outcome and predictor raw scores was 0.00 in the first place, in which case residualizing the focal variable is unnecessary). If researchers followed traditional practices and used correlation coefficients to establish a framework for interpreting the focal variable's construct, the fact that residualized outcomes and original (raw score) outcomes have different patterns of correlations requires the residualized outcome to be interpreted differently than the unresidualized outcome. Although an exhaustive survey has not been done, I estimate only a handful of thousands of articles and reports acknowledge this difference. In other words, using statistical procedures to improve focus on a variable actually has blurred focus because the variable interpreted is not the variable as it exists after it has been residualized. Interpretations of residualized variables are out of focus in proportion to the degree to which they covary with variables on which they have been residualized.

Borsboom, Mellenberg, and van Heerden (2004) take the issue of focus in a different direction. They argue the bold claim that validity cannot be examined through correlations (except in one rare case). Here is their description about interpreting scores on items appearing on a test:

> If something does not exist, then one cannot measure it. If it exists but does not causally produce variations in the outcomes of the measurement procedure, then one is either measuring nothing at all or something different altogether. Thus, a test is valid for measuring an attribute if and only if (a) the attribute exists and (b) variations in the attribute causally produce variations in the outcomes of the measurement procedure ... correlations between test scores and other measures cannot provide more than circumstantial evidence for validity. What needs to be tested is not a theory about the relation between the attribute measured and other attributes but a theory of response behavior. (pp. 1061–1062)

The upshot for research on instruction and in the learning sciences more generally is that accounts of how factors of instructional design "cause" learning have to "get inside" the time period between the independent variable and the dependent variable. This is addressed in the next section on granularity.

Failing to Meet Challenges of Granularity

In research studies designed in accord with models sampled in this chapter — teacher effects, cognition, or self-regulated learning — students' individual differences have played important parts (see Corno et al., 2001). For example, all three models pay respect to motivation as a powerful influence on how learners learn and what they learn.

The issue of granularity arises in these kinds of studies not because of the operational definitions of experimental variables, but because researchers intend to model *how* an individual student learns. The preferred procedure is to do a true experiment with random assignment of participants to groups. Arrange for participants in each group to experience an intervention (including a placebo and whatever is "natural"). Then administer a test or inventory to learners, score items, sum items to form a total, and correlate that total with other variables of interest. For instance, level of motivation might be used as an exogenous variable in a structural equation model accounting for achievement as outcome variables.

A problem with such methods, beyond the previously discussed issue of using variables to partial out variance in other variables is exposed by Borsboom, Mellenberg, and van Heerden (2003): "between subjects variables do not imply, test, or support causal accounts that are valid at the individual level"(p. 213). The reason is that there is no account in the data of *how* differences among, say, students' motivation affects individual students' (a) cognition during learning, (b) knowledge they acquire (or not), or (c) how or whether learners retrieve knowledge when they are tested. It is merely assumed that every individual student's pattern of cognition involving motivation is identical in these events or, if there is variance, that it is random and not consequential. Were it otherwise, a researcher discussing results would examine results using *several* models for *each* randomly formed group. For example, within the experimental treatment group, one model might be posited for learners below the median and another model for learners above the median. This sort of multiple modeling is not to be found often in the literature. Rather, quantitative analysis at a coarser grained level — the group — is generalized without warrant to the level of the individual (Borsboom et al., 2003).

Are there Remedies for these Problems?

Starting with Thorndike's work in the early 1900s, hundreds of researchers have striven to develop powerful and general models of learning and motivation that happens in laboratories, classrooms, and the workplace. I chose three significant traditions to represent the last 50 years of this research — teacher effects, cognition, and self-regulated learning. Each of these approaches to scientifically investigating learning from instruction faces multiple challenges, three of which were examined in this chapter. Problems of misspecifying models concern the appropriate presence of variables in models and the degree of their influence. Problems of focus refer to issues of how researchers try to separate influences that in the data are woven together for purposes of investigating separate and isolated theoretical constructs. Problems of granularity are problems that arise because researchers use data at one level to describe events at another level even though the former provides blurred or no basis for describing the latter.

Can researchers apply methods that respond to these challenges? I believe we must and we can. One path that might be taken begins with Borsboom and colleagues' (2003) recommendation to develop and test theories of response behavior. In this context, they observe:

> psychological research has adapted to the limitations of common statistical procedures (e.g., by abandoning case studies because analysis of variance requires sample sizes larger than 1) instead of inventing new procedures that allow for the testing of theories at the proper level, which is often the level of the individual .... Clearly, extending measurements into the time domain is essential. (p. 215)

Taking up their suggestion, I propose a general method to supplement, not replace, conventional approaches to experiments and correlational studies. It is an extension of Campbell and Stanley's (1963) time-series experiment with an addition to their recommendation about how to analyze the data.

> The essence of the time-series design is the presence of a periodic measurement process on some group or individual and the introduction of an experimental change into this time series of measurements, the results of which are indicated by [analyses that identify] a discontinuity in the measurements recorded in the time series. (p. 207)

Campbell and Stanley allowed that a time-series experiment might collect data about a group, but they also allowed that data could be collected about an individual. Campbell and Stanley suggest one approach to analyzing time-series data: look for a discontinuity in the level of measurements. For example, if knowledge is low across several time intervals, then increases steadily after introducing a treatment, this would be taken as evidence that the intervention caused increases in knowledge. Another track may be fruitful, one that strives to expose *how* events lead to changes when researching learning from instruction.

Gather Fine-Grained Data Describing How Learners Go about Learning

To research how learning activities promote the development of knowledge, it is necessary to gather extensive data over time about *how* each *individual* engages with or participates in an intervention (i.e., experimental change). Gather data that map onto a model of *how* responses are generated. What does a learner do? What methods does the learner use to interact with information over the course of a session in which learning may (is supposed to) be happening? For example: Does the learner search for particular information? Does the learner monitor some particular information in relation to some specific standards? Does the learner assemble two heretofore-unlinked propositions to create a larger structure of information? (See Winne, 2001, 2004 for further descriptions.) If data correspond to a model's causal events, chances are decreased that the data are out of focus.

As much as possible, record the occurrence of *every* event, those within a model of possible influences on or causes of an outcome in a model of response behavior, as well as other events that can be imagined. In particular, consider intermediate "steps" that lead up to a final product; that is, model nascent components or premature forms of a product. This lessens chances that the granularity of the data does not correspond to the granularity of events that play the role of cause in the model.

For instance, consider a model of learning that describes metacognitive monitoring as a causal factor that promotes comprehension and retention. Events representing metacognitive monitoring can be recorded. For example, every time a learner highlights text in a passage and writes an annotation about that highlighted text, I interpret this indicates or traces (Winne, 1982; Winne, et al., 2002) metacognitive monitoring. A variety of observable traces might cluster as indicators of metacognitive monitoring. Or, suppose my model specifies that the probability of storing information that can be retrieved is a function of the number of re-views of content. This can be recorded if software provides a search tool for learners. For every occurrence of a term the learner searches for, the software shows the occurrence of the term plus a few words preceding and following the term, the term's "local context." When a learner clicks the local context, the software scrolls to the paragraph containing the term and highlights the full sentence in which it occurs. My colleagues and I are developing software that records these events. It traces how a learner interacts with information and stamps each event with the time it occurs (Winne, Hadwin, Nesbit, Kumar, & Beaudoin, 2005).

One Plan for Analyzing Data to Describe How a Learner Learns

After collecting time-stamped trace data, draw a timeline of the recorded events. From this representation, compute for every event the conditional probability that it is followed in time by every other event, including itself. For example, suppose the events are designated as A, B, C, D, and E. Figure 12.1 shows a timeline for these events and two representations of conditional probabilities: a table of transitions and a map of transitions.

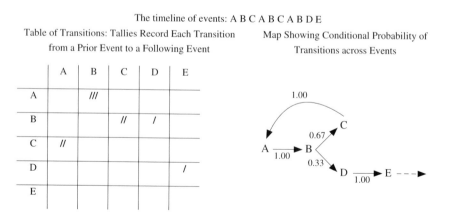

Figure 12.1: Transforming data about a series of events into conditional probabilities.

In this simple example, the conditional probability that an occurrence of event A is followed by an occurrence of event B is $3 \div 3 = 1.00$. The conditional probability that an occurrence of event B followed by an occurrence of event C is $1 \div 3 = 0.33$.

On the basis of this (fictitious) data, it can be interpreted that A is a proximal and reliable of cause B. B is proximal to D but more likely to cause C than D. E is caused proximally by D but D is the result of a "path" A → B. If traced events are tightly coupled to theoretically causal factors, focus can be achieved without statistically distorting the sense of an event, as happens when variance-partitioning methods are applied. If traced events reflect every action a learner can perform on information — those within a model and those not part of the model but which can be represented by traces — it is more likely that the researcher can surmount challenges of model misspecification and of having only of coarse-grained aggregates of events when theory refers to fine-grained events.

Nesbit and I (Winne & Nesbit, 1995; see also Winne, Gupta, & Nesbit, 1994) have developed quantitative methods for characterizing qualities of relations using methods borrowed from graph theory. A software program performs these calculations (Hadwin, Winne, Nesbit, & Murphy, 2005). As well, the "temporal span" of conditional probabilities can be expanded to explore distal effects. This can be done by framing rules such as, "When N events intervene, what is the conditional probability event A influences (or causes) event D?" This widens the focus on a relationship between variables. After the researcher has investigated relational properties at the level of individual, aggregation to form groups can occur *post hoc* on the basis of data rather than assumption.

Trace data should be analyzed in the first instance at the level of the individual. Only after analysis at this level should data or individuals be aggregated *post hoc*. The warrant for aggregation is based on the similarity of observed events and patterns of events. My proposal stands in contrast to the usual practice of aggregating data *a priori* (e.g., a frequency count, a sum of items on a test) or aggregating people *a priori* (e.g., experimental group, placebo group). Such *a priori* aggregation relies on randomness to balance out factors that are actually of interest to the researcher and, importantly, the intent to balance out such factors probably has an extremely small chance of working as intended (see Winne, 2004, 2005).

Conclusion

I judge most models of learning from instruction and many models in the learning sciences generally fail to surmount the challenges of misspecification, focus, and granularity. By changing methodological practices that prevail in today's research, these problems can be ameliorated but they almost surely never will be erased fully. The changes recommended are interrelated and form a gestalt. Adopting only one change may not be very productive.

Recommendation 1. Be more attentive to modeling *events*, traces of cognitive operations and their resulting products that constitute learners' responses to instruction rather than measuring just the level of factors that may covary with changes in levels of a response. For example, in addition to researching *whether* comprehension covaries with opportunity to review or the frequency of monitoring, model *how* comprehension develops over time in reference to traces of events. Granularity of the data comes into better alignment with the granularity of models that are intended to describe how learning happens.

Recommendation 2. Trace as many kinds of fine-grained events as possible. Do not limit the data collected only to measurements of factors that a model highlights *a priori* as "the" factor(s) that affect learning. How does a learner interact with information? How does a learner engage with features that comprise an intervention? Computer software that logs learners' engagements with information and tools can help reach this recommendation. By characterizing what happens during learning, the likelihood of misspecification can be lowered.

Recommendation 3. Generate models of learning-on-the-fly using trace data that describe each learner's engagement in learning over time. Timelines of events, tables of transitions, and maps of transitions can reveal relations about learning processes that are entirely masked by composites such as "a treatment group" or frequency counts of events. These kinds of analyses help to achieve focus.

Adopting these recommendations helps to defeat the challenges of misspecification, focus, and granularity. Adopting these recommendations also will increase complexity in research on learning from instruction because these practices multiply the information available to researchers about how learning unfolds. This complexity *is* information. It stands in contrast to the absence of information that arises when researchers rely on randomness to balance out possible causes or dependence on the often dubious homogeneity of composite measures, such as counts of events and sums of item scores on tests. If I am right that scholars in this field enjoy complexity, having information rather than disregarding it should be simultaneously more pleasing and scientifically fruitful.

References

Alexander, P. A., & Winne, P. H. (Eds). (2006). *Handbook of educational psychology* (2nd ed.). Mahwah, NJ: Erlbaum.

Baddeley, A. D. (1986). *Working memory.* Oxford: Oxford University Press.

Borsboom, D., Mellenbergh, G. J., & van Heerden, J. (2003). The theoretical status of latent variables. *Psychological Review, 110,* 203–219.

Borsboom, D., Mellenbergh, G. J., & van Heerden, J. (2004). The concept of validity. *Psychological Review, 111,* 1061–1071.

Campbell, D. T., & Stanley, J. C. (1963). Experimental and quasi-experimental designs for research. In: N. L. Gage (Ed.), *Handbook of research on teaching* (pp. 171–246). Chicago: Rand McNally.

Charters, W. (1963). The social background of teaching. In: N. L. Gage (Ed.), *Handbook of research on teaching* (pp. 715–813). Chicago: Rand McNally.

Corno, L. (Ed.). (2001). *Education across a century: The centennial volume* (Vol. 100, Part 1). Chicago: University of Chicago Press.

Corno, L., Cronbach, L. J., Kupermintz, H., Lohman, D. F., Mandinach, E. B., Porteus, A. W., & Talbert, J. E. (2001). *Remaking the concept of aptitude: Extending the legacy of Richard E. Snow.* Mahwah, NJ: Erlbaum.

Craik, F., & Lockhart, R. S. (1972). Levels of processing: A framework for memory research. *Journal of Verbal Learning and Verbal Behavior, 11,* 671–684.

Cronbach, L. J. (1975). Beyond the two disciplines of scientific psychology. *American Psychologist, 30,* 116–127.

Di Vesta, F. (1987). The cognitive movement and education. In: J. A. Glover, & R. R. Ronning (Eds), *Historical foundations of educational psychology* (pp. 203–233). New York: Plenum Press.

Dunkin, M. J., & Biddle, B. J. (1974). *The study of teaching.* New York: Holt, Rinehart and Winston.

Encarta World English Dictionary. (1999). [software edition]. Microsoft Corporation.

Flavell, J. H. (1979). Metacognition and cognitive monitoring. *American Psychologist, 34,* 906–911.

Gage, N. L. (1963). *Handbook of research on teaching.* Chicago: Rand-McNally.

Gage, N. L. (1972). *Teacher and teaching effectiveness. The search for a scientific basis.* Palo Alto, CA: Pacific Books.

Hadwin, A. F., Winne, P. H., Nesbit, J. C., & Murphy, C. (2005). *LogReader: A toolkit for analyzing Study log data and computing transition metrics* (version 1.0) [computer program]. Burnaby, BC: Simon Fraser University.

Jenkins, J. J. (1978). Four points to remember: A tetrahedral model of memory experiments. In: L. S. Cermak, & F. I. M. Craik (Eds), *Levels of processing and human memory.* Hillsdale, NJ: Erlbaum.

Lakatos, I. (1978). The methodology of scientific research programs. In: J. Worrall, & G. Currie (Eds), *Philosophical papers* (Vol. 1). Cambridge: Cambridge University Press.

Medley, D., & Mitzel, H. E. (1963). Measuring classroom behavior by systematic observation. In: N. L. Gage (Ed.), *Handbook of research on teaching* (pp. 247–328). Chicago: Rand McNally.

Michel, J. (1997). Quantitative science and the definition of measurement in psychology. *British Journal of Psychology, 88,* 355–383.

Miller, G. A., Galanter, E., & Pribram, K. H. (1960). *Plans and the structure of behavior.* New York: Holt, Rinehart & Winston.

Mitzel, H. E. (1957). *A behavioral approach to the assessment of teacher effectiveness.* Unpublished mimeograph. Division of Teacher Education, College of the City of New York.

Newell, A., & Simon, H. (1972). *Human problem solving.* Englewood Cliffs, NJ: Prentice-Hall.

Popper, K. R. (1963). *Conjectures and refutations.* New York: Harper.

Spearman, C. (1904). General intelligence, objectively determined and measured. *American Journal of Psychology, 15,* 201–293.

Winne, P. H. (1982). Minimizing the black box problem to enhance the validity of theories about instructional effects. *Instructional Science, 11,* 13–28.

Winne, P. H. (1983a). Training students to process text with adjunct aids. *Instructional Science, 12,* 243–266.

Winne, P. H. (1983b). Distortions of construct validity in multiple regression analysis. *Canadian Journal of Behavioral Science, 15,* 187–202.

Winne, P. H. (2001). Self-regulated learning viewed from models of information processing. In: B. J. Zimmerman, & D. H. Schunk (Eds), *Self-regulated learning and academic achievement: Theoretical perspectives* (2nd ed., pp. 153–189). Mahwah, NJ: Erlbaum.

Winne, P. H. (2004). Students' calibration of knowledge and learning processes: Implications for designing powerful software learning environments. *International Journal of Educational Research, 41*(6), 466–488.

Winne, P. H. (2005). Researching and promoting self-regulated learning using software technologies. In: P. Tomlinson, J. Dockrell, & P. H. Winne (Eds), *Pedagogy: Teaching for learning. Monograph Series II: Psychological Aspects of Education, 3*(pp. 91–105). Leicester, UK: British Psychological Society.

Winne, P. H., Gupta, L., & Nesbit, J. C. (1994). Exploring individual differences in studying strategies using graph theoretic statistics. *Alberta Journal of Educational Research, 40,* 177–193.

Winne, P. H., & Hadwin, A. F. (1998). Studying as self-regulated learning. In: D. J. Hacker, J. Dunlosky, & A. C. Graesser (Eds), *Metacognition in educational theory and practice* (pp. 277–304). Mahwah, NJ: Erlbaum.

Winne, P. H., Hadwin, A. F., Nesbit, J. C., Kumar, V., & Beaudoin, L. (2005). *gSTUDY: A toolkit for developing computer-supported tutorials and researching learning strategies and instruction* (version 2.0) [computer program]. Burnaby, BC: Simon Fraser University.

Winne, P. H., Jamieson-Noel, D. L., & Muis, K. (2002). Methodological issues and advances in researching tactics, strategies, and self-regulated learning. In: P. R. Pintrich, & M. L. Maehr (Eds), *Advances in motivation and achievement: New directions in measures and methods* (Vol. 12, pp. 121–155). Greenwich, CT: JAI Press.

Winne, P. H., & Marx, R. W. (1977). Reconceptualizing research on teaching. *Journal of Educational Psychology, 69*, 668–678.

Winne, P. H., & Marx, R. W. (1982). Students' and teachers' views of thinking processes for class-room learning. *Elementary School Journal, 82*, 493–518.

Winne, P. H., & Nesbit, J. C. (1995). *Graph theoretic techniques for examining patterns and strate-gies in students' studying: An application of LogMill.* San Francisco, CA: American Educational Research Association.

Withall, J., & Lewis, W. W. (1963). Social interaction in the classroom. In: N. L. Gage (Ed.), *Handbook of research on teaching* (pp. 683–714). Chicago: Rand McNally.

Yule, G. U. (1897). On the theory of correlation. *Journal of the Royal Statistical Society, 60*, 812–854.

Chapter 13

System Theoretic Designs for Researching Complex Events

William Winn

The Complexity of Learning and the Dangers of Simplification

Learning is naturally beset by three kinds of complexity: The complexity of the material to learn, the complexity of the learner, and the complexity of the environment in which learning occurs. The purpose of this chapter is to look at how we can study learning without losing sight of these three kinds of complexity. The discussion is primarily concerned with learning in computer-generated environments. The approach to research that is required is "systemic" as much as it is "analytical" (Salomon, 1991). To study learning in its natural, complex state we need to consider many more of the factors that affect learning processes and outcomes than has usually been the case, which requires us to think of students and learning environments as complex systems.

At first, the task of simply describing learners, what they learn and how they learn it, let alone of building explanatory models of their behavior, may seem daunting. However, complexity itself has become the object of scientific study, which has developed analytical methods that make it possible, albeit difficult, to describe and understand complex systems. These methods arise from recent studies of complexity, which call a system complex if it is impossible (or very difficult) to predict its future behavior because its initial states cannot be known with sufficient accuracy; *not* if it comprises purely random events (Blomberg, 2004; Gribbin, 2004). This chapter is therefore about the study of learning processes and outcomes that are assumed to be deterministic, explainable through theory and sources of testable hypotheses. It does not focus primarily on purely descriptive inquiry that can, at times, come dangerously close to being atheoretical.

Like a teacher or instructional designer, a researcher setting out to study learning is tempted to simplify the content learners are to study, or the assumptions made about the learners, or the learning environment itself. While sometimes justifiable, each of these simplifications has its particular problems.

Handling Complexity in Learning Environments: Theory and Research
Copyright © 2006 by Elsevier Ltd.
All rights of reproduction in any form reserved.
ISBN: 0-08-044986-7

Simplifying content has been an approach common to both instruction and research. But to study students' learning about pulley systems with weightless ropes and frictionless pulleys, for example, falls into the trap of what Spiro, Feltovich, Jacobson, and Coulson (1992) have called "reductive bias" — the tendency to reduce complexity in order to make something easier to learn, teach, or study. There is nothing wrong in principle with starting from easy material and working toward the more difficult. A problem arises when the simplification, as in this example, removes key concepts that *always* affect the behavior of what the student is to learn and cannot simply be ignored.

Simplifying the assumptions made about learners is also a common practice for teaching and research. In classrooms, it is usually impractical to provide different instruction for every student. This is not always a problem. Most students can learn from strategies that are somewhat misaligned with their abilities and preferences by drawing on their informal knowledge (Bransford, Brown, & Cocking, 2000). In experiments too, blocking subjects on achievement, aptitude or some other relevant measure is standard procedure and produces useful data. However, Clark (1990) has documented cases where making the wrong assumptions about students can lead to the use of supposedly better instructional strategies that cause students to learn *less* than they might using another strategy. Likewise, misunderstanding students we are studying can lead to misinterpretation of research data. The temptation to let students decide for themselves how to learn as a way around this problem is equally unsatisfactory. By definition, students do not know all they need to know. They need explicit guidance about subject matter, how to use it to solve problems and how to interpret what they observe (de Jong & Van Joolingen, 1998). Moreover, given a choice, students often opt for the method they are least likely to learn from well (Clark, 1982) because they shy away from strategies that require effort.

Simplifying the learning environment is also common. Any computer model is a simplification of what it models (Box, 1979). In many cases, though, computer-supported learning environments are unnecessarily over-simplified. Belland (1985) has made the case that beginners need the best possible tools to learn with, because they lack the competence to make up for the sub-standard tools typically given them. The myth that younger students are not capable of using complex computer simulations has been effectively dispelled (Edelson, Salierno, Matese, Pitts, & Sherin, 2002; Winn et al., 1999) in studies where children as young as fourth grade have successfully used "professional strength" data and software.

Studying Complexity in Education

In the 1980s, a number of educational researchers spoke out against this tendency to simplify content, assumptions about students and learning environments because it severely reduced the ecological validity of educational studies (Howe, 1985; Phillips, 1983). Educational scholars were encouraged to move away from laboratory experiments to the study of learning in context, giving up experimental control to preserve the authenticity of the context in which learning took place. In one direction, this has led to design experimentation (Cobb, Confrey, diSessa, Lehrer, & Schauble, 2003; Collins, Joseph, & Bielaczyc, 2004), where learning tools and methods are tried and iteratively refined in the settings where they are intended to be used. However, concern for ecological validity has sometimes led us to overlook accepted standards for evidence, objectivity, and procedural rigor. Fox (2006) has claimed that these approaches to research, which he loosely labels "Constructivism", have led to confusion, because there is no consistent definition of Constructivism, and have failed either to build on strong theoretical bases for research or to build a theory of their own. Perhaps Fox's criticism is too harsh. Unfortunately, many educators were ill-equipped to work outside the experimental paradigm as ethnographers or anthropologists, and research was conducted that fell short of accepted scientific standards (Shavelson & Towne, 2002). However, other approaches to educational research allow us to confront the complexity of learning and its setting head on. This chapter focuses on System Theory.

System Theoretic Approaches to Learning Research

System theory was developed to explain the structure and function of living organisms (Von Bertalanffy, 1968) and human organizations (Forrester, 1980). It has been proposed as a set of framing concepts for educational technology (Heinich, 1970) and has been applied to the practice of instructional design (Tennyson, 1997). In all of these cases, the role of system theory has been to describe and explain interactions among many connected components and processes, and thus embodies many ideas that are important to the study of complex learning events. These important ideas include the following:

Emergence. Complex systems cannot be described simply in terms of the behavior of their individual parts. The study of everything from ant colonies (Gordon, 1999), to the "behavior" of cities (Jacobs, 1961), to activity in the human brain (Kelso, 1999) reveals that systems exhibit complex organic behaviors that defy explanation in terms of the usually far simpler behaviors of their individual parts. For the study of learning, this means we must describe and explain the behavior of the entire system that includes the student and the learning environment, as well as individual learning events.

The corollary to emergence is that complexity arises from simple laws applied iteratively through feedback (Gribbin, 2004). Each successive state of a system depends on its previous state. However, the rule that predicts the next state is not just to sum previous states. This makes complex systems highly sensitive to their initial states, even minute changes in which can lead to large changes in later states (Gribbin, 2004).

Self-organization. Emergent behaviors of natural systems are typically organized, coherent, and purposeful. Examples include the orchestrated flashing of fireflies (Strogatz, 2003), the emergence of fractal structures in nature (Mandelbrot, 1983) and the regular behavior of many cellular automata (Wolfram, 2002). When we study learning, self-organization appears when learners become able to explain complete, multivariate phenomena. This can happen even when the concepts and rules upon which they build understanding are incorrect. In our work, we have recorded cases where students' explanations of ocean tides and currents have impeccable logic and consistency but are assembled from ideas that are completely wrong.

Structural levels. The structure and behavior of systems can be studied at many levels (Hauhs & Lange, 2004). An ant colony can be usefully studied as a single system, as a set of subsystems made up of different castes (workers, soldiers) each with unique roles, or at the level of individual ants. Likewise, learning can be studied usefully at many levels (Anderson, 1990), from the synapse to the society in which the learner lives.

To view learning systems in levels has two important implications. First, causality can be bi-directional. Experimental research on learning has tended to be reductionistic, seeking explanations of learning in its component processes. System theory suggests that why and what students learn may be equally the result of the organic behavior of the whole system of which the student is a part, a phenomenon that Campbell (1974) called "downward causation". Thus a student's understanding of evolution may be determined as much by an epistemological position held in the community as by knowledge of the fossil record or genetics. Second, it is not always necessary to decide where the boundaries of systems lie. It is sometimes best to think of the student and the learning environment as two separate but interacting systems, and at other times as one tightly coupled system whose emergent behaviors cannot be explained in terms of the separate properties of each (Clark, 2004; Winn, 2003). In the former case, learning occurs when information is exchanged between the student and the environment, and the researcher, observing the exchange, can ascribe environmental causes to learning effects. In the latter case, causality is often difficult to determine because changes are observable only at the level of the whole system, where the learner and the environment are indistinguishable, a situation that Clark (1997) has called "continuous reciprocal causation".

Determinism and predictability. Largely as a result of popular but incorrect accounts of Chaos theory, the uncertainty principle, and quantum mechanics, educational researchers, like many others, have confused determinism with predictability (Csiko, 1989). Chaos is indeed a condition that some complex systems can get into. But all that chaos implies is that it is not possible to predict how a system will behave, either because the initial state of the system is not sufficiently well known, or because it takes longer to compute the system's new state than it does for that state to evolve. It does not mean that the behavior of the system is random. Greater precision in measuring the system's initial conditions improves the accuracy of predictions about its future behavior, though not necessarily very efficiently (Strogatz, 1994). This means that learning events that may appear to be undetermined in fact are not. To find such events, we look for patterns in seemingly random data that reveal higher-level structure.

Dynamics. One thing all theories of learning agree on, however conflicted they may be about everything else, is that learning is a change over time (Van Gelder, 1998). We commonly measure learning by examining students periodically to see how they have changed between examinations. Educators espousing systems theory argue that the moment-to-moment dynamics of the changes that occur during learning — their rhythm and pace — reveal important information that is missed between traditional pre- and posttests (Thelen & Smith, 1994; Van Gelder & Port, 1995) and should therefore be continuously monitored to provide a complete account of learning.

Mathematical modeling. Finally, system theory provides tools for modeling complex systems mathematically, at any degree of complexity, at any level, and often to simulate their behavior with a computer. Two difficulties are writing the equations that describe the system's behavior, and then solving them. Scientists and engineers successfully write and solve systems of differential equations to predict tides, to simulate airflow over an airplane wing, to predict the weather, or to guide spacecraft. Yet these models produce results that, while within acceptable tolerances, are nonetheless approximations. As we mentioned earlier, the behavior of systems cannot be predicted with equations that just sum their successive states.

This means that most system behavior is "nonlinear" and that the systems of equations are impossible to solve analytically (Strogatz, 1994). Graphical approaches to describing complex dynamic systems (Abraham & Shaw, 1992) are useful and provide insights that computation cannot produce. But they cannot be used as the basis of computer models.

Van Gelder and Port (1995) offer the learning researcher three options. The first is, indeed, to build systems of equations that describe dynamic learning events. As we have seen, this is essentially impossible because, in all but trivial cases, the systems they describe are nonlinear and cannot be solved analytically. The second is to make the case that some aspect of learning is analogous to a system for which equations or a simulation already exist, and to use that to describe learning. (My own attempt to do this many years ago (Winn, 1975) assumed that the intake of information and production of knowledge by learners could be described by Von Bertalanffy's (1968) equations for organisms' metabolic processes.) The third is simply to acknowledge that learning is dynamic and complex, where learners and learning environments behave as systems, and therefore the researcher must expect to find interrelated and complex behaviors in learners that are likely to be emergent and self-organizing, difficult to predict, and continuously changing. None of these suggestions is completely satisfactory, but even very simple attempts to describe dynamic learning behavior systematically can produce useful insights.

Research Design and Methods

To detect, observe, and analyze the above-mentioned properties of systems in learning, learners, and learning environments, research studies must meet four criteria. First, researchers must study realistically complex learning environments and activities. Second, since complexity arises from the multivariate nature of learning, studies must gather a detailed record of all events in the learning environment. Third, new methods for analyzing data must be used alongside older established methods. Fourth, inferences must be made and conclusions drawn from several sources of data, not just one or two.

This section looks at each of these requirements. Illustrations are given from two projects currently under way at the University of Washington.

Study Realistically Complex Learning Environments

As we have seen, the reason we must study learning systemically is that content, students, and learning environments are complex. The reason is *not* that the most effective way to learn is through the unguided discovery of phenomena, which simply does not work (Mayer, 2004). Also, the complexity of authentic tasks often exceeds the student's cognitive capacity available for the time they have to learn them. Instructional strategies should reduce cognitive load, especially demands on working memory (Sweller, Van Merriënboer, & Paas, 1998; Van Merriënboer, Kirschner, & Kerster, 2003). Realistically complex learning environments must therefore include guidance. This might make the learning environments more complex, but including guidance results in necessary, or "germane" cognitive load (Paas, Tuovinen, Tabber, & Van Gerven, 2003), rather than load from the unrealistic expectations placed on learners to manage on their own. The two projects we use as illustrations, Virtual Puget

Sound (VPS) and INFACT/PixelMath, are learning environments that meet the criterion of realistic complexity.

Virtual Puget Sound. VPS (Windschitl & Winn, 2000; Winn et al., 2006) consists of interactive, animated, three-dimensional (3D) visualizations of data produced by a model of the physical oceanography of Puget Sound, Washington. VPS simulates water movement for a complete 24-h tidal cycle compressed into approximately 10 s. Tidal currents can be shown as animated vectors (arrows) placed at 12 depths on a 600 × 900-m grid, or as tracers that students can release into the water at any location or depth. Students move above and below water using the mouse or jumping to preset locations. Their toolkit includes an animated tide chart, cutting planes that show salinity values projected as colors onto movable vertical surfaces that can be placed anywhere, a set of virtual instruments for measuring properties of the ocean, and control over the rate at which time passes. VPS has been used in laboratory experiments comparing immersive virtual reality with desktop learning experiences, in college-level classes and with middle and elementary school students.

INFACT and PixelMath. Our other examples are from studies of a set of on-line computer tools used in freshman courses to teach basic computer science with a focus on image processing (Tanimoto, 2000; Tanimoto, Winn, & Akers, 2002). The students use two tools: The on-screen "PixelMath Calculator", into which they enter formulae or lines of code written in the Scheme language that transform images by altering and moving pixels; and an on-line forum, INFACT (interactive networked facet-based assessment capture tool), where they post answers to class and homework exercises and communicate about group projects. Students enrolled in the course are required to make predictions about what will happen to an image if a particular formula is used to transform it, or to write formulae that will bring about prescribed transformations. The PixelMath system allows students to control both the nature (color, brightness) and the positions of pixels, allowing them to magnify, shrink, rotate, or flip the image. The suite of tools includes a simple sketchpad that allows them to draw with the mouse what they predict an image will look like after they have applied a formula to it.

Gather a Complete Record of Learning Events

Both VPS and the INFACT/PixelMath systems create detailed files of student activity, saved as time-stamped event logs. In the case of VPS, the student's position and distance above or below water, the state of the system and all actions taken by the student are continuously recorded. We have also gathered think-aloud protocols, video and audiotapes of student activity and dialog, and have used a variety of pre- and posttests. Since students work with problem-based scenarios, their strategies and whether they are successful or not are also important sources of data. To assess these, we have students make predictions about the ocean by marking on maps, and by debriefing them also with reference to maps. Finally, we have conducted studies of courses where we have observed students using VPS in class and performing the same exercises at sea.

The PixelMath system logs formulae entered into the on-screen calculator, scheme code entered into the interpreter, all use of menus and tools and all mouse movements detected when the student uses the sketch tool. In addition, all posts students make to the INFACT forum are saved in a database. Our classroom studies always gather data from on-line pretests, midterms, and posttests of the content, and questionnaires about students' relevant experiences. Student classroom assignments, homework, and final projects, which are all posted to the forum, are also important in our analyses. During the four years we have offered the course, we have on an occasion interviewed students and the instructors, and conducted structured observation in the classroom.

Use a Variety of Tools to Analyze Data

Different data sources require different analysis techniques, encompassing the use of graphics to represent the data, analysis of text and video, and quantitative methods. One of the most productive sources of data in our two projects has been the time-stamped, detailed logs of student actions.

Logs of student activity allow reconstruction and analysis of what they do at any level of detail. For example, at the end of a two-week unit learning about the marine environment of Puget Sound with a lost Orca named Luna, students were asked to measure water depth, tidal currents, and salinity at various locations, and to guide the whale from one point to another. Figure 13.1 shows the routes taken by a Grade six student performing these exercises, laid over an outline map of Puget Sound. The left-hand panes show where he went. The right-hand panes show his position above or below the water surface. The vertical lines in the top right-hand pane show his return to the default position after completing each exercise, which was a view from space. The top left-hand panes show him visiting appropriate places to make his measurements. The second two panes show just the last exercise that required him to take the whale along prescribed routes. Note that he did so without surfacing to get his bearings. This is evidence that the student developed a reliable mental model of Puget Sound, an impressive feat given that the sound's bathymetry was not modeled in great detail and contained very few obvious landmarks. Other students performed almost as well. Without the ability to construct student activities from log files, none of this information would have been available.

INFACT/PixelMath log files have allowed us to obtain different kinds of information about learning. The system logs of mouse movements during sketching let us replay the act of drawing in real or accelerated time and examine the state of the sketch at any point during its construction. Among the most interesting events are where students erase or modify their sketches once their picture has begun to form on the screen. Figure 13.2 illustrates how. The student had to predict the effect of a formula that produced a rotation of 180° of the Mona Lisa. The figure shows plots of the x-, y-, and z-mouse positions. The top left image in Figure 13.2 shows the x- and y-mouse coordinates as the student drew them on the screen. The z-axis, representing time, runs into the page and is therefore not visible. Notice in particular the curved lines in Mona's lap that show the position of her arm, perhaps, or a fold in her clothes. The second image shows the student's sketch rotated partly into the third dimension so that the z-axis (time) becomes visible running left to right. The third image shows a complete rotation with the y-mouse positions plotted against time. The patterns formed in this rotation show that the student drew the complementary parts of each image in the same order. What is most important, though, is that from this rotated plot we can see that the lines in Mona's lap were drawn last in the sketch of the second, transformed, image, and added to the first sketch after that. It seems that the student used these lines as an orientation cue. Without them, the two sketches are more or less symmetrical.

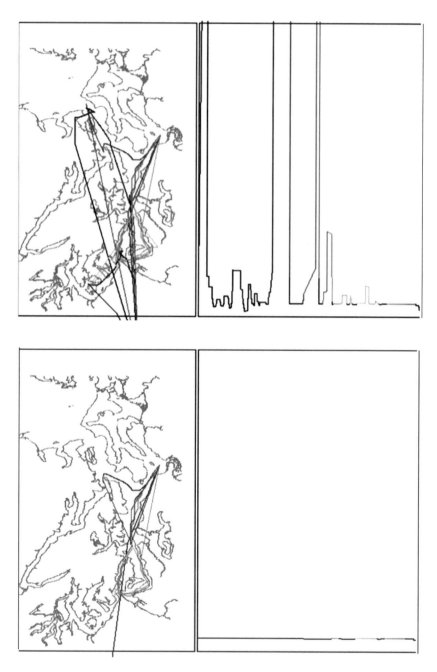

Figure 13.1: Plots of the movements of a Grade six student constructed from logs of his activity in VPS. The second two panes show where he took the whale, without looking for landmarks above the water surface.

Figure 13.2: Three-dimensional plots of mouse events that occurred while a student was drawing a figure before and after a 180° rotation using the PixelMath calculator. The top left picture shows mouse positions sampled from the screen as he drew. The top right picture shows a partial rotation into three dimensions, with time running left to right. The bottom picture shows mouse y positions plotted against time.

With them, it is clear that the student has predicted the image will be rotated through 180°, not flipped vertically, in which case the orienting lines would have been on the left side of the second sketch not the right. Once the student saw his work on the screen, he saw that he needed to add the orientation cue so that it was clear that the image was rotated, not flipped. We could not have learned this from just the final sketch.

Plotting events over time is another useful graphical technique. An example is Teng's (2004) study of concept mapping. Teng had students use the PixelMath sketch tool to draw concept maps describing what they knew about computer image processing. Building on concepts and techniques developed by Beatty and Gerace (2002), Teng plotted when words were typed into the map (when the "enter" key was pressed) on a time line. Like Beatty and Gerace, he observed that terms formed clusters in time. These temporal clusters corresponded to the way in which students organized their concepts spatially on the screen. The mean time between ending one cluster and starting a new one was significantly longer than that between the entry of words within clusters, demonstrating that the rhythm, which a student uses to construct a concept map, is a valid measure of concept organization.

Triangulate Data from many Sources

Considering just two data sources together can often tell us a great deal more than each can singly. Here, we consider data logs and posts to the on-line class discussion obtained in the INFACT/PixelMath project. Students in the course had to post their prediction of what would happen to an image when it was transformed by: (a) adding 100 to each pixel's x coordinate, (b) adding 100 to the y coordinate, (c) subtracting 1 from the x coordinate, and (d) subtracting 1 from the y coordinate, when the source and destination images were the same. The outcomes are not as easy to predict as they seem. To see why requires a short digression into how PixelMath works.

Like most graphic programs, PixelMath uses the "pull" method for manipulating images. This means that the x- or y-values point to where the pixel is *taken from* in the source image not where it is put in the destination image. Two results from this are counter-intuitive. First, since adding something to the x coordinate selects pixels part way in from the left side of the source image, adding moves the destination picture to the left not the right as most students expect. Second, students assume that subtracting from x will make the image move in the opposite direction. This is not the case when, as here, the source and destination images are the same. Subtracting any value from x or y selects as the first destination pixel one that lies outside the source image (when $x = 0, x - 1 = -1$), which defaults to gray. This gray pixel is then selected at the next iteration and replaces the pixel in the second position, then the third, the fourth and so on until the entire image is over-written with gray pixels. The image does not move left. It disappears.

Here are student JQ's predictions about the transformations required in exercises a, b, c, and d above, and the event log that accompanies them. The "Source1" part of the formula simply applies it to the first of two possible source images.

> I guess I cheated and used pixel math to see what would happen. At first I thought a statement like Source1$(x+100, y)$ would shift the picture to the right by 100 pixels. After testing it out, however, I saw that it went in the other direction. So now my guess is that Source1$(x+a, y+b)$ means that on any given x, y it is going to use the pixel it found at $(x+a, y+b)$ instead. So things would end up shifting opposite of what +100 would suggest in this coordinate system. So here we go:
> (a)   Moves picture 100 pixels to the left.
> (b)   Moves picture 100 pixels down.
> (c)   Moves picture 1 pixel right.
> (d)   Moves picture 1 pixel up.

Note that JQ begins by admitting he held the common misconception that adding to x would move the image right, but reports that he observed that it moved in the opposite direction. Note, too, the generalization that subtracting from x (or y) will move the image right (or up).

JQ's log file shows what he actually did. The first column is time in seconds. The statements in square brackets are comments, not part of the log.

4.97   Opened the Mona Lisa image.

15.44   Source1($x + 100$, y) [He tries the first formula.]

24.73   Source1($x - 100$, y) [He wasn't asked to do this. The image disappears.]

36.78   Source1($x + 100$, y) [A 12-second pause followed by three rapid attempts to recover the image by adding 100, which do not work.]

37.58   Source1($x + 100$, y)

38.20   Source1($x + 100$, y)

50.39   Opened the Mona Lisa image. [Starts over after a pause.]

55.61   Source1($x - 100$, y). [Subtracts 100 again. Image disappears.]

64.42   Undo [Recovers original image.]

71.75   Source1($x + 100$, y) [The image moves 100 pixels left.]

There are a number of points to make. Note that JQ did not try to explain in his post why Source1($x - 100$, y) and Source1(x, $y - 100$) made the image disappear, even though his log shows he saw it happen. Nor did he try using formulae with $x - 1$ and $y - 1$, even though he said he did. (Logs often show that students do not always do what they tell you they do!) The three Source1($x + 100$, y) in quick succession at 36.78 s exemplify two common behaviors. The first is the attempt to recover from an action by reversing the mathematical operation that it used. If subtracting 100 makes the image go away, maybe adding 100 will make it reappear. This does not work here. The second is what we call "superstitious behavior". If something does not work as expected, students will often simply repeat the same operation, assuming that "maybe it will work properly next time".

This episode shows how important it is to examine student activity from more than one source. If all we had to go on was JQ's post to the forum, we would not know that he had seen the image disappear when values were subtracted from x and did not understand why. (Here and elsewhere we have established that a pause after something does not work as predicted often indicates puzzlement.) We would not know that he thought this particular transformation had an inverse that would restore the original image. Nor would we know that he did not try one of the operations he said he had.

This last point is critical. We must always validate our inferences with data from other sources. Another example from the PixelMath project brings this home. Students were required to come up with a formula that would create a color gradient for the entire color spectrum. UP tried the following: "If $x < 20$ then 0 else if $x < 40$ then RGB(100, 50, 20) else if $x < 60$ then RGB(200, 100, 75) else if $x < 80$ then RGB(175, 50, 200) … else 255". This produces vertical stripes, not a smooth color gradient. UP experimented with different RGB values, using "undo" after each. Then, after a pause of 6 min and 38 s, he tried: "RGB($x + x$)*log(y) $-$ tan (y max) +log (x)". This formula does indeed produce a color gradient. UP's post to the forum explained the shift from the original "if then else" construction to the more elegant formula using log and tan functions:

> If I had to create an image of a spectrum, I would find a formula so that
> color red, green and blue components depended on the color [*sic*] and then
> I would color the screen using that formula. I found one such formula at
> [gives URL] and modified it a bit to suit my requirements and came up with
> this formula
> $RGB((x + x)*\log (y) - \tan (y \max) + \log (x), (y + y)*\log (x) - \tan (x \max) + \log (x), (x + y)*\log (x) - \tan (x \max) + \log (y))$

So during the 6-min pause, UP was on the Web looking for a better formula! We must be very careful what we conclude from single sources of data students are doing.

Our data contain many other examples of how one source of data can clarify or even change what we conclude from another. Here are some more brief examples.

Think-aloud data, interview, and log files can work well together. The log of an undergraduate working with VPS rapidly repeated many salinity measures at the mouth of Puget Sound. This is typically a sign that a student cannot figure out what is happening. His think-aloud transcript showed him saying, "Something isn't right here. I'm going to have to change my theory …" During the post-experience interview he was asked what his theory was and how he changed it. He explained that he assumed the water in Puget Sound was more saline than the water in the open ocean, because the Sound is a relatively small body of water and its salt will be concentrated by evaporation. (While this is true for the Dead Sea and for the Mediterranean, it is not the case in Puget Sound, which gains more fresh water from rivers than it loses through evaporation.) He went on to say that he changed his assumption to the correct one, and his measurements then made sense, even though his original theory was logical and valid in other contexts.

Another student's log file showed him having difficulty understanding how tidal currents vary according to the width of the passage through which they flow. During his interview, he stated that he thought water slowed down when it went through a narrow passage. (In fact, it speeds up.) His reason was that the arrows showing the current "clogged" the passage when they got longer as the current increased and that, "when I drive down the expressway and there's lots of traffic it slows down". Not only did this reveal a misconception, it also brought to light that the vector metaphor for current speed was itself a source of misunderstanding.

A middle school student who thought that the ocean gets warmer the deeper you go, when in Puget Sound it gets colder, drew an underwater volcano in his sketch of tidal movement after working in VPS. He explained that these thermal vents, which are found off the Washington coast not in Puget Sound and which had recently been in the news, heat the water at the bottom of the ocean.

Finally, here is another example from a PixelMath exercise. As we saw earlier, the system's use of the "pull" method for image manipulation can produce results that are counterintuitive. More than one student thought that an image disappears when you subtract from an *x*- or *y*-value because the pixels are *removed* from the source image — a "cut" rather than a "copy" operation. Going back to posts on INFACT forum showed this to be the reason for several wrong answers on a midterm exam.

In all of these examples, we have started out with student errors or difficulties that have appeared in either their observed or logged performance or on tests. In each case, we were able to establish that the reasons for the misconceptions were perfectly logical, even leading to what would have been correct solutions in different circumstances. Yet without cross-checking with other data sources, neither the logic nor the source of the misconceptions would have been discovered.

A Broader View: Other Relevant Research

Our own research, from which we have selected just a few examples, has provided a mere glimpse of the ways in which we can use ideas from system theory in research on learning. Other scholars are working in ways that are directly and indirectly contributing to this enterprise. We now look at three of these.

Complexity in the learning environment: Multimedia. As computers allow us to build ever more complex learning, Mayer and Moreno's (2003) "cognitive theory of multimedia" provides a conceptual framework that accounts for the integration of input from different senses and active student learning, bearing in mind the limited capacity of working memory. While not explicitly espousing a system-theoretic approach to research, rigorous study of hypotheses predicted from the theory (for example, Moreno & Valdez, 2005) demonstrates that complex learning environments are certainly amenable to experimental study. It is to be hoped that the recent increase in interest in what video games can tell us about learning from complex environments (Gee, 2003) will likewise develop testable theories.

Student-environment coupling: Self-regulation. As students become more expert in what they are learning, they can develop the ability to monitor and change how they learn. Such self-regulation can be measured and studied (Winne & Perry, 2000). What is more, the essential guidance students need when learning in complex environments can be designed into the environments to promote self-regulation. Lajoie and her colleagues (for example, Lajoie, 2003; Lajoie, Faremo, Wiseman, & Gauthier, 2005) have developed computer-based environments that, among other things, require medical and nursing students to provide justifications for solutions to problems that they can then compare to experts' knowledge. Studies have shown that this approach can develop metacognitive skills, which in turn evolve into self-regulation and improve performance. Students can therefore learn to adapt effectively to unpredicted and local variation in the learning environment as our systemic view of learning requires.

Looking for emergent patterns: Log-file analysis. The examples of how we use log files in our research showed that we rely on inspection and graphical representation to interpret them as much as numerical analysis. A variety of tools exists for analyzing student activity recorded in logs in more rigorous quantitative ways. Bayesian analysis of event logs (Martin & Van Lehn, 1995; Mislevy, Almond, Yan, & Steinberg, 1999) allows us to organize learning events into clusters, in this case by estimating the probabilities that they occur together. Neural network tools have also been used to analyze student performance. For example, McKnight and Walberg (1998) used the neural network program "Galileo", to analyze student essays. The program identified patterns of words that fell into meaningful clusters on the basis of the strengths of the associations among them. Methods like these identify groups of data points that form patterns. In so doing, they all identify emergent properties of learning that might otherwise escape detection and analysis.

Conclusion: Research Questions and Methods

Does a system theoretic approach to research on learning allow us to ask and answer questions about complex events that we could not otherwise consider? Certainly, we are a long way from writing systems of equations that describe how students learn complex material in complex environments. But even the simple awareness that the behavior of students coupled to learning environments, like that of all systems, is hierarchical, emergent, self-organizing, and hard to predict can lead us to take different approaches to research.

The approach described most fully here — the collection of detailed information about learning events in log files and the graphical and computational methods for analyzing them — certainly works well to detect emergent patterns of behavior and understanding that would otherwise go undetected. It therefore makes it possible to answer research questions about the ways in which students' learning strategies develop at levels of detail that have hitherto not been extensively examined. Most interesting, as we have seen, are cases where students stumble around, trying different approaches, before making the decision about how to solve a problem, which is often all we get to see from them. When these false starts form the basis of immediate feedback, the ground is laid for developing skill in self-regulation, a line of research that is important to pursue as we study the tight, systemic coupling of students and learning environments.

The systemic approach also emphasizes the influence of context on learning. In contrast to descriptive, ethnographic methods, the tools of system theory allow more precise graphical and computational analysis of how coupled student-environment systems change dynamically. To date, much of the relevant research has focused on robots and intelligent agents (Beer, 1995), with research on humans confined to fairly basic tasks (Kelso, 1999; Thelen & Smith, 1994). Nonetheless, this work is leading to tools that will help us answer questions about the mutual influences of students and learning environments, whether we consider the student and the environment to be two interacting systems with one-way causality, or one tightly coupled system where causality is reciprocal.

The systemic view of learning acknowledges that learners change their environment as they "externalize" cognition (Scaife & Rogers, 1996; Winn, 2003). We saw a good example of this earlier, where the student added an orientation cue to the rotated Mona Lisa. Important research questions are therefore the extent to which students rely on off-loading intermediate ideas into the environment as they think through problems, and how they learn to do so. The moment-by-moment examination of their actions is an excellent way to answer these questions, as we have seen.

Nearly all learning environments contain people, be they students, teachers, or others. In the systemic view, this means that a student is coupled to other people who can provide different degrees of support (or hindrance) as the student learns. This social nature of learning has been stressed by several of the authors cited above (Collins et al., 2004; Edelson et al., 2002). The systemic approach allows us to shed new light on the social dimension of learning. The INFACT project, in particular, has allowed us to monitor and document in great detail what students share with other members of their work group, through on-line posts, and what they choose not to make public. As students work first individually and then collectively on problems, we can trace the development of ideas as they appear privately in log files and publicly on-line. Our data include examples ranging from simply copying from another student to thoughtful and productive collaboration and discussion.

Finally, a number of the tools we have mentioned for analyzing complex datasets have been developed as alternatives to tests of student achievement. It is ironic that these tools appear to make traditional assessment techniques somewhat redundant. If we can watch students as they learn, moment to moment, we can determine what they know at any particular point. Assessment is no longer something that needs to occur separately from learning. Yet we still need to assess long-term retention and transfer of knowledge and skill, both of which require measurement of what students know at some distance in time and space from where they learned it. An important question, then, is whether the tools used for the systemic study of learning are valid for assessment, in its summative role, as a basis for academic and professional advancement. Two relatively recent developments suggest that they might be. First, these tools allow us to look beyond the answer a student gives on a test to the reasons for giving it. Second, the developing ability to automate the scoring of constructed rather than objective responses to test items means that it will soon be feasible to monitor student activity while taking a test and to determine with much greater accuracy what students actually know, based on more than one source of data.

The complexity of studying students while they learn remains daunting. But, if nothing else, the systemic view tells us that what often appears to be random, or wrong, is in fact not so. We therefore need to pursue system theoretic approaches to learning research as far as we can. Even if we are not as successful as physical scientists have been in this task, system theory will still yield important new insights into how students learn complex material in complex environments.

References

Abraham, R. H., & Shaw, C. D. (1992). *Dynamics: The geometry of behavior*. New York: Addison-Wesley.

Anderson, J. R. (1990). *Adaptive character of thought*. Hillsdale, NJ: Erlbaum.

Beatty, I. D., & Gerace, W. J. (2002). Probing physics students' conceptual knowledge structures through term association. *American Journal of Physics*, *70*, 750–758.

Beer, R. D. (1995). Computation and dynamical languages for autonomous agents. In: R. F. Port, & T. Van Gelder (Eds), *Mind as motion: Explorations in the dynamics of cognition* (pp. 121–147). Cambridge, MA: MIT Press.

Belland, J. C. (1985). The inverse tool principle. *Educational Communication and Technology Journal*, *33*, 51–57.

Blomberg, C. (2004). Aspects of fluctuations in non-linear biological systems. In: W. Klonowski (Ed.), *Simplicity behind complexity: Proceedings of the 3rd European interdisciplinary school on nonlinear dynamics for system and signal analysis* (pp. 25–60). Miami: Pabst Scientific Publishers.

Box, G. E. P. (1979). Robustness is the strategy of scientific model building. In: R. L. Launer, & G. N. Wilkinson (Eds), *Robustness in statistics* (pp. 201–236). New York: Academic Press.

Bransford, J., Brown, A., & Cocking, R. (2000). *How people learn: Brain, mind, experience and school: Expanded edition*. Washington, DC: National Academy Press.

Campbell, D. T. (1974). "Downward causation" in hierarchically organized biological systems. In: F. J. Ayala, & T. Dobzhansky (Eds), *Studies in the philosophy of biology* (pp. 179–186). New York: Macmillan.

Clark, A. (1997). *Being there: Putting brain, body and world together again.* Cambridge, MA: MIT Press.

Clark, A. (2004). *Natural born cyborgs.* Oxford: Oxford University Press.

Clark, R. E. (1982). Antagonism between achievement and enjoyment in ATI studies. *Educational Psychologist, 17*, 92–101.

Clark, R. E. (1990). When teaching kills learning: Research on mathemathantics. In: H. N. Mandl, N. Bennett, E. De Corte, & H. F. Friedrich (Eds), *Learning and instruction: European research in an international context* (Vol. 2, pp. 1–22). London: Pergamon.

Cobb, P., Confrey, J., diSessa, A., Lehrer, R., & Schauble, L. (2003). Design experiments in educational research. *Educational Researcher, 32*(1), 9–13.

Collins, A., Joseph, D., & Bielaczyc, K. (2004). Design research: Theoretical and methodological issues. *The Journal of the Learning Sciences, 13*, 15–42.

Csiko, G. A. (1989). Unpredictability and indeterminism in human behavior: Arguments and implications for educational research. *Educational Researcher, 18*(3), 17–25.

de Jong, T., & Van Joolingen, W. R. (1998). Scientific discovery learning with computer simulations of conceptual domains. *Review of Educational Research, 68*, 179–201.

Edelson, D. C., Salierno, C., Matese, G., Pitts, V., & Sherin, B. (2002). Learning-for-use in earth science: Kids as climate modelers. Paper presented at the annual meeting of the national association for research in science teaching, New Orleans, LA.

Forrester, J. W. (1980). System dynamics: Future opportunities. In: A. A. Legasto, J. W. Forrester, & J. M. Lynes (Eds), *Studies in management science: System dynamics* (pp. 7–21). New York: North-Holland Publishing Co.

Fox, E. J. (2006). Constructing a pragmatic science of learning and instruction with functional contextualism. *Educational Technology Research and Development, 54*(1), 5–36.

Gee, J. P. (2003). *What video games have to teach us about learning and literacy.* New York: Palgrave Macmillan.

Gordon, D. (1999). *Ants at work: How an insect society is organized.* New York: Free Press.

Gribbin, J. (2004). *Deep simplicity: Bringing order to chaos and complexity.* New York: Random House.

Hauhs, M., & Lange, H. (2004). Modeling the complexity of environmental and ecological systems. In: W. Klonowski (Ed.), *Simplicity behind complexity: Proceedings of the 3rd European interdisciplinary school on nonlinear dynamics for system and signal analysis*, Miami: Pabst Scientific Publishers (pp. 85–109).

Heinich, R. (1970). *Technology and the management of instruction.* Washington, DC: Association for Educational Communication and Technology.

Howe, K. R. (1985). Two dogmas of educational research. *Educational Researcher, 14*(8), 10–18.

Jacobs, J. (1961). *The death and life of great American cities.* New York: Vintage Books.

Kelso, J. A. S. (1999). *Dynamic patterns: The self-organization of brain and behavior.* Cambridge, MA: MIT Press.

Lajoie, S. P. (2003). Transitions and trajectories for studies of expertise. *Educational Researcher, 32*(8), 21–25.

Lajoie, S. P., Faremo, S., Wiseman, J., & Gauthier, G. (2005). Promoting self-regulation in medical students through the use of technology. Paper presented at the annual meeting of the American educational research association, Montreal, Canada.

Mandelbrot, B. (1983). *The fractal geometry of nature.* New York: Freeman.

Martin, J., & Van Lehn, K. (1995). Student assessment using Bayesian nets. *International Journal of Human-Computer Studies, 42*, 575–591.

Mayer, R. (2004). Should there be a three-strikes rule against pure discovery learning. *American Psychologist, 59*, 14–19.

Mayer, R., & Moreno, R. (2003). Nine ways to reduce cognitive load in multimedia learning. *Educational Psychologist, 38*, 43–52.

McKnight, K. S., & Walberg, H. J. (1998). Neural network analysis of student essays. *Journal of Research and Development in Education, 32*, 26–31.

Mislevy, R. J., Almond, R. G., Yan, D., & Steinberg, L. S. (1999). Bayes nets in educational assessment: Where do the numbers come from? In: K. B. Lashley, & H. Prade (Eds), *Proceedings of the fifteenth conference on uncertainty and artificial intelligence* (pp. 437–446). San Francisco: Morgan Kaufmann.

Moreno, R., & Valdez, A. (2005). Cognitive load and learning effects of having students organize pictures and words in multimedia environments: The role of student interactivity and feedback. *Educational Technology, Research and Development, 53*, 35–45.

Paas, F., Tuovinen, J. E., Tabber, S. H., & Van Gerven, P. W. M. (2003). Cognitive load measurement as a means to advance cognitive theory. *Educational Psychologist, 38*, 63–71.

Phillips, D. C. (1983). After the wake: Postpositivism in educational thought. *Educational Researcher, 12*(5), 4–12.

Salomon, G. (1991). Transcending the qualitative-quantitative debate: The analytic and systemic approaches to educational research. *Educational Researcher, 20*(6), 10–18.

Scaife, M., & Rogers, Y. (1996). External cognition: How do graphical representations work? *International Journal of Human Computer Studies, 45*, 185–213.

Shavelson, R., & Towne, L. (Eds). (2002). *Scientific research in education*. Washington, DC: National Academy Press.

Spiro, R. J., Feltovich, P. J., Jacobson, M. J., & Coulson, R. L. (1992). Cognitive flexibility, constructivism, and hypertext: Random access instruction for advanced knowledge acquisition in ill-structured domains. In: T. M. Duffy, & D. H. Jonassen (Eds), *Constructivism and the technology of instruction* (pp. 57–75). Hillsdale, NJ: Erlbaum.

Strogatz, S. H. (1994). *Nonlinear dynamics and chaos*. Cambridge, MA: Perseus Books.

Strogatz, S. H. (2003). *Sync: The emerging science of spontaneous order*. New York: Hyperion.

Sweller, J., Van Merriënboer, J., & Paas, F. (1998). Cognitive architecture and instructional design. *Educational Psychology Review, 10*, 251–296.

Tanimoto, S. (2000). Supporting assessment-intensive pedagogy: The design of INFACT — The interactive networked facet-based assessment capture tool. *Proceedings of CILT 2000*, Washington, DC: Center for Innovative Learning and Technologies.

Tanimoto, S., Winn, W. D., & Akers, D. (2002). A system that supports using student-drawn diagrams to assess comprehension of mathematical formulas. Paper presented at diagrams 2002: International conference on theory and application of diagrams (Diagrams02), Callaway Gardens, GA.

Teng, C. E. (2004). The message behind the canvas: Exploring the dynamics of concept maps. Paper presented at the annual meeting of the American educational research association, San Diego, CA.

Tennyson, R. D. (1997). A systems dynamics approach to instructional systems design. In: R. D. Tennyson, F. Schott, N. Seel, & S. Dijkstra (Eds), *Instructional design, international perspective: Vol. 1. Theory, research and models* (pp. 413–426). Mawah, NJ: Erlbaum.

Thelen, E., & Smith, L. (1994). *A dynamic systems approach to the development of cognition and action*. Cambridge, MA: MIT Press.

Van Gelder, T. (1998). The dynamical hypothesis in cognitive science. *Behavioral and Brain Sciences, 21*, 615–665.

Van Gelder, T., & Port, R. F. (1995). It's about time. In: R. F. Port, & T. Van Gelder (Eds), *Mind as motion: Explorations in the dynamics of cognition* (pp. 1–43). Cambridge, MA: MIT Press.

Van Merriënboer, J., Kirschner, P., & Kester, L. (2003). Taking the load off the learner's mind: Instructional design for complex learning. *Educational Psychologist, 38*, 5–13.

Von Bertalanffy, L. (1968). *General system theory.* New York: Braziller.

Windschitl, M., & Winn, W. D. (2000). A virtual environment designed to help students learn science. Paper presented at the international conference of the learning sciences, Ann Arbor, MI.

Winn, W. D. (1975). An open system model of learning. *AV Communication Review, 23,* 5–33.

Winn, W. D. (2003). Learning in artificial environments: Embodiment, embeddedness and dynamic adaptation. *Technology, Instruction, Cognition and Learning, 1,* 87–114.

Winn, W. D., Hoffman, H., Hollander, A., Osberg, K., Rose, H., & Char, P. (1999). Student-built virtual environments. *Presence: Teleoperators and virtual environments, 8,* 283–292.

Winn, W. D., Stahr, R., Sarason, C., Fruland, R., Oppenheimer, P., & Lee, Y.-L. (2006). Learning oceanography from a computer simulation compared with direct experience at sea. *Journal of Research in Science Teaching, 43*(1), 25–42.

Winne, P. H., & Perry, N. E. (2000). Measuring self-regulated learning. In: M. Boekaerts, P. Pintrich, & M. Zeidner (Eds), *Handbook of self-regulation* (pp. 531–566). Orlando, FL: Academic Press.

Wolfram, S. (2002). *A new kind of science.* Champaign, IL: Wolfram Media Inc.

Chapter 14

The Systemic vs. Analytic Study of Complex Learning Environments

Gavriel Salomon

The Meaning of "Learning Environments"

While it is difficult to clearly define "learning environments" as they entail a wide variety of instances, we nevertheless have an idea of what we mean by that concept. For one thing, we know that learning environments pertain to some real environment and for another that learning takes place there. As discussed here, learning environments are synonymous to instructional environments. But we can be even more specific in our understanding of learning environments and thus know how "learning environments" differ from other instances such as a pedestrian crossing where a toddler learns to wait for the green light, or a supermarket where we learn how to detect the shortest line at a counter. A street corner is an "environment", as is the supermarket, and some learning does take place there. They are not what we mean by a "learning environment" because both instances lack deliberate instruction. Indeed, from the point of view of instructional theory, a learning environment is a setting in which guided learning takes place — whether by a live teacher, computerized instructions, printed instructions or a voice recorded guide in a museum. A learning environment may often be "collaborative" in the sense that more than one learner is involved, although the learners are not always working jointly (Dillenbourg, 1999). Recently, the so-called constructivist learning environments have been designed and studied in which actual collaboration takes place (e.g., Wilson, 1995). At the same time other environments are evolving whereby learning takes place in the solitude of one's home, interacting with virtual others or with learning materials via electronic means (e.g., Smith & Hardaker, 2000). Still, whether it is constructivist or traditional, a classroom in a school or an Internet-based e-learning course, the learning environment is a real place with physical attributes where deliberate instructions are provided and where learning activities are supposed to take place.

    Despite this diversity, all learning environments share a number of characteristics such as learners with their individual traits, habits, preferences and proclivities, instructions, learning materials, learning activities, social interactions and relations, rules and regulations, norms and climates. In this sense, all learning environments — classrooms, museums, school field trips, afternoon clubs, soccer training sessions – are complex composites and thus need to be described, analyzed and studied as such.

Learning Environments as Complex Systems

Learning environments are complex by whatever criterion one uses to measure them. Based on Edmonds (1999), we might say that a learning environment is complex by virtue of the difficulty to describe its overall actions and behaviors on the basis of even complete information about its components and their interrelations. Thus, even when given the fullest possible description of a teacher's instructional behavior, her way of interacting with the students, interactions among students and the like, we still do not receive a full account of the classroom's changing complexity. Similarly, a learning environment can be seen to be complex because of the amount of computational resource (e.g., time or memory) that is needed to solve a problem that afflicts it (Hinegardner & Engleberg, 1983). This in turn relates well to the conception of complexity as entropy (Standish, 2001), in which learning environments are understood to have low levels of organization, thus making it difficult to predict one part of the system of components that comprise the LEs from knowledge of other components. Luckily enough, most learning environments are not totally random organizations of components and hence are not totally unpredictable. They are thus complex but manageably so. More recently, Berliner (2002) highlighted the complex nature of learning environments by pointing out the ubiquity of many high-order interactions that take place in them, thereby making generalizations and predictions rather temporary and incomplete.

Three Characteristics of Learning Environments

Close examination of typical learning environments reveals three important but not particularly surprising attributes. The first attribute is that learning environments are comprised of numerous components such a student characteristics, teacher–student interrelations, activities, rules and regulations, etc. One could group these into categories such as student characteristics, teacher characteristics, student–teacher interactions, student–student interactions, learning activities, learning materials, rules and norms, and so on (e.g., Hertz-Lazarowitz, 1992). The second attribute is that these components interact with each other, *affecting each other and giving meaning to each other.* The third attribute is that these interactions and their consequences are in constant flux, thus defying any attempt to describe a classroom as a static, easily predicted social entity (e.g., Berliner, 2002).

Concerning the multiplicity of components, one could easily show that this is not unique to learning environments or, for that matter, to any entity of interest to educational research, be it an individual, an attitude or a learning activity. Whatever entity we examine — separate cognitions, motivations, anxieties, chemical processes in the brain or interactions in a group — it is always comprised of smaller units which interact with each other. Nevertheless, what can be explained on one level, such as one's mode of learning, cannot be reduced to and explained by its constituent components, such as brain chemistry (Bandura, 1991). Thus, complex systems need to be studied as such.

Indeed, as the term was initially coined by Bartlett (cited by Iran-Nejad, McKeachie, & Berliner, 1990), the process of *simplification by isolation*, decontextualizes the processes and activities under investigation, often stripping them of their original meanings. As the philosopher Searle (1992) has commented, "Suppose that we tried to say that pain in 'nothing but' the pattern of neurons firings. Well, if we tried such an ontological reduction, the essential features of the pain would be left out" (p. 117). In this sense, studying the way a team of students goes about solving a new problem while searching the Internet would yield one meaning when studied in isolation as a stand-alone activity and another when studied in light of the way the students appear to perceive the ultimate goals of their joint activity. As Lizzio, Wilson, and Simons (2002) show, students' perceptions of the assigned workload and appropriateness of assessment affects how seriously they take their studies, making their perceptions a better predictor of learning than their prior knowledge.

The second attribute of learning environments as complex systems — the interaction between their components — involves three qualities of importance. First, the combination of a component such as teamwork with a particular kind of assignment produces a unique outcome which differs from what another combination would yield. This much is trivial. Less trivial is the possibility that more than two factors are involved and that the learning outcome of such or of an even richer combination of factors affects them reciprocally in a dynamic spiral of mutual determination. The poor learning that results from the collaboration between team members whose task is to solve a particular problem in physics who perceive it as unimportant and who dislike working together, may affect the way they continue to approach their collaboration as well as their next assignment. Such a spiraling of influences suggests that treating teamwork, assignments or social relations as independent variables and learning as a dependent variable misses the point as the variables affect each other reciprocally. In fact, we are entering here what Lee J. Cronbach (1975) has so succinctly described as "a hall of mirrors that extends to infinity".

More specifically, the different components, factors or variables that comprise the learning environment and affect each other reciprocally *give meaning* to each other. Thus, as Altman and Rogoff (1987) pointed out —

> ... the whole is composed of inseparable aspects that simultaneously and conjointly define the whole ... the root metaphor is historical event — a spatial and temporal confluence of people, settings, and activities that constitutes a complex organized unit. The aspects of a system, that is, person and context, coexist jointly and define one another and contribute to the meaning and nature of ... the event. (p. 24)

The meaning on-line learners may assign to their activity of preparing a joint project (important in their eyes?) may greatly depend on the meaning they assign to the virtual instructor's actions (supportive? dominating?), which is influenced by the meaning given to the overall social atmosphere as more or less supportive of helpful task-oriented cooperation (e.g., Oren, Mioduser, & Nachmias, 2002). Goddard and Goddard (2001) demonstrate the central role played by a collective sense of efficacy; it predicts variations in teacher efficacy better than such contextual factors as socioeconomic status and student achievement. Other studies reveal a number of additional variables that play important roles in characterizing a learning environment: Empowerment, student support, professional interest, mission consensus, resource adequacy and work pressure, student affiliation, interdependence, cooperation, task orientation, order and organization, individualization and teacher control (Dorman, Fraser, & McRobbie, 1997). Thus, such aspects of learning environments — collective and individual — turn out to be the engines that link each other to the different components of the learning environment and allows them to affect and define each other.

Learning Environments as Composites

In light of the above, it becomes clear why learning environments should be regarded as complex *composites* rather than just collections of variables that can be studied one by one. But what does this actually mean? The idea of studying a number of learning environment variables as a cluster (e.g., the variables that jointly constitute "classroom climate") is not new. Fraser, Anderson, and Walenberg (1982) and Haertel, Walenberg, and Haertel (1981) did so years ago. But studying one or another variable, or studying a cluster of related variables, does not address the complex nature of a learning environment as a composite.

Composites are not simply lists of variables or clusters. They are comprised of *relations* among these constructs. When we speak of a composite we mean something like a Gestalt, a configuration, or a "system" which has components that are structured in some organized manner. In this sense, a composite's structure, the organization of its components, is its main characteristic *as a composite*. Thus, a description of a learning environment as a complex composite of variables or elements must include its structure, that is — the way its variables are organized and related to each other. This need was felt by Barros, Verdejo, Read, and Mizoguchi (2002) who attempted to describe the ontology of learning environments that are inspired by activity theory (AT). Their main point was that "This ontology is defined within the AT framework (which underlines the importance of *relating* and *integrating* its components), and its nodes correspond to the main concepts in an AT activity: tools, rules, division of labor, community, subject, object (goal) and outcome" (p. 304).

Herein lies the unique contribution of addressing learning environments as composites. Usually, variables or clusters thereof are studied one by one as they relate to some dependent variable. For example, Dorman, Adams, and Ferguson (2002) correlated each of a number of mathematics learning environment variables such as student cohesiveness, teacher support and investigation with academic math efficacy. Similarly, comparisons between learning environments are usually based on the contrast of variables — the average of social interaction in one learning environment vs. another, or the mean of a competitive climate in one learning environment vs. another (e.g., Dryden & Fraser, 1996).

Patterns of Differences vs. Differences of Patterns

Acknowledging the need to look at the interrelations among variables, and their configuration, changes the focus of analysis. It is not just a study of the *patterns of differences*
between means, but rather it becomes a study of the *differences of patterns*. The difference between the two is profound. In the case of studying patterns of differences we look
at how learning environments differ from each other in terms of the strength of particular variables — how high or low these variables are. On the other hand, when we study
differences of patterns we look at the way the variables are organized. Thus, for example, Hicks (1993) carried out a study of a new learning environment around the use of a
computerized Writing Partner that provided semi-intelligent metacognitive-like guidance during essay writing. Analysing the *pattern of differences* between that learning
environment and a control one (writing with only a word processor), she found that the
tendency to write more mindfully accounted for 9% of the writing quality variance in the
experimental classes, but only for 1% in the control classes. Moreover, while general
ability (ITBS) accounted for only 5% of the variance in the experimental classes, it
accounted for 24% in the control ones. So much for *patterns of differences*. When the
differences in patterns were examined, Hicks found that mindfulness became a central
feature in the configuration of variables in the experimental classrooms whereas ITBS
scores were quite peripheral. The opposite was the case in the control classrooms
(Figures 14.1 and 14.2). Examination of the two maps, where distances signify correlations among the variables, suggests that the experimental and the control learning environments are two entities with entirely different structures. More will be said about these
maps later on.

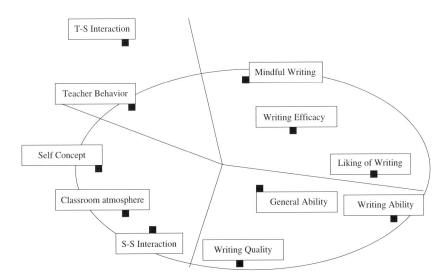

Figure 14.1: Small space analysis of Hick's (1993) control classrooms.

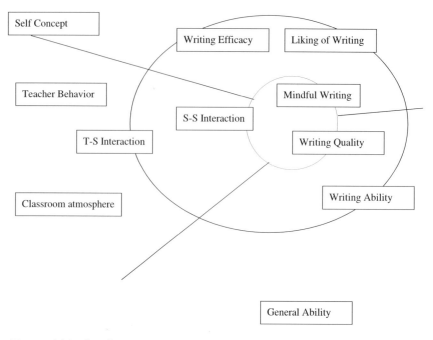

Figure 14.2: Small space analysis of Hick's (1993) experimental classrooms.

Analytic and Systemic Approaches

The distinction between studying *patterns of differences* and studying *differences of patterns* deserves some elaboration. When we want to study, for example, the extent to which more or less structure of the task affects the way teams learn cooperatively, the purpose is to estimate the net effect of this variable on teams' learning. This would constitute an *analytic approach* to studying learning environments (Salomon, 1991); it attempts to single out one or another variable or cluster of variables to examine its possible causal contribution to some dependent variable. This recalls Bronfenbrenner's (1977) quote of his professor according to whom to understand something one would be well advised to change it. Banaji and Crowder (1989), arguing with Ulric Neisser about the study of memory in real-life settings, claimed that complex systems ought to be studied more under controlled conditions (where variables can be isolated and manipulated) and less under conditions of natural complexity. They illustrate their claim with the studies by Milgram on obedience to authority and by Latane on the bystander phenomena, studies in which variables of importance were isolated and usefully manipulated to examine their causal function.

By traditional criteria, the pattern of differences between experimental groups that emerges from the analytic approach might well be a valid test of causality (Campbell, 1988). However, it will tell us very little about the learning environment as a composite and how the introduction of one or another important variable affects its overall nature. To the extent that the variable of interest is of any importance, and assuming that it enters a "cloud of correlated variables" with other variables (Scarr, 1985), to that extent would we need to examine the way the learning environment as a composite changes as a function of the introduction of that variable. This then, would call for a *systemic approach* of studying the learning environment (Salomon, 1991), an approach that would allow examination of the differences of patterns.

The analytic and systemic approaches to research are not just two different research strategies; they are based on a different sets of assumptions which, epistemologically at least, are mutually exclusive. Table 14.1 presents a brief contrast of the two different sets of assumptions.

Common to the assumptions of the analytic approach is the idea that one can explain "change and process by the actions of material things already existing at the commencement of change" (Gibbs, 1979), hence the ability and desirability of singling out and manipulating variables so that complex systems can be better understood (e.g., Banaji & Crowder, 1989). According to this view, elements of the system have meaning in and of themselves, can be isolated and their net contribution to the system can thus be observed. On the other hand, the systemic approach assumes that "Behavior is serial, not a mere succession. It can be resolved — it must be — into discrete acts, but no act can be understood apart from the series to which it belongs" (Dewey, 1930, p. 412). Hence, the need to study learning environments in their entire complexity as composites that are experienced and understood as "package deals". A fitting metaphor would be the study of architecture — the art and science of composites.

Actually Studying Complex Learning Environments

How then can one study complex learning environments? Two answers come readily to mind. One answer concerns the use of a qualitative, narrative description of a learning

Table 14.1: Contrasting assumptions of the analytic and the systemic approaches.

The analytic paradigm	The systemic paradigm
— You can break down complex situations and processes into their constituent components	— Situations and processes are viable entities and cannot be reduced to their components
— Single variables have meanings in and of themselves, independent of each other	— Variables come as "clouds of interrelated events", affecting and giving meanings to each other
— Hypothesis pertain to single variables	— Hypotheses pertain to whole Gestalts
— Behavior and learning are a function of what you can manipulate	— Behavior and learning are part of reciprocal interactions
— Manipulation of a variable leaves all others unchanged	— Changing one important variable is changing the whole configuration

environment and the way it changes when a new instructional element or a new social organization is introduced (e.g., Bredweg & Winkels, 1998), and a quantitative systemic approach of the kind that Louis Guttman developed on the basis of his facet theory (e.g., Shye, 1998). One of the offsprings of that approach is the *Small Space Analysis* (SSA; later called *Similarity Structure Analysis*) through which a spatial map showing the distances (correlations) between all variables is produced. SSA creates a spatial representation of the learning environment's variables and places them in "regions", making possible the systematic investigation of the environment's Gestalt-like structure. Figure 14.2 above is a case in point, showing that whereas in the Writing Partner experimental environment mindfulness and student–student interactions are very much at its core and closely related to writing quality, these variables are relatively peripheral and unrelated to each other in the control environment, which does not have much of a core except for students' general ability.

The qualitative narrative may offer a so-called full-blooded and highly plausible description (Bruner, 1990), but it may lack what Shavelson, Phillips, Towne, and Feuer (2003) call verifiability; it may be long on authenticity but short on certitude. As Shavelson et al. point out, a narrative approach to the description of new learning environment designs does not easily rule out alternative narratives, and hence alternative explanations. On the other hand, a Guttman-like SSA, while yielding an interesting picture of the configuration of variables in a learning environment, allowing comparison with alternative learning environments as to what is central and what is peripheral, what goes with what, etc., cannot show the dynamic changes among the environment's components. It yields a static configuration. This is of particular concern, given the claim made earlier that one of the important characteristics of a learning environment is its ever changing nature.

In fact, from a research point of view our wish list is not very modest. We want a detailed description of learning environments that will manifest their complexity, we want a modicum of exactitude and certitude concerning the interrelations among its component variables, we want to have a sense of its changing nature, and we want to gain understanding of the causal relations between the variables. In short, we want to be able to answer such questions as how does this or that learning environment function? What is important (central) in its life and what is not? Which variables relate more closely to which ones? How does the introduction of x change other variables? How does its introduction change the whole configuration? How do students' thoughts, perceptions, preferences or dislikes affect the way that x is handled? How do we explain the way x changes the learning environment?

It becomes evident that no single method or approach can answer all these and similar questions. The need to combine a variety of research approaches that complement each other is compelling; inviting a mixed methods research paradigm (Johnson & Onwuegbuzie, 2004) or a rich tool box of such. The causal link between variables that a controlled experiment or clinical trial can show does not take care of the ubiquity of interactions between the variables; such studies can show with relatively satisfactory certitude the amount variance accounted for by this or that isolated variable, thereby contributing to our causal understanding. On the other hand, Guttman's SSA can show the structure of the environment's configuration of variables and how the structures of two environments differ from each other as composites. To complement these two approaches, a detailed narrative can highlight the roles that changing meanings and perceptions play in the dynamic development of a learning environment. Obviously, to fully understand the way a learning environment functions, how it is experienced and what in it causes success or failure, we would need all three approaches.

This mosaic of approaches, based as it is on entirely different sets of epistemological assumptions, may be only a tentative solution. Once we come to fully acknowledge that learning environments are complex composites of ever changing relations among variables, a new approach will have to be developed.

References

Altman, I., & Rogoff, B. (1987). World views in psychology: Trait, interactional, organismic and transactional perspectives. In: D. Stokols, & I. Altman (Eds), *Handbook of environmental psychology* (pp. 7–15). New York: Wiley.

Bandura, A. (1991). Human agency: The rhetoric and the reality. *American Psychologist, 46,* 157–162.

Banaji, M. R., & Crowder, R. G. (1989). The bankruptcy of everyday memory. *American Psychologist, 44,* 1185–1193.

Barros, B., Verdejo, M., Read, T., & Mizoguchi, R. (2002). Applications of a collaborative learning ontology. In: *Second Mexican international conference on artificial intelligence, MICAI 2002* (pp. 301–310). Mérida: Springer.

Berliner, D. C. (2002). Educational research: The hardest science of all. *Educational Researcher, 31*(8), 18–21.

Bredweg, B., & Winkels, R. (1998). Qualitative models in interactive learning environments. *Interactive Learning Environments, 5*(1–2), 1–18.

Bronfenbrenner, U. (1977). Toward an experimental ecology of human development. *American Psychologist, 34,* 513–531.

Bruner, J. (1990). *Acts of meaning.* London: Harvard University Press.

Campbell, D. T. (1988). *Methodology and epistemology for social science: Selected papers.* Chicago: University of Chicago Press.

Cronbach, L. J. (1975). Beyond the two disciplines of scientific psychology. *American Psychologist, 30,* 116–126.

Dewey, J. (1930). Conduct and experience. In: C. Murchism (Ed.), *Psychologies of 1930* (pp. 410–429). Worcester, MA: Clark University Press.

Dillenbourg, P. (1999). What do you mean by collaborative learning? In: P. Dillenbourg (Ed.), *Collaborative-learning: Cognitive and computational approaches* (pp 1–19). Oxford: Elsevier.

Dorman, J. P., Adams, J. E., & Ferguson, J. M. (2002). Psychosocial environment and student self-handicapping in secondary school mathematics classes: A cross-national study. *Educational Psychology, 22,* 499–511.

Dorman J. P., Fraser B. J., & McRobbie C. J. (1997). Relationship between school-level and classroom-level environments in secondary schools. *Journal of Educational Administration, 35*(1), 74–91.

Dryden, M., & Fraser, B. J. (1996). Use of classroom environment instruments in monitoring urban systemic reform. Paper presented at the annual meeting of the American Educational Research Association, New York.

Edmonds, B. (1999). Capturing social embeddedness: A constructivist approach. *Adaptive Behaviour, 7,* 323–347.

Fraser, B. J., Anderson, G. J., & Walberg, H. J. (1982). *Assessment of learning environments: Manual for learning environment inventory (LEI) and my class inventory (MCI)* (3rd version). Perth: Western Australian Institute of Technology.

Gibbs, J. C. (1979). The meaning of ecologically oriented inquiry in contemporary psychology. *American Psychologist, 34*, 127–140.

Goddard, R. D., & Goddard, Y. L. (2001). A multilevel analysis of the relationship between teacher and collective efficacy in urban schools. Teaching and *Teacher Education, 17*, 807–818.

Haertel, C. D., Walberg, H. J., & Haertel, E. H. (1981). Socio-psychological environments and learning: A quantitative synthesis. *British Educational Research Journal, 7*, 27–56.

Hertz-Lazarowitz, R. (1992). Understanding students' interactive behavior: Looking at six mirrors of the classroom. In: R. Hertz-Lazarowitz, & N. Miller (Eds), *Interaction in cooperative groups: The anatomy of group learning* (pp. 71–102). New York: Cambridge Press.

Hicks, D. L. (1993). *Cultivating metacognitions within learning environments: The case of the computerized writing partner.* Unpublished dissertation. The University of Arizona.

Hinegardner, R., & Engelberg, J. (1983). Biological complexity. *Journal of Theoretical Biology, 104*, 7–20.

Iran-Nejad, A., McKeachie, W. J., & Berliner, D. C. (1990). The multisource nature of learning: An introduction. *Review of Educational Research, 60*, 509–515.

Johnson, R. B., & Onwuegbuzie, A. J. (2004). Mixed methods research: A research paradigm whose time has come. *Educational Researcher, 33*(7), 14–27.

Lizzio, A., Wilson, K., & Simons, R. (2002). University students' perceptions of the learning environment and academic outcomes: Implications for theory and practice. *Studies in Higher Education, 27*(1), 27–52.

Oren, A., Mioduser, D., & Nachmias, R. (2002). The development of social climate in virtual learning discussion groups. *International Review of Research in Open and Distance Learning, 3*(1), 1–19.

Salomon, G. (1991). Transcending the qualitative-quantitative debate: The analytic and systemic approaches to educational research. *Educational Researcher, 20*(6), 10–18.

Scarr, S. (1985). Constructing psychology: Making facts and fables for our times. *American Psychology, 40*, 499–512.

Searle, J. R. (1992). *The rediscovery of the mind.* Cambridge, MA: MIT Press.

Shavelson, R., Phillips, D. C., Towne, L., & Feuer, M. J. (2003). On the science of education design studies. *Educational Researcher, 32*(1), 25–29.

Shye, S. (1998). Modern facet theory: Content design and measurement in behavioral research. *European Journal of Psychological Assessment, 4*, 160–171.

Smith, D., & Hardaker, G. (2000). E-learning innovation through the implementation of an internet supported learning environment. *Educational Technology & Society, 3*(3), 1–16. Retrieved March 12, 2005 from http://ifets.ieee.org/periodical/vol_3_2000/e04.html

Standish, R. K. (2001). On complexity and emergence. *Complexity International, 9*, 1–6.

Wilson, B. (1995). Metaphors for instruction: Why we talk about learning environments. *Educational Technology, 35*(5), 25–30.

Chapter 15

Hypothesized Performance on Complex Tasks as a Function of Scaled Instructional Strategies

M. David Merrill

Introduction

Instruction involves directing students to appropriate learning activities; guiding students to appropriate knowledge; helping students rehearse, encode, and process information; monitoring student performance; and providing feedback as to the appropriateness of the student's learning activities and practice performance.

Instructional design is the technology of creating learning experiences and learning environments which promote these instructional activities. (Merrill, Drake, Lacy, Pratt, & ID2_Research_Group, 1996, p. 5)

Does instruction work? What is the evidence? Can we find out what is learned from instruction? Can we determine what makes instruction efficient, effective, and engaging? Is it possible to conduct evidence-based research to determine if students have learned and how they have learned?

Like other sciences, instruction is verified by discovery and instructional design is extended by invention. Instructional science, the foundation for the technology of instructional design, is the discovery of instructional strategies. Instructional science involves identifying the variables to consider (descriptive theory), identifying potential relationships between these variables (prescriptive theory), and then empirically testing these relationships in the laboratory and the field.

> Instructional science is concerned with the discovery of the principles involved in instructional strategies; and instructional design is the use of these scientific principles to invent instructional design procedures and tools. (Merrill et al., 1996, p. 5)

This chapter maintains that it is possible to ascertain if learners have acquired specified knowledge and skill from instruction. Merrill (2002a) identified a set of instructional strategy principles that are prescribed by a number of different instructional theories and recommended practices. While many of these instructional design principles have been supported by individual experimental studies the author has been unable to find an integrated body of research that supports these interrelated principles as a whole. This chapter proposes an interrelated set of hypotheses based on these first principles of instruction. It is hoped that this set of hypotheses might provide a basis for a systematic program of research designed to validate these prescribed instructional design principles and their interrelationships.

Instructional Principles

A first principle of instruction is a prescriptive strategy that promotes effective, efficient, and engaging instruction for the acquisition of complex tasks. It is a relationship that has been identified by a number of different instructional theorists and supported by research. Merrill systematically reviewed a number of different instructional design theories and abstracted from these theories a set of interrelated prescriptive instructional design principles (Merrill, 2002a, 2006a, 2006b). One of these papers (Merrill, in press-a) quoted similar principles that have been identified by other authors (Allen, 2003; Andre, 1997; R. C. Clark, 1999, 2003; R. C. Clark & Mayer, 2003; R. E. Clark, 2003; R. E. Clark & Estes, 2002; Dembo & Young, 2003; Foshay, Silber, & Stelnicki, 2003; Marzano, Pickering, & Pollock, 2001; Mayer, 2001, 2003; O'Neil, 2003; Reigeluth, 1983, 1999; Rosenshine, 1997; Tennyson, Schott, Seel, & Dijkstra, 1997; van Merriënboer, 1997). Many of these authors cited relevant research support for their principles while other authors based their prescriptions on their experience in designing and evaluating instructional products. The reader is encouraged to review this synthesis paper (Merrill, in press-a) and the works by the authors cited above for their prescriptions and the research base for these principles.

From this effort, five fundamental principles were identified. Learning is promoted when the learner: observes a demonstration — demonstration principle; applies the new knowledge — application principle; undertakes real-world tasks — task-centered principle; activates existing knowledge — activation principle; integrates the new knowledge into their world — integration principle. These five principles are elaborated via the following corollaries:

Demonstration principle: Learning is promoted when learners:
- observe a demonstration of the skills to be learned — demonstration principle;
- observe demonstrations that are consistent with the content — consistency;
- receive guidance that relates instances to generalities — guidance;
- observe media that are relevant to the content — media.

Application principle: Learning is promoted when learners:
- apply their newly acquired knowledge or skill — application principle;
- undertake practice that is consistent with stated or implied objectives — consistency;
- receive intrinsic or corrective feedback — feedback;
- are coached but gradually receive less coaching with each subsequent task — coaching.

Task-centered principle: Learning is promoted when learners:
- do real-world tasks — task-centered principle;
- observe the whole task they will be able to do — outcome;
- acquire component knowledge and skill — components;
- undertake a progression of whole tasks — progression.

Activation principle: Learning is promoted when learners:
- activate relevant cognitive structures — activation principle;
- engage in relevant experience — experience;
- recall, describe, or demonstrate relevant prior knowledge — prior knowledge;
- acquire or recall a structure for organizing the new knowledge — structure.

Integration principle: Learning is promoted when learners:
- integrate their new knowledge into their everyday life — integration principle;
- reflect on, discuss, or defend their new knowledge or skill — reflection;
- create, invent, or explore personal ways to use their new knowledge or skill — create;
- publicly demonstrate their new knowledge or skill — go public.

These principles may seem obvious. It has often been argued that these principles are well known and frequently used. However, a recent study (Barclay, Gur, & Wu, 2004) analyzed over 1400 web sites in five countries that claimed to provide instruction on marriage relationships. Each site was scored on a 15-point scale indicating the degree to which the first principles of instruction were implemented. The highest score on any site was 7.0 indicating that even the best site implemented less than half of these principles. The average scores[1] indicate that most of these sites do not implement any of these principles. The result is that these so-called instructional web sites fail to implement the principles that instructional design theorists have identified as fundamental for effective, efficient, and engaging instruction. However, this research merely indicates whether or not these principles are implemented, it does not provide information about the contribution of these principles to student performance or whether those sites that score low teach less than those sites that score high on the implementation of these principles.

A study (Thompson_Inc., 2002) conducted by NETg (a company that provides training courses for computer applications) compared their standard off-the-shelf Excel course with a new task-centered course designed by the application of first principles found that students on the new task-centered course completed complex spread sheet tasks significantly ($p. < 0.001$) more efficiently (29 min vs. 49 min) and effectively (89% vs. 68%)

---

[1]The average scores by country indicate almost no implementation of these instructional principles. $N=$number of sites analyzed, highest score, average score. Possible score is 15. Australia, $N=202$, 6, 0.11; China, $N=551$, 2, 0.02; France, $N=257$, 6, 0.12; Turkey, $N=42$, 6, 0.17; USA, $N=410$, 7, 0.13.

than students in the off-the shelf course. Effectiveness was measured by the learners' ability to complete three complex tasks which required them to develop three different spread sheets given a set of data and analysis requirements.

Another series of studies in the Netherlands (Collis & Margaryan, 2005, 2006) has also rated a number of courses in Shell Oil Company on the degree to which they implement first principles. Data are currently being collected to determine if those courses who rate high, result in better performance than those who rate low on their implementation of first principles.

Are these principles of equal value? Do they contribute equally to learning effectiveness or efficiency? Are some of these principles more fundamental than others? How are these principles related to one another? What is the relative contribution of these principles to the acquisition of the skill and knowledge necessary to complete complex real-world tasks? This chapter hypothesizes the relationship among these first principles of instruction. This chapter hypothesizes the relative contribution of these principles to performance on complex real-world tasks.

Performance Scaling

If research is to be able to assess the hypothesized relationships among these first principles, it is necessary to be clear about the type of learned performance that is promoted by these principles. Instructional objectives are often so vague that it is difficult to know what evidence might be relevant. When the outcome is to learn an unspecified goal from an unspecified experience, then, as advised by the Cheshire cat[2], it really does not matter which theoretical path you take or what evidence you collect. But unspecified learning from unspecified experience is not instruction. Instruction requires a specific goal to acquire a specific skill. If outcomes are carefully specified then appropriate evidence can be collected. Once a complex task has been clearly specified the level of skill to perform this task can be measured. But that does not mean it is easy. Measuring performance level in complex tasks is in itself a complex task. Too often, the measures used assess only the component of skill or individual actions rather than the level of performance on the whole task.

---

[2]From Lewis Carroll, *Alice in Wonderland*, Chapter VI Pig and Pepper. Quoted from the Internet
http://sabian.org/alice.htm
"The cat grinned when it saw Alice. It looked good-natured, she thought: still it had very long
claws and a great many teeth, so she felt that it ought to be treated with respect.
" 'Cheshire Puss,' she began, rather timidly, as she did not at all know whether it would like the
name: however, it only grinned a little wider. 'Come, it's pleased so far,' thought Alice, and she
went on. 'Would you tell me, please, which way I ought to go from here?'
" 'That depends a good deal on where you want to get to,' said the Cat.
" 'I don't much care where –' said Alice.
" 'Then it doesn't matter which way you go,' said the Cat.
" '-so long as I get somewhere,' Alice added as explanation.
" 'Oh, you're sure to do that,' said the Cat, 'if you only walk long enough.' "

Instructional research for the principles identified in this chapter requires a careful definition of a real-world complex task. In the real world we are required to complete integrated tasks to produce an artifact, solve a problem, or bring about a desired consequence. Such tasks usually require a variety of different kinds of knowledge and skill — all brought together in an interrelated way to complete the task. Too often, in instruction, we assess only pieces of the task, fragments of knowledge, or sub skills rather than the whole task. Such partial assessment often misses much of the complexity that characterizes authentic, real-world tasks.

Instructional research for the principles identified in this chapter requires that performance measures must be based on whole-task performance. These first principles of instruction form an integrated set of prescriptions, which are designed to promote the acquisition of all the knowledge and skill necessary for the learner to complete whole, integrated, complex tasks. The common types of measurement that require learners to remember-what-I-told-you, or to perform individual steps in isolation from a whole procedure, or to make isolated predictions from a limited set of circumstances are not sufficient forms of measurement to get at the complexity of real-world tasks or to assess the contribution of instructional strategies based on these first principles of instruction.

When performing a complex real-world task, there is no such thing as a simple right/wrong answer. Complex tasks allow for many levels of performance. At first, the learner may only be able to complete simple versions of the task. As skill increases, the learner can complete more and more complex versions of the task. In solving problems, early solutions may be unsophisticated and may consider only a portion of the factors involved. As the learner gains skill the solutions become more elegant, more complex, and take into consideration more and more factors. Measurement of task performance must reflect this gradual acquisition of skill. Bunderson (2003) described the need for a domain theory, which is a scaled measurement of increased levels of performance in a given subject matter domain. Adequate measurement of performance in complex real-world tasks requires that we can detect increments in performance demonstrating gradually increased skill in completing a whole complex task or solving a problem.

What is a complex task? For purposes of this discussion, a task that is performed with the same steps in virtually the same way each time is not a complex task. Simple data entry probably does not qualify as a complex task since the only increase in skill is efficiency in performing the same steps. On the other hand, using a word processor to write reports probably does qualify as a complex task since each report may require different operations; these operations can be performed in a variety of ways, and learning advanced operations may increase the efficiency and quality of the resulting report. In this case, the word processing of a series of reports can be scaled such that reports early in the series require only few operations and each subsequent report may require more operations and use of more complex operations to attain the required efficiency and quality of the resulting product.

Assessment of incremental expertise is relatively straightforward in well-defined tasks such as chess, athletic, or musical performance. Assessing incremental performance in less well-defined domains is more of a challenge but must be done if we are to assess the contribution of scaled instructional strategies to the acquisition of skill.

What are the possible procedures for designing scaled measurement of performance level in complex tasks? Three possible approaches are briefly described below. There is no doubt that researchers undertaking the research, based on the hypotheses of this chapter, will find additional effective methods for scaling performance on complex tasks.

(1)   Identify a progression of tasks, arranged so that the number or complexity of operations required for completion increases incrementally. For each task in the progression, establish a rubric of acceptable performance. The learner then completes the tasks in succession until they are unable to complete a task. The learner might also be given a task somewhere in the middle of the range. When learners are unable to complete a task, they are moved back in the progression until they are successful. Following successful task completion, they are moved forward in the progression until they are again unable to complete a task. Appropriate scoring measures the highest level in the progression of tasks at which the student completes the whole task in an acceptable manner.

(2)   For some domains, reducing task complexity may not be an option, tasks in the domain may all be relatively complex, making a progression of successively more complex tasks difficult to identify. In this situation, the learners are given a task with various levels of coaching available. When the learner is unable to proceed, the first level of coaching is provided. If the learner still has difficulty, the second level of coaching is provided and so forth until the learner is able to complete the task. The score is an inverse of the amount of successively more elaborate coaching required for the student to solve the problem or complete the task. Vygotsky (1978) called the difference between what a learner can do with help and without help — the *zone of proximal development*. In this case, it is not a progression of tasks that is scaled but the amount of help required within a task.

(3)   For some domains, it may be possible to use a single nested complex task to assess increasing levels of performance. This is similar to the task progression previously described but in this situation, solving the problem or completing the task can proceed incrementally. Each stage toward the complete solution requires an incremental increase in expertise for completion. A student is scored on the number of stages completed toward the problem solution. In other words, in this type of complex task, completing the first stage is solving a single whole task and each succeeding stage adds complexity, and hence requires an increment in expertise.

All these procedures may give some measure of performance level in completing complex tasks. Determining such task progressions is not a trivial activity and will require considerable empirical trials to get the progression so that it does indeed reflect the level of performance.

Instructional Strategy Scaling

In the following discussion, only one or two words are used to represent the principles involved. The reader should refer to the list of principles in the introduction to this paper for the full statement of the principle under consideration.

It is hypothesized that instructional strategies can also be scaled so that the level of instructional strategy employed correlates with the level of effective and efficient performance on scaled complex real-world tasks. It is hypothesized that instructional strategy scaling is determined by the degree to which an instructional strategy implements these first principles of instruction as described in the remainder of this chapter.

Presenting information is assumed to be the base-line (level 0) instructional strategy. Most of the web sites analyzed in the Barclay et al. (2004) study were level 0, information-only, instructional strategies. This chapter hypothesizes that performance on complex real-world tasks will be incremented when an instructional strategy implements each of the first principles in turn. Adding consistent demonstration to information promotes the first increment (level 1) in learning effectiveness, efficiency, and engagement. Adding consistent application with corrective feedback to information with demonstration adds a second increment (level 2) in learning effectiveness, efficiency, and engagement. Using a task-centered instructional strategy adds the third increment (level 3) in learning effectiveness, efficiency, and engagement.

Activation added to level 1, 2, or 3 will add an additional learning increment. Integration added to levels 2 or 3 will also add an additional learning increment. In the following paragraphs, this chapter will try to elaborate each of these instructional strategy levels and a very brief explanation of why it is hypothesized that each level correlates with increased levels of performance on scaled real-world tasks.

Subject matter content can be represented by both information and portrayal. Information is general, inclusive, and refers to many specific situations. Portrayal is specific, limited, and refers to one case or a single situation. Information can be presented (tell) and recalled (ask). A portrayal can be demonstrated (show) and submitted to application (do). Subject matter content can be represented in five categories: information-about, parts-of, kinds-of, how-to, and what-happens. Table 15.1 indicates the information and portrayal that is appropriate for each content category.

The base-line instructional strategy is *information-only*. Information-only includes presentation alone or presentation plus recall. An information presentation tells learners associations among two or more pieces of information; the name and description of one or more parts; the defining characteristics of a class of objects, situations, or processes; the steps and sequence to carry out a procedure; or the conditions and consequence for the events in a process. If recall is added it asks learners to recognize or recall the information

Table 15.1: Information and portrayal for categories of learning.

	INFORMATION		**PORTRAYAL**	
	PRESENT (TELL)	**RECALL (ASK)**	**DEMONSTRATE (SHOW)**	**APPLY (DO)**
Information-about	Associations (facts)	Associations (facts)	***	***
Parts-of	Name + description	Name + description	Location	Find location
Kinds-of	Definition	Definition	Examples	Classify examples
How-to	Steps + sequence	Steps + sequence	Procedure	Execute a procedure
What-happens	Conditions + consequence	Conditions + consequence	Process	Predict consequence Find conditions

that was presented. Information-only instructional strategies are very common in all educational environments whether schools, industry, or government. The author has been quoted[3] as saying, "Information is not instruction." For this chapter information-only will be considered as the most primitive form of instruction. It is a level 0 instructional strategy whether or not recall is included.

Hypothesis 1: Consistent Demonstration. *A level 1 instructional strategy that adds consistent demonstration to a level 0 information-only strategy promotes a higher performance level on scaled complex tasks.*

An information strategy presents the general information such as definitions, steps, or if ... then relationships. For a level 1 strategy to this information is added demonstration. A demonstration is one or more worked examples of all or a part of the task that shows how the information is applied to specific situations. To be effective, the demonstration must be consistent with the kind of task: location with respect to the whole for parts; examples of the various categories for concepts; showing the execution of the steps together with the consequence for a procedure; and illustrating a specific process by showing the portrayal of the conditions and consequences (Merrill, 1997).

The rationale for this hypothesis is as follows: because information-only is stored in associative memory, until learners construct a schema for the information, their only recourse is recall. Without a demonstration learners may fail to construct a schema or may construct an incomplete or inadequate schema. Even though they can remember the information, when asked to apply the information in a new situation they do not have or cannot create an adequate mental model to complete the task resulting in a lower level of performance on a scaled complex real-world task.

An application can also serve as a demonstration. Adding a consistent application to an information-only strategy will also result in an increment in performance. If the application is accompanied by corrective feedback, (essentially a worked example), then it is equivalent to a demonstration and will likely result in a similar increment in performance (Renkl, 1997). Except for very simple tasks, adding application with only right/wrong feedback but without corrective feedback will not promote as large an increment in performance on the final complex task as will demonstration for the same portrayal. A strategy that consists of information plus consistent application with corrective feedback is also a level 1 instructional strategy.

Problem-based strategies may not serve as suitable demonstration strategies. Providing information and then having the student attempt to apply that information to the performance of a complex task is also an information-only strategy; but it is still a level 0 strategy and is unlikely to promote an increment in the performance level on complex tasks (Mayer, 2004). A strategy that has learners to solve a complex problem after an information-only presentation is not the same as the task-centered strategy described below. Problem-based learning often involves giving learners a complex task, some resources (information), and expecting them to figure out a way to complete the task. There is a difference between this

---

[3]http://www.learningcircuits.org/2000/feb2000/Kruse.htm

type of a problem-based learning strategy and the task-centered or problem-centered instructional strategy described below. Merely asking learners to complete a complex task after presenting information is not likely to promote any increased performance levels on other complex tasks unless the task is used as a demonstration as described for application in the previous paragraph. For the same reasons explained above, simply presenting the information is unlikely to lead to adequate or complete schema representations. Attempting to complete the whole task, given the information-only instruction, especially in situations that are unfamiliar to the student, will likely result in incomplete or inadequate schema construction. If there is corrective feedback for the whole task then the situation is similar to application with corrective feedback, which is in fact the same as a demonstration and may result in a similar increment in effective performance. However problem-based strategies *per se* are not likely to result in efficient learning.

In summary, when scaling an instructional strategy adding consistent demonstration to an information-only strategy (a level 1 instructional strategy) is the most effective first step to promote an initial increment in level of performance on complex tasks.

This chapter also hypothesizes that instructional strategy scaling can also occur within levels. The following hypotheses suggest increments within demonstration.

Hypothesis 1.1: *Adding learner guidance to demonstration promotes an additional increment in the level of efficient and effective performance on complex tasks.*

Guidance focuses the student's attention on those elements of a given portrayal that correspond to the general information presented. For *kinds-of* tasks, guidance focuses the learner's attention on the portrayal of each of the defining properties used to determine class membership. For *how-to* tasks, guidance focuses the learner's attention on the execution of each step in the demonstration. For *what-happens* tasks, guidance focuses the learner's attention on the portrayal of each of the conditions leading to a given consequence. In short, guidance helps the student to relate the specific portrayals to the more general information.

The rationale for this hypothesis is as follows: appropriate attention focusing guidance directs attention to relationships among information and portrayals thus enabling learners to more readily relate abstract information to specific instances. Without this guidance, learners often fail to see the relationships thus forming an incomplete schema or one that is difficult to generalize because they do not have the abstract information associated with the concrete example. In addition, this guidance helps cognitive load by reducing the amount of effort required to locate critical relationships thus allowing more time for the learner to build appropriate schema and transfer the relationships to long-term memory.

Hypothesis 1.2: *Relevant media included in a demonstration promotes learning efficiency, effectiveness, and engagement. Irrelevant media included in a demonstration results in a decrement in learning efficiency, effectiveness, or engagement* (Clark & Mayer, 2003; Mayer, 2001).

Graphics are one kind of possibly relevant media. It is probably true that a picture is worth a thousand words. Graphic information that enhances and illustrates the information being presented facilitates learning. Graphic information that is irrelevant, (i.e., not directly related to the information being presented), increases cognitive load and results in a decrement in learning (Schnotz & Bannert, 2003). Irrelevant graphic information include illustrations that do not carry any information directly relevant to the information being presented and extraneous sound effects or music that is not a critical element of the information being taught. Processing extraneous information increases cognitive load thereby increasing processing time and requiring the learner to take time to determine the relevance of the information contained in the graphic material.

Another form of irrelevant media that results in a performance decrement is the use of audio to read text when both text and graphic material are presented together. Learners can process both auditory and visual information at the same time (Mayer, 2001), but they cannot process both written text and nontextual graphic material at the same time since both use the visual channel. When the audio reads displayed text, it focuses the learner's attention on the text rather than on the graphic material. If the graphic material carries some of the instructional information then this diversion of attention makes it difficult for learners to process the graphic information. However, when audio without text is used with a graphic both the audio and graphic information can be processed simultaneously. In this situation, learners can simultaneously study the details of a graphic diagram while the audio is providing explanation of what the learner is observing.

Hypothesis 2: Consistent Application. *A level 2 instructional strategy that adds consistent application with corrective feedback to a level 1 instructional strategy consisting of information plus demonstration promotes an additional level of performance on complex real-world tasks.*

Application requires learners to use their knowledge or skill to accomplish specific tasks. Consistent application for *parts-of* tasks is to locate the part with respect to the whole; for *kinds-of* tasks is to sort examples into appropriate categories; for *how-to* tasks is to execute a series of steps; and for *what-happens* tasks is to predict a consequence, given a set of conditions or find faulted conditions, given an unexpected consequence.

This hypothesis is based on the following rationale: Application allows learners to tune their schema. Given information plus consistent demonstration assist the learners to form an appropriate schema. Using this schema to do a new task requires them to check the completeness and adequacy of their schema. When errors result and these are followed by corrective feedback, then learners can adjust their schema. The initial application usually results in the most dramatic adjustment of the schema. If the schema is very incomplete or inadequate then learners may be unable to complete the task. If the task is too similar to the tasks that were demonstrated then learners merely do the task but engage in very little reconstruction of their schema. The challenge is to find new tasks for application that challenge the student but are not so challenging that their schema is inadequate to complete the task.

In summary, when scaling an instructional strategy adding consistent application with corrective feedback to an information plus consistent demonstration (level 2 instructional strategy) is the most effective second step to promote an additional increment in level of performance on complex tasks.

Hypothesis 2.1: *Adding gradually diminishing coaching to application promotes an additional increment in learning efficiency, effectiveness, and engagement.*

Coaching means that the instructional system or instructor does some of the cognitive processing for the student. Such coaching often takes the form of hints. A simple task may require only a single hint but complex tasks may require a series of more and more complete hints as described for complex-task scaling in previous paragraphs.

This can be explained as follows: If a task is too complex, the student may be unable to complete the task causing discouragement and eroding confidence. It is not always possible to sequence tasks in an optimal progression of difficulty. In order for the learners to complete the task, the instructional system does some of the "thinking" for learners and allows them to complete the remainder of the task. If this coaching is always present, learners exercise their right to be lazy and begin to depend on the coaching rather than tuning their schema to be able to complete the task on their own. When confronted with a task that is not accompanied by coaching their previous reliance on hints prevents sufficient schema development for them to complete the task. If this coaching is gradually withdrawn with each subsequent task the students are gently led to rely more and more on their own resources to solve the problem or do the task. When the coaching is finally completely withdrawn, learners will have sufficiently developed their own schema to allow them to complete the task without assistance.

Hypothesis 3: Task-Centered Instructional Strategy. *A level 3 instructional strategy that consists of a task-centered instructional strategy that includes consistent demonstration and consistent application with corrective feedback, promotes an additional increment in the level of performance on complex tasks.*

A task-centered instructional strategy is not the same as problem-based learning or case-based learning as they are typically described in the instructional literature. Problem-based or case-based learning are often far less structured than a task-centered strategy. Problem-based instructional architecture often involves presenting a complex task or problem to a learner or group of learners, providing some resources or links to possible resources, and allowing the learners to interact among themselves and with the available resources to solve the problem or complete the task.

A task-centered instructional strategy (see Figure 15.1) is much more structured. It involves presenting a specific complex whole task to the learners, demonstrating a successful completion of the task, providing information, demonstration, and application for each of the instructional components required by the task, and then showing learners how these instructional components are applied to the task. It also involves a progression of successively more complex tasks with successively less guidance provided with each subsequent task until learners are completing the tasks on their own. The 4C/ID model represents a very sophisticated version of a task-centered instructional strategy (van Merriënboer, 1997).

A task-centered instructional strategy requires consistent demonstration and consistent application at both the whole task level and at the level of the individual instructional components of the whole task. A task-centered instructional strategy is a significant modification

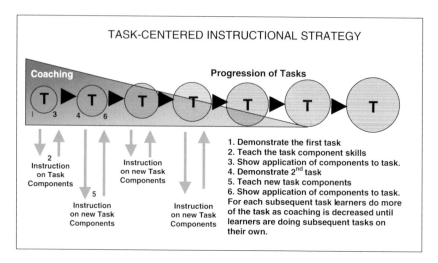

Figure 15.1: Task-centered instructional strategy.

of an information-only strategy and is likely to result in a much larger performance increment than merely adding demonstration or demonstration plus application.

The rationale for this hypothesis is as follows: When instructional components are decontextualized, students are often admonished with "You won't understand this now but later it will be very important to you". As a result the motivation to learn the material is significantly reduced. Further, when learners must retain many instructional components without a context for their use they must often resort to associative memory and are likely to forget or fail to recognize the relevance of the information when confronted with the whole task and thus will be unable to retrieve the required information when it is needed. At the best, they will construct schema for the individual skills. They are unlikely to incorporate the component into a schema for the whole complex task. When instructional components are presented just-in-time for their application to a real-world complex problem then the need for the knowledge or skill is apparent and the motivation to learn the knowledge or skill is increased. When the components are immediately applied to a complex problem then the student can construct a schema for the whole task rather than separate schemas for the individual instructional components.

In summary, a level 3 instructional strategy consisting of a task-centered approach is the most effective instructional strategy to promote a high level of performance on complex tasks.

Hypothesis 3.1: *Adding task progression to a task-centered instructional strategy promotes an additional increment in learning efficiency, effectiveness, and engagement.*

A task-centered instructional strategy that consists of a single complex task may be an effective strategy but a single task is far less effective than a progression of increasingly more complex tasks.

The following reveals the rationale for this hypothesis: A family of complex tasks, while sharing many similarities, is also characterized by subtle differences. Learning to complete a single task leaves, the learners with only one view of the task, and when confronted with a task from the same family but with differences from the original learning task, they may fail to recognize that it is from the same family of tasks or they may not have sufficiently tuned their schema to enable them to adjust the solution process to accommodate the differences found in the task. If the training task is a less complex task than the new task, then learners may have not developed the nuanced schema necessary to tackle the more complex task. A progression of tasks that are progressively more complex during training with the student performing more and more of the steps to task completion on their own enables them to tune their schema so that when confronted with yet a different or more complex task from the same family they are able to move forward toward task completion.

Hypothesis 4: Relevant Experience Activation. *Providing or recalling relevant experience promotes an additional increment in learning efficiency, effectiveness, and engagement when added a level 1, level 2, or level 3 instructional strategy.*

A level 1 demonstration-enhanced instructional strategy is hypothesized to promote a substantial increment in level of performance on complex tasks when compared to an information-only strategy. A level 2 application-enhanced instructional strategy is hypothesized to promote yet a second increment in level of performance. A level 3 task-centered instructional strategy is hypothesized to be the most effective in promoting performance on complex tasks. Strategy enhancements such as appropriate guidance and use of relevant media for demonstration or gradually diminishing coaching for application should increase the amount of the performance increment. These hypotheses, however, assume a precision of measurement that is rarely achieved in instructional or learning research. A regression analysis usually shows that the first two or three variables account for the majority of the variance and that subtle enhancement such as those just described, while contributing to effective learning, may be very difficult to measure.

A similar measurement problem confronts the researcher when attempting to determine the contribution of the activation principle. Significant effects may only show up when these enhancements are added to a level 0 or perhaps a level 1 strategy. As the instruction becomes richer, the relative contribution of these additional principles becomes less apparent. Nevertheless, it is hypothesized that effective activation of relevant experience does increment learning.

Adding activation to an information-only strategy may promote an increment in performance if the student has developed relevant schema from the previous experience. This schema can then be used as the basis for the construction of revised schema given the information. The more familiar the new task is to previously learned tasks the larger the affect from activation of this previous learning. Unfamiliar new tasks, for which the previous experience is only tangentially related, are less likely to promote an increment in performance.

This can be explained as follows: Adding relevant-experience-activation to level 1, level 2, or level 3 instructional strategies should facilitate the formation of an appropriate schema by allowing learners to build on existing schema. On the other hand, activating an inappropriate schema by activating experience that is not relevant may actually promote a decrement in performance. Attempting to add to an inappropriate existing schema may result in misconceptions that interfere with efficient and effective task completion. From a measurement standpoint, it may be easier to detect the detrimental effects of inappropriate relevant-experience-activation than the other way around.

Hypothesis 5: Structure Activation. *Providing activation-structure promotes an additional increment in learning efficiency, effectiveness, and engagement when added to level 1, level 2, or level 3 instructional strategies.*

One way to help students form an appropriate schema or mental model for completing a complex task is to provide a framework that can be used to organize the information required. One form of such a structure is an advanced organizer (Mayer, 1984). Other forms of structure have also been suggested (Marzano et al., 2001; Merrill, 2002c). This structure can form the basis for an appropriate task schema. When left to their own resources, learners often use less effective structures for organizing the information. When the instructional system provides an effective structure that learners can use to store and process the information their ability to retrieve and use this information in subsequent situations is improved. Providing a structure is especially effective for students who may have had little or no relevant prior experience that can be used as a basis for a new schema for the family of tasks.

Hypothesis 6: Reflection Integration. *Adding reflection integration to any of the above instructional strategies promotes an additional increment in learning efficiency, effectiveness, and engagement.*

It has often been demonstrated that amount and level of learning is a function of the amount of effort and time learners expend to acquire the required skill (e.g., Carroll, 1963). Providing an opportunity to reflect, review, go back over the information, and portrayals of the information increases the level of effort, provides additional opportunity for solidifying an appropriate schema, and allows learners to explore areas of possible misconception or ambiguity. This additional effort provides a tuning for learners' schema increasing the probability that it will be more effective in completing subsequent tasks.

Hypothesis 7: Create Integration. *Adding create-integration to any of the above instructional strategies promotes transfer of the newly acquired knowledge and skill to performance on similar tasks in the real-world beyond the instructional situation.*

Create is the opportunity for learners to think ahead to find ways that the newly acquired knowledge and skill might be applied in their subsequent real-world activities. Create probably is more related to long-range transfer than to task performance immediately following instruction. The effects of create are more likely to show up in transfer situations or later performance on the job. The logistics of measuring the effect of create integration are often impractical and difficult. Nevertheless, the ultimate goal of most instruction goes beyond the end-of-course performance to performance on-the-job or in the real world.

Hypothesis 8: Go Public Integration. *Adding integration — go public to any of the above instructional strategies promotes engagement that in turn promotes an additional increment in learning efficiency, effectiveness and engagement.*

It is hypothesized that engagement is only temporarily gained by graphics, animation, video, audio, and other multimedia enhancements. These superficial qualities of an instructional program often do little or nothing to promote long-term engagement. It is hypothesized that learning itself is the most significant determiner of long-term engagement. People love to learn but only when they can see their learning progress. When they perceive that they have acquired skill that was not present when they started the instruction then there is a desire to show what they have learned. Going public means that there is an opportunity to "show off" learning to significant others. Knowing that they will be going public early in the instruction provides an increased incentive for learners to be engaged in the learning process so that they will be able to ably perform for others when the opportunity is presented. It is also hypothesized that if learners are informed that they will be required to go public and if, because the instructional strategy is ineffective (level 0), the learners cannot perceive learning progress, then engagement will turn to frustration or anxiety with a resulting decrement in learning effectiveness and efficiency.

Conclusion

Figure 15.2 illustrates the hypothesized relationship among levels of instructional strategy and performance on complex tasks. Level 0, information-only, is shown in the left column, adding demonstration is shown in the second column, adding application is shown in the third column and adding a task-centered strategy is shown in the right column. The dashed line is the basic demonstration strategy plus learner guidance and/or appropriate media, the basic application strategy plus diminishing coaching, and the basic task-centered strategy plus a progression of tasks. The dotted line is the effect of adding strategy enhancements to the basic plus strategies i.e., relevant experience activation, structure activation, reflective integration, create integration, and/or go-public integration. The relationships illustrated in Figure 15.1 are merely relative rather than parameter predications. The initial

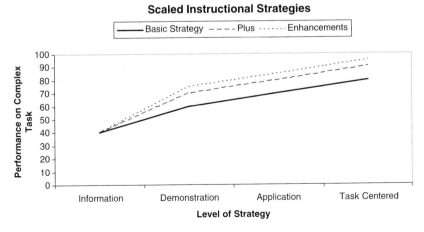

Figure 15.2: Hypothesized contribution of scaled strategies to performance on complex tasks.

basic and basic plus strategies will no doubt account for much of the variance and the enhancements will contribute significantly less as the instruction becomes richer.

References

Allen, M. W. (2003). *Michael Allen's guide to e-learning*. New York: Wiley.

Andre, T. (1997). Selected microinstructional methods to facilitate knowledge construction: Implications for instructional design. In: R. D. Tennyson, F. Schott, N. Seel, & S. Dijkstra (Eds), *Instructional design: International perspective* (Vol. 1, pp. 243–267). Mahwah, NJ: Erlbaum.

Barclay, M. W., Gur, B., & Wu, C. (2004). The impact of media on the family: Assessing the availability and quality of instruction on the World Wide Web for enhancing marriage relationship. Paper presented at the world congress of the family: Asia Pacific dialogue, Kualalumpur, Malaysia.

Bunderson, C. V. (2003). How to build a domain theory: On the validity centered design of construct-linked scales of learning and growth. In: M. Wilson (Ed.), *Objective measurement: Theory into practice*. Stamford, CT: Ablex Publishing.

Carroll, J. B. (1963). A model of school learning. *Teachers College Record, 64*, 723–733.

Clark, R. C. (1999). *Developing technical training* (2nd ed.). Washington, DC: International Society for Performance Improvement.

Clark, R. C. (2003). *Building expertise: Cognitive methods for training and performance improvement* (2nd ed.). Washington, DC: International Society for Performance Improvement.

Clark, R. E. (2003). What works in distance learning: Instructional strategies. In: H. F. O'Neil (Ed.), *What works in distance learning* (pp. 13–31). Los Angeles: Center for the Study of Evaluation.

Clark, R. C., & Mayer, R. E. (2003). *E-Learning and the science of instruction*. San Francisco: Jossey-Bass Pfeiffer.

Clark, R. E., & Estes, F. (2002). *Turning research into results: A guide to selecting the right performance solutions*. Atlanta: CEP Press.

Collis, B., & Margaryan, A. (2005). Merrill plus: Blending corporate strategy with instructional design. *Educational Technology, 45*(3), 54–59.

Collis, B., & Margaryan, A. (2006). Evaluating flexible learning in terms of course quality. In: B. Kahn (Ed.), *Flexible learning*. Englewood Cliffs, NJ: Educational Technology Publications.

Dembo, M., & Young, L. G. (2003). What works in distance education: Learning strategies. In: H. F. O'Neil (Ed.), *What works in distance education*. Los Angeles: Center for the Study of Evaluation.

Foshay, W. R. R., Silber, K. H., & Stelnicki, M. B. (2003). *Writing training materials that work: How to train anyone to do anything*. San Francisco: Jossey-Bass Pfeiffer.

Margaryan, A., & Collis, B. (2005). Design criteria for work-based learning: Merrill's first principles of instruction expanded. *British Journal of Educational Technology, 36*, 725–738.

Marzano, R. J., Pickering, D. J., & Pollock, J. E. (2001). *Classroom instruction that works: Research-based strategies for increasing student achievement*. Alexandria, VA: Association for Supervision and Curriculum Development.

Mayer, R. E. (1984). Twenty-five years of research on advanced organizers. *Instructional Science, 8*, 133–169.

Mayer, R. E. (2001). *Multimedia learning*. Cambridge: Cambridge University Press.

Mayer, R. E. (2003). What works in distance learning: Multimedia. In: H. F. O'Neil (Ed.), *What works in distance learning*. Los Angeles: Center for the Study of Evaluation.

Mayer, R. E. (2004). Should there be a three-strikes rule against pure discovery learning? *American Psychologist, 59*(1), 14–19.

Merrill, M. D. (1997). Instructional strategies that teach. *CBT Solutions*, (Nov/Dec), 1–11.

Merrill, M. D. (2002a). First principles of instruction. *Educational Technology Research and Development, 50*(3), 43–59.

Merrill, M. D. (2002b). A pebble-in-the-pond model for instructional design. *Performance Improvement, 41*(7), 39–44.

Merrill, M. D. (2002c). Knowledge objects and mental models. In: D. Wiley (Ed.), *The instructional use of knowledge objects* (pp. 261–280). Washington, DC: Agency for Instructional Technology and Association for Educational Communications & Technology.

Merrill, M. D. (2006a). First principles of instruction: A synthesis. In: R. A. Reiser, & J. V. Dempsey (Eds), *Trends and issues in instructional design and technology* (2nd ed., Vol. 2). Upper Saddle River, NJ: Merrill/Prentice-Hall.

Merrill, M. D. (2006b). First principles of instruction. In: C. M. Reigeluth, & A. Carr (Eds), *Instructional design theories and models III* (Vol. 3). Hillsdale, NJ: Erlbaum.

Merrill, M. D., Drake, L., Lacy, M. J., Pratt, J., & ID2_Research_Group. (1996). Reclaiming instructional design. *Educational Technology, 36*(5), 5–7.

O'Neil, H. F. (2003). *What works in distance education.* Los Angeles: Center for the Study of Evaluation.

Reigeluth, C. M. (Ed.). (1983). *Instructional-design theories and models: An overview of their current status.* Hillsdale, NJ: Erlbaum.

Reigeluth, C. M. (Ed.). (1999). *Instructional-design theories and models: A new paradigm of instructional theory* (Vol. 2). Mahwah, NJ: Erlbaum.

Renkl, A. (1997). Learning from worked examples: A study on individual differences. *Cognitive Science, 21*(1), 1–29.

Rosenshine, B. (1997). Advances in research on instruction. In: E. J. Lloyd, E. J. Kameanui, & D. Chard (Eds), *Issues in educating students with disabilities* (pp. 197–221). Mahwah, NJ: Erlbaum.

Schnotz, W., & Bannert, M. (2003). Construction and interference in learning from multiple representations. *Learning and Instruction, 13*, 141–156.

Tennyson, R. D., Schott, F., Seel, N., & Dijkstra, S. (Eds). (1997). *Instructional design international perspective: Theory, research, and models* (Vol. 1). Mahwah, NJ: Erlbaum.

Thompson_Inc. (2002). *Thompson job impact study.* Naperville, IL: Thompson NETg.

van Merriënboer, J. J. G. (1997). *Training complex cognitive skills: A four-component instructional design model for technical training.* Englewood Cliffs, NJ: Educational Technology Publications.

Vygotsky, L. S. (1978). *Mind in society: The development of higher psychological processes.* Cambridge, MA: Harvard University Press.

Conclusion

When Less Is More: Research and Theory Insights about Instruction for Complex Learning[1]

Richard E. Clark and Jan Elen

Introduction

In the past, complexity has been defined in terms of the number of elements and relationships that must be mastered in order to perform tasks in specific contexts. So for example, we often assume that adding two, single-digit numbers is less complex than adding two, two-digit numbers. Most of us would also assume that it is much less complex to learn to succeed at learning to play checkers than learning to play chess (Chase & Simon, 1973). This understanding has led us to make the reasonable suggestion that performing more complex tasks is necessarily more difficult and so requires more support, than performing simpler tasks.

This task-focused definition of complexity has been challenged by recent studies of learning and instruction based on cognitive architecture (Anderson, 1983, 1993; Newell, 1990; Sweller, this volume, Chapter 1; Mayer, this volume, Chapter 7; van Merriënboer, Sluijsmans, Kalyuga, Paas, & Tattersall, this volume, Chapter 11; Winne, this volume, Chapter 12), and by research on the interaction of implicit (automated procedures) and explicit (declarative) knowledge systems during learning (Sun, Slusarz, & Terry, 2005) and instruction (Depaepe, De Corte, & Verschaffel, this volume, Chapter 5; Vermunt, this volume, Chapter 9; Elen & Clarebout, this volume, Chapter 10; van Merriënboer et al., this volume, Chapter 11; Merrill, this volume, Chapter 15); a variety of studies focused on the dynamics of automated cognitive motivational processes that are thought to occur during learning (Wegner, 2002; Clark, Howard, & Early, this volume, Chapter 2; Cress & Hesse, this volume, Chapter 4; de Jong, this volume, Chapter 6) and the continued evolution of cognitive load theory (Sweller, Chapter 1, this volume) and its implications for instruction

[1]We offer this final chapter with thanks to our colleague Joost Lowyck for his many contributions to our developing understanding of complexity in learning and instruction over a long and very productive career of research and clinical practice. His colleagues and students have benefited from his work and we believe that the investment he has made will continue to pay intellectual and social dividends for many generations to come.

(Mayer, this volume, Chapter 7; van Merriënboer et al., this volume, Chapter 11). From the perspective of research in these several areas, complexity can only be determined by reference to the unique past experiences of an individual who is engaged in a task (e.g., Clark et al., this volume, Chapter 2; Seel, this volume, Chapter 3). Any one task may be very complex for one person yet very simple for another. Moreover, when a task is very complex for someone at one point in time it may be much less complex later after more experience handling the task.

Cognitive Definitions of Complexity

When attempting to determine the amount of complexity learners experience in any given learning task, the number of elements and relationships in a task may be less important than the number that must be consciously processed by learners to achieve learning goals (Sun et al., 2005; Winne, this volume, Chapter 12). This approach assumes that when familiar tasks are handled, we unconsciously call on automated cognitive procedures or productions (Anderson, 1993), which are performed very fast and require almost no mental effort to use (van Merriënboer et al., this volume, Chapter 11). These procedures (learned in past encounters with similar tasks) help us to decide and act in a way that will achieve the goals of the task without drawing on limited working memory capacity. As we confront more novel tasks, automated procedures interact with conscious, declarative processes and new knowledge is learned (Anderson, 1983, 1993; Newell, 1990).

 Extending the example started in the introduction, if someone has prior learning about addition that has resulted in highly automated procedural knowledge, the amount of complexity in one- and two-digit addition is most likely at a similar and very low level. Yet for children who are learning to add two, one-digit numbers the first time, the task is significantly more complex. It is most likely also that for a chess master who also plays the game of checkers, neither game requires a great deal of mental effort for success when compared with a novice or intermediate player. Thus, the general hypothesis that supports the cognitive theories could be stated as: "The more automated procedural prior knowledge a student has that is relevant to new learning, the less complex the new learning and the more we can expect internal, task-specific strategies to aid in task processing".

Chapter Goal

The goal of this chapter is to review what appears to be a number of research and practice consequences of the cognitive approach to complexity described by the various authors in this book and others. The goal of the review is to make suggestions for current and future research and practice on handling complexity in learning environments.

Implications of the Cognitive Approach to Complexity for Research and Practice

We turn next to a discussion of the implications of these new insights about complexity and their implications for both research and practice. Each section of the discussion is headed with a statement about a different implication that has been suggested or implied by one or more of the chapter authors and/or by current research. The chapter begins with a discussion about the two types and cognitive representations of knowledge described in current descriptions of our cognitive architecture for learning.

> Handling complexity in research and instruction requires the ability to distinguish between declarative and procedural knowledge. Declarative knowledge is complex but automated procedural knowledge is simple and more or less effortless to use. Our nearly total emphasis on declarative knowledge and our failure to acknowledge the overwhelming importance of so-called "implicit" or automated procedural knowledge during learning and problem solving is a barrier to improving our understanding of complexity.

When Schneider and Shiffrin (1977) published their groundbreaking paper on controlled and automated processing, it was difficult to anticipate all the learning and instructional consequences of the cognitive system they were describing. They proposed, and subsequent research has validated (Anderson, 1983, 1993; Newell, 1990; Schneider & Chein, 2003), that two types of knowledge can be learned about nearly any task: controlled knowledge and automated knowledge. Additionally, nearly all learning requires that these two types of knowledge interact in ways that we seldom acknowledge in either instructional research or practice. This distinction is critical to advancing our understanding of learning because it suggests that we may only be aware of the novel and complex components of tasks because they are available for conscious inspection. "Consciousness" is in part the capacity to observe ourselves thinking and remembering declarative knowledge. Yet we are only indirectly aware of our constant use of automated, unconscious procedural knowledge, which we can observe only by noticing the consequences of its operation. For example, when we see a problem such as "(8 × 105)" and immediately think of the solution "840" most adults are not aware of the automated process that produced the solution. Only the unautomated portions of the solving procedure are conscious and therefore open to conscious inspection. Some readers may have multiplied eight by five and added 800 to get the solution; others may have immediately realized the answer "840." Those who performed the operation in two conscious steps experienced more complexity than those who immediately realized the answer.

These two types of knowledge are very different ways to represent the same event. For example, if a child is learning the concept (event) of an equilateral triangle (ET) — she can learn a declarative representation of the definition of ET (the sides are of the same length and all of the internal angles are 60°) or a classification procedure for how to identify ET's (Condition: Given a triangle and a request to classify its form — Step 1: Are the sides of this triangle of the same length?; Step 2: Are all of the internal angles 60° ?) or both. Each of these two ways to understand the ET event is both a different type of knowledge and a different representation of knowledge about the same event. There is evidence that they are also stored in different memory systems and they operate in different cognitive "locations" during learning and problem solving since declarative knowledge operates in working memory, and automated procedures do not (Anderson, 1993).

What is most important is that the declarative components of learning or problem solving may only be the "tip of the iceberg". It is likely that the teaching and learning of most tasks require an understanding of a large number of task-specific automated processes that support the handling of the conscious components of tasks. These unconscious components may be unknown and unconsidered by both instructional researchers and practitioners. In order to appreciate the importance of this insight, we must first examine the difference between controlled and automated knowledge.

Declarative Knowledge

This type of knowledge is conscious (we are aware of it when we recall it and/or think about it) and it is controllable in that it can be changed or modified quickly. Merrill's (this volume, Chapter 15, 1983) component-display theory described four kinds of declarative knowledge — facts, concepts, processes and principles. Declarative knowledge is the only type that we are aware of using or learning. We are aware of accessing it when we "think" or "remember". Estimating the amount of declarative knowledge is difficult but the current estimates range from 10 (Bargh, 1999) to 30 percent (Glaser & Chi, 1988) of the total knowledge possessed by most adults.

Procedural Knowledge

This type of knowledge tends to take the form of step-by-step action and decision steps required to achieve task sub goals under specific conditions. It is estimated that procedural knowledge varies from 90 to 70 percent of the total knowledge possessed by adults. As procedural knowledge is learned and applied successfully, it gradually becomes unconscious and procedural (it cannot be monitored and we are largely unaware of its use) and it is more or less unmodifiable once it has become automated (Anderson, 1993). We apparently need automated procedural knowledge to circumvent the limitations of working memory. In the past we had estimated our "thinking capacity" at approximately seven (plus or minus two) chunks of declarative knowledge but that number has been cut in half by Cowan (2001), who lowered it to three (plus or minus one). So the benefit of procedural knowledge is that it allows us to express effective routines while leaving working memory space to handle the novel components of tasks.

An Example

A simple test of the inaccessibility of procedural knowledge, consider the following armchair experiment. Most of the European and North American readers of this chapter would be able to quickly and accurately classify cats and dogs when presented with a variety of small mammals. Yet how many readers could quickly provide an accurate definition for a cat or dog (or accurately describe the differences between the two species)? Automated procedural knowledge, developed over time by trial and error, allows us to make a rapid and accurate classification but since we have no need for the conscious declarative knowledge about the definitions of species membership, we do not "know" it. It is most likely that when it is not used, the declarative knowledge that initially supported the development of a classification procedure for identifying cats and dogs decays faster than the more frequently used and automated procedure (Tunney, 2003).

Types of Procedural Knowledge

While there have been no systematic attempts to create a typology of procedures, Clark and Estes (2002) suggest two types: classification procedures (a procedure for automated classification of events — such as picking cats and dogs from a large variety of mammals) and change procedures (actions and decisions that modify events — such as how to treat a sick cat). They suggested that procedures are best viewed as the automated form of declarative knowledge. Classification procedures are the automated form of facts and concepts whereas change procedures are the automated form of processes (how things work) and principles (cause and effect).

Presumably, all human performance on nearly all tasks represents an interaction between conscious declarative knowledge and automated, unconscious procedural knowledge (Sun et al., 2005). Recent evidence from neuroscience has helped to deepen our understanding of these two types of knowledge by providing evidence about functional and anatomical differences in their processing in the brain (Jansma, Ramsey, Slagter, & Kahn, 2001).

The evidence for these two types of knowledge suggests a second implication that was suggested or implied by a number of chapter authors.

> Handling complexity in research and instruction requires that all of us (including researchers, teachers and students) are largely unaware of most of what they know about how to perform a familiar task or tasks that have familiar components (including learning, teaching and the design or interpretation of research) and therefore are unreliable when we describe the novelty or complexity of what we know, how we think or analyze problems or what we may have learned from instruction or experience.

The growing body of research on the development of expertise and the contextualized nature of knowledge structures indicates that most of us may be unaware of what we know.

Experts Are Only Aware of Approximately 30 Percent of Their Own Expertise

The largely unappreciated consequence of our increased awareness of these two types of knowledge is that even highly perceptive psychologists, who studied cognitive processing are largely unaware of their own automated knowledge (Besnard, 2000). For example, Feldon (2004) studied the self-awareness of personal research design strategies used by a number of well-published psychologists who teach research design. He found that the psychologists were approximately 70 percent unaware of the primary analytical strategies they were using when designing experiments. More evidence for the hypothesis is that expertise is largely automated and unconscious comes from the studies of task analysis and other self-report protocols conducted with experts. For example, Chao and Salvendy (1994) studied the errors made by a number of top programming experts during systematic task analysis interviews. When a number of top experts were asked how to solve and debug specific programs, each expert was only approximately 31 percent accurate in their conscious recall of the successful strategies they use constantly and successfully. Hoffman, Crandall, and Shadbolt (1998) and Besnard (2000) have described other studies that reported similar data.

Velmahos et al. (2004) found that when surgery professors taught medical students to perform surgery, the professors tended to accurately describe their own visible actions but were consistently mistaken while describing (or omitting) the cognitive decisions they made during surgery. Clark (personal communication) one of the co-authors of the Velmahos study suggests that when asked how they describe a surgery to students, teaching surgeons indicated that they work from a visual image of themselves or others performing the surgery and report what they "see" in the image. Since we cannot directly or indirectly observe our own automated decision-making processes it is most likely therefore that we will be largely unable to describe automated decision knowledge.

While the research on this issue has focused primarily on experts who teach, we must assume that all of us are unaware of a large segment of knowledge that has a critical function when we learn or solve problems.

Teachers and Trainers Often Provide Wrong or Incomplete Information

The evidence for our lack of awareness of our own procedural knowledge sheds doubt on many of our most closely held assumptions about instruction and learning. Teachers are selected for their expertise at all educational levels from the early schooling to the most advanced doctoral programs. Teachers are expected to "teach what they know". If teachers are an average of 70 percent unaware of their procedural knowledge, what might be the consequence for their students? Is it highly likely that students with lower ability levels and/or less prior knowledge and/or lower motivation to learn might be more vulnerable to learning difficulties when instruction is incomplete or gives inaccurate knowledge?

Self-Regulatory Studies may be Focused on the Wrong Type of Knowledge

The current popularity of "self-regulation" skills in education is another area where a focus on automated knowledge might modify our approach (Winnie, this volume, Chapter 12). Self-regulation is generally defined as the capacity to deliberately exercise conscious, deliberate control over attention, emotions and learning (Schunk & Zimmerman, 1997; van Merriënboer et al., this volume, Chapter 11; Vermunt, this volume, Chapter 9). The enthusiasm for research and instruction on self-regulation is in part an attempt to avoid the presumed negative impact of highly controlled instructional settings. The goal of self-regulation studies is to encourage students to learn to deliberately control their own performance by recognizing when they must implement self-control strategies that will permit them to direct their attention, apply effective study strategies and control their motivation so that they persist and achieve performance goals.

While the goal of this research is laudable, we wonder if it is pursued in a reasonable fashion given the arguments about cognitive control processes (Wegner, 2002) and evidence that self-regulatory skills may not always be used very effectively (Peverly, Brobst, Graham, & Shaw, 2003). Wegner (2002) for example, argues persuasively that human beings misperceive themselves as the agent of most of their own behavior when in fact, most behavior is automated and under the control of external conditions. And since much of the research on self-regulation asks learners to report on the regulatory strategies they have learned and used (Vermunt, this volume, Chapter 9; Schunk & Zimmerman, 1997; Wolters, 1998) it is doubtful that the results of self-report data accurately reflects the actual cognitive regulatory mechanisms that underlie learning. It is easy to agree that all of us need to learn effective strategies that support our motivation and learning. Yet, it may be the case that all effective strategies must be learned as contextualized procedures that will operate automatically and outside of our conscious awareness to overcome the limits on working memory. Assessing the use and effective operation of these automated regulatory strategies requires new approaches

The evidence that we are largely unaware of a large body of our own knowledge, suggests that we need a more effective way to capture the advanced expertise of experts.

Handling complexity in research and instruction requires that since self report protocols appear to be flawed, we should consider the more extensive use of cognitive task analysis to correct errors and provide missing information for instruction.

Research on the use of cognitive task analysis (CTA) to capture and identify the automated knowledge used by experts has grown in recent years (Clark & Estes, 1996; Schraagen, Chipman, & Shalin, 2000). As an evidence of the instructional value of using CTA to identify automated and unconscious expert knowledge, Lee (2004) performed a meta-analytic study of the instructional effectiveness of CTA-based training and performance improvement studies. She reported an overall median percentage of post-training performance gain of 75.2% with an effect size of 1.72 for CTA training when compared to more traditional training design using behavioral task analysis.

Velmahos et al. (2004) studied the expertise of expert surgeons in a medical school and their efforts to pass on their surgical knowledge to medical students. In a controlled study, half of a randomly assigned group of 24 medical students were taught in a traditional modeling and practice strategy by expert surgeons. These students' post-training performance was compared with the other half of the medical students who were trained with information gathered from experts with a "cognitive task analysis" (Clark & Estes, 1996; Schraagen et al., 2000) interview technique designed to expose automated routines and make them available for training. It was clear from the analysis that the information provided to the traditionally taught students contained significant omissions and errors, and primarily focused on essential decisions and problem-solving strategies that were never discussed or were incorrectly described by the experts.

After training, whenever the medical students performed the routines with patients in the following year, they were observed and evaluated by judges who were unfamiliar with their experimental status. Not only did the experimental group with CTA training outperform the expert-taught control group on all analytical (diagnostic) and many performance items by over 50 percent, the traditionally trained doctors caused four medical emergencies and those with CTA training made no mistakes. Equally important was the finding that students taught with CTA training learned 24 percent faster than the traditionally instructed students. This time saving appears to happen often in CTA-based studies and suggests that we should become more interested in the time it takes learners to learn and perform.

It is clear that CTA may serve to correct some of the errors and omissions found in expert-based teaching and ineffective task analytic procedures. It is also important to note that these studies and studies of the development of advanced expertise (Ericsson, 1998) report large-scale time-savings. In addition, recent research on motivational processes in learning (Pintrich & Schunk, 2002) indicates that the investment of "mental effort" to learn may be considerably different for different learners on the same learning task. The discussion of automated expertise suggests another consequence of the cognitive approach to complexity — the addition of time and mental effort required to learn in our assessment of learning.

> Handling complexity in research and instruction requires that we should consider adding speed and secondary measures of mental effort to our assessment of learning.

At the present time, instructional researchers and teachers assess learning with measures that attempt to determine whether learners can perform a task after instruction that could not be performed before they were taught. Considering the literature on the importance of automated procedural knowledge, it appears that the speed of performance and the amount of mental effort required to perform may be critical indicators of developing expertise. As Camp, Paas, Rikers, and van Merriënboer (2001) note, "when only performance is used as a selection parameter, no difference is made between people who perform well and indicate a high mental effort and people who also perform well, but indicate a low mental effort" (pp. 579–580). As task performance is practiced and improved over time, it gradually automates. As automation increases, speed also increases (Anderson, 1993) and the mental effort required for performance decreases (Camp et al., 2001).

It is assumed that complexity is correlated with mental effort, which is considered to be an index of cognitive load and is defined as "the number of non-automatic elaborations necessary to solve a problem" (Salomon, 1984, p. 231). As skills become less effortful with practice, they move toward automaticity, require less mental effort and impose less cognitive load. Thus, the more mental effort required to learn, the less learning strategies and tasks are automated (Sweller, 1994). Early empirical findings suggested a reliable, linear correlation between subjects' self-report of mental effort and other load measurements (Paas, 1992). However, more recent research (Clark, 1999; Flad, 2002; Gimino, 2000) has provided compelling evidence that self reported mental effort may not be a reliable indicator of actual effort expended to learn. As tasks become more complex self-reported mental effort scores continue to increase. Yet when tasks become excessively complex and working memory capacity is exceeded, self reported mental effort continues to increase but secondary measures of mental effort (such as the speed with which learners respond to irrelevant visual or auditory cues) start to decrease.

The slower the performance and the greater the amount of mental effort required to learn, the more external instructional support students require to succeed. This leads us to the issue of how much and what kind of instruction is needed to support the learning of complex knowledge — our fifth and final consequence of the cognitive approach to complexity.

Handling complexity in research and instruction requires that we consider whether, in instruction, "less is more". In light of the cognitive research on learning of complex knowledge, one of the most general implications for instruction is that less task complexity, less irrelevant mental load and less learner control of the learning environment may be more beneficial for learning and motivation to learn.

All learning is novel and therefore complex. Thus, our goal must be to reduce the complexity in a learning task to provide very minimal amounts of task relevant information so that instruction does not exceed students' working memory capacity. Cowan's (2001) estimate of a processing limit of three or four chunks for adults (the estimate is smaller for younger children) reduces by 50 percent of our former estimate (Miller, 1956) of seven to nine chunk working memory capacity. This very much lower capacity estimate is further reduced by learner anxiety or distracting and task irrelevant sources of cognitive load (Sweller, this volume, Chapter 1; Mayer, this volume, Chapter 7). In addition to the number of chunks of information we provide, other more surprising factors increase the cognitive load of instruction. Among the less appreciated factors are various cultural and ethnic differences among students and between students and the design of learning environments (Depaepe et al., this volume, Chapter 5) and in the many motivational challenges that stem from different student values for learning and either low or excessively high self-efficacy (Clark et al., this volume, Chapter 2). This evidence suggests that we must try to understand the "fit" between students' motivational and cultural outlook on the one hand, and the context, rationale and climate of instructional environments on the other. This attempt to adjust instruction to student needs is what is intended by the goal of "learner centered education".

A second sense in which "less is more" concerns the amount of conscious self-regulation of learning activities we ask of students as they are learning. The more unguided "discovery" or cognitively "constructed", the learning experience we provide for students, the more mental load we impose on them to perform cognitive processing that most often could have been performed externally (Elen & Clarebout, this volume, Chapter 10; Kirschner, Sweller, & Clark, in press). This view swims upstream against a very popular but mistaken belief that when students are given learning goals and resources and are asked to discover how and what to learn, the result is a more durable learning and a more independent learner. The best evidence over the past half century of research on instruction and leaning is that instructional guidance that reduces cognitive processing so that it fits with learner capacity is the most beneficial (Mayer, 2004). While there are a number of research-based approaches to cognitive, capacity-focused instructional design, few are as well developed as van Merriënboer's 4C/ID design system (van Merriënboer, 1997). We are also attracted to David Merrill's (2002, this volume, Chapter 15) review of the five key components of a number of research-based and capacity-focused instructional design systems that attempt to provide students with: (1) authentic problems that gradually increase in complexity; (2) connections to relevant prior knowledge to reduce cognitive load; (3) demonstrations of worked problem-solving examples to provide an accurate procedure to be learned; (4) practice and feedback on the application of the procedures; and (5) a wide integration of new knowledge in whole task practice on increasingly difficult problems.

A third way in which "less is more" is concerned with the amount of instructional control we give to learners while they are learning. The new electronic instructional media permits the design of learning environments where students are able to have an extraordinary level of control over their own learning activities. It is possible and now common, for example, to allow students to change the order of lessons, activate animated pedagogical agents that will help them pursue additional information about lesson goals, choose to listen to background music or sounds and/or video segments that elaborate on instructional information, increase or decrease the amount of structure in lessons and pace themselves as slowly or as fast as they wish. The evidence best supports the claim that except for control over pacing, most of these "learner control" devices actually reduce learning for most students (Mayer, this volume, Chapter 7; Clark & Feldon, 2005). van Merriënboer (van Merriënboer et al., this volume, Chapter 11) has recommended what he calls the "training wheels principle" where learners are very gradually given more control over their own learning as their learning-goal specific knowledge base grows and becomes more extensive over time. Yet in all but rare instances, the evidence still supports the generalization that higher levels of learner support is best for most students, most of the time when they are handling complexity.

Finally (for this discussion), we must consider teaching less declarative knowledge and instead focus more of our instructional goals on the learning of procedural knowledge (actions and decisions that will achieve the goal of tasks). One of the best examples of research that can support our move to teaching and supporting the learning of more procedural knowledge is Anderson's (1993) ACT-R theory of cognitive architecture. He makes the compelling argument that declarative knowledge is useful primarily for the development of accurate and efficient procedures. His 30-year record of systematic research on learning has provided a very clear map of the stages learners experience as they develop, edit and gradually automate knowledge as they pursue learning sub goals and main goals (Anderson, 1995). At each of the stages he identifies, the type of support students need to succeed changes somewhat. His research has found its way into a number of the best contemporary instructional design systems. Now we must find a way to encourage the use of these contemporary instructional design systems in a wider range of educational and instructional settings.

Conclusion

The perspective with which we view complexity is in transition from a task-focused view to a more cognitively based understanding of the mental architecture and processes we use to handle complexity. As we slowly adopt a cognitive approach, our understanding of complexity and ways to help people handle it in education, are undergoing a surprising and somewhat ironic transformation.

One of the more ironic aspects of new developments in this area is our recent appreciation of how much of our own learning and problem solving is hidden from our conscious awareness. Current estimates suggest that we cannot directly monitor from 70 to 90 percent of our cognitive processing that occurs when we learn or solve even novel and complex problems. The reason for this handicap is presumably the severe limits on the information capacity of our working memory where all new knowledge is elaborated and integrated with our prior knowledge. Sweller (this volume, Chapter 1) hypothesizes that our limited working memory capacity has evolved to protect us from the potentially destructive consequences of the rapid and impulsive learning of large amounts of new but inaccurate and damaging knowledge. Complicating this problem is equally compelling evidence (Wegner, 2002) that we mistakenly believe that we exercise constant, conscious and willful control over our cognitive processing. So it appears that we have ignored mental operations that we are not able to directly monitor.

As we gradually find ways to infer and indirectly measure these unconscious and powerful cognitive processes (Winnie, this volume, Chapter 12), we will begin to change our approach to research and practice on instruction and learning. Some of the changes we anticipate are an increase in the emphasis on the teaching and learning of procedural knowledge, an enlarged awareness of the needs of learners at various stages in their learning and the automation of knowledge. One dominant need is for instructional environments that reduce the amount of irrelevant cognitive load to a minimum through an increased awareness of the individual and cultural factors that influence cognitive processing. Clearly then, theory and research on the relation between automatic and controlled processes in learning may advance our capacity to handle complexity in learning environments.

References

Anderson, J. R. (1983). *The architecture of cognition*. Cambridge, MA: Harvard University Press.

Anderson, J. R.(1993). *Rules of the mind*. Hillsdale, NJ: Erlbaum.

Anderson, J. R. (1995). ACT: A simple theory of complex cognition. *American Psychologist, 51,* 355–365.

Bargh, J. A. (1999). The unbearable automaticity of being. *American Psychologist, 54,* 462–479.

Besnard, D. (2000). Expert error. The case of trouble-shooting in electronics. *Proceedings of the 19th international conference SafeComp2000*, Rotterdam, The Netherlands (pp. 74–85).

Camp, G., Paas, F., Rikers, R., & van Merriënboer, J. (2001). Dynamic problem selection in air traffic control training: A comparison between performance, mental effort and mental efficiency. *Computers in Human Behavior, 17,* 575–595.

Chao, C. -J., & Salvendy, G. (1994). Percentage of procedural knowledge acquired as a function of the number of experts from whom knowledge is acquired for diagnosis, debugging and interpretation tasks. *International Journal of Human–Computer Interaction, 6,* 221–233.

Chase, W., & Simon, H. (1973). Perception in chess. *Cognitive Psychology, 4,* 55–81.

Clark, R. E. (1999). Yin and yang: Cognitive motivational processes operating in multimedia learning environments. In: J. van Merriënboer (Ed.), *Cognition and multimedia design* (pp. 73–107). Heerlen, The Netherlands: Open University Press.

Clark, R. E., & Estes, F. (1996) Cognitive task analysis. *International Journal of Educational Research, 25,* 403–417.

Clark, R. E., & Estes, F. (2002). *Turning research into results: A guide to selecting the right performance solutions*. Atlanta: CEP Press.

Clark, R. E., & Feldon, D. F. (2005). Five common but questionable principles of multimedia learning. In: R. Mayer (Ed.), *Cambridge handbook of multimedia learning* (pp. 97–117). Cambridge: Cambridge University Press.

Cowan, N. (2001). The magical number 4 in short term memory: A reconsideration of mental storage capacity. *Behavioral and Brain Sciences, 24*, 87–114.

Feldon, D. F. (2004). *Inaccuracies in expert self report: Errors in the description of strategies for designing psychology experiments.* Unpublished doctoral dissertation. Rossier School of Education, University of Southern California, USA.

Flad, J. A. (2002). *The effects of increasing cognitive load on self-report and dual-task measures of mental effort during problem solving.* Unpublished dissertation. University of Southern California, USA.

Gimino, A. E. (2000). *Factors that influence students' investment of mental effort in academic tasks: A validation and exploratory study.* Unpublished dissertation. University of Southern California, USA.

Glaser, R., & Chi, M. T. H. (1988). Overview. In: M. T. H. Chi, R. Glaser, & M. J. Farr (Eds), *The nature of expertise* (pp. xv–xxviii). Mahwah, NJ: Erlbaum.

Hoffman, R., Crandall, B., & Shadbolt, N. (1998). Use of the critical decision method to elicit expert knowledge: A case study in the methodology of cognitive task analysis. *Human Factors, 40*, 254–276.

Jansma, J. M., Ramsey, N. F., Slagter, H. A., & Kahn, R. S. (2001). Functional anatomical correlates of controlled and automatic processing. *Journal of Cognitive Neuroscience, 13*, 730–743.

Kirschner, P., Sweller, J., & Clark, R. E. (in press). Why minimally guided learning does not work: An analysis of the failure of discovery learning, problem-based learning, experiential learning and inquiry-based learning. *Educational Psychologist, 41*(2).

Lee, R. L. (2004). *The impact of cognitive task analysis on performance: A meta analysis of comparative studies.* Unpublished EdD dissertation. Rossier School of Education, University of Southern California, USA.

Mayer, R. E. (2004). Should there be a three-strikes rule against pure discovery learning? *American Psychologist, 59*(1), 14–19.

Merrill, M. D. (1983). Component display theory. In: C. Reigeluth (Ed.), *Instructional design theories and models* (pp. 279–333). Hillsdale, NJ: Erlbaum.

Merrill, M. D. (2002). First principles of instruction. *Educational Technology Research and Development, 50*(2), 50–59.

Miller, G. A. (1956). The magical number seven, plus or minus two: Some limits on our capacity for processing information. *The Psychological Review, 63*, 81–97.

Newell, A. (1990). *Unified theories of cognition.* Cambridge, MA: Harvard University Press.

Peverly, S. T., Brobst, K., Graham, M., & Shaw, R. (2003). College adults are not good at self-regulation: A study on the relationship of self-regulation, note-taking, and test-taking. *Journal of Educational Psychology, 95*, 335–346.

Salomon, G. (1984). Television is "easy" and print is "tough": The differential investment of mental effort in learning as a function of perceptions and attributions. *Journal of Educational Psychology, 76*, 774–786.

Schneider, W., & Chein, J. W. (2003). Controlled & automatic processing: Behavior, theory, and biological mechanisms. *Cognitive Science, 27*, 525–559.

Schneider, W., & Shiffrin, R. M. (1977). Controlled and automatic human information processing: 1. Detection, search, and attention. *Psychological Review, 84*, 1–66.

Schraagen, J. M., Chipman, S. F., & Shalin, V. L. (2000). *Cognitive task analysis.* Mahwah, NJ: Erlbaum.

Schunk, D. H., & Zimmerman, B. J. (1997). Social origins of self-regulatory competence. *Educational Psychologist, 32,* 195–208.

Sun, R., Slusarz, P., & Terry, C. (2005). The interaction of the explicit and the implicit in skill learning: A dual-process approach. *Psychological Review, 112,* 159–192.

Sweller, J. (1994). Cognitive load theory, learning difficulty, and instructional design. *Learning & Instruction, 4,* 295–312.

Tunney, R. J. (2003). Implicit and explicit knowledge decay at different rates: A dissociation between priming and recognition in artificial grammar learning. *Experimental Psychology, 50,* 124–130.

van Merriënboer, J. J. G. (1997). *Training complex cognitive skills: A four-component instructional design model for technical training.* Englewood Cliffs, NJ: Educational Technology Publications.

Velmahos, G. C., Toutouzas, K. G., Sillin, L. F., Chan, L., Clark, R. E., Theodorou, D., & Maupin, F. (2004). Cognitive task analysis for teaching technical skills in an inanimate surgical skills laboratory. *The American Journal of Surgery, 18,* 114–119.

Wegner, D. M. (2002). *The illusion of conscious will.* Cambridge, MA: MIT Press.

Wolters, C. A. (1998). Self-regulated learning and college students' regulation of motivation. *Journal of Educational Psychology, 90,* 224–235.

Author Index

Subject Index